From Tian'anmen to Times Square

From Tian'anmen to Times Square

Transnational China and the Chinese Diaspora on Global Screens, 1989–1997

GINA MARCHETTI
Author of *Romance and the "Yellow Peril"*

TEMPLE UNIVERSITY PRESS
Philadelphia

GINA MARCHETTI is Associate Professor in the School of Cinema and Photography at Ithaca College and a Visiting Researcher at the University of Hong Kong. She is the author of *Romance and the "Yellow Peril": Race, Sex, and Discursive Strategies in Hollywood Fiction*, which won the 1995 Association for Asian American Studies National Book Award in Cultural Studies.

Temple University Press
1601 North Broad Street
Philadelphia PA 19122
www.temple.edu/tempress

Copyright © 2006 by Temple University
All rights reserved
Published 2006
Printed in the United States of America

♾ The paper used in this publication meets the requirements of the American National Standard for Information Sciences—Permanence of Paper for Printed Library Materials, ANSI Z39.48–1992

Library of Congress Cataloging-in-Publication Data

Marchetti, Gina.
From Tian'anmen to Times Square : transnational China and the Chinese diaspora on global screens, 1989–1997 / Gina Marchetti.
    p.   cm.
Includes bibliographical references and index.
ISBN 1-59213-277-4 (cl. : alk. paper) — ISBN 1-59213-278-2 (pbk. : alk. paper)
1. Popular culture—China. 2. Chinese—Foreign countries. 3. Mass media. I. Title.

HM621.M362 2006
791.43'6251—dc22   2005054746

2   4   6   8   9   7   5   3   1

Dedicated to the memory of
my mother, Frances Stone Marchetti (1916–2000), and
my father, March Peter Marchetti (1915–1999)

Contents

List of Illustrations

Preface

TIAN'ANMEN SQUARE IN BEIJING and Times Square in New York City are worlds apart. While Tian'anmen represents centuries of the public exercise of Chinese power, Times Square signifies the ephemeral and superficial nature of American capitalism and image-based consumer culture. After 1989, Tian'anmen becomes a point of departure, a symbol for what has been left behind, and the reason for exile, whereas Times Square symbolizes the hope and despair of a real and imagined destination in an America obsessed with itself, vulgarly commercial, overwhelming, and often violent. Both squares provide spaces for the movement of people, for the public display of images, for the performance of identities, and the juxtaposition of these two squares, geographically and historically distinct, emphasizes the important link between global China and the American metropolis. With its massive outdoor screens, Times Square is an internationally recognized symbol of American commerce, theatricality, and image production that can contain both the satellite media event of Tian'anmen and the commercial environment in which images of China/the Chinese circulate globally. In the postmodern moment, time and space warp, and Tian'anmen and Times Square move closer together connected by an instantaneous stream of motion pictures.

Certainly, the ways in which the world has imagined China and the images the Chinese have used to depict themselves have changed dramatically since 1989. The media spotlight placed on Beijing during the spring of 1989 created repercussions that continue to affect how China is seen globally, how it sees itself, and how the Chinese outside the People's Republic see themselves. At around the same time, other events were forcing many Chinese outside the People's Republic to reposition themselves economically, politically, and culturally in relation to Beijing and to one another. The impact of the Joint Declaration between London and Beijing that would return the Crown Colony of Hong Kong to Chinese jurisdiction became subject to even greater anxiety and public debate as the people of Hong Kong turned out in record numbers to protest the June crackdown in Tian'anmen.

The number of those committed to leaving both mainland China and Hong Kong increased, and Chinese communities in the United States, Canada, Australia, and elsewhere swelled dramatically. Also in the 1980s, the KMT (Kuomintang), the ruling party in Taiwan, finally ended decades of martial law and strict control of domestic politics. The decline of the ruling KMT's power (hastened by the U.S. normalization of relations with China in the late 1970s) opened up the island for democratic reform and the provocative possibility of official independence from China. Social tensions between families that arrived on Taiwan after the Chinese civil war ended in 1949 and those who had lived on the island for centuries before the KMT took control escalated, and the allure of emigration for the former increased significantly. The transfer of sovereignty of Hong Kong became an important turning point for Taiwan as well, increasing pressure on the island to consider itself part of China or suffer the consequences. Hong Kong as a buffer between Beijing and Taipei was eliminated, and the People's Republic increased pressure for Taiwan to also return to mainland Chinese sovereignty.

Economically, as China continued its policy of encouraging capital investment, money from the "overseas" Chinese began to flow into China, as Chinese goods became even more visible within the global marketplace. Chinese Americans, Chinese from the Nanyang (Southeast Asia), as well as the Chinese in Hong Kong, Taiwan and elsewhere had compelling economic reasons to form transnational alliances. Cheaper air travel, telecommunications, and the rise of the Internet enabled networks to form more easily across borders. A sense of a "global" China began to become part of the Chinese diaspora, so that tensions between local Chinese identities and a global sense of a transnational cultural identity began to emerge.

Much of the economic euphoria of the period came to an end in 1997 with the Asian economic crisis and devaluation of currency all over the region. Also, Deng Xiaoping died that year, symbolically marking another terminus in the history of Greater China. Thus, 1997 marks more than just the transformation of Hong Kong, British colony, into Hong Kong, Special Administrative Region.

Screen culture has played a significant role in these transformations. Films, television shows, and digital materials have taken up the spring 1989 events in Tian'anmen as shorthand for many of these alterations. These changes include the threat of exile, the lure of emigration and assimilation into other countries and cultures, the contradictions between economics and politics among the Chinese globally, the quest for freedom sometimes within and sometimes outside Chinese tradition, and so on. Other screen works have taken up the 1997 change of sovereignty of Hong Kong as the allegorical basis for dealing with these questions of Chinese identity within the current economic and political maelstrom. Using these two events as markers, this book investigates how screen culture has represented Chinese identity in flux and has intervened actively to reposition the Chinese at the end of the millennium.

In some respects, *From Tian'anmen to Times Square* takes up where my previous book, *Romance and the "Yellow Peril": Race, Sex, and Discursive Strategies in Hollywood Fiction* (1993), left off. Like my earlier book, this project looks at the contradictory ways race, ethnicity, nation, class, generation, gender, and sexuality insinuate themselves into visual narratives. However, whereas *Romance and the "Yellow Peril"* deals exclusively with Hollywood fiction features involving interracial romances between Euro-American and Chinese, Japanese, Vietnamese, and Asian American characters, *From Tian'anmen to Times Square* examines a range of motion picture representations from around the world. However, this book also has a more narrow focus in that it deals with a much shorter period in cinema history, 1989–97, and exclusively with works that screen global China.

The films and other texts included in this book represent a range of work by media artists working within China, Hong Kong, Taiwan, Singapore, on transnational coproductions involving those places, from other positions within the Chinese diaspora (including Chinese America), and work produced on China by non-Chinese. Hong Kong has dominated the attention of film scholars in recent years and film from the People's Republic had its critical vogue earlier. However, the interconnections among these works and these various national and transnational media formations have only begun to be explored in scholarship on global Chinese media.

This is neither a chronology nor an exhaustive study of Chinese screen culture between 1989 and 1997. Rather, this book provides a look at some key filmmakers and media artists and the impact of political, social, economic, and cultural changes on their oeuvres. The book offers critical exegeses of selected films and other media texts as well as interviews with filmmakers involved in representations of China and the Chinese on screen. These interviews balance the close analyses by providing breadth and context to the discussion, thereby expanding the book's scope. All the interviews were conducted in English between 1997 and 2002.

This book examines only a few critical themes within the enormous change that has taken place in Chinese screen culture during this time period. Highlighting questions of the circulation of images, people, and commodities, the book explores the important interconnections involving questions of race, ethnicity, gender, and sexuality on global screens. Beginning and ending with Tian'anmen and world image culture, a portrait emerges of momentous change and persistent challenges facing media and filmmakers working within "Greater China."

A Note on Romanization

Because *From Tian'anmen to Times Square* deals with a wide range of Chinese-language communities and preferred systems of Romanization, no standard method is followed. Generally, *pin yin* is used for names and terms associated with the People's Republic and Wade-Giles for Taiwan. Given the variety of dialects referenced in the book, the most common Romanization of names in Cantonese and other dialects is used. When proper nouns like "Tian'anmen," "Mao Zedong," and "Guangdong" have become more common in pin yin than earlier renderings, the pin yin is used. However, other proper names are rendered in their more commonly used forms; for example, Chiang Kai-shek. Although most Chinese names are presented with the surname followed by the given name, some individuals prefer the given name to precede the surname. In this book, the preferences of the individuals are followed when possible (e.g., "Ning Ma"—surname last—rather than "Ma Ning"—surname first). However, the preponderance of the Chinese names presented in this book follow the Chinese custom of surname first, given name last (e.g., Mao Zedong). Quoted material maintains the system used by the author in the original. Any renderings that may cause confusion include a note or alternate transliteration for clarification.

Acknowledgments

SINCE I FIRST BECAME seriously interested in Chinese screen culture in 1982, so many wonderful people have encouraged my research in this area that it is impossible to thank all those who have gone out of their way to help me. Since my days in graduate school, Chuck Kleinhans has been a tremendous help and source of constant inspiration. I must also thank the other editors at *Jump Cut*, particularly Julia Lesage and John Hess, for their support of my interest in Chinese film. I am also very grateful to Robert Kolker for his unflagging support of my work and his encouragement when I began to venture into the realm of the digital and cyberspace.

My editor at Temple University Press, Micah Kleit, has been the model of patience and good sense. I also must thank Eric Smoodin, formerly of the University of California Press, for his invaluable help at the early stages of the development of this project as a book. Jerome Ng and Tad Doyle were both particularly helpful as the book began to take shape. Others, including Qin Hong Anderson, Qu Jiao-jie, Kelley Clements, Evan Cony, and Maureen Denis, among others, have also worked in various capacities during the preparation of the manuscript by transcribing interviews, tracking down books and articles in the library, photocopying, and in other essential duties.

When I first began to work on Hong Kong cinema, Tony Rayns, Ian Jarvie, Ming Tam, Li Cheuk-To, Norman Wang, Roger Garcia, Evans Chan, Allen Fong, and Ho Chi-Kuan were incredibly generous with their knowledge and time. Vivian Huang, Shu Lea Cheang, Peggy Chiao, Yeh Yueh-Yu, Yang Ming-Yu, Jeff Yao, Scarlet Cheng, and Edward Yang were extraordinarily helpful as I began to become more interested in Taiwan screen culture. Hong Jingyi, Zhang Lihui, Ma Ning, Xie Fei, Xie Jin, and Stephanie Donald were all very encouraging during the early stages of my research in cinema in the People's Republic.

I would never have been able to persevere without the support of the Asian Cinema Studies Society; the efforts of Mira Binford, who got it started; and John Lent, who has kept it going. I want to particularly note my debt to the late Cynthia Contreras, who was so wonderful to me the last time we met in Trent. I miss her. I am grateful for all my colleagues who have participated in the ACSS over the years, including Carol Slingo, Chris Berry, Jenny Lau, Esther Yau, Ramie Tateishi, Joelle Collier, Peter Rist, Jyotika Virdi, Jyotsna Kapur, Kathe Geist, Linda Ehrlich, George Semsel, Poonam Arora, Tony Williams, Lalitha Gopalan, Priya Jaikumar, Aaron Park, Adam Knee, Sheldon Lu, Anne Ciecko, and Suzie Young. I am particularly indebted to Sumiko Higashi, Marina Heung, Frances Gateward, and David Desser, who have always been so supportive of my work in Asian cinema over the years. They have gone through a lot with me, and I am grateful for their friendship. Tan See-Kam has become a close collaborator, and I am so thankful to have his tremendous depth and breadth of knowledge to draw on as well as his surprising energy. Peter X Feng has also become a collaborator, and I am beholden to him and all the other pioneers in Asian American film studies who have inspired me, including Phebe Chao, Kent Ono, Darrell Hamamoto, Chris Choy, and Renee Tajima-Pena.

I want to thank all my colleagues who have been generous with their support over the years, particularly Tom Waugh, David James, Linda Dittmar, Lucy Fischer, Dana Polan, Marcia Landy, Manju Pendakur, Gary Okihiro, Suzanne Regan, B. Ruby Rich, Caren Kaplan, Ella Shohat, Ann Martin, Patricia Erens, and Linda Williams. Patricia Zimmermann and I have been in the film studies trenches together for more than twenty years, and she has been a wonderful friend and pillar of strength during my time at Ithaca College. Chris Holmlund, Chris Straayer, Claudia Springer, Gretchen Bisplinghoff, Jane Shattuc, and Diane Waldman have been hanging in there with me, so I know I am not alone. The younger recruits, like Christina Lane and Anna Siomopoulos, have also been a joy and an inspiration.

Although it no longer exists as such, Asian American Arts and Media (AAAM) of Washington, DC, still figures as a force in my life and work, and I am very grateful to all those who worked with me on the Asian American International Film Festival of Washington, DC, as well as to those who continue to promote Asian and Asian American film in the area now. I particularly want to thank Do Linh Khai, Chris Li, George Liao, Hiro, Franklin Chow, Dorinda Capole, Inbum Chung, Seth Silberman, Joe Schaub, Katrien Jacobs, Tad Doyle, Wendy Lim, Terry Huynh, and Theo Feng. I am also grateful to Asian CineVision and the Asian American International Film Festival of New York City for their continuing support. Vivian Huang, Risa Morimoto, Angel Shaw, Curtis Tsui, Cindy Wong, Peter Hitchcock, Jessica Hagedorn, John Woo, Jeff Yang, Ho Yuet-Fung, Wendy Lidell, Masa Yoshikawa, Somi Roy, and Kyoko Hirano have all been particularly encouraging over the years in their various roles in the media arts in New York City. Aruna Vasudev, Wang Shujen, Shih Shu-Mei, Yau Ching, and Jon Moritsugu have also been very supportive.

A considerable amount of the research that appears in this book was collected while I was on faculty at Nanyang Technological University in Singapore. I am very grateful to Dean Eddie Kuo for giving me the opportunity to live and work in Singapore, and I feel fortunate to have been able to work with my colleagues there, including Chua Siew-keng, Duncan Holaday, Jamason Chen, Kathy Frith, and the entire faculty in the School of Communication. I was honored to have the opportunity to work with outstanding students like Ray Ng, Abel Ang, Michael Lee, and the other graduate and undergraduates at NTU who made my experiences in Singapore so rewarding. I am also very grateful to everyone at the Singapore International Film Festival and to the Substation for their support. Philip Cheah, Eric Khoo, and Audrey Wong were all extremely helpful to me while I was in Singapore.

I want to thank all those who supported my work at Ithaca College under the leadership of President Peggy Williams. In addition to the enthusiastic backing of

Patricia Zimmermann, I want to single out Peter Bardaglio, Garry Brodhead, Tanya Saunders, John Keshishoglou, Zillah Eisenstein, Larry Shinagawa, Asma Barlas, Carla Golden, Sandra Herndon, John Hochheimer, Barbara Adams, Naeem Inayatullah, Steve Tropiano, Traevena Potter-Hall, Gordon Roland, Rebecca Lesses, Aron Gutman, Michael Faber, Meg Jamieson, Vaun Monroe, Simon Tarr, and all those involved in Cinema on the Edge. At Ithaca College and Kino, Rodrigo Brandao has provided enormous support. Portions of the research for this book were supported by a Pendleton Faculty and Staff Research and Production Grant, Ithaca College, 2000 and 2003–2004; a Faculty Diversity Book Award, Ithaca College, 2002; a Summer Research Grant, Ithaca College, 2001; Reassigned Time, Center for Faculty Research and Development, Ithaca College, 2000–2001, 2001–2002, 2002–2003; and a Small Grant for Faculty Research/ Scholarship, Ithaca College, 2000.

The final stages of this book came to fruition at the University of Hong Kong with the support of a Fulbright Lecturing/Research Award, 2003–2004. So many people made this year particularly valuable, including Law Kar, Richard Stites, Lance Sung, Staci Ford, Priscilla Roberts, Peter Cunich, Amy Lee, Nicole Hess, Gordon Slethaug, Mette Hjort, Jason Ho, and Esther Cheung. Special thanks go to Yau Ka-Fai.

Sizable inspiration for this book came from my involvement in Asian martial arts, particularly Jow Ga kung fu. I owe a tremendous debt to Si-gong Chan Man Cheung, the current grandmaster of the system, as well as to the many teachers who have helped me over the years, including Sifu Ho Hin Chong, Sifu Ho Gin Hong, Sifu Lim Chin Kim, Si-heng Chris Henderson, Si-heng Howard Bryant, Si-heng Yee Rong Yuan, Si-heng T. Brighthaupt, and fellow students Huang Can-Ye and Huang Sun-Jan (Shang-Jing). I must also thank those practicing other arts for their encouragement and friendship, including Mike Young, Fred Degerberg, Edmund Lin Yiu Fai and Hu Xiang-gan.

Many people were helpful in locating stills, including Vivian Huang, Rodrigo Brandao, the Hong Kong Critics Society, Li Cheuk-to, Wendy Lidell, Vanessa Domico at Women Make Movies, Evans Chan, Eric Khoo, Xie Jin, and Jerry Ohlinger. All those who granted interviews—Paul Lee, Allen Fong, Edward Yang, Eric Khoo, Evans Chan, and Carma Hinton—were extremely kind and generous with their time.

Special thanks to all the editors who worked so diligently on earlier versions of the material collected here, including David Desser, Poshek Fu, Sheldon Lu, Murray Pomerance, Esther C. M. Yau, Yeh Yue-yu, Michael Tapper, and Robert Kolker. They all contributed enormously to this project. I would also like to thank David Li and Darrell Hamamoto for their careful reading of the manuscript.

I am grateful for the friendship of Stephanie Hoare, Traci Smith, and Lisa Bernstein. Certainly, this book would not have been possible without friends and family. Cao Dong-qing and Luca sacrificed a lot to enable me to complete this project. I can never thank them enough for their love and support.

Portions of this book have been published in other forms as follows:
Chapter 2: "Buying American, Consuming Hong Kong: Cultural Commerce, Fantasies of Identity, and the Cinema," in Po Shek Fu and David Desser, eds., *The Cinema of Hong Kong: History, Arts, Identity* (New York: Cambridge University Press, 2000), pp. 289–313. Reprinted with permission of Cambridge University Press.
Chapter 4: "Taiwanese Triads in the Transnational Imagination: *Mahjong* and *Goodbye South, Goodbye*," *Film International* 9 (2004), pp. 28–41.
Chapter 5: "Global Modernity, Postmodern Singapore, and the Cinema of Eric-Khoo," in Sheldon H. Lu and Yeh Yueh-Yu, eds., *Chinese-Language Film: Historiography, Poetics, Politics* (Honolulu: University of Hawaii Press, 2005), pp. 329–61.
Chapter 6: "Transnational Exchanges, Questions of Culture, and Global Cinema: Defining the Dynamics of Changing Relationships," in Esther C. M. Yau, ed., *At Full Speed: Hong Kong Cinema in a Borderless World* (Minneapolis: University of Minnesota Press, 2001), pp. 251–60. (Shortened version of "Transnational Cinema, Hybrid Identities and the Films of Evans Chan," *Postmodern Culture* 8:2 [January 1998], available online at http://jefferson.village. virginia.edu /pmc with a new introduction.) Reprinted in Esther M. K. Cheung and Chu Yiu-wai, eds., *Between Home and World: A Reader in Hong Kong Cinema* (Hong Kong: Oxford University Press, 2004), pp. 196–223.
Chapter 7: "The Gender of GenerAsian X in Clara Law's Migration Trilogy," in Murray Pomerance, ed., *Ladies and Gentlemen, Boys and Girls: Gender in Film at the End of the Twentieth Century* (Albany: State University of New York Press, 2001), pp. 71–87, courtesy of SUNY Press.

1   China and the Chinese on World Screens, 1989–97

TIMED TO COINCIDE WITH the change of sovereignty of Hong Kong from Britain to the People's Republic of China (PRC) in 1997, the James Bond thriller *Tomorrow Never Dies* (directed by Roger Spottiswoode) takes an ironic look at capitalist lust for Chinese screens. The Rupert Murdoch–like villain,[1] Elliot Carver (Jonathan Pryce), stages an international incident between the United Kingdom and the PRC to worm his own way into total control of world media, including recalcitrant China's screens. James Bond (played by Pierce Brosnan) steps in to sort out the mess, and Wai Lin (Michelle Yeoh), a female agent sent by the Chinese government, helps foil the plot. Although a hedonist who certainly enjoys the "good life" promised by capitalism, Bond has always spent more time going after rogue villains like Carver, usually hungrier for power than money, than fighting the Cold War in any substantial way. Thus, it seems natural to pair Bond with an attractive PRC operative in a symbolic union of East and West, old colonialism and revivified nationalism, capitalism and communism to combat postmodern globalization.

By doing away with the excesses of capitalism represented by the monopoly-mad Carver, Bond and Wai Lin make the world "safe" for the peaceful transfer of Hong Kong and the maintenance of capitalism without the intrusions of global media. Although they may appear to be strange bedfellows, the British and Chinese governments are on the same side after all, and global media must be imagined as tools of imperialist intrusion into the Chinese market rather than as a means for dissident voices to be heard on world screens. If *Tomorrow Never Dies* comments on the transformation of Hong Kong from a Crown colony into a Special Administrative Region (SAR), it obliquely puts to rest any ghosts that may linger involving the events in Tian'anmen Square in 1989 and the media's involvement in bringing those events to light outside of China.

Certainly, the global media were not in the People's Republic of China in May 1989 to cover a demonstration, even though the protests had been heating up in Tian'anmen since the death of Hu Yaobang a month before. An out-of-favor Party official, Hu became a symbol of reform around which various protesters could rally, and Deng Xiaoping found himself in the embarrassing position of having the world watch a mass movement occupy Tian'anmen Square. Mikhail Gorbachev had achieved a historic rapprochement with Deng, another reform-minded Communist head of state, and global interest centered on the Soviet leader's visit to China that May. Four years before, CNN inaugurated its global news network, and in 1987, it set up a news bureau in Beijing.[2] Real-time satellite broadcasts of world events had become common in 1989, and the events leading up to the June 3–4 violent suppression of the protests received the global immediacy of satellite coverage. With the Internet in its infancy and satellite broadcasts virtually impossible to pick up by television viewers in China, faxes flew across continents to feed information to the demonstrators about world press coverage of the protests. The visual and spatial seat of power in Tian'anmen, China's most public square, shifted from the official reforms of the Communist bureaucracy (envisioned by the meeting of Deng and Gorbachev) to the control of the square by students, workers, artists, intellectuals, and activists involved in the protests. The world watched, and the demonstrators and the government leaders knew the power China had as the cynosure of global media.

In 1989, Tian'anmen Square—the core of the capital of China, *Zhong Guo*, the "central kingdom," and the purported heart of the Chinese world, which had recently claimed Hong Kong through the 1984 British-Chinese Joint Declaration, welcomed "back" overseas Chinese investors who may be generations removed from the mainland, and tried to rope in its wayward province of Taiwan and the government in exile of Tibet—could not afford the world to see chaos in the square. American-owned global media saw things differently. Rather than seeing demonstrators with demands specific to their positions within a rapidly changing economic and political structure in China, television screens narcissistically reflected the "Americanization" of the Chinese, and thus the world, as the Goddess of Democracy, a postmodern sculptural citation of New York's Statue of Liberty, made her appearance on Ted Turner's satellite broadcasts. The contradictions between nationalism and processes of globalization, as well as the ways in which global capitalism could reinforce national interests, were placed in high relief.

New technologies transformed the moment, and this visualization of the spring Tian'anmen demonstrations marks the way in which China has been subsequently seen and screened worldwide. The image of the lone man confronting a line of tanks in the streets of Beijing speaks volumes as a celebration of the individual against the state (a shorthand for Reagan-Bush policies suspicious of "big" government at home and "evil empires" abroad), a symbol of hope on a par with antigovernment movements as diverse as People Power in the Philippines, anti-apartheid in South Africa, and Solidarity in Eastern Europe, or as an icon of hopelessness for Chinese around the globe who continue to lament the "sorrow" fated to China condemned to face impossible odds head on. The long history of the People's Liberation Army (PLA), the waves of political changes associated with the Communist Party, and the legacy of demonstrations and individual protests dating back centuries to figures like Qu Yuan, whose suicide is celebrated annually on Dragon Boat Day, or the demonstrations on May 4, 1919, in Tian'anmen, which ushered in the modern era of Chinese culture, fade from view.

The image of the man standing alone against the tanks resonates with another prominent image produced in China around the same time. In Zhang Yimou's *Ju Dou* (codirected with Yang Fengliang, 1990), the title character, played by actress Gong Li, turns her head to look at her in-law, Tianqing (Li Baotian), who has been spying on her bathing. Battered by an impotent husband who blames her for his own sexual inadequacy, Ju Dou bathes her wounded body as Tianqing looks at her through a peephole. She turns, returns Tianqing's gaze, and displays her wounds to him. As Jenny Lau points out in her analysis of the scene:

> One finds that the explicit erotic content of the film—beginning when Judou deliberately turns around to expose her naked body to the peeping Tianqing—is not derived from a simple act of narcissism. Indeed, her tired, dirty, and bruised body, together with the melancholy accompanying music, offers no 'visual pleasure' for Tianqing or the film audience. Judou's turning around represents a decisive move against the gerontocratic and patriarchal rule that operates against her.[3]

In the course of the film, Tianqing's look turns from voyeuristic pleasure to embarrassed compassion, and Ju Dou/Gong Li has been transformed from an object of erotic desire to a wounded being confronting Tianqing/the world and silently asking for (or perhaps demanding) justice.

Given the events of 1989, *Ju Dou*'s acerbic treatment of decrepit old men oppressing the younger generation to the point of mutual annihilation seems to allegorize the Party's treatment of the demonstrators. As film scholar Dai Jinhua notes referring to the film: "In a certain way, it relates the heavy and painful emotions associated with the Tiananmen Square crackdown to the China of the nineties."[4] Given that downtrodden women have often signified the Chinese nation, beaten and in need of liberation, in the Chinese cinema, looking at Ju Dou as a bloody but defiant China seems appropriate. Reluctant to put a stop to his older relative's abuse of his young wife, delighted to share in the power the old man has over her by spying on her nude body, Tianqing represents complicity with power, and when Ju Dou turns, she confronts her line of tanks in the form of Tianqing. In fact, *Ju Dou* provides the reverse shot of the face of the oppressed that the footage of the anonymous man facing the line of tanks in Beijing does not offer. This time, the camera, the audience, and the world share Tianqing's point of view, and this moment of confrontation extends beyond a remote village in China of the 1920s to the present, post-Tian'anmen representations of China and the tacit challenge in Ju Dou's gaze as she/an oppressed China confronts global complacency and complicity.[5]

Not surprisingly, the Chinese censors banned *Ju Dou*. (The PRC ban on the film was lifted after Zhang made the more politically agreeable *The Story of Qiu Ju* in 1992.) However, even before it began production, *Ju Dou* had already bypassed the domestic film industry as a Japanese-Chinese coproduction. Nominated for a Golden Palm at Cannes and the first film from the PRC to be nominated for an Academy Award for Best Foreign Film in the United States, Miramax picked up *Ju Dou* for distribution. The fact that the China Film Bureau attempted to withdraw the film from consideration for the Academy Award only helped boost its visibility in the press, and *Ju Dou* won considerable international critical acclaim. With perfect timing, Zhang Yimou shifted from domestic funding to transnational financing, from a subject of the power of the Chinese government to a winner in the global market economy. As Ju Dou gazes back at Tianqing and the world, Zhang Yimou takes command of global screens with a film that implicitly comments on the Tian'anmen demonstrations and the government's repressive response.[6] As Rey

Chow notes, Zhang Yimou's films cross borders because of their ability to shift gears as they circulate on different screens globally: "The wish to 'liberate' Chinese women, which seems to be the 'content,' shifts into the liberation of 'China,' which shifts into the liberation of the 'image' of China on film, which shifts into the liberation of 'China' on film in the international culture market, and so on."[7]

Screens do not provide a neutral medium for the transmission of images. They screen out as much as they reveal, shielding the viewer from sight, ensuring anonymity, and filtering out particular sights that do not fit in with the interests of the government or media moguls. As David Morley and Kevin Robins note in *Spaces of Identity: Global Media, Electronic Landscapes and Cultural Boundaries*:

> The screen is a powerful metaphor for our times: it symbolizes how we now exist in the world, our contradictory condition of engagement and disengagement. Increasingly we confront moral issues through the screen, and the screen confronts us with increasing numbers of moral dilemmas. At the same time, however, it screens us from those dilemmas. It is through the screen that we disavow or deny our human implication in moral realities.[8]

The screen is then a separation, a shield, a protection.[9]

Like the door screens that still guard some traditional Chinese homes, media screens keep out evil influences that cannot turn corners to avoid them. Images on screen, therefore, have more to do with projected fantasies than actual conditions. Although a picture may be worth a thousand words, images can also be vexingly silent, like the Beijing man confronting the tanks or the mute Goddess of Democracy. Screens reflect, like mirrors, back on the viewers and producers of images. However, as Jean Baudrillard points out, screens also produce the viewer who, within postmodernity, has become "a pure screen, a switching center for all the networks of influence."[10] Global screens provide "ways of seeing" suitable to the interests of a transnational economy,[11] and images become commodities for consumption, subject to the same disciplines and ideological strictures of the agora as any other mass-marketed goods. Writing with respect to films by China's Fifth Generation, Xudong Zhang notes the following paradox:

> The paradox is that its immediate situation invites the intervention of a global network of symbolic capital, which endows it with social prestige, cultural distinction, ideological legitimacy and, in some extreme cases, political identity. The invisible background is ultimately the bourgeois global (cultural and material) market in whose value system an elevated style makes sense beyond its immediate social context.[12]

When the lights went out on the night of June 3–4, the reporters banished, and the tanks moved in, images of China fractured, and the meaning of China became hotly contested throughout the ethnic Chinese world and beyond. As Chris Berry notes, "At and after this moment of shock, it is not possible to be simply one of the Chinese people, and that collective noun is shattered into a series of positions in relation to the massacre."[13] Screens may reveal, conceal, reflect, and project, but they also represent sites of struggle over images and ideas. The broadcast of the TV series *River Elegy* (aired in 1988),[14] for example, opened up heated debate over the ills of China before the spring 1989 events in Tian'anmen, and the appearance of one of the show's producers, Su Xiaokang, in the square during the demonstrations seemed to point to the link between earlier representations of China and the creation of a current vision of the "people of the Yellow River" to be presented on world screens during the demonstrations.

Images of Tian'anmen began to circulate on global screens attached to widely varying significations. Hollywood picked up Tian'anmen as a link in a narrative causal chain that could explain the violence at the heart of a string of action-adventure plots in need of rationalization because the end of the Cold War had done away with an important aspect of the formula. (See Chapter 8.) Conveniently, China became the new "evil empire," linked with all sorts of other more concrete evils like drug trafficking, prostitution, and illegal immigrant labor, that held greater meaning for global working class audiences more suspicious of the ex-cesses of transnational capitalism than the more remote oppressiveness of the Chinese state.[15]

With a number of Hollywood regulars having strong personal ties to Tibet, Buddhism, and specifically to the exiled Dalai Lama, global interest in China as a result of the Tian'anmen demonstrations and their suppression led to the pro-duction of films like *Red Corner* (1997),[16] starring Richard Gere, a prominent Hollywood supporter of the Dalai Lama; *Seven Years in Tibet* (1997), in which the Nazis seem preferable to the Chinese Communists; and Martin Scorsese's *Kundun* (1997), which chronicles the Dalai Lama's early years and exile. Not coinciden-tally, all three films coincided with the change of sovereignty of Hong Kong, reminding the world of America's prerogative to question Chinese legal institu-tions and claims to sovereignty. Of course, the PRC countered with several anti-colonial films released the same year, including *Red River Valley* (1997) about the British in Tibet and *Opium War* (1997) (discussed in Chapter 2).[17]

The impact of Tian'anmen on global screen culture outside of Hollywood has been far more complicated and contradictory. The status of Hong Kong became a particularly perplexing issue. As Esther Yau notes, "For many who followed the worldwide reportage on China in June 1989, Hong Kong became a question and an unfinished story . . . the interest in Hong Kong as a last colonial site/sight was a secret longing for disaster—a dramatic news sequel to the Tiananmen Square episodes."[18] Even before the signing of the Joint Declaration and long before 1989, Hong Kong cinema began to show signs of what Stephen Teo terms a "China syndrome"[19] and Esther Yau calls "1997 consciousness."[20] Many films began to reflect anxiety about the change in sovereignty. For example, the main-land gangs attempting to take over Hong Kong in Johnny Mak's popular *The Long Arm of the Law* (1984) and his brother Michael Mak's sequel (1987) appear to encapsulate a more general anxiety about the Chinese takeover. However, few filmmakers could directly address these feelings or the political issues surrounding them due to Hong Kong's censorship restrictions. Specifically, Hong Kong colo-nial censorship regulations stipulated that the cinema may not offend its neighbors, expressly, the People's Republic of China, and films that may displease the Chi-nese government have been routinely banned. In fact, in May 1987, a new Film

Censorship Bill was passed, as John Lent observes, "to ensure that filmmakers did not use Hong Kong as a propaganda base against China."[21] Thus, even before 1989, sentiments in opposition to the transfer of sovereignty to the People's Republic of China began to be taken very seriously by the colonial administration in preparation for 1997.

After the signing of the Joint Declaration, Hong Kong's New Wave directors,[22] including Ann Hui, Allen Fong, Tsui Hark,[23] and Yim Ho, began to explore the implications of the inevitable change in sovereignty in relation to Hong Kong's unique identity in their films. Yim Ho based most of his career on coproductions set in the mainland, including *Homecoming* (1984), which looks at the bittersweet return of a Hong Kong woman to her native town in China. Comparing *Homecoming* to *The Long Arm of the Law*, Lisa Odham Stokes and Michael Hoover observe that the two films

> represent polarized approaches to the Hong Kong/China question: romantic melo-drama/violent actioner, bucolic virtue/urban anomie, hopeful about the return/cynical about the handover. The meditation of the former conveys educated and efficacious middle-class humanism; the rant of the latter communicates underskilled and alienated working class cynicism.[24]

In fact, Hong Kong films made between 1984 and 1989 evidence a range of emotions with respect to 1997 from hope to ambivalence to suspicion and downright apprehension. Based on a novel by the prolific Eileen Chang, *Love in a Fallen City* (directed by Ann Hui, 1984), for example, hints at parallels between the fall of Shanghai and Hong Kong to the Japanese during World War II and the inevitable demise of Hong Kong as a colony in 1997.[25] In both cases, the British are fated to lose. Ann Hui also produced a trilogy on Vietnam culminating with *Boat People* (1982), in which parallels between Vietnam's Communist government and China seem difficult to ignore particularly because *Boat People* was made in China on the island of Hainan with scores of mainland extras.[26] In addition, Allen Fong explored the pros and cons of immigration to the United States in *Just Like Weather* (*Mei Guo Xin*, literally *American Heart*, 1986).

Hong Kong's second wave directors, including Stanley Kwan, Clara Law, Mabel Cheung, Alex Law, and Eddie Fong, took up many of the same themes in their work in the late 1980s. Mabel Cheung's *Eight Taels of Gold* (1989), for example, resembles *Homecoming*. Several films about immigration to the United States also emerged from the group, including Cheung's *Illegal Immigrant* (1984) and *An Autumn's Tale* (1987) as well as Kwan's *Full Moon in New York* (1989).[27] Other films, like Kwan's *Rouge* (1986), take a nostalgic view of Hong Kong that Ackbar Abbas has discussed, following Paul Virilio,[28] as part of a "future anterior" cinema "déjà disparu,"[29] characteristic of Hong Kong on the verge of 1997. These films look at Hong Kong's historic identity in relation to the fears attendant on the change of sovereignty.[30]

After 1989, anxieties increased. Hong Kong emigration jumped, and many in the film industry, following the trend, left, prepared to leave, or solidified their ties to places like Taiwan, Japan, England, Canada, Australia, and the United States, where they could go if needed. For many, 1989 hit harder than the actual signing of the Joint Declaration, and several filmmakers mentioned that they rethought their films in light of the June crackdown. Born in Vietnam, Tsui Hark, for example, uses that country as a backdrop for a story of characters desperate to escape in *A Better Tomorrow III: Love and Death in Saigon* (1989), which includes a chilling confrontation with a tank. In addition, John Woo's *Bullet in the Head* (1990), set in pre-1975 Saigon on the verge of its own Communist future as Ho Chi Minh City, visualizes the graphic violence Woo imagined happening in Tian'anmen that only partially emerged from the news blackout. In fact, Woo cites the bloody suppression of the demonstrations as key to changes he made during the film's production:

> For the second half of the film I was influenced more by the massacre at Tiananmen Square in Beijing in 1989. I was very sad and very upset and felt very ashamed of our country. It was so inhuman to kill all those students. And so I put that pain into the movie, I change the whole second half of the script—the scenes when they first arrive in Vietnam and they see the students demonstrating. When I shot the movie I almost went crazy because I shot the film with pain. I kept thinking about the tragedy. The original idea for the story didn't have the Vietnam part. I just used it as the future of Hong Kong.[31]

Clara Law, in production with *Farewell China* (1990) around the same time, also changed her original conception in the wake of the events in Tian'anmen. The concluding image of the film features a replica of the Goddess of Democracy made by supporters of the demonstrators residing in New York City. By bringing the political and emotional issues associated with Tian'anmen to New York, Law makes Chinese events global concerns by reinforcing the importance of key images on transnational screens. (See Chapter 7.)

Not surprisingly, Woo and Law both relocated to other countries (the United States and Australia, respectively) before 1997. Transnational filmmakers like Evans Chan, dividing his energies and resources between the United States and Hong Kong, dealt more directly with the impact of Tian'anmen on Hong Kong and its people in *To Liv(e)* (1991) and *Crossings* (1994). (See Chapter 6.) Hong Kong–born experimental filmmaker Yau Ching made *Is There Anything Specific You Want Me to Tell You About?* (1991), an epistolary film about exile, and *Flow* (1993), a portrait of a Chinese artist exiled in the United States. She made these short films while living in New York (although she subsequently returned to Hong Kong). Trinh T. Minh-ha reworked *Shoot for the Contents* (1991) to take the Tian'anmen demonstrations and their media depiction into account during the production of the film. As a counterpoint, she puts contemporary Chinese cinema in the mix by including an highly stylized interview with former Xi'an studio head, Wu Tian-ming, a strong supporter of the Fifth Generation, outspoken during the 1989 demonstrations, who immigrated to the United States afterward.[32] Shu Lea Cheang, unable to enter the People's Republic to record the spring 1989 events, focused instead on an analysis of reportage in Taiwan on the Tian'anmen demonstrations in *How Was History Wounded* (1990).

Hong Kong filmmakers Shu Kei and Ann Hui also explored the effects of the Tian'anmen demonstrations in documentaries that included strong ties to Taiwan. Ann Hui produced a documentary for Hong Kong television on Taiwanese singer Hou Dejian, who played an active role in the spring demonstrations in Beijing and was later arrested and deported back to Taiwan. Made in collaboration with Taiwanese screenwriter Wu Nien-Jen, Shu Kei's documentary *Sunless Days* (1990) looks at the impact of the previous spring's events on a variety of people living around the world, including Taiwan's Hou Hsiao-hsien, several members of the Hong Kong film community involved with the demonstrations, and members of his own family. Narrated in English and financed by Japanese television NHK, *Sunless Days* insistently makes Tian'anmen a global issue, with implications beyond its significance for Hong Kong because of 1997 or for Taiwan because of continuous pressure to reunite with the People's Republic.

Indeed, like most of the Chinese world, Hong Kong has been torn between the demands of the "two Chinas" since the end of World War II. Both the ROC and the PRC have exerted considerable influence on virtually all aspects of life in Hong Kong, and the film industry is no exception.[33] In fact, many Hong Kong filmmakers act as go-betweens for mainland and Taiwanese interests. After the lifting of martial law in Taiwan in 1987, a few Taiwanese filmmakers even made films about the reunion of families separated for decades, such as Yu Kanping's *People between Two Chinas* (1989), using Hong Kong as "neutral" ground.

Also released in 1989, Hou Hsiao-hsien's *City of Sadness* became the first feature film made in Taiwan to address directly the February 28, 1947, massacre of demonstrators dissatisfied with the Nationalist/Kuomintang (KMT) occupation of the island. As the last stronghold of Chiang Kai-shek after the KMT loss of the Chinese civil war in 1949, Taiwan came under the absolute authority of the Party until martial law was lifted in 1987. As the first to narrate the impact of the white terror within a family saga that covers the history of Taiwan in the years immediately following the end of Japanese colonial rule, *City of Sadness* generated considerable acclaim as well as controversy. As many artists and intellectuals in Taiwan attempted to distance themselves from the mainland, from the fact of the KMT and the threat of the Chinese Communist Party (CCP), Hou's depiction of the white terror profoundly resonated with recent images of the violence in Tian'anmen in spring of that year.[34]

Just as Shu Kei's "casting" of Hou in *Sunless Days* draws Taiwan into the orbit of concern in the aftermath of Tian'anmen, Hou's casting of Hong Kong actor Tony Leung as the mute protagonist in *City of Sadness* draws Hong Kong, and the rest of the Chinese world, into the drama of February 28.[35] A photographer, Leung's character both witnesses and documents the era, but he remains silent. The impact of Tian'anmen, like the horrors of the white terror, left many unable to articulate their thoughts and feelings. In many respects, after June 4, 1989, Chinese metropolises became what Gilles Deleuze has described as "any space whatever" that characterized the postwar European city:

The post-war period has greatly increased the situations which we no longer know how to react to, in spaces which we no longer know how to describe. These were "any spaces whatever," deserted but inhabited, disused warehouses, waste ground, cities in the course of demolition or reconstruction. And in these any-spaces-whatever a new race of characters was stirring, kind of mutant: they saw rather than acted, they were seers.[36]

While many remained mute, Tian'anmen united and polarized the Chinese-speaking world in profound and sometimes unexpected ways. Many dissidents fled China or decided to permanently stay abroad if they were away during 1989. Hong Kong emigration escalated. Parallel to this, many children of the KMT saw their privileged days numbered after the end of martial law, and they formed another wave of semi-political, semi-economic exiles from the "other" China. Political and economic changes in Singapore, Malaysia, the Philippines, Indonesia, Thailand, and Vietnam fueled other waves of Chinese emigration, and Chinatowns around the world began to change dramatically. Familial, linguistic, economic, social, and cultural relations within the diaspora often competed with the influence of the PRC, Taiwan, and Hong Kong on these diverse communities. Thus, for example, links among a single extended Chinese family living in the United States, Canada, Indonesia, and Holland may be stronger than any ties to the Chinese cultural "centers."[37] In New York's Chinese communities, for example, Chinese cultures from around the globe cross-pollinate, and what has been called "transnational," "Greater," or "global" China emerges as a phenomenon that crosses national as well as cultural borders.[38]

The most direct cinematic indictments of the 1989 crackdown have come from filmmakers working with people living within this transnational cultural sphere. Michael Apted's *Moving the Mountain* (based on Li Lu's memoir of the same title, 1994) and Carma Hinton and Richard Gordon's *Gate of Heavenly Peace* (1995) stand out as attempts to reframe the demonstrations and their impact.[39] *Gate of Heavenly Peace*, in addition, brings the continuing implications of Tian'anmen from the cinema theater to the video screen and to the Internet, considerably expanding access to information about the demonstrations and their suppression. (See Chapter 9.)

Even without direct mention of 1989, images of Tian'anmen evoke different associations as a consequence of the crackdown. When Sixth Generation filmmaker Zhang Yuan looks at the daily life in Tian'anmen in *The Square* (codirected with Duan Jinchuan, 1994) or interrupts the loose narrative of *Beijing Bastards* (1993) to allow the camera to move through Tian'anmen Square in the rain, 1989 haunts the images.[40] Circulating as a photograph or a memory in films as diverse as *Out of Phoenix Bridge* (Chapter 3) and *Twelve Storeys* (Chapter 5), Tian'anmen also functions as an absent presence in myriad films. The desperation of Chinese émigrés in green card romances may remain unexplained. Chinese artists suddenly appear painting pictures of tourists in Times Square, and the terror that swept through the avant-garde art communities in the aftermath of the June crackdown need not explicate their presence.

Although films decrying the excesses of the Great Proletarian Cultural Revolution (1966–76) had become a formulaic staple in the Chinese-speaking world earlier, they took on a new dimension after 1989. Crowds in Tian'anmen shouting, students gripped by political fervor, violence erupting from demonstrations became images that spoke more to conditions in 1989 than to the era of the Cultural Revolution. The critique of the Communist Party for the "excesses" of the Cultural Revolution began to take on elements of the 1989 demonstrators' condemnation of the Party's corruption, insensitivity, and myopia. Xie Jin's *Hibiscus Town* (1986) won accolades for condemning the Cultural Revolution,[41] but a string of films made after 1989 on the topic became sore points for the censors, including Zhang Yimou's *To Live* (1994) and Tian Zhuangzhuang's *Blue Kite* (1993). Dai Sijie's *China My Sorrow* (1989)[42] and Wang Xiaowen's *The Monkey Kid* (1995), with European and American backing, respectively, also resonated differently, as did the scenes featuring the Cultural Revolution in films as diverse as David Cronenberg's *M. Butterfly* (1993) and Chen Kaige's *Farewell My Concubine* (1993). However, the television series *Yearnings* (first aired in 1990), used the Cultural Revolution to move away from politics and became an immensely popular media event in mainland China.[43] Although popular author Wang Shuo was visibly involved with *Yearnings*, another film based on his vision of the Cultural Revolution, *In the Heat of the Sun* (1995), directed by Jiang Wen, took the history of that era in a very different direction with its fragmented depiction of a group of delinquent boys on their own. Wu Wenguang's *My Time in the Red Guards* (1993) also dealt with that era with similar candor.

In fact, the 1960s and early 1970s provided the backdrop for many Chinese-language films made after 1989. In addition to the trauma associated with the Cultural Revolution, this period represented the time in which many of the New Wave filmmakers of Chinese cinema (from the "first" and "second" waves of Hong Kong's and Taiwan's New Cinema to the Fifth and Sixth Generation in the People's Republic) went through childhood or came of age as young adults. As Hong Kong and Taiwan reexamined their identities vis-à-vis the People's Republic after 1989, the complexities of the 1960s—from labor unrest, student and worker riots, demonstrations against the war in Vietnam, the impact of youth countercultures, and the anxieties surrounding Hong Kong as a British colony and Taiwan as part of the American military's sphere of influence during the Cold War—enabled filmmakers to look at their current situation with regard to the People's Republic through the prism of a previous era. For example, Wong Kar-Wai's *Days of Being Wild* (1991), Edward Yang's *Brighter Summer Day* (1991), Wu Nien-jen's *A Borrowed Life* (1994)[44] and *Buddha Bless America* (1997),[45] as well as several of Hou Hsiao-hsien's films all take place in the 1960s with a keen eye to the ways the vicissitudes of that period, from political turmoil and economic uncertainty to the massive influx of American popular culture into Asia, reverberate with questions of identity in the 1990s. Ann Hui's *Song of the Exile* (1990), scripted by Wu Nien-jen, provides one of the most telling examples. Roughly autobiographical, the narrative depicts Ann Hui's relationship to her Japanese mother and Chinese relatives and recounts travels and memories that include Manchuria, Japan, Macao, Hong Kong, England, and mainland China. When Cheung Hueyin (Maggie Cheung) goes to China to visit her paternal grandparents, who have been

FIGURE 1. Still from *The Blue Kite*. The child Tie-tou (Zhang Wenyao) witnesses waves of political strife as he grows up in the People's Republic of China. (Courtesy of Kino International.)

repatriated during the Cultural Revolution, she discovers the old couple living in appalling conditions and caring for a mentally handicapped boy. When the disturbed boy bites the hand that tries to feed him, the allegorical implications seem clear as Hong Kong confronts a "backward" and violent China to which it is related—no matter how distantly.[46]

Films set during the Republican era, particularly those featuring "old Shanghai," the Japanese occupation, and the civil war before 1949 also allegorized the 1989–97 period. Zhang Yimou's *Ju Dou* (1990) and *Raise the Red Lantern* (1991), for example, were set during the Republican period. Sek Kei, in his essay "Hong Kong Cinema from June 4 to 1997," characterizes Yim Ho's *Red Dust* (1990) as an allegory of June 4.[47] Loosely based on Eileen Chang's life, the film deals with the chaos of life in China immediately before Mao's victory in 1949 in a story about the love affair between a woman novelist and a Chinese agent working for the Japanese. Other films, like Ye Daying's *Red Cherry* (1995), from the PRC, demonize the Axis powers (in this case, the Germans), but remain strikingly raw in their depictions of violence, opening up various readings. In the film, the Nazi commander takes possession of the young Chinese Communist victim, Chuchu (Guo Keyu), by forcibly tattooing her back. Given that the film is based on an actual historical incident, the possible interpretations extend beyond the film itself into the historical memory of the Chinese body politic. Whether interpreted as a call for Chinese ethnic solidarity in the face of European aggression, as a reminder of the suffering that went into the creation of the Chinese Communist state, or as a

FIGURE 2. *Red Cherry*. Billboard in Singapore. "A soft-core visualization of sadistic excess for export." (Photo by author.)

soft-core visualization of sadistic excess for export, *Red Cherry* opens up another window on Chinese history that seems to elevate nationalism above dissent and stands in marked contrast to other films' use of the era to allegorize June 4.

Old Shanghai, in particular—divided among various colonial powers before 1949, cosmopolitan, economically vibrant, corrupt, riddled with urban vices, a base for gangsters as well as political dissidents—became the setting for several films that chronicled Chinese society on the verge of momentous change.[48] Although pre-1949 Shanghai had been on global screens before 1989 with films like Steven Spielberg's *Empire of the Sun* (1987), based on J. G. Ballard's semi-autobiographical novel of his childhood under Japanese occupation in China, interest in Shanghai stepped up after Tian'anmen. Ulrike Ottinger's documentary, *Exile Shanghai* (1997), documents the lives of Jewish exiles in Shanghai during World War II. Zhang Yimou's *Shanghai Triad* (1995), Chen Kaige's *Temptress Moon* (1996), Poon Man-Kit's *Shanghai Grand* (1996), Leong Po-chih's *Shanghai 1920: Once upon a Time in Shanghai* (1991) all deal with the dark side of Shanghai's economy; Li Shaohong's *Blush* (1994) looks at the "reform" of Shanghai prostitutes after 1949. Wong Jing's *God of Gamblers II* (1991) sends its hero back to Shanghai in 1937, the year of the Japanese invasion, and the Austrian/Chinese coproduced television series *Shanghai 1937* (1996) is set in the same year.

In two films made the same year, Taiwan's Stan Lai evokes old Shanghai in *Peach Blossomland* (1992),[49] using a play-within-a-play structure, and Hong Kong's Stanley Kwan looks at the career of Shanghai silent film star Ruan Lingyu

FIGURE 3. Still from *Red Cherry.* Chuchu (Guo Keyu) displays her tattoo back to back with her Nazi tormentor. (Courtesy of Wellspring.)

in relation to contemporary Hong Kong in the person of the actress who plays Ruan in the present, Maggie Cheung, in *Centre Stage* (1992). As Lisa Odham Stokes and Michael Hoover note: "The image of woman, through Ruan individually and the roles she played and through women generally, becomes for Kwan a meditative ground for circumscribing Hong Kong."[50] Based on a novella by Eileen Chang, Kwan's *Red Rose White Rose* (1994) also uses Shanghai in the 1930s as a backdrop for its story of a man torn between two women—one "modern" (i.e., influenced by the West) and one "traditional"—and the pull between Europe and China. Hong Kong, of course, like a man with two lovers, experiences the same frustrations as it negotiates its identity in the years before 1997. Mabel Cheung's *The Soong Sisters* (1997) also uses the political history of the earlier part of the century to comment on the present moment by following the choices made by the three most famous sisters in contemporary Chinese history—Soong Meiling (Vivian Wu), who married Chiang Kai-shek and ended up as the first lady of the Republic of China on Taiwan, Soong Qingling (Maggie Cheung), young widow of Sun Yat-sen, who remained in the People's Republic of China after 1949, and Soong Ailing (Michelle Yeoh), who ended up with her banker husband in Hong Kong.[51] Also covering decades, Clifton Ko's *The Mad Phoenix* (1997) spans the years from the 1930s to the 1980s to look at momentous changes in Chinese society against the backdrop of Cantonese opera. Using the political arena, the stage, and the screen, these films offer the opportunity for reflection on the past in the light of the present moment; that is, in anticipation of July 1, 1997.

OUT OF CHINA

Even though contact between the United States and China increased considerably after Richard Nixon's visit to Beijing and meeting with Mao Zedong in 1972, Jimmy Carter's official normalization of relations in January 1979 opened up a floodgate of economic, cultural, educational, and even military contacts. A number of films made in the United States featured reunions of families split apart as a result of the Communist victory in 1949.[52] Peter Wang's *A Great Wall* (1986), for example, portrays the reunion of a Chinese American businessman and his Asian American family with his relatives in the People's Republic. Born in Taiwan, Wang, as an actor, has also played a prominent role in films by Hong Kong/Asian American director Wayne Wang and Hong Kong director Allen Fong, bridging Taiwan, Hong Kong, and Asian American film cultures.

Although transnational links among the cinemas of China, Hong Kong, Taiwan, and the United States escalated after 1989, the nature of the narratives shifted. Films did continue to feature family reunions—for example, *The Joy Luck Club* (Wayne Wang, 1993) and *My American Grandson* (directed by Ann Hui, scripted by Wu Nien-jen, 1990), among others. Evans Chan's documentary *Journey to Beijing* (1998) also featured a group of walkers on a trip to the mainland to raise money for charity. However, these narratives diminished in number in comparison to stories dealing with people leaving China. Legal and illegal émigrés from the mainland began to people global screens. Although the stretch of mainland authority might be benevolent as in the *Her Fatal Ways* series (beginning in 1991), starring Dodo Cheng as the "biao jie" /country "cousin" police officer from the PRC in Hong Kong or as the pathetic mainland mistress as in Sylvia Chang's *Mary from Beijing* (1992),[53] the mainland émigré, from "China bride" (Chapter 5) to political exile (Chapter 9) to gangster (Chapters 6 and 7) to working stiff desperate to get ahead invaded world screens after 1989 with a vengeance. The popular mainland television series *A Beijinger in New York* (1993), for example, depicts the struggles of émigrés from the PRC in New York City,[54] and Xia Gang's melodrama *Yesterday's Wine* (1995) deals with a complex relationship between a young woman from the PRC and her Chinese American boyfriend, who happens to be her first lover's son, separated from his mainland family as a boy.

Perhaps Peter Chan's *Comrades: Almost a Love Story* (1996) provides the definitive telling of the story with its sweeping tale that spans the ups and downs of two mainland émigrés as they travel from Hong Kong to the United States, meeting up with Taiwanese gangsters, Thai prostitutes, alcoholic English teachers, and a range of mainlanders in search of the Hong Kong/American dream. (See Chapter 2.) In fact, although it may be reassuring for the Hong Kong audiences to see the mainland Chinese characters move on from Hong Kong to supposedly greener pastures in the United States, film screens saw no shortage of Chinese characters from Hong Kong, Taiwan, Singapore, and other Chinese communities on the move. Just as so many filmmakers are themselves multiple migrants,[55] Chinese characters tend to be on the move, forced to travel because of political or economic hardship or inclined to travel for other reasons. By 1997, characters on the screen and filmmakers behind the scene found themselves increasingly mobile, "flexible citizens."[56] For example, Chinese martial arts hero Wong Fei-hung (played by Jet Li) goes to the Old West in the Hong Kong film *Once Upon a Time in China and America* (directed by Sammo Hung, written by Tsui Hark, 1997),[57] and all three (Beijing-born Li, Hong Kong-born Hung, and Vietnamese-born Tsui) end up working in Hollywood. Wong Kar-Wai takes his Hong Kong characters to Argentina in *Happy Together* (1997), and although the film concludes in Taiwan, Hong Kong itself is only pictured, upside down, as a fleeting thought, from the other side of the world.

Stepping back, filmmakers look at the way their Chinese characters fit into a global picture, and the PRC, Taiwan, and Hong Kong drift to the background as the Chinese diaspora, Asian America/Canada/Australia/Eurasia and more cosmopolitan, multicultural relationships move to the fore. (See Chapters 2, 6–8.) Film artists map out global processes and their impact on individuals in films that chart the global flow of people, goods, images, and ideas.[58] Just as Chinese characters travel around the globe, the "centers" of Chinese civilization become more cosmopolitan. Filmmakers in the People's Republic depict the changes taking place in increasingly cosmopolitan Chinese cities in films like Ning Ying's *For Fun* (1993), on the lives of Beijing opera-obsessed retirees; *On the Beat* (1995), on the impact of reform on the duties of China's police;[59] Huang Jianxin's satiric trilogy, *Stand Up, Don't Bend Over* (1993), *Back to Back, Face to Face* (1994),[60] and *Signal Left, Turn Right* (1996), as well as in several films based on novels by Wang Shuo.[61] Subsequently, Beijing (Chapters 3 and 9), Hong Kong (Chapters 2, 6, and 7), Taipei (Chapter 4), and Singapore (Chapter 5) begin to host narratives strikingly similar to those found in New York (Chapters 6 and 7) and Australia (Chapter 7). Borders become more porous, and stories about the movements of Chinese people, money, and cultural artifacts pop up around the globe. Thus, the chronicle of migrant labor from the Chinese countryside to Beijing in the documentary *Out of Phoenix Bridge* (Chapter 3) resonates with similar stories of the transnational movements of Chinese labor in *Comrades: Almost a Love Story* (Chapter 2) and *Farewell China* (Chapter 7).

With the transnational movement of labor as well as capital, class positions increasingly require renegotiation. As overseas investment poured into the People's Republic of China and the market economy boomed, capitalism stratified Chinese society, enriching a few and impoverishing many. Overseas Chinese, who had been successful outside of the mainland, saw new competition coming from the "backwaters" of cities like Beijing and Shanghai. The economies of Hong Kong and Taiwan became increasingly dependent on mainland markets, labor, industrial goods, and raw materials. As a result, for many, the business climate appeared to be more welcoming abroad. However, moving outside of Asia, Chinese businesspeople, students, and laborers suffered from discrimination and often violent racism.[62] Many diasporic Chinese began to reinvestigate their identity based on a Eurocentric definition of race as well as class, and filmmakers began to look at the relationship between the Chinese and African Americans, for example, in new ways. (See Chapter 7.)

If racial categories destabilized, class hierarchies also changed. Many films dealt with these shifting class relationships and the difficulties of navigating a global marketplace in which Chinese ways of doing business may or may not be viable. (See Chapters 2–5.) Zhang Yimou's parable *The Story of Qiu Ju* (1992),[63] provides a case in point. A Hong Kong–PRC coproduction, the film tells the story of a peasant woman, Qiu Ju (Gong Li), looking for justice for her injured husband. The case begins, before the film, with a misunderstanding involving land use in the village when the village head Wang Shangtang (Lei Laosheng) refuses to let Qiu Ju's husband, Wan Qinglai (Liu Peiqi), build a shed to store chili peppers. After Wan taunts Wang with the fact he has only girls and no male heir, the village head kicks the chili farmer in the groin and beats him. The film begins with the pregnant Qiu Ju taking her husband to the doctor in town. Looking for an apology, she goes to the town official. The cadre does his best to smooth things over; however, reconciliation proves difficult when Wang agrees to pay Wan's medical bills but throws the money down in front of Qiu Ju to force her to bow to him to get her compensation.

In the film, two systems of dealing with personal disputes emerge—one based on traditional Chinese notions, specifically *guan xi* (discussed in Chapter 4),[64] and the other based on the rule of law. Although *Qiu Ju* takes place exclusively in the People's Republic, the fact that the film is a Hong Kong coproduction and that Hong Kong, in anticipation of the "one country, two systems" policy stipulated by the Joint Declaration, was attempting to eke out the guarantee of the rule of law for itself before 1997, merits attention. The film carefully shows that the backdoor system of guan xi connections actually works better to guarantee justice in the village than the elaborate legal hierarchy that represents the rule of law. After Wang saves Qiu Ju and her son in a difficult childbirth, the scales seem balanced. However, because she has filed a suit and involved the legal system in the case, the village chief finds himself sentenced to prison at the film's conclusion. The last shot of the film shows a helpless Qiu Ju unable to save Wang from this punishment that now seems excessive. Thus, guan xi relations, the traditional Chinese methods of handling things, in the film point to a superior method of handling disputes (through gifts accepted and declined, rules like the one-child policy broken through influence and others like the land use policy maintained somewhat arbitrarily) rather than a deeply ingrained practice of corruption. Confucian-based, hierarchical systems of mutual obligations vie with Western notions of money and legal justice to present a picture of China's entry into the global sphere that goes far beyond this story of village life. As *The Story of Qiu Ju* demonstrates, both Deng's notion of "socialism with Chinese characteristics" and Hong Kong's postcolonial status in relation to China and the West remain in need of careful contemplation.

Following Lee Kwan-Yu of Singapore, who called for Confucian-inspired "Asian values," and Confucian philosopher Tu Wei-Ming's notion of "cultural China,"[65] other leaders across Asia used a reinvigorated Confucian sensibility to justify everything from cuts to programs to aid the elderly (who should be cared for, of course, by filial sons and daughters) to family planning campaigns.[66] (See Chapter 5.) As Sheldon Lu notes:

The idea of Cultural China is closely tied to a revival of Confucianism. The identification with China is not a matter of legal or territorial consideration but a matter of
cultural affiliation. "Greater China," "Greater China economic zone," "East Asian
modernity," and "Cultural China" are notions that stake out a grand global role for
China at the end of the twentieth century and in the next century. Whether perceived
as a renewed Sinocentrism or a counterhegemonic discourse against Euro-American
domination, the idea of Cultural China fully articulates the ambition and reality of a
new transnational Chinese culture in the making.[67]

Particularly after 1989, films dealing with Confucian virtues and traditional Chinese social hierarchies based on the model of the dynastic state and the patriarchal
family attempted to navigate the way ethnic Chinese within the global economy
could or should operate differently than their non-Chinese counterparts. However,
as Peter Hitchcock has pointed out, "ethnicist economics mask the real relations of
the economic to its subjects."[68] Clearly, tensions persist, and films take up the
contradictions created by global capitalism.

Gangster films, for example, that deal with negotiations between the legitimate
and "unofficial" economies, hierarchical structures of criminal organizations,
divided loyalties, and mutual obligations (particularly among gang "brothers")
seem to point to the difficulties of reconciling Chinese tradition, the state, and
modern capitalist concerns. Of course, John Woo's gangster sagas represent this
tendency with their emphasis on filial devotion, loyalty and betrayal, and a Confucian sense of "manly" virtue based on brotherhood wedded to a heavy dose of
Christian symbolism, reflecting Woo's Christian education in Hong Kong and
infatuation with Hollywood cinema.[69] Although Confucianism was often at odds
with capitalism, the excesses of the new marketplace (embodied by the gangsters'
illegal enterprises) always came under the command of a traditional sense of
justice and virtue. Violently cleansed of any taint of injustice through elaborately
choreographed gunfights, society emerged, reinvigorated by the challenge posed
to Confucian values against the background of the West represented by the
physical presence of Christian churches in many of Woo's films.

However, another interpretation of *The Story of Qiu Ju* and these Hong Kong
gangster sagas is also possible. The characters in these films desperately attempt to
find a way of dealing with the authority of the state, whether in the form of the
village head or the chief of police or other figure of official, governmental power.
Furthermore, these films depict these relationships as strained and corrupt, and the
fact that these narratives resonate with other depictions of the excesses of authority
in the wake of the Tian'anmen crackdown in 1989 cannot be ignored.

GENDER CRISES

Of course, John Woo's films also portray masculinity—specifically Confucian-
inflected, Chinese masculinity—in crisis.[70] Particularly after 1989, male power,
represented by the old cadres of the Communist Party headed by Deng Xiaoping,
came under serious assault, as seen in Zhang's *Ju Dou* and *Raise the Red Lantern*.
The old male guard was losing its grip beyond Beijing. Hong Kong colonial

authority—British influence and potentially the wealth and power of the upper echelon of Hong Kong Chinese society that had built its fortunes on the colonial system—was nearly a thing of the past. In *Chinese Box* (1997), Wayne Wang captures the death rattle of the British Empire in the figure of John (Jeremy Irons), who slowly expires through the course of the film.[71] In British director Peter Greenaway's *The Pillow Book* (1996), Hong Kong embodies all the uncertainty and ambiguity associated with the end of British colonialism, the end of the millennium, and the transformation of the cinema by the digital revolution. Hong Kong, positioned between Japan and the West, becomes part of the canvas, the skin, on which the director writes his tale of sexually ambiguous relationships that seem to question patriarchal certainty as well as the position of Britain in relation to Asia through the story of Nagiko (played by Shanghai-born Vivian Wu), who journeys from Japan to Hong Kong and finds "herself" by writing on the bodies of young men to avenge her father's honor compromised by his sadistic publisher.

The KMT in Taiwan, reprieved by the 1996 elections, was also coming under attack for the first time since it took control of the island after World War II. Aging KMT patriarchs, for example, attempt to hang on to the slightest illusion of control in Ang Lee's "father knows best" trilogy (*Pushing Hands*, 1992; *The Wedding Banquet*, 1993; and *Eat Drink Man Woman*, 1994),[72] but, as Lee's own immigration to the United States highlights, the future in Taiwan does not seem bright for the aging mainlanders and their progeny.

Chinese women, like Qiu Ju (Gong Li), emerge, in many of these films, as the face of the new China—beaten down, stubborn, but pregnant with possibilities. Although the Goddess of Democracy crafted by the students for the demonstrations in Tian'anmen may not have many "Chinese characteristics," the fact that liberty should be embodied as a woman speaks to the power of the female form to allegorize Chinese aspirations. This tendency predates 1989. As Sheldon Lu succinctly states: "Woman in Chinese cinematic expression is the trope for the modern Chinese nation."[73] Changing gender roles and sexual crises, then, allegorize the nation at a crossroads within a shifting global culture. However, Chinese women on screen also operate outside of (or polysemically within) national allegories in films that comment on the impact feminism has had on shifting attitudes toward gender and female sexuality within the "scattered hegemonies" that characterize postmodern, transnational culture.[74] In genres as diverse as comedy, melodrama, fantasy, soft-core porn, and the martial arts action film, female protagonists take on the Chinese patriarchy and renegotiate their place within global Chinese society. (See Chapters 2, 3, 5–7.)

Many of these films use generational conflicts to explore the tension women experience between traditional expectations for women under the Chinese patriarchy and the demands of an increasingly globalized environment in which living within the Chinese diaspora may mean putting aside outmoded family structures modeled on Confucian principles (e.g., *Song of the Exile* and the films by Clara Law discussed in Chapter 7). Ann Hui's *Summer Snow* (1994), for example, shows an overextended middle-aged Hong Kong woman, May, at the end of her tether.

Played by veteran actress Josephine Siao, May must balance her obligations at her job at an import-export company with her demanding life at home as the mother of a teenager and primary caretaker of her father-in-law, who suffers from Alzheimer's disease.

Needing heroic strength to deal with quotidian demands, the Chinese martial heroine emerged to fit the bill.[75] Women warriors play a key role in Chinese folktales, classical literature, and traditional opera. These figures have been on Chinese screens since the silent era, and their appearance in Chinese-language films after 1989 does not mark any major departure from tradition. Rather, the *dao ma dan* (as she is known in opera) has always provided an exceptional figure for extraordinary times. Although an emblem of feminine strength, she does not challenge Confucian orthodoxy, and she only takes up the sword because all the men in her family have died, become disabled, or are too young to fight. Thus her filial obligations outweigh her gendered role as daughter, wife, and mother in the patriarchal household. Also, filial piety dictates that she must defend her honor (and by extension, the honor of her family) when assaulted, and the woman warrior may become a female avenger if raped or otherwise abused. In fact, the woman warrior only becomes villainous when she goes against Confucian notions of hierarchy and attempts to transform society in her own image. Whether in period costume as a *kung fu* adept or in modern dress as a police officer or government spy, the woman warrior on Chinese screens continues to function in much the same way as a locus of contradictions surrounding the tension between "proper" gender roles for women and the actual circumstances women face in a complex, chaotic world. Although they may appear to be exemplars of feminism perfectly able to handle themselves in any situation, even in contemporary film, the woman warrior remains bound to Confucian obligations to her family, employer, government, or martial arts master, and she seldom steps out on her own with impunity.

Whether comic as in the *Yes, Madam* series (featuring Michelle Yeoh and Euro-American martial arts adept Cynthia Rothrock),[76] comic/dramatic as in *Wing Chun* (also starring Michelle Yeoh, 1994), cartoonishly grotesque as in *Heroic Trio* (featuring Michelle Yeoh, Anita Mui, and Maggie Cheung, 1992), melodramatic as in Ann Hui's *Ah Kam* (a.k.a. *The Stuntwoman*, also with Michelle Yeoh, 1996), romantic as in *The Bride with White Hair* (starring Brigitte Lin, 1993), or fantastic and folkloric as in *Green Snake* (with Maggie Cheung, 1993), the martial heroine's physical prowess marks her as exceptional and, in her late-twentieth-century incarnations, able to transcend the dueling demands of Confucian obligations and postfeminist career expectations.

The woman warrior has also become a site for the projected fantasies of non-Chinese filmmakers and fans. In Olivier Assayas's *Irma Vep* (1996), for example, she becomes the blank screen for the projection of a range of desires.[77] In *Tomorrow Never Dies*, she is enlisted to free the world from media monopolies and seal the West's relationship with China with a kiss. Distantly related to the *biao jie* (country cousin) of Hong Kong's *Her Fatal Ways* series, the ex–cold war agent, formerly stripped of her sexuality by Jiang Qing and the Gang of Four,[78] has finally found her way to world screens as a dangerously sexy Bond girl.

FROM GENDER BENDING TO QUEER DIASPORAS

The reinvention of the Chinese woman warrior as the Bond girl does not drift too far from the formulaic presentation of Asian women in Hollywood as passive but erotic "lotus blossoms" or villainously dangerous, exotic "dragon ladies."[79] Hollywood has similarly vacillated from depicting Asian men as eunuchs or rapacious threats to white women.[80] After 1989, Chinese imperial eunuchs, transvestite spies, transsexual villains, and a variety of other gender-bending characters appeared on world screens at the same time that films began to treat Chinese gay men, lesbians, and queer issues openly for the first time.

Although, in some films these two aspects of "gender trouble" are intimately related,[81] in other films, gay life and queer critiques of heterosexual norms take a back seat to the use of gender-bending characters as political allegory. For example, Wai-tung (Winston Chao) in *The Wedding Banquet* (1993) seems to function less as a symbol of Chinese gay men's demands for recognition and liberation from compulsory heterosexuality and more as an allegory of Taiwan's troubled identity in relation to the PRC as well as the West.

Just as the woman warrior has traditionally had her place in Chinese culture, the "eunuch" has played a prominent role in narratives involving court intrigues and the corruption inherent in the imperial system. After 1989, Fifth Generation filmmaker Tian Zhuangzhuang produced *Li Lianying, The Last Eunuch* (1991) as his first cinematic statement after Tian'anmen, referring more to current power configurations than Qing decadence. Certainly, Bernardo Bertolucci had already established an interest in the sexual dynamics involved in the fall of the Qing court in *The Last Emperor* (1987), and Hong Kong's Jacob Cheung followed up with *Lai Shi, China's Last Eunuch* (1988). Eddie Fong, who scripted *Lai Shi*, went on to direct *Kawashima Yoshiko, The Last Princess of Manchuria* (1990), a film about the bisexual transvestite relative of Pu Yi, the last emperor, who worked as an agent for the Japanese. Questions of political loyalty, national sovereignty, gender roles, and sexual desire blend in these films to engage with broader social and political issues facing the Chinese.

In martial arts fantasies, "yin/yang" monsters representing unholy alliances of the feminine and masculine principles began to spring up and demand power in films such as *The Bride with White Hair* (1993), *The Heroic Trio* (1992), *Dragon Inn* (1992), *Tai Chi Master* (1993), and the *Chinese Ghost Story* series, among others. *Swordsman II* and *Swordsman III: The East Is Red* (1993), for example, feature Invincible Asia (Brigitte Lin) as a martial arts master who feminizes himself to attain a superior level of occult power.[82] The English subtitle of *Swordsman III*, referring to the Maoist classic, points directly to the allegorical significance of this martial arts fantasy. Fears of a primitive primordial Chinese power blend with anxiety about changing identities in these Hong Kong martial arts films that allude to the frightening changes that may happen when Hong Kong reverts to Chinese control. However, other interpretations of this trope are also possible, as Bhaskar Sarkar notes:

Castration alludes not just to the crisis of a partitioned China but also to the West's conception of Asia as feminine, spiritual, and mysterious. At another level, the castration may be interpreted as the abandonment by the various Asian nations of their avowed socioeconomic policies and their capitulation to the West's schemes for a global economic order.[83]

In Wong Kar-Wai's *Ashes of Time* (1994), based on Louis Cha/Jin Yong's martial arts novel, Brigitte Lin plays the dual female/male roles of Mu-rong Yin and Mu-rong Yang, roaming the hinterlands of the Chinese mainland. Again, gender uncertainty appears to stand in for a more general malaise associated with Hong Kong's identity crisis. In *At Full Speed: Hong Kong Cinema in a Borderless World*, Esther Yau notes a particular "androgynous" aesthetic associated with films made in Hong Kong in anticipation of 1997:

> Instead of holding on to a single identity tied to a small territory or replaying the norms of a bounded culture, the "culturally androgynous" film cites diverse idioms, repackages codes, and combines genres that are thought to be culturally, aesthetically, or cinematically incompatible. . . . These modes help break down the notion of bounded cultures, so that the cultural entities that once appeared to be historically and geographically intact are often taken apart and reassembled. This process of "disintegration" has contributed to the cultural androgyny of Hong Kong movies.[84]

Given the importance of transvestitism within the institution of Chinese opera, narratives featuring cross-dressing as an element of romance have a tradition that predates 1989 as well. Again, however, anxieties about identity, related to the changing roles of China and the Chinese as well as men and women in the global economy, fuel some of the increased screen attention given to these stories. In He Ping's *Red Firecracker, Green Firecracker* (1994), the female protagonist cross-dresses to solidify her claim on the family business. In the *Victor/Victoria*-inspired comedy by Peter Chan, *He's a Woman, She's a Man* (1994), and its sequel, *Who's the Woman, Who's the Man* (1996), Anita Yuen's character cross-dresses to establish her singing career in the competitive world of Hong Kong Canto-pop. The links formed between business and gender in these films point to issues that go beyond superficial changes in the Chinese patriarchal household and indicate recognition of the inextricable connection between gender and changing ways of doing business in contemporary society.

Although these films only tangentially depict homosexual characters and the homoeroticism associated with transvestite performances, others deal more directly with homosexuality in relation to Chinese entertainment, particularly the world of Chinese opera. *M. Butterfly* (1993) and *Farewell My Concubine* (1993), for example, portray homosexuality within the opera world. Cheng Sheng-fu's *The Silent Thrush* (1992) looks at lesbianism with Chinese opera as a backdrop. Other films displace lesbianism as a contemporary issue onto characters abused by patriarchal excess in the past, for example, Wang Jin's *Women Flowers* (1994), Jacob Cheung's *Intimates* (1997), and Huang Yu-shan's *Twin Bracelets* (1992).[85]

As Taiwan relaxed after the end of martial law, Singapore changed its censorship ordinances, and Hong Kong reexamined its regulations involving homosexuality before 1997, Chinese filmmakers began to make films dealing directly with gay and lesbian protagonists and with queer culture. Yon Fan's *Bugis Street* (1994), set in Singapore, Shu Kei's *A Queer Story* (1996), set in Hong Kong and including some interesting glimpses of gay life across the border with the mainland in Shenzhen, and Yu Kan-ping's *The Outcasts* (1986), set in Taiwan, all provide candid portraits of gay life in those places. Tsai Ming-Liang, born in Malaysia, takes up the experience of being young and gay in his films depicting life in contemporary Taipei. Although gay Chinese filmmakers had been producing films in the United States, Canada, and other countries outside of Asia for some time, Ang Lee's *The Wedding Banquet* made global audiences even more aware of gay life within the Chinese diaspora. Richard Fung, Paul Lee, Ming-Yuen S. Ma, Quentin Lee, and others working within the Chinese diaspora continue to wrestle with the specific problems of being queer and Asian in the West. Again, perhaps dealing more with political allegory than gay rights, Wong Kar-Wai's *Happy Together* (1997) takes its central gay couple from Hong Kong to Argentina to explore the "can't live with him, can't live without him" syndrome that characterizes Hong Kong's relationship to China on the eve of the handover.

Balancing the personal and the political, Kwoi's *Dark Sun, Bright Shade* (1993) depicts a gay love affair between a Chinese dissident involved with the 1989 demonstrations and his Chinese Canadian lover. Although Stanley Kwan's *Lan Yu* (2001) also deals with the juxtaposition of a gay relationship with the Tian'anmen protests, perhaps more than any other film, Zhang Yuan's *East Palace, West Palace* (1997) uses its story about gay life in Beijing to work through feelings surrounding the crackdown in June 1989. In this case, a young gay man, A Lan (Si Han), cruising the "palaces," the public washrooms frequented by gay men for surreptitious sex near Tian'anmen Square, gets hassled by a policeman. Seemingly on impulse, A Lan kisses the officer. Actually, the young man has a masochistic attraction to this figure of authority, and during the course of a night's interrogation, a relationship develops that has more to do with power than sex. As the images of the man confronting the tanks in Beijing or Ju Dou confronting Tianqing force a recognition of oppression, A Lan's direct address to this figure of Chinese governmental power speaks to contradictory sentiments, which had been percolating since 1989, involving complicity with forces of tyranny, a masochistic love of victimization, and the insistent urge to struggle against authority at any cost.[86]

GENERASIAN X AND EXPANDING SCREENS

For A Lan, the public lavatory is also a stage, and Tian'anmen Square again becomes a platform for the officially invisible to be seen and for the silenced to be heard. Like the demonstrators in Tian'anmen, A Lan steps out of the shadows to stand up and be publicly counted. As a Sixth Generation filmmaker, Zhang Yuan has an intimate association with the generation most visibly connected to the Tian'anmen demonstrations. Although a coalition of various groups and committed individual activists occupied the square, students took center stage as the principal representatives of the Tian'anmen demonstrations. In fact, Zhang Yuan and other Sixth Generation filmmakers became intimately associated with this generation as it suffered through the repercussions of the 1989 events.[87] For example, Zhang's *Beijing Bastards* (1993) features Cui Jian, a rock musician known around the world for his appearance in Tian'anmen in support of the demonstrations; Cui also cowrote and produced the film. Wang Xiaoshuai directed *Frozen* (1996), anonymously, as Wu Ming ("no name") in protest against the suppression of dissident voices in China. The film documents the suicidal performance of a young artist who plans to die on a block of ice to protest the "icy" conditions in China. Wang also deals with China's underground avant-garde arts community in *The Days* (1993), which chronicles the malaise at the root of the dissolution of a relationship. The film records the inevitable split and the alienation, self-destruction, and hopelessness of the generation surfaces.[88]

Jia Zhang-ke also paints a bleak portrait of this generation in *Xiao Wu* (1997), a film about a young, alienated pickpocket in the bleak city of Fenyang in Shanxi. The title character, Xiao Wu (Wang Hongwei), struggles to make sense of his place in the new market economy and rapidly changing social and cultural relations that result from the pressures of globalization. As such, he has much in common with other GenerAsian X characters that people films from Hong Kong, Taiwan, Singapore, and the far reaches of the Chinese diaspora. The young, petty crooks that appear in Fruit Chan's *Made in Hong Kong* (also 1997),[89] for example, have a great deal in common with Xiao Wu as they find themselves with little hope on the margins of Hong Kong society. Filmmakers as diverse as Edward Yang, Hou Hsiao-hsien, and Tsai Ming-Liang in Taiwan, Clara Law in Hong Kong, and Eric Khoo in Singapore have dealt with the trials and promise of GenerAsian X in their films. (See Chapters 4, 5, and 7.) Facing the new demands of global capitalism, the expectations of transnational consumerism, and the stifling legacies of the government crackdown in the People's Republic, the pall of the KMT in Taiwan, British colonialism in Hong Kong, the People's Action Party in Singapore, and racism throughout the diaspora, youth culture, from Canto-pop to Chinese rock, Japanese anime and Taiwanese bubble tea parlors, from the drug subcultures to the world of the avant garde and an emerging Asian queer culture, ekes out a transnational space for critique and the negotiation of competing demands.

Much of that critical culture finds its ways to screens outside the commercial mainstream. Although Hollywood has embraced talents as diverse as Ang Lee, Chen Kaige, Yuen Woo-ping, Jackie Chan, Michelle Yeoh, Jet Li, Chow Yun-fat, and John Woo, among many others, what Hamid Naficy has called "transnational independent cinema" has grown exponentially within "Greater China."[90] Intimately connected with the rise of the new American independent cinema, Asian American film has been fueled by talent from the Chinese diaspora. Several filmmakers have worked very successfully on the borders between Hong Kong and other industries, for instance, Evans Chan between New York and Hong Kong and Clara Law between Australia and Hong Kong. Although state-controlled studios still fund considerable production in Taiwan[91] and the People's Republic,[92] many prominent filmmakers have achieved greater independence by looking for funding elsewhere—including Japan as well as other parts of Asia. Although Hollywood increasingly dominates screens in most of Asia, Chinese films from Hong Kong, Taiwan, and the People's Republic continue to receive serious attention at film festivals and within the international art house circuit.[93]

In addition, Chinese filmmakers have made their presence felt in documentary and experimental film circles globally. Despite dramatic cuts in funding of arts and media organizations, which became particularly acute in 1989, as Patricia R. Zimmermann notes in *States of Emergency: Documentaries, Wars, Democracies*,[94] Chinese American filmmakers continue to contribute to alternative screen culture. Many have worked within what John Hess and Patricia Zimmermann have referred to as oppositional "transnational" documentaries:

> Adversarial transnationalism, then, as a reimaging of relations among media politics and the economy suggests a constant shuttle between domination and resistance, between hegemonic power and multi-oppositional alliances, between repression and hope. Films, videos, Web sites and CD-ROMs are emerging that operate within this new epistemological nexus—work that refigures the relationship between the local, regional, national and global as one of endless mediation, integration and negotiation rather than separation.[95]

Christine Choy, for example, has been involved in establishing alternative media production and distribution outlets in the United States since the 1970s. Working within a broad coalition of politically engaged filmmakers committed to a range of issues involving race, class, gender, and political activism, Choy also has close ties to Asian as well as Asian American filmmaking communities. She worked with Tsui Hark, for example, on *From Spikes to Spindles* (1976), a documentary on political activism in New York's Chinatown. Also involved in New York's vibrant media activist community, Shu Lea Cheang has produced a range of work on gender and racial politics, including *Fresh Kill* (1994). Directly challenging transnational capitalism, this film imagines the use the Internet may serve in providing an alternative means of communication for political change.[96]

In fact, moving from video and performance to CD-ROMs and the Web, Chinese media artists have become involved in new technologies, hybrid modes, and experimental forms to critique a society increasingly dominated by global capitalism, consumerism, and corporate control of the media. Many of these works fall within what Laura U. Marks has called "intercultural cinema": "'Intercultural' means that a work is not the property of any single culture, but mediates in at least two directions. It accounts for the encounter between different cultural organizations of knowledge, which is one of the sources of intercultural cinema's synthesis of new forms of expression and new kinds of knowledge."[97] These works are characterized by a radical "polycentric multiculturalism" that Ella Shohat and Robert Stam describe as being "about dispersing power, about empowering the disempowered, about transforming subordinating institutions and discourses. Polycentric multiculturalism demands changes not just in images but in power relations."[98]

From the lowest end of the video spectrum to the complexity of digital technology (e.g., Web site for *The Gate of Heavenly Peace*; see Chapter 9), new technologies have empowered alternative voices within Greater China. Although the Internet has certainly facilitated the dissemination of information on and distribution of Hong Kong popular film among a loyal coterie of "fan boys" like Quentin Tarantino,[99] the Web has also served to facilitate other subcultural formations around Chinese screen culture. In Michael Lee Hong Hwee, William Phuan Chee Hoong, and Tan Chee's *One or Zero* (1997), produced as a student project at Nanyang Technological University in Singapore, for example, the Internet, through e-mail, becomes a site for the exploration of repressed gay desire, and new technologies provide avenues for the expression of suppressed and marginalized voices.

With the Web site that accompanies the documentary *The Gate of Heavenly Peace* (1995), Carma Hinton and Richard Gordon expand access to the information provided in the video to viewers unable to screen the documentary. (See Chapter 9.) Reconfiguring global space for a critical voice on Tian'anmen, the Web site provides a place for reflection on the events of spring 1989 unbounded by the usual channels of broadcast television and video distribution often hindered by censorship, as in the case of *The Gate of Heavenly Peace*. Beyond efforts to block it with firewalls or force its ouster from film festivals, *The Gate of Heavenly Peace* (in its film, video, and digital incarnations) provides a mediated Tian'anmen Square for ongoing debate and political critique.

In fact, the presence of transnational China and the Chinese diaspora has exploded on the Internet. As the Web site for *The Gate of Heavenly Peace* indicates, this presence has considerable potential for the creation of a digital body politic. For instance, Ian Buruma characterizes the potential of Chinese cyberspace as follows:

> There, for the first time, Taiwanese, mainland Chinese, Hong Kong Chinese, and overseas Chinese can talk about politics everyday. The Internet has become a forum of worldwide Chinese opinion, posted on websites, transmitted by e-mail, debated in chat rooms. Geographical borders no longer count in the same way they did. Even minor barriers to smooth communication, such as the different ways of writing Chinese characters in mainland China and other parts of the Chinese-speaking world can be overcome with a simple change of font.[100]

However, the digital space open for any type of political discourse involving China and the Chinese diaspora remains limited by a number of critical factors. Class, education, and location radically diminish the number of people who have any access to Chinese cyberspace. Also, as Buruma notes, those with access do not necessarily use the Internet as a site for public debate. The question Zillah Eisenstein poses in *Global Obscenities: Patriarchy, Capitalism, and the Lure of Cyberfantasy* remains, therefore, open:

> Democratic media require open dialogue and discussion, as well as access to technologies for production and distribution. Imaging diversity is not enough. Global

capital must be exposed as an obscene system. This means moving beyond consumerist culture and transnational capital to a vision of democratized publics. It remains a crucial question whether the new technologies of cyberspace will be able to unleash this process.[101]

ORGANIZATION OF *FROM TIAN'ANMEN TO TIMES SQUARE*

From Tian'anmen to Times Square: Transnational China and the Chinese Diaspora on Global Screens, 1989–1997 approaches Chinese screen culture and the visualization of China and the Chinese on world screens by looking at a range of motion pictures that have appeared since the 1989 demonstrations in Beijing. In *An Accented Cinema: Exilic and Diasporic Filmmaking*, Hamid Naficy examines transnational filmmaking practices in terms of exilic, disaporic, and ethnic cinemas. Although fluid categories, subject to considerable overlap, each term emphasizes a different positioning of the film/filmmaker within global media culture. Thus an "exilic" film emphasizes the relationship of the filmmaker to the country of origin, a "diasporic" film underscores the connections among various communities within a specific diaspora worldwide, and "ethnic" film highlights links of the immigrant to the adopted country. When looking at transnational Chinese cinema, the circulation of film within Greater China, Chinese American film, and films about the experiences of the ethnic Chinese globally, all three categories operate in this study to examine a range of films, filmmakers, and aspects of global film culture.

All the films presented in this book cross cultural as well as national boundaries. In other words, not only do the films show the marks of circulation within a transnational economy, with international production crews, casts, funding, and distribution, they also cross cultural borders to comment on the diversity contained within Greater China based on national, linguistic, political, class, gender, generational, sexual, and other differences. As the films display the hybridity accrued from very different histories of colonialism, socialism, capitalism, migration, exile, and diaspora, they present no singular Chinese way of life but a cultural cornucopia associated with the ethnic Chinese globally.

Part I of this volume covers the impact that changing economic as well as political factors have had on films made in Hong Kong, the PRC, Taiwan, Singapore, Canada, and the United States. Focusing on issues of labor and the circulation of commodities in the official and unofficial economies of these countries, the films examined in this section provide a critical view of the relationship between Western economic and political interests and the hard facts of living and working within a globalized economy either within China, Hong Kong, Taiwan, or the Chinese diaspora.

Part II focuses on the impact this has on the creation of hybridized Chinese identities. Films analyzed in this section highlight issues of migration, exile, alienation, and deracination in relation to changing notions of gender, generation, family, and ethnicity within Greater China.

The book concludes with a close look at the way in which the various screens that form *The Gate of Heavenly Peace* project from film to video to computer monitors have opened up consideration of the May–June Tian'anmen demonstrations in Beijing to wider global audiences. More than fifteen years after the crackdown, 1989 continues to be a benchmark that anchors any consideration of global China within international media culture.

I. Global Economies, Commodities, and Labor

2   Buying American, Consuming Hong Kong: *Chungking Express, The Opium War, These Shoes Weren't Made for Walking,* and *Comrades: Almost a Love Story*

A BRIEF SHOT IN Wong Kar-wai's *Chungking Express* (1994) frames one of the principals (played by transnational star Brigitte Lin/Lin Ching-hsia),[1] dressed in a blonde wig, raincoat, and sunglasses, in front of a shop window brimming with toys, small electrical goods, and a variety of colorfully packaged gadgets. Despite the outlandish attire (that is, blonde tresses framing an Asian face, dark glasses and raincoat when it is neither particularly sunny nor raining), the character blends in perfectly with the backdrop. "Disguised" as a Marilyn Monroe look-alike, this drug dealer blends in by standing out. In fact, she embodies many of the ironies and contradictions, revolving around Hong Kong as the so-called melting pot of Asia, dealt with in the film. She becomes another aspect of the spectacle of global consumerism that forms the visual foundation for the film's vertiginous bricolage of American pop culture, British colonialism, and Asian commerce. In the background of the same shot, Faye (pop singer Faye Wong), the female protagonist of the film's second section, purchases an oversized Garfield stuffed toy. This brings the spectacle of display and the consumption of commodities together in a single image. Running parallel to the film's two love stories is a more general, all-encompassing story of markets, consumers, commodities, packaging, display, promotion, and exchange. The romantic entanglements are juxtaposed with fantasies that revolve more around the marketplace than the heart.

As debate surrounding Hong Kong's political status continues, the film industry's place as an arena for the formation of identity and forum for speculation about Hong Kong's future also comes into question. In this light, *Chungking Express* can be looked at as a cinematic entry into this discourse of speculation in economic as well as political terms. Although ostensibly a stylish love story, the parallel romantic plot lines of the film obscure (without concealing) other issues beyond the surface of plot and character. Hidden in shop displays, model airplanes, the Mamas and the Papas' tapes, and canned goods, the film tells another story about economics and the politics of identity. Commodities create and re-create individual identities, not only operating along the axis of sexuality but moving from the uncertainties of gender and romantic roles to the instabilities of international commerce,[2] American cultural penetration, and the national, ethnic, and linguistic hybridity that is Hong Kong.

Chungking Express can be read as a commentary on contemporary Hong Kong, as a meditation on its current state and speculation on its future metamorphosis.

FIGURE 4. Still from *Chungking Express*. In this production still, Faye (Faye Wong) takes a picture of herself as part of the spectacle that includes Brigitte Lin posing in blonde wig, sunglasses, raincoat, and heels. Both are framed by the shop window and put on display within the film frame. The toy helicopters, trucks, trains, and boats pick up on the themes of flight and travel, while the other toys point to the commodification of the quotidian in postmodern Hong Kong. (Courtesy of Miramax.)

This commentary can be teased out of the film's mise-en-scène through a close look at the choice, use, and organization of the commodified objects in the film. These objects create a spectacle that reveals, while it "pretends" to hide, and this creates a cityscape that comments on the "transnational" nature of Hong Kong's economy and the personal identity of the film's characters.

Many films produced in Hong Kong and by members of the overseas Chinese community (the Chinese diaspora) look at the way both personal and public identities are shaped through an encounter with American popular culture and, specifically, through the consumption of "American" commodities, often, "made in China." This chapter examines this current as it runs through films made in Hong Kong, such as *Chungking Express* and *Comrades: Almost a Love Story*, about Hong Kong, such as *The Opium War*, and within the Chinese diaspora (e.g., the Asian Canadian documentary *These Shoes Weren't Made for Walking*, and other Asian American short films).

ALLEGORY

Several critics have already discussed *Chungking Express* as an allegory of Hong Kong's return to China on July 1, 1997,[3] and as an exemplar of a postmodern sensibility linked to the instability of identity the change of sovereignty implies.[4] In fact, postmodern texts tend to favor allegory. Gregory L. Ulmer,[5] Craig Owens,[6] and Fredric Jameson,[7] among many others, have commented on the parallels between the slippery signifiers of allegory in which the sign always stands in for something else and the uncertainty and contingency that characterizes postmodernism. Given that political conditions in China historically have worked against direct expression of dissent, China, as Jerome Silbergeld points out, has a long tradition of allegory in the literary and visual arts: "Allegory, . . . by any name, is a well-conditioned cultural response that no politically sensitive Chinese artist, visual or textual, modern or traditional in period, has needed to think too much about in order to use."[8] This tradition certainly has had an impact on Chinese language film—including Hong Kong cinema. Because Hong Kong filmmakers have traditionally worked within the boundaries created by the colony's censors,[9] it is not surprising to find "sensitive" political issues, particularly involving Hong Kong's relationship to China, dealt with obliquely. In the case of *Chungking Express*, although no direct mention is made of the change in sovereignty, for example, the film's mood, themes, and overall sensibility point to feelings that have commonly been associated with 1997.

However, it must be kept in mind that *Chungking Express* operates within a postmodern sense of allegory. As Jameson notes, this newer type of allegory demands a process of interpretation that is "a kind of scanning that, moving back and forth across the text, readjusts its terms in constant modification of a type quite different from our stereotypes of some static medieval or biblical decoding, and which one would be tempted (were it not also an old-fashioned word!) to characterize as dialectical."[10] The structure of *Chungking Express* echoes this type of dialectical structure as it shifts between various contradictory positions arising from its division in two segments and parallel pairings of couples, places, and plot elements. Thus, the film appears to lend itself to the type of allegorical scanning Jameson describes in which signification cannot be absolutely pinned down.

Like many postmodern texts that allegorize speed, compression of time, and reconfiguration of the past as part of the present moment, *Chungking Express* has an obsessive interest in time and dates that also alludes to Hong Kong's preoccupation with July 1, 1997. The first segment of the film revolves around May 1 as a turning point, that is, an "expiration date" for the drug trafficker as well as the cop, Ho Chi-wu (Takeshi Kaneshiro), whose birthday falls on that date, marking a month since his girlfriend, May, left him on April Fool's Day. As Ewa Mazierska and Laura Rascaroli wryly observe, "One gets the impression that he does not want so much to arrest dangerous criminals as to 'arrest' time."[11] Clocks, expiration dates on cans, elements of the dialogue and voiceover monologues ("In 24 hours I will fall in love with this woman," etc.), even songs like Dinah Washington's "What a Difference a Day Makes," remind the viewer of the passing of time and the absolute demarcation of time by dates like July 1, 1997 (or June 4, 1989).

Concomitant with this preoccupation with time, *Chungking Express* deals with a pervasive sense of loss and abandonment as Hong Kong prepares to lose itself in its new identity as a Special Administrative Region (SAR). The film narrates two stories of jilted lovers. In the first, May has abandoned Cop 223, Ho Chi-wu, a regular at the Midnight Express carryout. Lovelorn, he engages in rituals like buying dated cans of pineapple, his ex-girlfriend's favorite fruit, to deal with his loss. One night, in a bar, he meets an unnamed woman (Brigitte Lin) and decides to fall in love with her. He has promised himself that he would fall in love with the next woman he sees, and he does not realize that she is a drug trafficker. In a plot to smuggle drugs out of Hong Kong, a group of South Asian couriers had duped her and stolen a very valuable shipment. She has been warned to rectify the situation or face her own "expiration date" of May 1. However, although the date may indicate the end of Cop 223's love affair, it does not mark the end of the drug trafficker. After spending a platonic night with Ho in a hotel, she kills her narcotics boss and escapes.

In the second part of the film, the narrative shifts to deal with the story of Cop 663 (Tony Leung Chiu Wai), who is also a victim of a broken heart. Like Cop 223, he carries out a series of rituals to help with his loss and demarcate the period of mourning. Also a regular at the Midnight Express carryout, Cop 663 becomes acquainted with Faye, a relative of the owner who works there. When his former girlfriend leaves a key to his apartment at the carryout, Faye secretly begins her own ritual of visiting the apartment, cleaning up, rearranging the place, changing labels on the canned food in the cupboards, and manipulating time as well as space by dissolving a sleeping pill in 663's bottled water to help him get over his former girlfriend by sleeping better at night. Eventually, Cop 663 discovers Faye in the act, and he decides to make a date with her. She breaks the date, becomes a stewardess, and returns a year later to see Cop 663 settling in as the new owner of the Midnight Express. Faye's return may or may not signal a fresh start to the relationship. Under the veneer of popular optimism about the future, there is a sense that Hong Kong has been abandoned and worse, that like the jilted lover, it has no power or say in this decision. As Jeremy Hansen observes:

> The heart of this sense of powerlessness lies in the tension, the hype, and the frustration that surrounded Hong Kong's handover from Britain to China in 1997. Wong's characters are powerless subjects of the same gusts of circumstance that the people of Hong Kong endured when Britain and China debated the territory's future—neglecting any formal consultation with its people.[12]

In addition to being swept around by the capriciousness of chance and fickle lovers, identity itself remains uncertain and constantly in flux. The sometimes nameless, sometimes faceless characters found in *Chungking Express* do not present themselves as the traditionally unified creations of classical Hollywood. The pop divas and movie stars who portray these characters bring their own baggage of recognition to their roles. In addition to the star power of Brigitte Lin and Tony Leung in film circles, Faye Wong and Takeshi Kaneshiro bring the world of Canto-pop and GenerAsian X chic into the mix.[13] Therefore, these characters have a theatrical aspect that keeps them at an imaginative distance. Looking directly at the camera, addressing the viewer with voiceovers, they display a self-consciousness that brackets their fictional personae and puts any fixed identity in doubt.

The characters constantly shift among occupations and recognizable types, again disallowing any firm sense of identity. Cop 223, a representative of the royal police and the British Crown, also happens to be a lovelorn, ineffectual dupe who befriends a drug dealer. The cop and the criminal become intimate. Authority dissolves with the state; legality becomes a nonissue. Cop 663 acts as a bastion of state authority but actually aspires to own a carryout joint. Faye escapes from her menial work for her cousin in the carryout only to be cast in the similar role of stewardess; she has essentially the same job with different clothes at a different altitude.

The film seems to ask if anyone can ever be certain of his or her identity in the shifting political and cultural climate of Hong Kong. A city of migrants at the borders of many nations, Hong Kong hybridity can be disorienting. The heavily accented Cantonese of Ho, explained away as a Taiwan education,[14] comes up against the accented English of the Mandarin-speaking drug trafficker in blonde wig and outlandish Western dress. The 1960s quality of Faye—her short hair and slight figure conjuring up both Jean Seberg and Twiggy, the Mamas and the Papas, and the "British Invasion"—plays against the official stiffness of Cop 663's police uniform and Faye's own transformation into a uniformed flight hostess.

As Ackbar Abbas has eloquently pointed out,[15] Hong Kong's shift from refugee way station to self-consciously unique place with its own local interests, language, and culture has been accelerating since 1984. He notes a shift after the signing of the Joint Declaration, stepped up since the 1989 events in Tian'anmen Square, in which Hong Kong citizens have been searching for a distinctiveness that exceeds that of exile (from the Qing court, the Japanese, the KMT, or the Communists) or marginal colonial subject to something that may go beyond the "floating" identity of the Hong Kong migrant. However, the global marks of colonialism and proximity to China continue to typify Hong Kong, and the hybridized characters in *Chungking Express* seem to be part of local Hong Kong and elsewhere as well. The use of language in the film makes this clear. Cantonese vies with English, Mandarin, and Japanese in accents coming from Taiwan, India, the People's Republic, America, and beyond. The search for an authentic Hong Kong identity seems futile within the hybridity of this cosmopolitan metropolis; the global has already claimed the local as its own as Hong Kong emerged out of the Opium Wars as separate from the Chinese nation-state.

Given the flexibility of identity, the vicissitudes of fate, and the cultural acumen that allows its polyglot inhabitants to thrive away from home, the fact that Faye and the other characters in *Chungking Express* should be "California dreamin'" about leaving Hong Kong comes as no surprise in light of the uncertainty surrounding 1997. The feeling of wanting to be elsewhere and living as if one were actually elsewhere is palpable in *Chungking Express*. Most of the principals have their boarding passes in hand, ready for a flight out of there. All are looking for a change. Although the actual date of July 1, 1997, does not come up in the film, tacit references to it make staying or leaving the main topic of conversation whether the object of flight happens to be a drug deal gone awry, a love affair gone stale, or a city on the brink of an uncertain future.

The prospect of the handover has occasioned economic uncertainty that can be felt in the film. The drug deal gone sour may be a sign of the beginning of the end of Hong Kong's role in the global circulation of goods. Cop 663 may be thinking of the future when he turns in his colonial police uniform to run a carryout. Although the "one country, two systems" mandate guarantees a certain autonomy for Hong Kong, the implications of this policy for cops as well as criminals in *Chungking Express* remain less than certain.

As Hong Kong ponders its new identity, *Chungking Express* turns back on itself as an object, reflecting on its creation, and the place of intellectual "property" under the new regime. The film self-consciously uses its structure to comment on the change. Thus, one country with two systems equals one film with two segments. Life becomes a literal, visual blur. The cinematography and editing—optical printing, jump cuts, hand held camera, and so on—create a vertiginous feeling of spatial/temporal disorientation. One particular technique, developed in collaboration with Wong's principal director of photography, Christopher Doyle,[16] stands out; Robert M. Payne describes it as follows:

> Between them, Wong and Doyle have developed a visual motif that appears in all of their films together: some strategic scenes are shot at a slower film speed ("undercrank" in Hollywood jargon), so the action is speeded up; then, the frames are *step-printed* at a slower speed onto the finished film, so the action is restored to its real-time duration. The undercrank/step-printing method gives these scenes a haunting sense of simultaneous animation and suspension. . . . Together, the director and the cinematographer have fostered a visual style that is self-reflexive without being completely alienating.[17]

Time and space, therefore, take on new qualities in the cinema as Hong Kong passes into a new type of existence.[18]

Through its distinctive visual style that alludes to Hong Kong as a fashion center and media hub, *Chungking Express* plays up the transnational associations that point to a cosmopolitan, urban culture. The film presents Hong Kong as diametrically opposed to the perception of mainland China as monolithic, isolated, "primitive," and out of the swing of the global economy. As such, *Chungking Express* fits into the category that Hamid Naficy has termed the border-crossing film: "hybridized and experimental—characterized by multifocality, multilinguality, asynchronicity, critical distance, fragmented or multiple subjectivity, and transborder amphibolic characters."[19] Crossing aesthetic as well as national boundaries, *Chungking Express*'s vision of Hong Kong as a hybrid, postcolonial border town at the pulse of postmodern world culture and the global economy allows the film to be read as a tacit entry in the list of works that have tried to eke out an identity for Hong Kong separate from the PRC and ROC (Taiwan) Chinese by celebrating Hong Kong's cosmopolitanism as its distinguishing feature.

Other scholars have examined all these elements in some detail, but it may be worth taking another look at some of these issues from a slightly different perspective. In this chapter, *Chungking Express* and the world of politics, culture, identity, time, and space conjured up in the film are examined in relation to Hong

Kong as a transnational entrepôt.[20] In many respects, the film narrates a tale about Hong Kong's defining role as a place for production, exchange, display, and consumption of commodities. From this point of view, *Chungking Express* tells its story of love, loss, and memory through the romance of goods.

THE COMMODITY

As Marx has pointed out, commodities operate like "fetishes." They appear to be concrete, absolute, knowable, tangible, and limited. However, appearances are deceptive. The commodity actually hides its history. The thing does not reveal the labor that went into its production, the relations of production that organized that labor, the ownership of the means of its production, and how and for whom its value is defined. As Marx states in *Das Capital*:

> A commodity is therefore a mysterious thing, simply because in it the social character of men's labour appears to them as an objective character stamped upon the product of that labour: because the relation of the producers to the sum total of their own labour is presented to them as a social relation, existing not between themselves, but between the products of their labour. This is the reason why the products of labour become commodities, social things whose qualities are at the same time perceptible and imperceptible by the senses.[21]

The commodity mystifies in its obviousness and banality. It acts as a fetish, standing in for something else that is not there, magically appearing out of nowhere to drift in a "free" marketplace that mysteriously determines its value. Standardized, mass produced, homogenized, circulating globally, the commodity erases its past and presents only a cheerful present moment to its consumer.

In the postmodern turn, the commodity can be stripped of its substance and become an image, which in turn becomes a commodity. *Chungking Express* freely plays with this mercurial relationship between goods and images. In this regard, the film owes a genuine debt to Pop Art. Like Andy Warhol, Wong Kar-wai takes a close look at mass produced, popular commodities, for example, cans of pineapple, sardines, stuffed toys, soda pop, beer, model planes, wigs, sunglasses, CDs, portable stereos, textiles and clothing, home furnishings and domestic goods, soap, toothbrushes, dish towels, and the list goes on. Although all have a place within the drama (i.e., characters talk to and about the commodities, use the commodities, buy and sell the commodities), these goods take on significance beyond the narrative as well. Isolated in close-up or cluttering and overpowering the characters in long shots, these commodities function as objects of specular contemplation.

By examining Dole pineapple cans or a giant stuffed Garfield doll in a diegetic universe brimming with manufactured goods, the film addresses the nature of our contemplation of the manufactured object. Like Pop Art, *Chungking Express* poses several questions: Why am I looking at this can of pineapple or sardines? Why does this glittering CD fascinate me? Is there an aesthetic pleasure involved in looking at something as banal as a beer bottle? Is the "poetry" in the everyday or in the artistry of the creator of the image? Which creator? The designer of the

Coca-Cola logo or the filmmaker representing it for us on the screen? Does the image critique or celebrate the manufactured commodity? Is the surface of things "superficial" or a profound contemplation of the (post)modern world? As Jameson might ask, do these images function as pastiche or parody?[22] Does the viewer laugh at or empathize with confronting a convenience store clerk with his cold-hearted disregard for the "feelings" of his expired cans or trying to console a "crying" wet dishrag? Does the contemplation of the commodity demystify it or simply add to its fascination and fetishization?

All of the questions posed stand unanswered in *Chungking Express,* as they do in Andy Warhol's oeuvre. Beyond these questions, however, there is another aspect to the play of commodities/images common to both the film and Pop Art that needs to be addressed. This involves the flattening of the political dimension of the image with its global circulation. Beyond soup cans, Warhol reproduced images of Marilyn Monroe, Elvis Presley, John F. Kennedy, and Mao Zedong. Media personalities and political figures circulate as commodified images, bought and sold through newspapers and magazines as well as through Warhol's prints and paintings. Moving beyond national borders, ideological allegiances, and historical moments, detached from movie fantasies as well as political realities, these images take on a resonance for some and exist as only emptiness and evacuation of meaning for others.

Like Steven Spielberg's *Jurassic Park* (1993), *Chungking Express* spends a significant amount of screen time contemplating commodities. In *Jurassic Park,* the commodities are dinosaurs in all their various manifestations from stuffed dolls to manufactured attractions that bite back, and the global surface of the manufacture and display of the commodity (dinosaurs in the third world created by a multinational cast of characters) takes on a particularly American quality when consumed (by two American kids in the film and by a global audience seeing a Hollywood production).

Garfield, Coca-Cola, Dole pineapple, the Mamas and the Papas, flannel shirts, Caesar salads, hot dogs, blonde "Monroe" wigs, model Boeing airplanes, and all similar objects in *Chungking Express* may be "made in China" but from a clearly American mold. American labels mark the commodities as "global" and the environment (as well as the people) they form as "modern" and "cosmopolitan" through an American frame of reference.

A Chinese saying seems to be creeping with increased frequency into the discourse of Hong Kong movies. Roughly translated, it goes as follows: "When they travel, goods become more precious and human life cheaper."[23] Circulation in patriarchal culture has traditionally cheapened women and their labor, as well as shortening the lives of migrant workers and others. In Hollywood cinema, women's images have also served as tokens of exchange among men, with female performers rarely enjoying the full profits of their exploitation. However, *Chungking Express* goes beyond the objectification and commodification of its female protagonists. The film draws all the characters into the spectacle of the manufactured environment. People function as commodified images for exchange. However, revealing the fetishization of goods through anthropomorphism, the film also elevates the commodity to the status of character, attributing thoughts and feelings to goods, allowing them to "speak" through close-ups. Commodities begin to reveal the secrets of human relationships that the mystification of the fetish tries to keep hidden.

Ho's relationship to canned pineapple can be taken as a case in point in the film. Separated on April 1, Ho decides to buy a can of pineapple every day with an expiration date of May 1. If his girlfriend, named May, does not return before May 1, Cop 223 will call the relationship "expired." When the convenience store no longer carries cans with an expiration date of May 1, Ho confronts the store clerk. The clerk feels it is unethical to sell cans that expire the next day. After confronting the clerk with his insensitivity and refusal to take the cans' feelings into consideration, Ho is given a box of expired cans and dismissed from the store. Outside, a bum refuses to take the cans because they have expired. All of this takes place in a busy composition with a neon sign saying "Okay" (the name of the store chain), and huge pictures of ice cream cones framing the store's entrance.

In his voiceover commentary, Ho queries, "Is there anything that doesn't have an expiration date?" Back in his apartment, Ho eats pineapple and watches his goldfish (ironically, a sign of fertility, according to Chinese lore). In a voiceover, he notes that he is eating his thirtieth can of pineapple and laments, "To May I'm just another can of pineapple." Eventually, he tries to get the dog to help him eat the pineapple. He notes he is lucky that "May isn't into durian." Although popular in Southeast Asia, durian (the "king of fruits," foul to the nose, but sweet on the tongue) is an acquired taste and not the best choice to circulate transnationally. Because of its pungent odor, some airlines even prohibit its transportation in passengers' baggage. The camera pans from the goldfish to a pile of empty pineapple cans, and the ease of transport of the pineapple, its portability and disposability mirrors May's ease of leaving her former boyfriend behind.

Ho ventures into a bar and vomits up the pineapple in the urinal. To "protect" himself, he asks the woman in the wig he has decided to woo on impulse if she likes pineapple. He tries the question in several languages until Mandarin provokes a response. Pineapple comes up as a summation of his ultimate inability to know someone—"pineapple one day, something else the next." Canned goods, then, act as a shorthand or code for human relationships. Although a critical edge to this may be expected, none is delivered. Commodities retain their mystery as the segment ends on an optimistic note that still hides as much as it reveals about human relationships understood through processed goods. When Ho receives a happy birthday greeting via his beeper, he remarks in voiceover, "If memories can be canned I hope this one never expires. If an expiration date must be set, I hope it's 10,000 years."

Film, of course, attempts to "can" memories through the mechanical reproduction of motion picture images. In the case of *Chungking Express*, Hong Kong goes into the film "can" as a cinematic commodity and serves as a spectacle for contemplation as well as an image for consumption. Made during a hiatus from Wong's martial arts epic *Ashes of Time* (1994), *Chungking Express* is an example of cinematic "just-in-time" production.[24] Whereas *Ashes of Time* took years to

FIGURE 5. Still from *Opium War*. Lin Zexu (Bao Guo-an) takes command of a task doomed to failure. (Courtesy of Xie Jin.)

complete with grueling location work in the People's Republic, *Chungking Express* went from initial conception to postproduction in a matter of a few months using some of the labor made available from the break in the production of the other film. Recycling part of the initial idea into his next film, *Fallen Angels* (1995), Wong wasted nothing and brought *Chungking Express* to the screen quickly, cheaply, and profitably. To signal its stylishness, the film makes its surface visible; canted angles, step-printing, slow motion, jump cuts, hand-held camera movements, startling ranges of under/overexposure, and play with light and filters foreground the technique involved in making the film. It is an object with a shiny, seductive surface like the tin of sardines it depicts. To guarantee its quality, stars like Brigitte Lin and Faye Wong are put on display—framed by store windows in the mise-en-scène, boxed in the cinema screen, and ready for consumption. Picked up by Miramax for distribution under Quentin Tarantino's Rolling Thunder brand, the film circulates in global markets,[25] perhaps "speaking" in unexpected ways like the "crying" dishrag within its diegesis.

THE OPIUM WAR

To have a better feeling for the presentation of commodities in *Chungking Express*, it may be useful to look at Wong's film in relation to Xie Jin's *The Opium War* (1997). Specifically, one scene in that film brings commodities to the fore in a spectacular display—the depiction of Lin Zexu's destruction of the opium. Made to commemorate the July 1 return of Hong Kong to the administration of the People's Republic, the film depicts the events surrounding Hong Kong's transfer from Qing to British jurisdiction during the first Opium War. Much maligned even before its completion as anti-British/pro-Communist/Chinese chauvinist propaganda,[26] *The Opium War*, the most expensive mainland Chinese film ever produced, should not be so simply dismissed.[27] If nothing else, the film reminds the world that Hong Kong's roots as a major port of trade are grounded in a drug deal gone sour. Antidrug czar Lin Zexu runs afoul of drug traffickers, corrupt petty customs officials, higher placed addicts, a corrupt Qing court, a vacillating emperor, power-hungry British military officials, and an English monarch devoted to "free trade" over the "public good." Hong Kong thus arose out of a war over the circulation of processed goods. For Xie Jin, who comes out of a socialist filmmaking tradition, the exchange of opium as a commodity stands in for the imperialist underpinnings of capitalism.

Beyond the pomp and circumstance of the imperial destruction of the opium (the incident that directly led to the start of the first Opium War) and the heroic Lin Zexu's apparent triumph over the foreign drug trade, there is a sensual delight in the destruction of the opium. Careful attention is paid to the details of the process, for example, the cutting of the black tar balls of opium with broadswords, the glistening of the light on the sweat-drenched bodies of the workers involved in the process, the texture of the water changed by the white smoke of the lime as it is poured into the quadrant of the river used for the event. The camera cranes up to give a sense of scale to the destruction and moves in to show closer details of the entire process. To enhance the spectacle, shots of officials, European merchants, and townspeople looking on as the event takes place compound the scene's visual allure. Firecrackers burst; drums and gongs sound. Lin Zexu looks proudly on as the detritus is flushed from the river into the bay.

Needless to say, the scene stands out much the same way the helicopter napalm attack on the Vietnamese hamlet in Francis Ford Coppola's *Apocalypse Now* (1979) does; that is, as a sensual moment of destruction that visually and viscerally overwhelms. However, unlike the destruction of the village, the delight in the destruction of the opium brings with it no moral ambivalence. Rather, Xie freely critiques capitalism as vociferously as he pleases, because the commodity in question is opium.[28] While drug trafficking is normally presented as an extreme form of capitalism, excessive and unrelated to more mundane forms of bourgeois relations, in Xie's *The Opium War*, the drug traffic becomes emblematic of capitalist and imperialist relations generally.

A noted master of the "woman's film" during the post-1949 reconstitution of the Shanghai film studios under the new regime, Xie still displays traces of a socialist suspicion of commodities and the hidden oppression of free trade. However, moving away from early accounts of the Opium War produced in the People's Republic, Xie fails to people his film with peasants and members of the working classes. Rather than show the ravages of the drug trade on the commoner, his version deals with the powerful, the wealthy, and the nobility. Even the victims of opium addiction are all courtiers and fallen nobles. Thus, his critique of capitalism is oblique and highly ironic.

He places the British rationalization for the Opium War in the mouth of Queen Victoria. A prim, youthful figure in bonnet and fiddling with a whip, she is better

FIGURE 6. Still from *Opium War*. Queen Victoria cuts the ribbon to usher in the modern age of British imperialism. (Courtesy of Xie Jin.)

informed than her ministers seem to know. Her remarks, throughout her brief appearance in the film, are intercut with close-ups of the astonished expressions of her aging male ministers. Opening an imperial railway line and holding office in her royal car, Victoria approves a stamp of her profile for distribution throughout the empire (where the sun never sets on her image). When asked for her approval of military force to handle affairs in China, she delivers the following speech:

> If I were in Lin Zexu's position, I would also burn all the opium. But now, it's not the opium issue, nor the issue of the lives and properties of a few merchants. It's not even a matter of the dignity of our British flag and royalty. If all the nations followed China's example and rejected free trade, the British Empire would no longer exist within a year. This is the reason for us to use force. We must teach them a lesson on free trade. Gentlemen, Britain has the responsibility to open up this last, largest territory in the East. I hope you won't tell me one day that this has been done by other countries. The fact is whoever gets hold of China will have the entire East . . . the nineteenth century.

The camera dollies in during the speech so that it finally rests on Victoria's face in close-up, half in shadow (profiled like her stamp) from the light coming in through the window next to her. She emphasizes free trade like a curse throughout the monologue.

Hong Kong emerges later in the film as a makeshift wooden sign announcing it as British territory. It is a ripple in the film and in the film's telling of the tale of the first Opium War; Hong Kong appears as little more than a dot on a map and then a few planks marking a nondescript piece of ground. Hong Kong itself, of course, like opium, is property to be exchanged. The making of *The Opium War* seems to be another episode in the saga of the British–Chinese relations, with Hong Kong still serving as booty to be lost or won, a token of China's lost national integrity.

Queen Victoria rationalizing the opium trade through reference to the free market has a curious resonance with the media discussion surrounding 1997, including fantasies at the edge of the political discourses involving July 1, like *Chungking Express*. A scene in the first segment of *Chungking Express* stands out in a way similar to *The Opium War*'s spectacle of the opium's destruction. The unnamed woman in the blonde wig organizes a group of South Asians in a drug-smuggling operation. A montage sequence shows the details of the packaging, concealment, and transportation of the heroin.[29] The spectacle of opium represents the hidden historical identity of Hong Kong as a place for the exchange of commodities. In this case, because the merchandise is heroin, what is normally hidden by the surface of commodities comes dramatically to the foreground, so that there is at least a partial appreciation of the human labor involved in the transportation and exchange of goods. Here, Hong Kong, the quintessential entrepôt, is depicted as a place where commodities are processed, repackaged, transported, and redistributed; raw materials and the initial stages of manufacture lie elsewhere. Hong Kong is in the middle as the merchant and go-between.

The drug trafficker in blonde wig, raincoat, sunglasses, and pumps is regal as she holds court in the Chungking Mansions flophouse. Seated next to a refrigerator, open for cooling, she fans the chilled air toward her face. Like Queen Victoria in *The Opium War*, a side light gives her an imperious profile. She speaks in English to people off-screen, "Are you sure you want to do it?" "Yes, yes" comes from off-screen. Passports are handed to her, and the drug-running montage begins. Synthesized music on the soundtrack holds the shots that follow together: Drugs are sown into clothes and shoes. Money (US$100 bills) is counted out. Shoes are made; scissors cut through seams; sewing machines whirl. Men in traditional Indian skirts on bunks count money happily. Shots show various shops with shoemakers, tailors, and seamstresses putting drug-filled plastic bags in heels of shoes, clothing, a toy stuffed bear. The woman in the blonde wig counts money; she then fills condoms with white powder. South Asian men go into the bathroom with the condoms and come out waddling.

Preparations continue around the bunks of the cramped room: scissors rip open new hiding places; a box marked VCR provides another possibility for hiding the drugs; a woman pretends to be pregnant with wadded cloth under her sari; another man comes out of the bathroom waddling. A shot of the airline flight board at the airport follows; the last of the drugs are wrapped up; jump cuts juxtapose various shots of luggage being closed. At the airport, the blonde smuggler leads the South Asians (men, women, and children) in a line behind her, pushing carts laden with boxes and luggage. One man carries an infant. The others follow behind toting baggage. Except for the woman leading the group, the picture represents a clichéd depiction of South Asians on the way back from a stint working abroad, laden with consumer goods, particularly electrical appliances, and an overall air of prosperity.

A baby cries; music plays. The trafficker goes to the ticket counter. The film cuts away to a stewardess (the girlfriend who jilts Cop 663 in the following section) waiting for a taxi. South Asian drum music comes up on the soundtrack; the trafficker turns around; her charges have vanished. Back at her supplier's bar, she receives a can of sardines with a May 1 expiration date as a sign of the amount of time she has to clean up the mess.

However, as the sequence ends, it remains unclear as to whose mess she must clean up. She ends up fighting her own opium war, facing both her Caucasian supplier and South Asian runners. As a go-between, she finds herself expendable. Her supplier/barkeep/boyfriend has already found a replacement for her; he elevates the newcomer to this position by crowning her with a blonde wig and a kiss. However, the trafficker's mercurial identity proves to be her salvation. Hidden behind wig, raincoat, and sunglasses, her identity evaporates, freeing her, at the end of the film, to escape. She kills all the principals in the drug transaction and leaves. However, she remains doomed to a selfless, anonymous existence defined only through commodities and her relation to them. When she throws off her wig after killing the supplier, she frees herself from one set of relations (i.e., associated with colonialism, Americanization, Western patriarchy), but her image remains a literal blur captured by a freeze frame; her identity stays a mystery.

Speaking Mandarin and English, clothed like Marilyn Monroe, drifting between the Anglo-American world of the barkeep/drug supplier and the (post)colonial world of the South Asian runners, this nameless character appears to be a mainlander who has drifted to Hong Kong and fallen in with the seedier side of the colony. However, she could be the opposite; that is, a Taiwanese gangster looking for greener pastures in Hong Kong.[30] It is impossible to tell. Commodities define her in their movements between places; her identity drifts with them between drug trafficker and survivor, blonde wig and black hair, raincoats when it is sunny and sunglasses on overcast days. When the goods are gone, nothing clear (or authentic) remains.

SPACE AND MARKETPLACE

The title of *Chungking Express* conjures up a locale and implies speed of motion. Not only does the title bring together the Chungking Mansions, where the South Asian drug runners live, with the space of the Midnight Express, where both Cop 223 and Cop 663 habitually stop, but it conjures up other associations as well. Chungking was the last stop on the train, so to speak, for the KMT fleeing the rape of their capital, Nanjing, by the Japanese during the Pacific War. It conjures up images of last resort, of a last place of exile before a further scattering in 1949 to Taiwan, Hong Kong, or elsewhere after the civil war. The title may also be read allegorically as Hong Kong speeding back to Chungking on the mainland.

However, Chungking here does not refer to the city but to a high-rise block in the tourist district of Tsimshatsui. Known for cheap accommodations (small hotels/backpacker dorms/flophouses) often owned by South Asians and frequented by a cosmopolitan blend of guest workers and very low-budget tourists, the Chungking Mansions provide the seedy environment for the scenes of drug trafficking. It is the urban "jungle" or wild "forest" referred to in the Chinese title of the film.

The English title conjures up still other associations, however. The "express" of the title brings up other relationships, closer to Hollywood than fast food, of the *Orient Express* (1934 and many other versions as well) and *Shanghai Express* (1932), of trains as conduits for Orientalist cinematic fantasies about the Westerner abroad. The fast food "express" operates as a more banal appropriation of the word for the serving up of "made in Hong Kong" American- and British-style fast food (hot dogs, pizza, salads, fish and chips, and the occasional South Asian savory) for the local crowd.

The title brings together mainland China and Hollywood in one breath, the Chungking Mansions and the local/global aspects of the express food joint in one thought. The title serves as an entry into the physical space of the film, a space in which commodities are displayed as spectacle and circulate rapidly as objects of exchange.

Much has been written on the presentation of urban space within postmodern film culture. For example, in *The Geopolitical Aesthetic*, Fredric Jameson examines the traditional, national, multinational, and transnational organizations of the urban space of Taipei in Edward Yang's *The Terrorizer* (1986):

> A foreigner and an outsider may be permitted to wonder whether this way of looking at urban experience does not have something to do with the "representation of totality" of a small island which is also a non-national nation state. The enclosed spaces in their range and variety thereby figure or embody the unevenness or inequality of the world system: from the most *traditional* kind of space . . . all the way to the *national* space of the hospital, the *multinational* space of the publisher's office (the media, surely of a global range, now housed in a great glass high-rise) and what I am tempted to call the equally *transnational* anonymity of the hotel corridor with its identical bedrooms.[31]

Drawing on Jameson, Curtis Tsui observes the following regarding *Chungking Express*:

> And these spaces also illustrate the inequality created by the global system that is present in the Crown Colony today, as the film goes from the "(multi)national" space of the ethnically-diverse Chungking House, to the "transnational" space of the airport, to the "personal/local" space of Cop 663's flat. With these spatial relations then (and with his heavy use of jump cuts, which further atomize the characters' lives temporally and spatially), Wong has created a film that completely visualizes the nature of Hong Kong (or practically any global city such as New York, Los Angeles, or Tokyo).[32]

Expanding on Tsui's observations, it may be useful to look at these spaces in *Chungking Express* in more detail in relation to how commodities in the film operate with respect to particular types of space in Hong Kong. As the Surrealists have shown, objects take on a different significance in different contexts. Sunglasses are just utilitarian objects to prevent sun glare until they are worn at night or with a raincoat. Cop 223 then hypothesizes that they signify blindness, pretentiousness, or a broken heart; he does not see the "caution" that the wearer ascribes to them, preparing her to deal with sunshine at a moment's notice. Thus, being out of place marks an object or a person in various ways; however, in a transient city like Hong Kong, it becomes difficult to discern what does not belong and precisely why it should be considered foreign.

As Jameson observes in his analysis of *The Terrorizer*, there is a range of spaces that need to be examined in the postmodern global metropolis. To embellish on his and Tsui's observations a bit, these spaces often exist as palimpsests—one on top of the other. The most "traditional," most "local" space can be the most global; i.e., a widely circulated picture postcard representation of a city. Also, in this case, there is a powerful dynamic played out spatially between the pre-colonial, colonial, neo-colonial and post-colonial spaces in the film.[33]

At its base, Hong Kong appears as the open hawker's market, small stalls run by aging Chinese merchants, handmade wicker baskets of produce carried on the shoulder, tailors and seamstresses working with older sewing machines, a single bare bulb for illumination. This is the Hong Kong of the waves of immigrant mainlanders who came to the Crown Colony seeking their fortune or looking for political exile. This Hong Kong speaks of cheap labor, hand craftsmanship, small merchants, and shopkeepers in the Chinese mold.

The colonial legacy asserts itself further in the presence of the South Asian population both in the Chungking Mansions and as workers at the Midnight Express. They represent another side of cheap labor, an additional facet of the international operation of empire. They provide a further take on the dynamics of trade among the colonies, through a vague reference to the history of the Opium War and the centrality of India in the British imperial system and the British Commonwealth.[34]

As a legacy of colonialism, these Chinese and Indian workers, small businessmen, and merchants continue to form the backbone of an important sector of the Hong Kong economy. The spaces that they occupy, from sweatshops to flophouses, appear "traditional" (i.e., ethnically marked by the sounds of Cantonese opera and Indian chanting) and therefore "precolonial." However, these spaces really feed into the workings of the global economy from the textile plush toys found in the film's shop windows to the "informal" sector of heroin trafficking.

Where "national" or clearly marked "colonial" modern space might be expected, there is a vacuum. Police officers circulate in the city without police stations or jails. The closest one gets to public space in *Chungking Express* may be the jogging track where Cop 223, alone and isolated, runs to drain his lovelorn tears from his system by sweating them out. The solid blocks of low income highrise housing move from the national to the private, for example, to Cop 663's apartment in the more swanky "Mid-Levels," situated by the shots of the escalator sidewalk outside his window.

This part of the project of modernity is missing from Hong Kong's history. It has never been a "nation" or an independent "state," with a uniquely defined precolonial past. Perhaps this is what makes the city postmodern—it easily by-passes the national and has always already been part of the global in terms of economic relationships and cultural formations. In the transnational cinematic imagination, Hong Kong goes from the wooden sign in Xie's *Opium War* to the decaying capitalist promise of the Chungking Mansions without passing through postcolonial modernity.

The multinational spaces in the film seem to be related to those international enterprises associated with the postwar turn to American domination of the world economy. With headquarters in the United States, these multinationals formed the bedrock of many contemporary transportation and telecommunications concerns. These neocolonial economic relations still have their power. In this case, the airlines (both Faye and Cop 663's former girlfriend wear the United Airlines uniform)[35] present spatial relations as centripetal forces drawing characters away from one another and from Hong Kong as well as defining intimate relations in precarious terms as constantly moving take-offs, landings, smooth skies, and se-ductions measured in thousands of feet above the ground. Airports and airplanes share uniformity worldwide, creating a global anonymity that would seem to run counter to domesticity, intimacy, and private life. However, here, in the form of uniforms and toy model airplanes, this neocolonial, multinational presence finds its way into the bedroom. Bare backs become landing fields after sex, and the model plane celebrates Faye's excitement during her surreptitious forays into Cop 663's apartment.

Other spaces have a transnational dimension, moving away from a neocolonial domination of the periphery by the center, to a more active play among "emerg-ing" economies, the third world, and a postcolonial reorganization of the cultural sphere. Spaces take on a global uniformity, rooted in the local economy, but appealing to an international flow of tourists, businesspeople, and a mobile, local middle class, either educated abroad or well traveled. The hotel room in which Cop 223 wolfs down salads as the blonde drug trafficker sleeps nearby could be any-where. Only the framed spaces of the TV playing old Cantonese movies and the cityscape outside the high-rise picture window mark the location as specific to Hong Kong. Otherwise, the impersonal room could be anywhere on Earth.

The bars, the convenience stores, and the electronics/toy shop function in a similar fashion. Contrasted to the traditional/colonial spaces of the hawkers' stalls, where Faye buys produce and Cop 663 eats local fare, and the sweatshops and flophouses frequented by the drug trafficker and her ilk, these spaces embody a different type of economic relationship. The local is poured into molds that can no longer be located in East or West, third or first worlds, periphery or center. For example, the Garfield toy and the boom boxes in the shop display are likely manufactured in China, designed by American or Japanese firms, bought and sold in entrepôts like Hong Kong, and finally used by a cosmopolitan consumer (either a local or tourist shopper). Aptly, the film ends with a shot of the portable stereo at the deli. The transnationals—JVC, Sony, or Motorola—have the last word.

In the convenience store, the display of commodities offers a similar vision of homogeneity; for example, sardines, pineapple, and beer are all poured into the

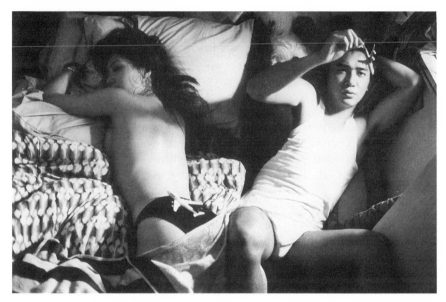

FIGURE 7. Still from *Chungking Express*. Cop 663 (Tony Leung) may dream of flight, but he remains rooted to his bed in Hong Kong as he uses his stewardess lover's rear as his landing strip. (Courtesy of Miramax.)

same cans and packages worldwide. The California Bar (frequented by Cop 663 and Faye) and the other bars (operated by the white drug lord and Cop 223's haunt where he encounters the blonde) express a similar sort of transnational organization of culture. CDs, beer bottles, ash trays, whiskey, cocktail and shot glasses, colored lights, mirrored bars all seem to be the same everywhere. (Only Faye's cousin moves on to the more regional KTV/karaoke entertainment establishment, particularly popular in East Asia, when he sells the Midnight Express.)

Finally, the Midnight Express itself, which cobbles together the two sections of the film, works as cultural glue that binds together the various economies and personal/productive relationships that appear throughout the film. The Midnight Express brings the local and global together in the arena of commerce. It serves Coca-Cola, coffee, salad, pizza, fish and chips, hot dogs, and other deli items to an international clientele—local police as well as English-speaking tourists. Behind the scenes, the film gives us a look at what goes into the production of these international food favorites. South Asian assistants, Chinese cooks, servers, and proprietor drag food in from the local market, cook it up in a culturally hybridized kitchen, and serve it up in the paper and foil containers of delicatessens everywhere. In a culture traditionally suspicious of "cold," raw food, Cop 223's and Cop 663's girlfriends' penchants for salads appear to be quite cosmopolitan. In this case, on the peripheries of the transnational exchange of goods, local production creates exotic commodities, such as the pizza (with its horrific—to the traditional Chinese palate—gobs of cheese)[36] and the salad. Cheese, raw lettuce, and

FIGURE 8. Still from *Chungking Express*. Faye, like the stewardess and the nameless drug runner, eventually manages to take off. (Courtesy of Miramax.)

Coca-Cola meet at Hong Kong's Midnight Express and become part of the local cultural environment.

The Midnight Express also serves as a fitting backdrop for Cop 223's numerous phone conversations. (Cops seem to hang out at the deli or at the convenience store everywhere.) The viewer hears only one side of the fragmented conversation, and the phone underscores the potentially alienating quality of the Hong Kong hybridized environment by concentrating on language and (mis)communication. The polyglot Cop 223, for example, switches from Cantonese to Mandarin to English to Japanese in search of a language to pick up women. The blonde drug trafficker uses English with the South Asians and Mandarin with the cop. However, most of the time, characters do not converse. Voiceover monologues replace conversation. American English blots out thought, and "California Dreamin'" blares at the Midnight Express to help Faye (and, later, former Cop 663) "not think."

Commodities—culturally mediated, tainted, fetishistic certainly, but concrete—remain the most certain conduit for the communication of personal feelings and desires. To get to know the blonde drug trafficker (whom he never knows), Cop 223 asks (in several languages) if she likes pineapple. Cop 663 recognizes and expresses his feelings for Faye by returning the CD of the Mamas and Papas' tunes he had misrecognized earlier as a gift from his ex-girlfriend. Faye expresses her feelings for 663 by redecorating his apartment, replacing his intimate possessions with objects of her own fancy, and speaking to him at a distance through commodities.

The last type of space depicted in *Chungking Express* involves domestic space. The female characters have a tangential relationship to this space, whereas the male characters are firmly entrenched within the household. For example, the blonde drug trafficker is shown only briefly in anything resembling a private space, and it appears to be a very impersonal hotel room. Cop 663's apartment frequently hosts his stewardess girlfriend and her personal effects as well as Faye's additions, but they never appear in their own homes. These women have "no room of their own," so to speak. The women drift and the men stay put in this film.

However, even if the women are cast adrift, they still manage to shop. The montage of the blonde drug trafficker shopping for all the containers and special clothing and trick luggage for the runners parallels the scenes featuring Faye reorganizing Cop 663's apartment with the commodities she has purchased. Faye expresses her passion through commodities: goldfish (a Chinese symbol of prosperity and good fortune), new sheets, old sardine labels on new cans of fish, new CDs, new soap, toothbrush and cup, new dishrags, sleeping pills (to help the lovelorn cop get some sleep); a giant Garfield replaces a white stuffed bear.[37] Faye transforms Cop 663's domestic realm, but only subtly and without upsetting the transcultural panoply of commodities that define his personal space. Cops 223 and 663, like most of Hong Kong's residents, do not need to leave home to see the world. They can stay put, put their feet up, and have the world tumble in on them. The toy airplanes in Cop 663's apartment operate as both sex toys and symbols of the interconnections between the Hong Kong locality and the global system.

FIGURE 9. Still from *Chungking Express*. Faye holds a bowl of noodles as she dodges Cop 663, outside his apartment off Hong Kong's famous Mid-Levels escalator. (Courtesy of Miramax.)

CALIFORNIA DREAMIN': ARE GLOBAL DREAMS "MADE IN AMERICA"?

In *Chungking Express*, the most intimate spaces display the marks of a global environment. However, although "made in China" commodities exhibiting an American or transnational label would be expected to be found in any urban center, the appearance of these same commodities may take on different meanings as they appear in different locations. In *Woman and Chinese Modernity*, Rey Chow points out a very important aspect of the relationship between identity and material objects in Asia:

> Unlike what Oriental things still are to many Europeans and Americans, "Western things" to a Chinese person are never merely dispensable embellishments; their presence has for the past century represented the necessity of fundamental adaptation and acceptance. It is the permanence of imprints left by the contact with the West that should be remembered even in an ethnic culture's obsession with "itself."[38]

Chungking Express's director, Wong Kar-wai, talks about being influenced by what he calls "Seventh Fleet culture."[39] During the years between the Korean War and Vietnam when American presence in Asia was waxing, Wong "bought the music, the cigarettes, the lifestyle; seeing big foreigners in the streets made a strong impression."[40]

Chungking Express is filled with this sort of culture. The blonde wig, sunglasses, high heels, and raincoat of Monroe and Hollywood in the late 1950s/early

1960s and the "California Dreamin'"[41] of the swinging late 1960s refer to a specifically American style. The airline uniforms have a timeless American aspect to them—sensible pumps, dark skirt, tailored blouse and tie, pinned-up hair.

Like Godard's *Breathless* (1959), *Chungking Express* relies on Hollywood as a backdrop. It becomes a pastiche of Hollywood genres like the policier, the gangster film, and the romantic comedy. It plays with a Hollywood/Hong Kong sense of stars and stardom, for example, Lin Ching-hsia as Monroe, Faye Wong as Jean Seberg, Tony Leung somewhere between Cary Grant and a John Woo hero. It self-reflexively recognizes itself as a commodity for exchange within the international market of "art films."

The song "California Dreamin'" promises an escape to the warmth and safety of Los Angeles—particularly for many Hong Kong filmmakers with Hollywood aspirations. Several questions come to mind. In Hong Kong, whose mind, given 1997, is not elsewhere? If the People's Republic, England, and Taiwan are part of that elsewhere, is America the "big elsewhere," the place where dreams come true or reach their dead-ends? Is the hybridity of Hong Kong just a new take on American cultural imperialism? Or, has America been "made in China?" Has California and Hong Kong's California Bar dissolved into one another and become interchangeable? Cop 663 thinks he has a date with Faye in Hong Kong's California Bar, but she has the state of California on her travel itinerary. Does she really dream of California or has the California of her dreams never existed? Faye, in fact, remarks when she returns to Hong Kong that California is "nothing much."

Commodities seem to be the key to this ambivalence. America is a global dream and a Hollywood illusion. However, it is also the structuring principle for identity. The carryout selling Coca-Cola and hot dogs is as marked by America as the stewardess in her uniform and sensible pumps. American goods move beyond the market to construct the individual.

GENDER AND COMMODITIES RECONSIDERED

Ackbar Abbas talks about *Chungking Express* as a "comedy of the fetish, a displaced detail. A fetish is a substitute, a surrogate, a neurotic symptom, but it can also be regarded as a defense against neurosis, in that it is a less harmful kind of neurosis."[42] Taking a cue from Abbas and moving from Marx to Freud on the nature of the fetish, it may be worth looking at the commodities that populate *Chungking Express* as different sorts of fetishes. Going back to Freud, the fetish exists as a phallic object used symbolically to belie the mother's lack of a penis, and thus to disavow the possibility of the male's own castration.[43]

Both Cops 223 and 663 encounter women who threaten their egos. Each one deals with loss, abandonment, and rejection by these women. Pain (the pain of symbolic castration) turns into fetishistic encounters with commodified objects— canned pineapples, soap, dishrags, stuffed toys, and so on. All of this comes back to another aspect of postmodernity evident in *Chungking Express*, that is, a crisis in the authority of the patriarchy and in traditional notions of masculinity. All the women in the film fly off (in the case of the drug trafficker, the stewardess, and

Faye, whose name sounds like the word for "to fly" in Chinese, quite literally in airplanes) and leave the men to fend for themselves. Officially (on the police force) or economically (as small businessmen), the men are grounded, whereas the women move freely in the "new" service (airline hostess) and "informal" (drug trafficking) parts of the global economy.

More flexible, the women circulate more freely. As Gayle Rubin has pointed out in her work on women as objects of exchange, men, under patriarchy, allow women to circulate according to male rules.[44] The patriarchy defines the extent and nature of exchange among groups; that is, exogamous marriage for women implies a relationship between families, clans, communities, nations, and races. As postmodernity sees a weakening of all of these old relationships, women, traditionally more likely to circulate among various groups in patrilocal communities in which men stayed put, now, riding on the advances of feminism, can venture even further from hearth and home.

In *Chungking Express*, this leaves the men to hang out the laundry, mop up the floor, and wring out the dishtowel. Within the Western imagination, however, the association of Asian men with domesticity is not a recent development. Rey Chow, in her analysis of Bernardo Bertolucci's *The Last Emperor* (1987), talks about the China of the Orientalist imagination as a "feminized space."[45] Masculinity becomes problematic as it enters this space. However, as Ella Shohat and Robert Stam have shown in *Unthinking Eurocentricism*,[46] filmmakers outside the West create strategies for combating these Orientalist presuppositions promulgated by Hollywood's cinematic hegemony. From this perspective, the fetish and the domesticated male do not necessarily point to a world hopelessly out of balance but to a place of hopeful potential. Abbas sees the film as fundamentally comic, and Tsui reads it as a hopeful allegory of the changeover. However, the film can also be seen as a description of a postmodern/postcolonial/transnational culture in the making in which gender roles are radically redefined.

If nothing else, commodities and consumers are slippery characters—mystifying material relations of production, subject to the whims of fashion, creatures of the marketplace, capricious with disposable income. Cop 663's stewardess girlfriend learns a lesson from the world of consumption. She was satisfied with eating the salads her boyfriend brought her until the owner of the Midnight Express talked him into giving her a choice. Manipulating the consumer, he devilishly persuades Cop 663 to buy both the salad and the fish and chips to give the poor woman a choice. Rather than being grateful and satisfied with these food choices, the stewardess decides to try the same market strategy in her personal life and switches from man to man. The proprietor tells the cop that she will come back for more of her old favorites when she tires of the novelty of the new goods. However, Cop 663 does not have the same faith in the dynamics of the market. He leaves her letter unopened and lives with the illusion that she may be hiding in the wardrobe of his apartment; finally, his lack of contact with actuality leads him to think she has come back to rearrange his apartment (when, in fact, Faye has rearranged the stewardess out of the cop's life by erasing her message from the answering machine).

Cop 223 complains that May treats him like "a can of pineapple." In *Chungking Express*, the men see themselves as the commodities. Women are the consumers. As in the case of Edward Yang's meditations on contemporary Taipei (e.g., *The Terrorizer*), *Chungking Express* shows women as key players in these new relationships of exchange—more malleable, better at bouncing back, more proactive than the men, who are more emotional and nostalgic, trying to hang onto the past, wanting to stay put. Do these postmodern, supposedly postfeminist characters really inherit the world economy? Or are they themselves commodified images packaged to sell the "new" look of old relations of production, exchange, and consumption?

SHOPPING ABROAD: *THESE SHOES WEREN'T MADE FOR WALKING*

As Sumiko Higashi[47] and Larry May[48] have pointed out in their books on American silent film, there is a long tradition in American film of linking the acquisition and display of commodities not only to wealth and social standing but also to "Americanization" and the promise (implicitly to immigrants) that an American identity can be purchased and acquired through goods. Over the decades, this has had a particular appeal to women, who have been socialized to link personal identity with fashion. Clothing and make-up make and unmake (in the case of *Chungking Express*'s drug trafficker, for example) the woman.

In Hollywood fantasies about Hong Kong, there has been a continuing interest in Asian women's clothing. As I have pointed out in *Romance and the "Yellow Peril": Race Sex and Discursive Strategies in Hollywood Fiction*,[49] in both *Love Is a Many-Splendored Thing* (1955) and *The World of Suzie Wong* (1960), two films set in Hong Kong during the Cold War, the female protagonists run afoul of their male love interests (played by William Holden in both cases) because of their attraction to Western dress. The non-Asian clothing style threatens the romance with the taint of Western independence, female control, and, perhaps, "feminism."

This linking of Asian women, gender identity, sexuality, and clothing finds its way into works by several Chinese American/Chinese Canadian filmmakers. These works have ranged from feature films, like Mina Shum's *Double Happiness* (1994),[50] to fictional shorts like Pam Tom's *Two Lies* (1989) and documentaries like Deborah Gee's *Slaying the Dragon* (1987).

In *Sewing Woman* (1982), Chinese American filmmaker Arthur Dong centers his documentary on the life of his mother, Zem Ping, who worked in the American garment industry for over thirty years. In this case, Dong provides a look at the other side of the relationship between Asian women and American commodities, that is, as laborers rather than consumers. In this film, the sweatshops that produce the consumer goods behind the constructed image of American femininity become a prominent part of the picture, exposing the fetishism of the commodity.[51]

Sharon Jue's *My Mother Thought She Was Audrey Hepburn* (1989), a short, autobiographical work, looks at the construction of Asian female identity within the Chinese diaspora. Through interviews with three of her friends and extensive voiceover commentary, Jue explores the relationship between public image and

FIGURE 10. Still from *These Shoes Weren't Made for Walking*. Clothing tells the story of the Chinese diaspora. (Courtesy of Paul Lee.)

internalized "racial self-hatred." Looking at family photographs, she examines several phases her mother went through in the creation of her own identity, including periods influenced by Audrey Hepburn, Jackie Kennedy, and, later, the remarried Jackie Onassis. Within a culture where self-definition rests on media spectacle and the acquisition of the appropriate style through consumption, Jue asks the question: "Why be Chinese when you could be white?" This question, in fact, led her mother to seek out an eye operation to better conform to Euro-American conceptions of beauty.[52]

In her own punk-inspired group of friends, she finds an understated but insistent racism revolving around ethnic jokes and an internalized self-image of the "banana" (white on the inside, yellow outside). Disjointed and roughly edited, this montage of impressions, like the contradictory images of self constructed through commodities, never comes together in any semblance of organic unity. Rather, the film, filmmaker, and principals stand as fragmented, scrambled constructions, pieced together from clichés about race, Hollywood ideals, and available goods. Jue concludes the film by stepping back a generation and reflecting on her grandmother: "I never looked to see if she had bound feet."

Asian Canadian filmmaker Paul Lee does look to see if his grandmother has bound feet in *These Shoes Weren't Made for Walking* (1995). In this documentary on four of the women in his family, Lee uses his relatives' attitudes toward feet and shoes as a thread to link together their various positions within the extended family and within the Chinese diaspora, stretching over a century from southern China to Vietnam, Hong Kong, England, Australia, and Canada. He weaves talking head interviews together with family photographs, home movies, staged shots of feet and shoes, on-the-street footage, and an occasional dramatic reenactment of a remembered incident. All the women address Lee implicitly as grandson, son, nephew, and brother; however, he remains off-screen and silent as the women reply to the questions he is assumed to have asked. Many of these questions deal with shoes, that is, wearing them, buying them, touching them, dreaming about them.

The film provides a striking visualization of the changes in Chinese women's lives across the generations from the three-inch lotus slipper for bound feet to the designer running shoe of today. Moreover, the shoe, as a handicraft and manufactured object, also operates as an icon for Hong Kong, the place in which these four women find themselves most firmly rooted. Stylish, ephemeral, necessary, and practical, the shoe represents the contradictions inherent in Hong Kong's materialism and consumerism, that is, its comforts and frustrations. No one shoe ever seems to fit entirely, and none of the women ever seem to fit into the world outside of Hong Kong entirely, either. However, they are also uncomfortable and alienated in Hong Kong on the verge of the 1997 change in sovereignty. Their feet are always ready to get up and go—shoes or no shoes. As in *Chungking Express*, the shoe becomes a synecdoche for Hong Kong women's sexuality and mobility. In the Wong film, for example, Cop 223 thoughtfully polishes the drug trafficker's high heels as she sleeps, to freshen her up to move on the following morning, and the film closes in more than once on pumps worn by Faye and Cop 663's former girlfriend in their airline hostess garb.[53]

These Shoes Weren't Made for Walking begins with a high angle close shot of feet in a pair of red Western-style pumps. Split edges of a *cheong sam* gown can be glimpsed over the edges of the shoes. The simple pumps are dressy, but not exceptional. They only stand out in contrast to the Chinese gown, creating a certain hybridity through fashion. This image sets up what will follow as an exploration of shoes as representations of gender, ethnicity, class, and modernity.

The story of the Lee family's relationship to shoes begins with the testimony of the filmmaker's grandmother, Mrs. Wong. She talks about her grandmother binding her mother's feet, but unbinding them after Sun Yat-sen finally made the practice officially illegal with the establishment of the Chinese Republic after the fall of the Qing Dynasty in 1911. Before that time, bound feet and three-inch shoes signified more than a crippled, submissive femininity. The deformed feet also meant wealth and a household affluent enough to have servants to do the heavier chores.

An interview with the filmmaker's mother, Betty Lee, follows. She talks about her childhood in French colonial Vietnam in a wealthy Chinese family. When the fortunes of the family fell, Betty Lee went from an affluent life in a boarding school in Canton to the struggle to make ends meet in Hong Kong. It was a period when there were a lot of American GIs in Hong Kong, and Wanchai, the red light district, was booming. Lee mentions *The World of Suzie Wong*; Hollywood became involved in a style still associated with Hong Kong women and perceptions about their sexuality worldwide.

A struggling schoolgirl, Betty Lee tutored the bar hostesses to make enough for her school tuition fees. She remembers one episode in particular because of her pupil's bright red fingernails complemented by red slippers, which dangled from her feet as she studied. Lee envied the slippers and swore to buy a pair as soon as she had enough available cash. In the following shot, she holds a pair of fancy red bedroom slippers, the kind with pompoms that can be found in catalogs like Frederick's of Hollywood. Lee confesses that when she finally bought the slippers, they were not suitable, because she was much older. A shot of young feet kicking off the slippers accompanies the voiceover remark, "The thrill of the slippers was not there anymore."

In this story, Lee reveals another side of what the slippers as a commodity hide. Associated with a style linked to the sexual availability of Chinese women for an international film public, the slippers here signify a certain level of luxury, if not affluence, and an insouciance connoting youth. However, the slippers remain an empty sign; the "thrill" of the commodity as an emblem of self-identity vanishes with the ability to acquire the material object. As in *Chungking Express*, the commodity's significance is slippery. The meeting of identity, personal style, and manufactured object happens by chance and is constantly in flux. Though *The World of Suzie Wong* may ossify a look, an attitude, and an ideology through commodities, the actual circulation of those images and goods among the women of the Chinese diaspora takes on different significances.[54]

Betty Lee trades her dream of red boudoir slippers for sensible nurse's shoes and, then, wedding shoes. After the birth of her two children and death of her husband, Lee immigrates to Canada. As she describes walking in the snow and the agony of acclimating to Canadian winters, a staged re-creation appears on screen. Lee struggles up an incline in the snow, carrying groceries. A voice off-screen shouts racial slurs, and Lee plucks off one of her heavy boots and hurls it toward the camera at the off-screen voice. The glamour of the shoe fades, as it becomes a token of survival and resistance.

The testimony of the filmmaker's paternal aunt, Terry, picks up on the possible infusion of footwear with elements of resistance. Terry appears in a tilt up from a shot of two pairs of shoes—one a highly polished pair of men's shoes, the other a pair of low-heeled women's pumps. Dressed in trousers, with short hair and a deep voice, Terry is seated next to her partner, Ellen, wearing a dress, with long hair loosely permed. Terry describes her life abroad—schooling in Hawaii and England, and her commitment to Ellen in Hong Kong. She mentions that she has not worn a dress in eighteen years.

In a scene that parallels Betty Lee's discussion of the bar girl's red slippers, Terry talks about her relationship to men's shoes. Accompanied by still photos of Terry in various stages and styles of cross-dress, she reminisces about her experiences shopping for men's clothing on Bond Street and in Oxford Circus in London. She says she prefers Baly's men's shoes, because "they last longer," although she has experimented with different styles, including the very pointed-toe shoes associated with the punk/new wave subculture. Over an image of a foot in such a shoe rubbing out a cigarette butt, Terry mentions that she never wore chains with the shoes, as some did.

For Terry, the mundane commodity of the Western men's shoe marks a site of gender transgression and struggle for an identity out of keeping with most representations of Asian female sexuality found in global media. As in Betty Lee's case, the commodity here signifies beyond its usual associations. Speaking of lesbian eroticism and a type of freedom from tradition occasionally found within the diaspora, the men's shoe betokens a sense of self as gendered beyond the limits of either Chinese or Euro-American notions of "proper" female roles.[55]

The filmmaker's sister, Carol, has a more ambivalent attitude toward her shoes. Beginning with a tear as she remembers a pair of shoes her father (now deceased) bought her as a child, Carol also discusses her fondness for tennis and sports shoes, which give her a feeling of power and control. Later, her voiceover discussion of her career as an accountant is punctuated by shots of a Hong Kong shoe store and a pair of legs provocatively propped up next to a computer terminal sporting black heels. As she talks about being treated as a sex object rather than a professional in mainland China, these shots of shopping and visual display at the workplace underscore her words.

All the women's shoes bring up mixed messages about their relationship to Hong Kong and future plans to stay or leave. Grandmother Wong, an Australian citizen, states, "We are all Chinese people. There is no need to run away," as the screen shows the well-known video image of the protester standing in front of the tank in the aftermath of the 1989 demonstrations. Carol, however, is given the last word, which seems to comment on shoes, diasporic identities, as well as political choices: "If I had a choice between running shoes and heels, I don't think I would want to restrict myself to running shoes or heels. I would want to wear whatever, wherever. I just want to be myself." *These Shoes Weren't Made for Walking* leaves the question of where the shoes will eventually lead Chinese diasporic women unanswered.

A Final Look at Cultural Goods:
Comrades: Almost a Love Story

Returning to Hong Kong films that drift away from Hong Kong, it is important to note that *Chungking Express* is in no way exceptional in its interest in American commodities, consumerism, and the shaping of Hong Kong identity. Rather, this film serves as one example within a body of works that take up these themes and marry them to the issue of 1997 and emigration. Within a range of films dealing with border crossings between Hong Kong and the mainland, Hong Kong and America, and among various countries in Europe and Asia as traversed by Hong Kong émigrés, Peter Chan's *Comrades: Almost a Love Story* (1996) stands out for several reasons. In addition to sweeping the Hong Kong International Film Festival awards and making money at a time when the Hong Kong film industry had encountered a serious slump, the film also manages to bring together two key preoccupations of recent Hong Kong film—mainland Chinese coming to Hong

Kong and emigration from Hong Kong to America. Both themes play with the anxiety surrounding 1997 when Hong Kong may be "overrun" by mainland émigrés, economically depressed by the influx, and immigration to America the only resort for the survival of the Hong Kong middle class. Because this fantasy must appeal to Hong Kong viewers, characters that alight in Hong Kong are luckily more enamored of the American Dream than any Hong Kong reality.

Like *Chungking Express*, *Comrades* offers a picture of Hong Kong formed from American commodities: McDonald's restaurants, Mickey Mouse, and English classes where students learn to say, "Jump, you son of a bitch, jump," from American Westerns. As these American icons float transnationally, they come in contact with commodities that have a distinctive and sentimental Chinese aspect. Bottles of soy milk and the commodified music of the transnational Chinese pop star Teresa Teng (Deng Lijun)[56] circulate within the film, too. In fact, Teresa Teng's song, "Tian Mi Mi" ("Sweetness") provides the film with its Chinese title, linking it with Teng's Mandarin love songs and a pull away from the vacuous cheerfulness of Mickey Mouse. Teng represents a bittersweet sense of fate in *Comrades*. Her music sets apart the mainlanders in the film, because Teng is presented as being appreciated almost exclusively by Chinese from the mainland. Born in the mainland, Teng established her career in Taiwan and within the overseas Chinese communities of Southeast Asia. After the Cultural Revolution, Teng's music swept through the People's Republic and achieved a great deal of popularity while Canto-pop became the music of choice in Hong Kong.

When Li Xiao-Jun (Leon Lai) and Li Chiao (Maggie Cheung), the PRC "comrades" of the film's title, are drawn together, it is through their common appreciation of Teresa Teng. As Kwai-Cheung Lo notes:

Her popularity was even comparable to another Deng: the engineer of the modernization campaign and the political leader at that time, Deng Xiaoping. Because of this time lag in the reception of the same cultural products among the Chinese, their choices and tastes easily reveal their different local identities. Chan's film cleverly appropriates this delicate difference in tastes in pop song to rethink the question of Chinese cultural identity . . . .

As new immigrants suffering from culture shock, poverty, and discrimination, the protagonists have achieved a transcendent unity and a community of one not by any traditional folk-cultural forms but, ironically, through an "alien" commercial Taiwanese song.[57]

At the end of the film, the couple meets in front of a shop window in New York City, pulled together by a TV report on Teng's death. Teng, as a dead pop icon on a collection of flickering tubes, stands in for the characters' lives and emotions, their "almost" love story.

Whistling Teng's music had brought them together earlier along with the debacle of Li Chiao's poor judgment in buying Teng's music for resale in Hong Kong. Hoping to make a profit on the fact that Hong Kong is filled with "mainlanders," she opens a booth to sell Teng's music during the New Year holidays. She falls into debt, however, when she fails to bank on the fact that the mainlanders (referred to as "Uncle Chinas" in the film) try not to be spotted by indulging openly in the purchase of goods shunned by the cosmopolitan Hong Kong population. Teng makes the Uncle Chinas stand out in a crowd. Furthermore, the sense of the vicissitudes of fate embodied in Teng's songs and by her premature death permeates the film, pushing its protagonists from the mainland to Hong Kong and on to New York.

However, when commodified, the sentiment of Teng's music flattens. Like *Chungking Express*, *Comrades* is difficult to pin down in its own sentiments. On one hand, it offers a fantasy to the Hong Kong audience of the mainland, represented by the naive Xiao-Jun and the ambitious but unlucky Li Chiao, as simply sojourners on their way somewhere else. However, it also offers a point of identification for the Hong Kong viewer who may indeed be on the way somewhere else, too, either by staying put and becoming part of the People's Republic or by emigrating. The promise of prosperity of Hong Kong and New York is undercut by the harsh conditions for immigrants in both places, represented by a roller-coaster ride of the characters' economic ups and downs in Hong Kong and by the even bleaker picture of a New York associated with violent death and sudden loss. Although the characters' fortunes and the future of Hong Kong can be dismissed as questions of fate, any sense of nostalgia, sentimentality or fatalism empties of its affect as *Comrades'* images empty out onto flickering TV screens that multiply Teng's death as so many images, muted further by the reflections of a shop window.

This postmodern draining of the image finds a parallel much earlier in the film with the introduction of Xiao-Jun's aunt, Rosie (played by veteran Hollywood actress Irene Tsu). A former Hong Kong Wanchai bar girl, Rosie now helps run a bordello; however, she remains obsessed with William Holden, whom she may or may not have met during the filming of either *The World of Suzie Wong* or *Love Is a Many-Splendored Thing*. Hollywood's image of Hong Kong surfaces again to stand in for the Hong Kong version of the American Dream.

Rosie has a shrine to William Holden on her bedroom wall. In addition to newspaper clippings and photos of him in diverse poses (in various states of dress and undress), the shrine includes a formal portrait of the actor. When the camera frames Xiao-Jun and Rosie in a mirror hanging on the same wall, Holden's image is juxtaposed with their reflection and with a crucifix and a picture of Jesus Christ in the extreme background. Surrounded by Western icons of salvation, the images point forward and back to a mainland/Hong Kong/American future in the figure of Xiao-Jun and a mainland/Hong Kong/American past in Rosie.

Working in the sex trade where her body had been commodified within the colonial economy of Hong Kong, Rosie reveres another commodity, Hollywood icon Holden, as her savior. The objects she associates with Holden take on a fetishistic quality, offering a magical cure-all for those who come in contact with them. For Rosie, clothes make the man, and she lends Xiao-Jun one of "William's" suits for a job interview, telling him to dry-clean it later because "William" will be back. A close-up shows the monogram "William H." in the collar of a shirt. Xiao-Jun seems flattered when Rosie mentions he looks like William, and the camera lingers on Xiao-Jun's reflection superimposed over Holden's image after Rosie has been called away and leaves the shot. In the next scene, one of Rosie's acquaintances informs Xiao-Jun that William is a drunk Rosie picked up, undercutting the magic of Holden's image that had captured Xiao-Jun's imagination in the previous scene.

However, later in *Comrades*, Rosie reappears to discuss her relationship with William further. She tells Xiao-Jun the story of meeting William Holden while he was in Hong Kong shooting *Love Is a Many-Splendored Thing*. As she shows souvenirs of their relationship in the form of knickknacks from the swanky Peninsula Hotel, a Hong Kong colonial landmark, the plausibility of her story increases. Later, Rosie's memories seem to be justified by a snapshot Xiao-Jun finds of the two together. However, the truth or self-delusion behind Rosie's relationship with Holden remains unimportant. Rather, through William Holden *Comrades* looks at Hollywood's imagination of Hong Kong as the home of the exotic Suzie Wong as well as Hong Kong's view of Hollywood/America as a savior in the form of William Holden, who is placed on a visual par with Jesus Christ.

Rosie's memories/delusions are presented in an ambivalent way—grotesque, satiric, nostalgic, bittersweet, ironic, sentimental, genuine, and false. *Comrades* accesses these feelings through the commodified image of Holden—through the relationship between the American image/commodity and the Chinese/Hong Kong/Hollywood character/actress. However, Holden, the American "savior," and Teng, the "heart" of a (displaced) China, fade in significance in the transnational cultural marketplace where meaning can so easily be drained through commodification and the whims of fashion.

Comrades' reflection on Holden in Hong Kong brings the discussion of consumerism, commodities, Hong Kong, and America full circle. Xiao-Jun melts into the image of William Holden as completely as Faye and the blonde drug trafficker blend in with the panoply of commodities in the shop window in *Chungking Express*. Global products with American labels define the cultural landscape of both films.

Film itself is a special kind of commodity for Hong Kong. Both *Comrades* and *Chungking Express* are self-conscious of their status as images and as commodities. In fact, *Comrades* includes several references to the work of Wong Kar-wai. To cite only one example, *Chungking Express*'s principal director of photography, Christopher Doyle, plays the drunken English teacher in *Comrades*.[58] Both films seem to be "about" Hong Kong and 1997, while saying nothing directly about the change in sovereignty. They display commodities circulating around the globe, bouncing between Hong Kong and the United States, Hong Kong and Taiwan, Hong Kong and the People's Republic, and Hong Kong and the United Kingdom/British Empire/Commonwealth. Surface and the display of the marketplace play their roles, but more fundamental issues of identity and self-determination also come into play. Like most postmodern texts, *Chungking Express* and *Comrades* remain elusive and equivocal, and, ultimately, ambivalent.

Other questions come to the fore when looking at independent works arising out of the Chinese diaspora in relation to Hong Kong. For those people cast adrift in a new wave of the Chinese diaspora, these images may carry a different significance. The consumption of commodities promises a new identity; however, the commodity may insistently shape that identity in unexpected and unappreciated ways. As the echoes of Hollywood in Hong Kong seem to indicate, cinema plays a role in the display of people and goods transnationally. The hybridity that marks Hong Kong draws its people and its products away from its center as it absorbs images and commodities back into itself. As the interconnections between Hong Kong and "Greater China" become more complex, the images that circulate to define those relationships begin to reveal the roots of power in the exchange of people, commodities, and images on global screens.

Interview with Paul Lee

How did you get involved in filmmaking?

I was born in 1963 in Hong Kong; my father died when I was seven. At that point, my mom decided to move to be closer to her family. Most of them were in Toronto, so, in 1974, when I was twelve, we moved to Toronto. I went through school, and I graduated with a BSc in biology/genetics from University of Toronto; an MA in anthropology also from the University of Toronto; an MBA in arts and media administration; and then an MFA in film. I went back for my MFA only a few years ago. After I had made my first and second films, I realized that I better learn all the theories and concepts, so I know what I am talking about on the set. Now, I am finishing my Ph.D. coursework in education. [Lee earned his Ph.D. in June 2001.]

Is your Ph.D. at the University of Toronto, too?

Yes, in arts education and curriculum, and I use film as my medium of education, so my thesis is going to be film-related. In fact, I started with filmmaking quite by accident. I finished my MBA in 1989, and the first job I got was to set up a very small independent film festival in Toronto, the first lesbian/gay festival in Toronto, which is celebrating its tenth anniversary this year. I worked with a collective, and, in that collective, there were quite a few filmmakers. A lot of filmmakers were asking me to go into the editing room to look at their films. That was really how I got a film education, because, when I first got my job, I had no idea about the difference between 35mm, 16mm, or video. I knew nothing, so that is how I really learned the business. I applied for funding from the National Film Board and other Canadian grant programs for my first film, *Thick Lips Thin Lips*. Very fortunately I got every single grant I applied for. I asked for maybe two or three thousand dollars for each one, and I got all the grants. It took only one day to shoot the film and three days to edit it. From beginning to end, it only took about six months to put it together. The film premiered at the Berlin Film Festival in 1994, and it has gone to over 120 festivals so far, and it has won eight awards. I was very pleased with how it turned out; it was beyond my wildest expectations.

   In 1994, after I finished that film, I started my next project, *These Shoes Weren't Made for Walking*, which was an experimental documentary about my family—four women in my family: my grandmother, my aunt, my mother, and my sister. It is a purely subjective documentary from a very personal perspective, based on the stories I have heard from them since I was a child. I had just turned thirty, and I was realizing that these people may not be with me all the time; they're getting old and I really want to have a record of their stories for myself. I applied for some grants, and I got most of the funding I applied for, again I was quite lucky. My crew of three went to Hong Kong to shoot in March 1994. We shot for five days there. Most of the

Hong Kong footage we shot on video, because it was cheaper and faster, and most of the Canadian footage we shot on film. I started editing in June, and it was finished in November of that year, but, because I ran out of money to complete it, I did not finish it until May of 1995. It has not been as well received as the first one.

Why do you think that is?

Documentary. People are just not into documentaries; they like fiction. It is long, twenty-six minutes, a TV half-hour. Also, it is quite raw, a lot of it shot on video. It is subtitled, the bulk of it is in Cantonese, and it is just not the type of film people watch for entertainment. It did well at documentary film festivals and Asian film festivals.

Thick Lips Thin Lips and *These Shoes Weren't Made for Walking* were shown in Hong Kong at the Hong Kong International Film Festival and also at the Hong Kong Independent Film Awards. *These Shoes* did very well in the educational front, because it is in the collections of over fifty universities. That gave me a lot of motivation to go on making documentaries. In 1996, I started my third project that was a ten-minute short film called *The Offering*, a film with no dialogue, shot on 35mm. [*The Offering* premiered at the 1999 Berlin International Film Festival. Since then, it has screened at over 280 film festivals and has won forty-three awards.]

Chinese cinema has changed considerably in recent years, particularly in terms of the presentation of gay and lesbian issues. Could you talk about the intervention you personally have made into that area, and why you think the change has happened?

I never really set out to make a gay film, but I was informed by the politics and certain aesthetics of queer cinema. I knew if I made a gay-themed film then I have a whole dimension that other films may not have. It is difficult for gay filmmakers to make films, to have the financial resources to put their voices and their images on screen. I thought, if I do have the opportunity, why not address that as part of the film, it definitely serves a need, and it is something that audiences seemed to be hungry for, at that point, anyway.

With *Thick Lips Thin Lips* I was making a film about resisting homophobic violence, and the racist portion of it I encountered personally when I first came to Canada. All the heckling in the film, the racist remarks, I heard them personally or they were directed towards me at different times on the streets in Toronto. When I first came to Canada, there were very few Asians here—not like now with seven or eight Chinatowns and Asians as one of the largest minorities. It was a very different kind of atmosphere at that time. It was much more puritanical at that point, and much more white, a very WASP type of culture.

The gay culture I encountered first in my teenage years. I was eighteen, nineteen, going to university, and, at that time, things were changing quite rapidly. Still, racism has always been a part of everyday experience. Going to school, for the first two or three years, you'd never know what they were going to say to you. If they said something that could be taken as ethnically or racially motivated, even if it were just an offhand remark, you would find yourself always second-guessing people's motives and intentions. Nothing was really for sure, whether it was racially motivated or not, and that is a pretty dangerous way of viewing things. A lot of people were saying that these immigrants come in and use up all our precious resources and time, take away all our jobs, but it was so difficult to arrive in a new country and not speak the language, not know anybody, and start life over again. On top of that, it was a tough struggle with the injustice and the intolerance of racism. That really was my starting point for filmmaking—to express that kind of concern, frustration, and probably anger, too.

Somehow the gay and lesbian issues crept into the films, too. In *Thick Lips Thin Lips*, after I put the racist remarks in, I thought there were other issues, such as homophobic violence. In *These Shoes Weren't Made for Walking*, I also explore racism in Canada.

Was your family resistant to making the film? Did they really want to tell their stories? Did the filmmaking change your relationship with your family?

It did, and this is quite personal. Because it was such a personal story to me and also to them, it took quite a bit of convincing for them to do it. At that point, they thought I was making this amateur film; no problem there. . . . I actually had a crew with me when I shot the interviews. I brought the crew from Toronto, but everybody spoke Cantonese, so that put my family at ease, and they really had no clue how well my first film did, and they thought this would be just another little project. I was pestering them to let me shoot their stories because I wanted to remember them. My sister was very resistant. She was working, so she was afraid that people would see her in the film and work against her in some way or gossip about her. My mother is a very private person, so she was not too open or revealing about her life. My aunt, for obvious reasons, did not want to talk about her life with her partner, so that was difficult all around. I went to Hong Kong twice before the actual shooting just to make sure.

Did structuring the film around shoes and clothes help? Do you think that talking about their lives in terms of how they dressed and what they were wearing helped to break down some of these barriers or made it easier for them?

Beyond the campy aesthetics of it all, I just thought that the shoes represented very well different stages of how their lives evolved, how their expectations of their lives changed as they went through different phases with their shoes. It was a nice elliptical way to discuss their lives, and it was easier for them to talk about their way of dressing or their shoes. Instead of asking them what they did at a specific period in their lives and how they felt about things, the feelings came through when they were talking about their stories of how they related to their belongings. I do not think it could have turned out any other way because my family would not have opened up. The idea to focus on shoes came before I actually applied for money, so the funders of the film knew that I was going to shoot a film around the women's relationship with their shoes.

It is also an interesting way to examine women's sexuality in terms of fashion. Not everybody is interested in my family, but everybody has shoes, and everybody has mothers who wear shoes, and grandmothers who wear shoes. Maybe viewers can relate to the topic in some broad way and find something interesting in the film.

One of the most striking scenes involves your aunt's shoes. Was it difficult to get her to open up about purchasing men's shoes?

Yes, it was, and actually, my grandmother was quite upset with me after the film was released, because I exposed that aspect of the family to the outside world. I think the thing that the family remarked on was that it was better not to be seen than to be seen. That is just part of the Chinese culture, my family, and the way the family handles this kind of situation.

Was this representation of lesbianism in Hong Kong striking to people who saw it in Hong Kong at that time? I know Twin Bracelets *screened around the same time; however, even now, lesbianism in Chinese film represents rather new subject matter.*

In relation to *Twin Bracelets,* I could not believe lesbians were always portrayed in the same way. They either killed themselves or they killed each other; the husbands killed them or someone killed them to put them in their place. I thought that was just not right, it was not the way things are, and we cannot always present this kind of negative portrayal in the cinema. I decided, with my film, to just focus on a relationship. This relationship involved two people who found each other in their teenage years, lost each other, and then found each other again. It was quite a lovely love story.

My aunt was dressing like a man before the film was made, long before, years and years before. I think it was a personal choice that she made, which she never regretted. It was that way or no way, and I wanted her in the film because of her strength and pride in who she was.

When gays and lesbians from Chinese backgrounds travel around the world, they sometimes can express their sexuality in a different way in a foreign context than they can in a Chinese context. Was it difficult for your aunt, for example, to return to Hong Kong?

She really did turn heads when she first returned from England, and there were people who were convinced that she was a man. In restaurants, for example, it used to be very upsetting for my grandmother. Waiters would wager whether she was a man or woman, and my grandmother got really upset about these things because she felt personally responsible for how my aunt dressed. When the film came out, in Hong Kong especially, a lot of people actually thought maybe "the man" in the film, my aunt, was the filmmaker. However, at the gay and lesbian film festivals, there was quite an overwhelmingly supportive response from the lesbians, who had never really seen Asian lesbians portrayed that way.

Still, my family is not happy about the film. In terms of family dynamics, it has been a hurtful experience for all of us.

How has your mother dealt with it? How does she feel about the way she is portrayed in the film?

She was not happy. I think she was not happy because she felt that people would judge her based on the poverty in her life. She felt they would judge her decisions about moving, marrying my father, not getting married again after he died; she felt very open to criticism. Her life became so exposed on the big screen, and strangers were watching it. She felt that she would be exposed to gossip, criticisms, and judgments, which she is not very happy about, and my sister feels the same way.

Your sister seems to embody the relationship between Hong Kong and the People's Republic. How does she feel about staying in Hong Kong after 1997? Does she still have the same trouble with her business connections in the PRC?

She is still in Hong Kong, she works there, and she has changed. She no longer has to go to China. She is much happier about that. They handle delicate situations involving gender issues very differently in the PRC. For example, sometimes she would wake up in the morning, and a male hotel employee would be in her room, standing there watching her. This type of intrusion is just not acceptable in North America, or even in Hong Kong. When the film came out, she thought people who saw the film would think she had negative feelings about China and Chinese clients. She felt that her managers would not want her to work with Chinese clients because of the way her attitude was portrayed in the film, but of course, that was one of the most powerful things she said in her interview.

All of my films to this point are very personal. I think I have changed after working on *These Shoes*, in terms of thinking about consent for interview material, because my family thought that I had not properly obtained the consent to use the kind of intimate personal information I put in the film. It is hard to define the boundaries, especially in a family context, where one would draw the line between what hurts people, what offends people, and what is acceptable, so that is the one thing that is stopping me from making more documentaries.

My grandmother passed away in the summer of 1998. The film had been out for about three years by then. I did not have a chance to see her after the film was released. The family did not really feel very good about the film after it was released, so I stayed away for a year or two. In the summer that I was supposed to go back to see them, she passed away in her sleep. She was about to turn seventy. I do not know how I relate to the film at this point because of losing my grandmother. I am very happy that I have the memory of her and the intimacy that was so special about our relationship. I can feel that intimacy whenever I watch that film, so that is very important to me. However, it saddens me that I did not have the opportunity to properly resolve the situation about the film with her before her death. Since then, my family has viewed the film quite differently. They think it is a good thing to have the film, since grandmother is not here anymore. Their negative emotions towards the film have toned down a little bit.

What project are you working on now?

I developed my new project with the assistance of the Asian Community AIDS Services in Toronto, and I wrote a script using some of the research I did through speaking with some of their clients. They spoke with me about the experience of living with AIDS for Asian gay men and lesbians, which informed part of the film. When I was writing the film last year, I was struggling to deal with the loss of my grandmother. The main character is actually a filmmaker dealing with the loss of her grandmother, and, within the film itself, I bring back the interviews of my grandmother from *These Shoes*. The relationship between the filmmaker and the mother is a fictionalized version of the dialogue with my mom in *These Shoes*. A lot of it is based on personal experiences of the struggle of coming to a new place and not knowing if one has made the right decision.

Are you looking for funding in Canada or elsewhere? Will the film be in English and Cantonese?

Hopefully, in both languages. The Cantonese part is really tricky because, in general, it is difficult to fund a film with subtitles. I am hoping to get the funding from the Canadian film agencies and arts councils, although there has been such a severe budget cutback for arts funding in the past three or four years in Canada that it is no longer that easy to get funding for any kind of film projects. Also, progressing from shorts to a first feature is a very difficult point in a filmmaker's career. I was actually thinking of probably having to shoot quite a bit on video just to make it affordable. I think that digital video/DV can provide intimacy, too. I would much rather make something in DV and be able to produce it within two or three years than wait ten years to shoot it on film.

How do you envision yourself making an intervention within the different communities in which you work?

When I write a script, I do not tell myself that I am going to write an issues-oriented film, or that I am going to write a gay film, or that I am going to write a women's film, but the issues that are in my head somehow surface, first onto paper, then onto the screen. I do not consider myself a political activist, although my films have been used in many situations for AIDS activism, for campaigns against homophobic violence, for counseling, etc. It is wonderful that the films can be used in those contexts, and, if people think of my work as activist, then I am flattered and honored. I am doing something for the communities, even though I do not really set out intentionally to make the film as a political intervention. When I make my films, the stories have to be true to me, true to my experience, so my stories always seem to come from deep within.

April 15, 2000

3   Working Women in the People's Republic of China: *Out of Phoenix Bridge, Women from the Lake of Scented Souls,* and *A Little Life Opera*

ZHOU XIAO-WEN'S *ERMO* (1994) follows its eponymous protagonist (Aliya) on a quest for a television set—the biggest one in her remote village—to show up her more industrious next-door neighbors, who already own a set that makes them quite popular with the other villagers. Ermo works herself to exhaustion to attain her consumerist dream. She makes noodles by pounding on the dough with her feet, sells them, moves away from the village to work in town, sells her blood, and unwittingly sells herself (in an affair with her neighbor's husband) to buy the TV. In "*Ermo*: Televisuality, Capital and the Global Village," Anne T. Ciecko and Sheldon H. Lu describe the film as "a road map of the processes of globalization and capital accumulation in the Deng era's economic reform."[1] As the authors point out, the television symbolizes the village's entry into the global economy as Ermo's blood, sweat, and tears transubstantiate into a screen that transmits American popular culture and commercials for even more consumer products: "Television teaches Ermo how to be a good capitalist."[2] In "Blood Money: Woman's Desire and Consumption in *Ermo*," Beth Notar concurs: "Make money, consume—achieve urbanity, modernity, sexuality-the images on television beckon Ermo."[3]

Although it is fiction, *Ermo* does highlight actual aspects of China's new economy, including the use of migrant labor from the countryside, the exploitation of working women in the service sector, and the way global capitalism fuels new class hierarchies and exacerbates gender inequities. As *Ermo* travels around the globe, the film critiques the very processes that enabled its worldwide exhibition. Thus, global screen culture links Chinese women's labor to a critique of transnational capitalism.[4]

When Deng Xiaoping instituted his policies of economic reform in 1978, he embarked on a path diametrically opposed to Mao Zedong. Rather than work for national economic self-sufficiency, Deng encouraged foreign investment, joint ventures, and free trade zones to bring China into the global capitalist arena. Dismantling the commune system, Deng reinstated private ownership with the family farm as the main unit of production in the countryside. Controls on the movement of labor loosened, and unemployed peasants flooded major cities looking for jobs. Although these policies enabled some to become "gloriously" rich, displaced peasants, unemployed factory workers, and many who lost the security of socialist guarantees of health care, child care, and basic subsistence found themselves worse off under the new, booming economy. While students agitating for democratic reform received the lion's share of the global media coverage of the demonstrations in Tian'anmen Square in 1989, many of those protesters were there to agitate for a reexamination of economic policies that had left many workers in the lurch.

Certainly, the 1989 protests and subsequent crackdown dealt a blow to Deng's plans for economic growth and world recognition.[5] Though the bloody suppression of the demonstrations may have signaled strength in some quarters (e.g., among investors more comfortable with authoritarian regimes such as Singapore), it signaled instability and violation of human rights in other quarters (e.g., the United States, Western Europe). In 1992, Deng made another push to attract foreign investment and stimulate the market economy in China, and indeed, China's gross national product expanded considerably. However, while the quantity and variety of goods manufactured for export and available in the domestic market increased exponentially and dreams of a consumer paradise overshadowed agitation for political reform, a darker picture of the new economy began to emerge from various sectors of China's media culture.

Even before 1989, China's Fifth Generation entered the global economy of film production through official coproductions, foreign investment, and transnational distribution deals. After 1989, these transnational connections became even more important for the financing and distribution of films that were routinely banned by the PRC government for domestic exhibition. Also, under the influence of the new economic climate, studios increasingly insisted that films turn a profit. At the same time, as digital technologies and advances in video recording made the use of smaller, less expensive, easier-to-operate formats more widely available, an explosion in unofficial production took place. The Sixth Generation of filmmakers graduated from the Beijing Film Academy and found a very different world waiting for them in which even the possibility of going to an out-of-the-way studio like Xi'an to direct a film no longer existed; an "underground" filmmaking movement began to spring up involving younger, formally trained filmmakers, avant-garde artists attracted to new motion picture technology; and alternative media producers anxious to provide a view of post-1989 China that differed from the official picture.[6]

As 1997 came closer and Hong Kong's return to Chinese sovereignty nearer, many in Hong Kong became more curious about conditions in the mainland. Coproductions thus not only provided filmmakers in the PRC with capital investment for their films, they also provided Hong Kong filmmakers with an entry into the Chinese distribution system and offered a glimpse of conditions across the border for Hong Kong audiences. Audiences throughout the Chinese diaspora, which formed the pool of much of the capital coming into the People's Republic through the connections of the overseas Chinese, also needed to know about or fantasize about economic conditions in the mainland. Therefore, the ups and the downs of the new economy provided an object of fascination for global Chinese audiences.

Although many of these films take a light-hearted view of the new economy,[7] others, like *Ermo*, have been more critical. However, few films link any social critique they may proffer of contemporary China directly to Deng's policies. Rather, an ambivalent and contradictory picture emerges of Deng's China in which the unequal distribution of wealth, social ills like prostitution and narcotics abuse, and "decadence" of various sorts may be tied to the necessary evils of Western contamination, bourgeois selfishness, or the annoyingly persistent threat of pre-1949 Chinese feudalism. Any actual link between global capitalism and Chinese social problems remains oblique. However, by looking at the margins of these films and highlighting what lies beneath the surface of these texts, a clearer picture of the consequences of China's tremendous economic growth emerges.

Li Hong's *Out of Phoenix Bridge* (1997), Xie Fei's *Women from the Lake of Scented Souls* (1993), and Allen Fong's *A Little Life Opera* (1997) are three films that look at Chinese women in the post-Deng economy. However, all three filmmakers take dramatically different approaches to their subject matter. A graduate of the Beijing Broadcast Institute, Li Hong is one of the leading figures of the Sixth Generation's new documentary movement, and *Out of Phoenix Bridge*, heir to the direct cinema/cinema vérité documentary tradition, takes a "reality TV" approach to looking at the lives of young working women in Beijing by living with them in their hovel. As a filmmaker and educator from the Fourth Generation, Xie Fei takes the opposite approach. He uses sumptuous cinematography and a melodramatic plot to look at the impact of globalization on a Chinese village. A member of the Hong Kong New Wave, American-educated Allen Fong takes a stylistic middle ground by approaching small town life in a way reminiscent of Italian neorealism, blending documentary with melodrama to provide an ethnographic presentation of the subject matter.

Working with established figures in Taiwanese cinema via the work of Ang Lee (e.g., Yang Kuei-Mei of *Eat Drink Man Woman* and Winston Chao from *The Wedding Banquet*), Fong draws on recognized faces within transnational Chinese film; however, he also works with local Fujian opera performers (i.e., Zeng Ji-Ping, who plays Liliang, is head of the Quanzhou Liyung Opera Troupe)[8] and, as is characteristic of his oeuvre, with other nonactors who work within the performing arts but who make their screen debuts in his films. Although stylistically distinct, all three filmmakers look at women in relation to issues of labor, class, gender, family structure, and Chinese tradition.

These cinematic representations of women from experimental video documentaries to feature length fiction offer a view of women within post-Tian'anmen China that exposes some of the contradictions inherent in the processes of economic change, urbanization, gender redefinition, class repositioning, and globalization at the root of contemporary Chinese society. By looking at the margins of these three films, a darker picture of Deng's economic policies begins to emerge.

Documenting Chinese Women's Labor

Representations of female laborers—specifically women factory workers, peasants, and soldiers—have always played key roles in the literary and visual works of Chinese progressive cultural circles from the May Fourth Movement beginning in

1919 through the left-wing cinema productions of the pre-1945 era and the socialist art establishment of the People's Republic since 1949.[9] Whether as allegorical figures of colonial oppression, feudal backwardness, and hope for liberation of the Chinese nation or, later, emblems of the traumas of the Cultural Revolution and vicissitudes of Chinese Communist political life, women laborers represent the backbone of China and concretize the nation's triumphs and tribulations.[10]

In fact, the three films examined here represent three traditions in which women's labor has been represented in Chinese cinema. *Out of Phoenix Bridge* comes out of the long tradition of documentary representations of women workers produced by studios like the Central Newsreel and Documentary Film Studio, Agriculture Film Studio, the August 1st Film Studio (run by the People's Liberation Army), Changchun Film Studio, as well as documentary units in all the major film studios.

Women from the Lake of Scented Souls figures within the genre of the Chinese melodrama devoted to women in village life that includes a resurgence of films in the 1980s, such as *The In-Laws* (1981), *Country Couple* (1983), *A Girl from Hunan* (codirected by Xie Fei, 1985), *Hibiscus Town* (1986), *Red Sorghum* (1987), and *Ju Dou* (1989). All these films look at women peasants and family structure in relation to the political vicissitudes of the day. Although similar in subject matter, films like *In the Wild Mountains* (1985) and *Ermo* take a more ironic view of village life and the impact of the new economy on sexual relations among the peasantry. In a similar vein, Peng Xiaolian's *The Women's Story* (1987) follows three peasant women as they go to town to sell yarn.

A Little Life Opera fits squarely within the backstage opera genre, devoted to comparing the traditional stories told on-stage to the parallel life experiences of the actors and actresses off-stage, which includes films such as *Two Stage Sisters* (1964) and *Farewell My Concubine* (1993).[11] Several films on the Cantonese opera world appeared around the same time as *A Little Life Opera*, including Shu Kei's *Hu Du Men* (*Stage Door*, 1996) and Clifton Ko's *The Mad Phoenix* (1997).

However, these three films take very different approaches to women's labor in contemporary China by looking at the challenges posed by the new market economy and the effects of globalization. *Out of Phoenix Bridge* deals with the transformation of women from the countryside into migrant laborers within Beijing's informal economy. *Women from the Lake of Scented Souls* looks at the increasing chasm between a newly emerging entrepreneurial class in the countryside and the impoverishment of other peasants due to the impact of China's entry into the global economy. *A Little Life Opera* looks at the emergence of a new class of small businessmen and -women in China and the impact these changes have had on women in Chinese society.

Out of Phoenix Bridge documents women involved in the informal economy that keeps the economic boom in Beijing going. The young women in this film work in the informal service sector as maids and waitresses. As the communal structures of the factory "work unit" and the rural commune break down, they are not replaced by the Western bourgeois ideal of the nuclear family or the Confucian ideal of the extended, patriarchal family. Rather, working women must find a way to stay on top of domestic chores as well as bring in the expected additional income in the family. For women entering the emerging middle classes and for single men in the city looking for opportunities unavailable in the home village, domestic chores prove to be an additional burden. Thus, although condemned as a sign of bourgeois decadence, the maid from the countryside has reappeared in the households of Beijing. Similarly, curbside eateries have sprung up to cater to the increasingly transitory population that may have limited access to cooking facilities and no time to make even a bowl of noodles before the workday begins, and these diners demand staff to cook, serve, and clean up. The cheap labor that fuels domestic work and the lowest sector of service work in the capital comes from the countryside.

In 1993, Li Hong became acquainted with a group of young women living together in a hovel in one of the *hu tong* in Beijing. Most of the older residences in the city cluster around maze-like alleys, called hu tong, which provide very narrow pathways from the main boulevards to the housing hidden from the view of the casual pedestrian. In a cluster of one-room shacks in one of these alleys, migrant workers from Anhui province rent housing. In fact, in many parts of Beijing and other large urban centers, mini-villages exist where residents from a specific province cluster together for mutual support.[12] Although people are required to have a permit to live and work in Beijing, enforcement of the residency rules can be uneven, corrupt, or simply not feasible due to the surging numbers of displaced workers and peasants looking for opportunities in the booming capital.

By moving in with her subjects, Li Hong paints an intimate and detailed picture of the lives of these migrant women laborers. She makes excellent use of portable video equipment to record in the cramped quarters of the workers' shack. Because of the nature of the location, Li favors close-ups, and the camera often lingers on the women's faces, occasionally too close for the image to be in focus, allowing the talking heads to directly address the live-in filmmaker and by extension, the audience.

The compositions are cluttered with the women's belongings. Most of the furniture consists of suitcases, and the women keep their belongings in plastic bags, piled around the shack, or on hangers above their beds. As temporary workers, they never completely settle in, and even if they wanted to, they have little to unpack. To provide background on their present circumstances in Beijing, the filmmaker makes several trips to the women's home village of Phoenix Bridge in Anhui. Through the course of the film, Li Hong makes clear the untenable circumstances in which these women find themselves; they have fled abuse in the countryside only to suffer in the city as well.

Indeed, the film uses direct observation to concretize labor issues that had been reported in the press as the volume of migrant workers coming to the city, particularly Beijing, increased during the decades of the 1980s and 1990s. Li Hong puts a very human face on these statistics, literally getting in bed with her shivering subjects, to go through, step by step, a litany of abuses and poor conditions the young women endure. Although the film can be read as a testament to the survival of the tough Chinese peasantry and the enduring power of the Chinese woman to live through even the most adverse circumstances, the specifics of these women's lives and their particular exploitation as undocumented or underdocumented (with recently expired permits) workers take the film beyond the timeless story of suffering and survival to the very timely story of the dark side of the new economy.

Out of Phoenix Bridge begins chaotically, with a narrow escape from an armed assailant in the alley, highlighting the marginal nature of the little shack and the disorienting quality of the life within. Dark and sequestered, the alley makes a perfect place for attackers to prey on the young women, who have little recourse to legal protection, because they themselves may be in Beijing illegally. Although the landlady arrives to try to smooth the situation over by offering alternative explanations for the man's threatening behavior, they remain frightened of the possibility of robbery, assault, and kidnapping. The young women also live in fear of the landlady, who often appears unannounced to scold them about sewage found in a drainage ditch (because the shack has no toilet) or the fact they have used too much coal or water (due to the lack of proper heating and running water). The women have no privacy. In their cramped quarters, even taking a bath (i.e., taking off clothes to wipe the body down with a washcloth) requires considerable advance planning to make sure curtains are secure, the door guarded, and the other women in bed to give the bather adequate room.

The shack does little to keep outsiders at bay. At one point, an official finds his way to the back alley for a crackdown on stolen bicycles. Although the young women have no or suspect papers, the policeman turns a blind eye to their residency status, just as he was nowhere in sight when Xiazi was assaulted. Regulation of property and the general belief that migrant workers steal bicycles, deal in stolen bicycles, and are the principal, gullible customers for stolen bicycles brings the official to the hu tong. Within the market economy, the state takes a greater interest in controlling property and preserving private property rights than in the general welfare of its citizens.

The women do menial labor for meager wages. One works at an outdoor restaurant and the others work as maids. They know no one in Beijing except for their employers and the landlords. Even though they have been working in the city for over a year, Li Hong is the first local to take them sight-seeing, photograph them in Tian'anmen Square, and take them shopping for new clothes to celebrate the New Year. Shy of people not from Anhui, their lives revolve around work and basic survival, and the bulk of their wages goes back to Phoenix Bridge to help support their parents and brothers. Thus their labor forms the conduit for the limited capital that funnels back to the countryside from Beijing.

Li Hong demonstrates that these women's role in the unofficial economy relates directly to their gender. Although men from the provinces also work on the margins of the Beijing labor force particularly in seasonal and temporary occupations like construction, women enter Beijing's undocumented labor force for different reasons, for poorer wages, with fewer opportunities, and with different familial expectations. In fact, the gender differences within the family life of the village narrowed these women's opportunities from childhood. The women in *Out of Phoenix Bridge*, for example, did not attend school because of the need to babysit younger brothers, and now, working in Beijing, the girls help build up the dowry for their brothers' weddings.

Li Hong develops the closest relationship with Xiazi and uses her circumstances as the primary focus of the film. Through Xiazi, the filmmaker presents a detailed picture of the relationship between gender and labor. Born in a cowshed because giving birth to daughters in a house is considered bad luck, Xiazi had difficulty growing up because of her stepfather's abuse of her mother. When it came time for her to marry, she refused two potential suitors because she preferred a boatman. However, her boatman suitor was too poor to be acceptable to the family, and he was engaged to another woman. During the argument over the relationship, Xiazi threatened suicide, but instead ran off to Beijing to work. In interviews in Phoenix Bridge with Xiazi's stepfather and mother, Li Hong exposes the anger that continues to sour their relationship with their daughter, whom the stepfather complains has "a dark side" and drifts like "duckweed."

Xiazi makes several attempts to improve her lot. Minimally trained as a hairdresser (her stepfather is the village barber), she attempts to apprentice herself at a beauty salon with no luck. Seeing a chance of a new marriage prospect arranged by her grandmother, Xiazi goes to the county seat to meet a young man studying driving and auto repair. However, the young man refuses to even meet Xiazi, and his family claims that he will not consider marriage until his studies have been completed. To make up for the misunderstanding, Xiazi's grandmother arranges for her to take a job in a wooden screw factory, which would enable her to live in the county seat of Wu-wei. However, when her parents learn about the low wages at the factory, they insist on her return to Phoenix Bridge to help out growing cotton for sale. Not wanting to do the hard physical labor of bringing the night soil to the fields and stooping to pick the cotton like her mother, Xiazi goes back to live in the hu tong in Beijing.

Most of the young women do eventually return to their villages to marry, but Xiazi's mother's difficult life points to the real possibility of unhappy marriages, lack of opportunity, and fear of poverty. In the barbershop, the village men gossip about the migrant women laborers, telling stories about women who marry much older men to stay in the city, and the gossips dismiss them as spineless sluts. However, they speak ill as well of women who choose not to marry and live indefinitely as maids in Beijing. They complain that educated women are too picky. Xiazi's younger aunt provides an example of an accomplished woman who cannot find a suitable match. Trained as a tailor and a middle-school graduate, the younger aunt is called a "Hong Kong woman." When she dared to make a Western-style outfit to wear, her grandmother tore it to shreds to prevent gossip. The young aunt repaired and wore it, but her marriage prospects declined dramatically after the incident.

In her mid-twenties, with failed ambitions as a hairdresser and two broken engagements behind her, Xiazi also has dwindling prospects for marriage. Although a few years before a factory job with a residence permit to live in the county seat would have guaranteed a modicum of security, the changing economy has made that a much less attractive possibility. As her parents worry about support in their old age when they can no longer work their small field or cut hair in the village, they also see the difficulties Xiazi may face without children to support her. Without the safety net of the communal farm or factory, with no "iron rice bowl" there for working-class women, the individual's welfare again depends on making a suitable marriage, having sons to bring in decent wages, and hoping for some security through traditional patriarchal family ties.

Out of Phoenix Bridge concludes with a shot of a photo Li Hong took of the young women under the portrait of Mao in Tian'anmen Square. The picture, diminished by its placement on a large gray wall, concretizes the irony of these young women's lack of opportunity. Although Mao's marriage reforms and insistence on women's equality held out hope for China's peasantry and proletarian laborers after the institution of legal reforms in 1950, those hopes have come to nothing, and the young women return to village life with little to show from their experiences in the new urban economy except a photo of Tian'anmen.

Women from the Lake of Scented Souls (a.k.a. *Woman Sesame Oil Maker*) makes a similar connection between traditional patriarchal structures and China's new market economy. In this case, like Xie Jin's *Hibiscus Town* and Hong Kong director Yim Ho's *The Day the Sun Turned Cold* (1994), the plot revolves around a small-town woman who has a knack for making a profit with the production of a local commodity. However, unlike the bean curd sellers in *Hibiscus Town* and *The Day the Sun Turned Cold*, the protagonist of *Women from the Lake of Scented Souls*, Xiang Ersao (Siqin Gaowa),[13] turns her sesame oil into a thriving local business without suffering the consequences of a series of political campaigns against bourgeois tendencies. Through the connections of her lover, Ren (Chen Baoguo), a provincial truck driver, Xiang sells her oil in the city and attracts the attention of a Japanese company represented by Shino Sadako, a highly placed manager in an import-export firm. As Xiang's oil enters the global economy and her profits increase, the pressure of patriarchal tradition forces her to take account of the future of her enterprise.

Married to a cripple, Xiang believes that her best hope for keeping the capital she has accumulated in the family rests with marrying off Dunzi, her mentally handicapped son (illegally, because a marriage certificate cannot be obtained officially for an epileptic)[14] and hoping for grandsons to take over the business. Although she has a daughter fathered by Ren, she cannot envision matrilineal inheritance or other ways to reorganize her family finances. Though it may be expected that her very traditional husband would oppose taking her daughter's education seriously, the fact that Xiang is blind to the possibility of allowing her daughter to continue the business testifies to her own belief in the patriarchal system that made her life a living hell. Even though she is beaten and abused by her alcoholic husband, Xiang hopes that the right daughter-in-law will somehow provide her with the grandson she craves.

Craftily, Xiang manipulates the system to achieve her goal. Very savvy about the way the new economy operates, she cajoles a lender into demanding repayment of a debt to get the overextended family of an attractive village girl, Huanhuan (Wu Yujuan), to agree to marry their daughter to Dunzi in exchange for relief from the

FIGURE 11. Still from *Hibiscus Town*. Selling bean curd can be tougher than it looks for this rural woman entrepreneur in the Chinese countryside. (Courtesy of Shanghai Film Studio.)

threat of foreclosure. Though capitalism has enriched Xiang with the investment of foreign capital, Huanhuan's family has not fared as well under the market system, because the money they borrowed to modernize their fishing business did not achieve the desired results. To get Huanhuan's boyfriend, one of Xiang's employees whose family is also not well off, out of the picture, Xiang arranges for the young man to open a sesame oil shop in town and forces him to promise not to look for a girlfriend in the village, because that may distract him from making money. He gleefully agrees to her conditions for the opportunity to work in town, even though he knows he also gives up any chance at marrying Huanhuan in the bargain. With a couple of bottles of sesame oil, Xiang persuades the village head, a representative of the government, to turn a blind eye to Dunzi's impairment and declare him cured by the prospect of marriage.

Although surrounded by impotent and broken representatives of the Chinese patriarchy (e.g., a crippled husband, retarded son, impotent and corrupt party cadre, morally loose lover, and selfish, greedy young employee), Xiang still holds on to the patriarchy as if the institutionalization of women's equality under Communism had never happened. Ironically, the entry into the global market revives feudal marriage customs and the abuse of women. Rather than entering a modern system in which women's liberation can be taken for granted, global capitalism reminds the village it needs Confucian virtues and patriarchal structures to prosper and guarantee inheritance rights of private property.

Of course, Xiang's schemes do not achieve their desired results. Only able to beat Huanhuan in frustration, Dunzi remains impotent, and his epileptic episodes continue. Xiang and Huanhuan continue to help Dunzi urinate into a chamber pot at night and sleep clutching a rag doll. At one point, Huanhuan goes back to her family, but with a combination of gifts and threats, Xiang cajoles her into coming back to Dunzi. Ironically, the new adult pair of eyes in the household makes it increasingly difficult for Xiang to see Ren, and Ren decides to break off the affair. Even with Ren out of the picture, Xiang's husband becomes suspicious and beats her mercilessly when he discovers that she has been taking birth control pills and "robbing" him of additional heirs. When he points out that she need not fear another Dunzi because they have a healthy daughter, Xiang's silence confirms her husband's suspicion that Zhi'er, Xiang's daughter, is not his child. With the loss of her lover, the further disintegration of even the sham of a marriage, and Dunzi's impotence, Xiang realizes the hopelessness of her own situation. Seeing herself in Huanhuan, she offers to free the girl. However, Huanhuan is fatalistic, and she does not see much hope in finding a better husband after being tainted by her marriage to Dunzi.

The parallel between Xiang and Huanhuan becomes clear as they look off at the lake in silhouette. Earlier, Xiang had told the story of "souls' lake" to Ms. Shino. During the Qing Dynasty, two young women—one the daughter of a landlord, the other the daughter of a blacksmith—committed suicide by jumping into the lake at the same time. Legend has it that they turned into two birds and flew to heaven. The moral seems to be clear: Rich or poor, women have plenty of reasons to want to leave this world.

In *China into Film: Frames of Reference in Contemporary Chinese Cinema*, Jerome Silbergeld notes a connection between Deng's economic policies and the narrative question posed in *Women from the Lake of Scented Souls*:

> Deng Xiaoping's notion of "socialism with a Chinese face" implies in a most un-Marxian fashion that the socio-cultural superstructure can be uncoupled from its economic base, that China can undergo a so-called "second revolution" economically while retaining its traditional "Chineseness." The question that *Scented Souls* asks, by way of its female analogy, is not whether China *can* do this (in Marxian terms or otherwise) but whether it *should*. At the same time, while concluding that the social character of China *is* as much in need of a revolution as China's economy, it does not make clear any belief that this *can* be done.[15]

Approaching this question, *Women from the Lake of Scented Souls* opens up a number of contradictory interpretations. It can be seen as a critique of China's entry into the global market economy, because economic prosperity does little to alleviate suffering. In fact, Xie Fei made an even more direct critique of the impact of China's economic modernization and entry into global capitalism in his earlier film on urban life, *Black Snow* (1989).[16] However, *Women from the Lake of Scented Souls* can accommodate a diametrically opposed position that seems to favor globalization. From this perspective, the film indicates that if only the Chinese would let go of their "old," "backward" ways (e.g., if Xiang would let go of her hopes for the retarded Dunzi, her loyalty to her abusive husband, her dependence on her lover), China could become a "modern" nation on a par with Japan.

However, Ms. Shino's history seems to mitigate this reading—at least to a degree. Actually, Shino has a Chinese grandfather, speaks some Chinese, and serves as an icon of overseas Chinese investment. Therefore, ties to an imagined ancestral homeland explain foreign investment as something other than an attempt to profit from China's cheap labor costs. In fact, her Chinese ethnicity argues against Japanese economic imperialism replacing Japan's military ambitions during the Pacific War. Also, although she appears to be an accomplished, educated, independent woman, her involvement in global capitalism has not freed her from the demands of the patriarchy. When her lover calls for an unexpected assignation, she jumps, asks no questions, and rushes to him. Whether Shino prefers not to marry to further her career or whether she is taken advantage of because of her Chinese ethnicity remains unclear; however, her situation underscores the fact that global capitalism promises no end to patriarchal exploitation.

However, the film does not comment on whether the patriarchy is required for the smooth running of capitalism. If communes still existed, production would be less efficient, but women would "hold up half the sky" and not have much pressure to produce male heirs. However, *Women from the Lake of Scented Souls* does not wax nostalgic for the days before Deng's economic reforms. Rather, given the petty corruption and ineptitude of the Party's representative in the village and Xiang's history of an abusive marriage even before her business took off, the link between socialism and feminism breaks down and with it, the reverse reasoning that capitalism must be linked to the patriarchy. Even though Xiang could never have managed Dunzi's marriage without the profits from her sesame oil, the film seems to divorce the economy from the Chinese patriarchy and, as a consequence, shies away from any concrete critique of China in the global marketplace and the effects of privatization on women.

China's entry into global capitalism and its impact on gender roles and family organization also form the backdrop for *A Little Life Opera*. The vicissitudes of a local Chinese opera troupe chart the growth of the new economy. In *Women from the Lake of Scented Souls*, Xiang's husband passes his time in a floating tea house enjoying predominantly male forms of entertainment ranging from Chinese songs to Hong Kong soft-core porn Category III films.[17] Before the infusion of Japanese capital, he watches opera performed by a disheveled man in an undershirt; however, after the money begins to come in, an attractive woman sings accompanied by more professional musicians. Similarly, in *A Little Life Opera*, the revival of traditional opera under Deng's economic policies points to one of the cultural forms the nouveau riche use to display their good fortune publicly.

Xue Yan (Yang Kuei-Mei) works at a dismal outdoor food stall in a bustling town in Fujian. She also manages the Jinan Opera Troupe. When the troupe is commissioned to perform an opera in Xi Tang Village, Xue Yan jumps at the chance and gathers her troupe together to prepare for the performance. Of course, the troupe's fortunes depend on the material prosperity of the province and the willingness of those who have benefited from Fujian's booming import-export businesses to support the arts, because government subsidies for local operas are minimal. A coastal province, Fujian has always had extensive international business contacts, and many Chinese émigrés hail from that province. When the "overseas" Chinese return to invest, these points of ancestral origin often benefit most directly from foreign investment.

Although often dismissed as appreciated only by the elderly[18] or hopelessly lost during its suppression by the Red Guards during the Cultural Revolution, local operas continue to survive and sometimes thrive. However, the reasons for the resurgence of opera may have less to do with an appreciation of local arts and more to do with acceptable displays of newly acquired wealth. As *A Little Life Opera* makes clear, the opera provides a way to display personal success publicly. While driving a Mercedes or inviting business associates to gatherings at trendy KTV (karaoke) clubs signals financial success, the staging of an opera in the public square or in front of a temple to honor an elderly family member or celebrate a particular milestone roots that personal success in the dynamics of family and village life. Sanctioned by the Confucian tradition associated with the opera, any stigma connected with class privilege can be eliminated by patronizing the arts for the civic good. Traditional opera's roots in Confucian virtue and celebration of filial piety put to rest any question of the morality of private enterprise and the potentially corrosive influences of capitalism on the village.

For the *hua dan*, the female performers who anchor the local troupe featured in *A Little Life Opera*, these performances promise an escape from the drudgery of the service sector. Through opera, they hope to achieve a degree of recognition for their art and autonomy as "businesswomen," albeit in a marginal sector of the export-oriented industrial economy of the province. However, *A Little Life Opera* uncovers the difficulties of this entry into the global economy and exposes the contradictions that divide the material performance of the opera from the fantasy presented on the stage.

As the troupe publicizes the upcoming performance, Xue Yan runs into Li Sampeng (Winston Chao), whom she remembers as a musician and puppeteer. Li has become a successful businessman and factory owner, but the two recognize each other as kindred spirits because of their love of traditional performing arts. Ironically, although Xue Yan hid Li during the Cultural Revolution when all forms of traditional performances were suppressed, the couple solidifies their connection to the old days by singing a song from one of the model operas, *The Red Lantern*, favored by Mao's wife, Jiang Qing, during the Cultural Revolution. Incongruously, they also bond by waltzing in a popular KTV club, where Pabst Blue Ribbon beer is the drink of choice, and Western commodities and cultural forms clash with Chinese political history and traditional aesthetic sensibilities.

As a former artiste, Li seems out of place at gatherings of his contemporaries. Disdainful of making money, Li prefers to indulge his passions for photography and traditional opera, and he leaves most business dealings to his wife (Wu Xiao-Ting). Li's relation to the new economy and traditional culture is contrasted with that of his colleague, Mr. Jin (Ren Yong). Jovially, Jin tells the story of a man who borrowed money to build a factory and became so successful he was able to build a house. Because of his success, he also built a new road to the village and invited an opera troupe to perform for three days. Jin continues to make fun of this rich man's ostentatious display of wealth by imitating the way he shows off his gold watch and his cell phone.[19] All at the table joke that Jin is describing himself in these boastful as well as self-deprecating terms. However, Jin also reveals himself to be a phi-listine when he demands that Xue Yan's opera troupe perform a striptease as part of the entertainment he has commissioned. To help out Xue Yan, Li talks Jin out of his plan and offers to take everyone out for a night at the KTV club to smooth things over. Through his appreciation of Chinese opera, Li sets himself apart from the other successful businessmen, and the excesses of capitalism (e.g., delight in salacious spectacles, etc.) can be contained through the actions of this character.

However, although he argues against the striptease, Li has few inhibitions about fraternizing with Xue Yan and insinuating himself into the daily routines of the troupe. Leaving his wife to deal with the quotidian operations of the factory and with government pressure for the operation to come up with an accurate set of books for tax assessment, Li has the leisure to enjoy his opera companions with few restrictions. While his wife makes suspect transnational deals that violate tax regulations, Li begins to act like an opera patron from pre-Communist China, playing in the orchestra when it suits him, and even donning make-up to perform on stage with Xue Yan. As Li and Xue Yan watch one of the other hua dan perform *The Chant of the Good Widow*, which includes a reference to "high rank and fast promotion" as well as a widow's reluctance to cross the threshold to return the affections of a suitor (because traditionally, widows, if financially able, remained loyal to their husband's memory), stage events parallel the couple's developing relationship.

Although Li's wife confronts her husband about his relationship to Xue Yan, he counters by changing the subject to his wife's lust for money and lack of appre-ciation for the arts. In fact, to celebrate her ailing father's birthday, she plans an opera performance to cheer up the old man. Ignoring her husband's offer to pick a decent opera troupe, she gives the job to an underling. As plans are being made, trouble bubbles up in another marriage. In this case, Xue Yan's colleague and prima donna Liliang (Zeng Jing-Ping) has decided to leave the troupe, her hus-band, and young daughter and run off with another opera impresario. This rival troupe is commissioned to play at Li's father-in-law's party. However, the old man snoozes through the performance and complains about the quality of the show. Convinced that a good opera will help her father regain his health, Li's wife begs her husband to go to his friend to engage her troupe. Li agrees, but he sees the missing Liliang as a stumbling block.

Miraculously, Li, Xue Yan, and the other members of the troupe persuade Liliang to return to the troupe as well as her husband and family. Li personally picks the opera for the special performance, *The Powder Room*, which includes a scene in which a father, mistaken about a supposed transgression, mercilessly beats his daughter. Out of filial piety, the daughter submits to the blows. Li convinces his wife that her father will enjoy this operatic celebration of her filial

Figure 12. Still from *A Little Life Opera*. Xue Yan and Li share a common bond as devotees of traditional opera that transcends the vicissitudes of the burgeoning capitalist economy. (Courtesy of the Hong Kong Film Critics Society.)

obligation to him, and Liliang sees its performance as a way for her husband, Baotian (You Chun-Cheng), who plays the father, to berate and beat her publicly for her off-stage infidelity. Thus the opera's performance celebrates the triumph of Confucian morality, patriarchal privilege, and personal wealth as well as upholding the sexual double standard of punishment for the wayward wife, Liliang, and vindication for the roving husband, Li.

At this point, *A Little Life Opera* and *Women from the Lake of Scented Souls* seem to take slightly different perspectives on the supposed increase in extramarital affairs occasioned by China's new prosperity. In *Women from the Lake of Scented Souls*, Xiang appears to want to make a clear distinction between her own infidelity, the direct result of forced marriage and physical abuse, and the rise of the *xiao lao po/xiao tai tai*—the "little wife" or mistress. Her lover, Ren, talks about his colleagues who now can afford to have several mistresses along their routes due to the increasingly lucrative nature of their trucking business. Xiang, who claims never to have heard the term, becomes outraged by the implication that she may be like these "loose" money-hungry women. She does not consider the fact that these other unofficial relationships may be similar to her own. Xiang feels she has a right to Ren's affections because of the history of their affair. However, she has second thoughts about their relationship when she ponders Ren's decision to marry a woman in the city and have a son with her, solidifying his right to live outside the village. Indeed, his decision to break off the affair ostensibly because they are getting too old for that sort of thing, without stating the fact that the money he has made from his share in the sesame oil transportation business now enables him to indulge in pricier relationships if he so desires, seems to indicate that he does not place the same value on his long-distance affair with Xiang as he does on his other relationships.

More worldly and wise, Xue Yan never bothers to ask Li to leave his wife. Rather, Li's affair with Xue Yan makes his marriage stronger, at least from a patriarchal point of view. Asking for advice on the opera and openly acknowledging her husband's relationship with Xue Yan puts Li's wife squarely within her place in the Confucian order as subordinate to her husband and father. When Li takes the fall for his wife's failure to pay taxes on their business, he agrees to quit business and spend all his time with the troupe when he gets out of jail. Xue Yan has also given in to her daughter's desire to study opera in Beijing rather than learn foreign languages that would have put her at an advantage within China's transnational business environment. The celebration of her daughter and her adopted daughter's success at the arts academy coincides with the troupe's celebration of the lunar New Year and also acts as a farewell party for Li. As the police take Li away, the troupe, in full stage regalia, launches a hot-air balloon with a banner stating, "Opera—the love of my life." Although local opera seems to have won out over the allure of international business, the irony remains that the opera cannot survive without the burgeoning of local business due to the influx of foreign capital and the demand for cheap Chinese goods flowing through Fujian's ports. Without the global, the local would be something quite different, and Xue Yan's daughter may not be as keen to see a future for herself as a hua dan like her mother.

SCREEN SPECTACLES AND GLOBAL COMMODITIES

Certainly, part of what attracted Hong Kong filmmaker Allen Fong to Fujian involved the global migration of people from that province. Singing in a dialect understood by many in Taiwan, Singapore, and other diasporic communities around the world, the transnational production (with Taiwanese and PRC on-screen talent and a director from Hong Kong) strikes a familiar chord with many outside the mainland. Its story of the rise of the global market and the enduring power of traditional values and aesthetic sensibilities represented by the local opera also underscores some key points for the overseas Chinese. The excesses of the Communist Party fade with the memories of the Cultural Revolution that can be personalized (and trivialized) as reminiscence over an old tune. People in the People's Republic now respect the arts and need them to keep the vulgar influences of the West (e.g., striptease, a "modern" dance routine performed by elderly women, etc.) under control. Shady business practices become the mismanagement of an overly ambitious wife, and the government steps in, not as a corrupting influence but only to ensure that business dealings remain legitimate. Women's liberation may still be a problem (e.g., Li's wife's ambitions, Liliang's affair), but women in general (e.g., Xue Yan, the reformed Liliang) still appreciate Confucian values and accept male privilege (e.g., Li's affair).

The film presents the opera world as a relief from the market economy but inevitably dependent on capitalism and a traditional system of patronage. Women's labor has been aestheticized, the artiste Xue Yan held up over Li's capitalist wife, and the money that drives the global economy has been laundered for the transnational Chinese audience. However, the film can be approached from another perspective. Xue Yan and her fellow hua dan, who dominate the troupe, manage to carve out a space for their art and display strength through their performances that transcend the gender hierarchy or the transnational marketplace.

From this point of view, dependent on but also contemptuous of global consumerism, the opera performers only coincidentally enact Confucian principles. Rather, the heart of the opera enacts female autonomy, sisterhood, and skill. Unlike Beijing opera that had traditionally been an exclusively male realm, regional operas, particularly in the twentieth century, often admitted women, and these *dive* occasionally exerted considerable power on and off the stage. Although ostensibly conservative with their portrayal of operas about filial piety and their careful adherence to rituals like the burning of incense to the troupe's ancestral spirits and patron deities before performances, the troupe's existence also serves as a corrective to the excesses of consumerism and the erosion of Chinese culture in the face of Western commodities. In addition, opera celebrates the power of women to make a living outside the confines of the roles they enact in the theater or play on the stage of the global marketplace (e.g., as dutiful daughters or undervalued waitresses in street-side eateries).

The women continue to enact a tension that has always been at the heart of the Chinese opera world. Although they play idealized figures, royalty, and martial heroines, the women remain at the edges of society, on the margins linked to petit bourgeois artists, cultural workers, and the working classes. However, the stage does give them some autonomy from the world of global business, the local service economy, and the presumed monotony of working-class life in Chinese provincial cities. The opera offers a dream of transcending China's new class hierarchies, while turning away from its socialist past.

In one scene, Xiao Xue (Liu Shao-Xia), Xue Yan's daughter, and another young woman apprentice in the troupe, Lan Ying (Ke Shu-Ping), practice a martial arts routine with a *da dao*, a type of long-handled saber favored in the theater. One of the older women in the troupe comes by to show them how the routine is done. In the moonlight, the women practice, and only the sounds of their footsteps and the evening birds punctuate the opera movements. The ostensibly effortless aesthetic of the opera cannot be accomplished without the sweat and physical labor of the young women. As the light shining onto the courtyard from the door behind frames the performer, the magical quality of the opera transcends their daily cares, and the precision of the martial routine overshadows all else. In the scene that follows, Xiao Xue reveals her desire to continue to perform opera and not go to college to learn Western languages. As Xiao Xue and Lan Ying huddle together to sing an aria with the troupe's ancestral altar framed in the doorway behind them, a very traditional sense of duty and obligation to the art harmonizes with a more contemporary sense of sisterhood and struggle against expectations to enter into the global labor force.[20]

At the moment when the young woman holds her da dao in the doorway and freezes in a pose of martial vigor characteristic of traditional opera, the contradictions embodied by the spectacle she enacts transcend the global/local binary too often used to analyze the relationship between modernity and tradition in contemporary China. Rather, the power and restrictions of the stage allow for the female performance of martial roles while binding women to the patriarchal constraints of Confucianism on and off stage. In addition, the opera acts as a spectacular visual emblem of the ability to offer an alternative to Western consumerism while being dependent on global capitalism for its existence. Here these contradictions are accommodated by this single, contradictory image of a woman wearing sweatpants and performing the puissance and glamour of the *dao ma dan*, Chinese martial heroine role.

As they circulate in international film festivals and are screened in art cinemas, films from and about China often captivate viewers through spectacular visual displays that vie with the narrative for control of the film's meaning. For example, the strength of this moment of opera practice in *A Little Life Opera* captures the contradictions of the new economy, local traditions, women's labor, and individual desire quite succinctly and, coincidentally, turns that moment into a commodified image that circulates beyond China. The image can highlight or obscure these contradictions as it travels to showcase what Rey Chow has characterized as the "primitive" passions of traditional Chinese culture or act as a corrective to China's embrace of global consumer capitalism.[21]

The spectacle circulates as a commodity, but the profits rest on the display of contradictions that cannot be too easily relegated to the reified realm of Chinese primitivism. In *Women from the Lake of Scented Souls*, a strong parallel exists between the circulation of the sesame oil within the narrative and the way the film travels as a commodity on global screens. As Laura Marks notes in *The Skin of the Film: Intercultural Cinema, Embodiment, and the Senses*: "The further the product (both the oil and the film) travels ... the more its meanings become rarefied and distanced from their material origin."[22] As in *A Little Life Opera*, *Women from the Lake of Scented Souls* makes women's labor a rarefied object of spectacular display. Although Dunzi and Jinhai also work at the small sesame oil factory, Xiang, Huanhuan, and, to a lesser degree, Zhi'er, become the primary human elements in the smooth running of the oil-making process. The film begins with images of labor: close-ups of sesame roasted over an open fire, the grinding of the seeds into oil, bodies bending over open fires, turning wheels, pounding mortars. The women work constantly in the film, and few bits of dialogue are unaccompanied by washing clothes, preparing food, selling sundries in the family store, babysitting, or other types of labor. Their pain becomes commodified through the sesame oil as well as through the images on screen, underscored in the film's denouement when Xiang and Huanhuan come to an understanding as Huanhuan's silhouette is projected onto a bed sheet she hangs up to dry, doubly framing her existence as a phantom on the screen.

In fact, the scenes that feature the performance of traditional ceremonies (e.g., weddings) bring the forces of the global marketplace and the power of feudal patriarchy together. Chinese wedding rituals and marriage customs, in fact, figure prominently in many films that circulate globally. Xie Fei's earlier *A Girl from Hunan* (codirected with U Lan, 1986) features a story about a young girl married to a toddler so that babysitting becomes part of the marriage contract, and similarly mismatched marriages are featured in Huang Jianzhong's *A Good Woman* (1985) and Wayne Wang's *The Joy Luck Club* (1993). The wedding sedan and subsequent relations with the palanquin bearer form part of the plot in Zhang Yimou's *Red Sorghum* (1987) and Huang Jianxin's *The Woodman's Bride* (1994). In the case of Huang's film, the bride's marriage to a wooden image as a substitute for her dead fiancé adds to the wedding complications. In Zhang's *Raise the Red Lantern* (1991), the bride forgoes the palanquin completely and just walks to her new home. In *Women from the Lake of Scented Souls*, the village children re-create a traditional wedding while playing in the river with large lotus plants used as props. Huanhuan, Jianhai, Dunzi, and the other young adults in the village look on and begin to joke about their own budding sexuality. However, unable to take part in the fun, Dunzi ends up attacking Huanhuan, and Xiang must be called to stop the assault. Play hides the violence of tradition that remains close to the surface in the film.

In fact, this scene strictly parallels Dunzi and Huanhuan's wedding ceremony. The detailed presentation of the spectacle of the wedding highlights the ceremony's emptiness and underlying violence. To display the family's wealth and legitimate a marriage that is technically illegal and based on coercion, Xiang has orchestrated an elaborate wedding that visually structures a new class order in the village with Xiang's family at its apex. Using expansive long shots and sweeping crane shots, *Women from the Lake of Scented Souls* creates a cinematic spectacle that graphically details the ceremony, including an orchestra composed of Chinese traditional instruments, plates of food, northern Chinese–style lion dancing, abundant firecrackers, boats draped in red for good fortune, the bride veiled in red and the groom wearing an oversized red ribbon for the same reason. Like *The Wedding Banquet* (also released in 1993), *Women from the Lake of Scented Souls* includes many of the traditional rituals used to create a sexually functional heterosexual couple out of two strangers. The bride and groom drink toasts at each table of assembled guests. The younger guests shower the inebriated couple with nuts to represent the bride's fertility, coerce the groom into carrying the bride on his back, and force the couple to bob at the same apple and piece of candy to encourage a kiss.

However, although *The Wedding Banquet's* narrative allows the illusion of a heterosexual couple to emerge from the raucous rituals, *Women from the Lake of Scented Souls* reveals the inefficacy of the ceremony. Dunzi emerges with Huanhuan's underwear, but Xiang later finds no blood as evidence of penetration. The spectacle remains an empty display, entertaining for the guests at the banquet as well as the viewers in the audience, but disturbingly so, because it visually signals the spectacular excesses of both a newly emerging capitalism and a deeply entrenched patriarchy. As in many of the films of China's Fifth Generation (e.g., Chen Kaige's *Yellow Earth*, Zhang Yimou's *Raise the Red Lantern*), actual and invented rituals punctuate films in which the plot works to uncover the violence under the visually seductive facade.

However, whereas women's work is aestheticized through opera in *A Little Life Opera* and through the display of oil manufacture in *Women from the Lake of Scented Souls*, women's labor is not glamorized in *Out of Phoenix Bridge*. Rather than turning struggle into spectacle, this documentary struggles to visualize an invisible part of the new Chinese economy. The intimacy of the video contrasts sharply with the visual distance of the oil-making process, the opera performance, or the wedding ceremony. In *Out of Phoenix Bridge*, the unofficial representation of the informal economy comes to the screen in marked contrast to the few official images that exist of undocumented women workers in Beijing, that is, the two still photographs included in the film of a prenuptial portrait and a tourist picture of a visit to Tian'anmen. In these representations, women's labor does not provide an appropriate subject for the camera, and Li Hong must fill in the gaps with her own unofficial labor as an underground documentary filmmaker, working outside the government-funded and regulated mass media to create a visual record of what otherwise remains undocumented.

However, as different as all three films are in their approach to visualizing Chinese women workers, all operate within a continuum that includes the use of Chinese women's bodies as spectacles for consumption and an ethnographic interest in detailing the quotidian indignities that these women suffer in Chinese cities, towns, and countryside. The highly polished, elaborately composed spectacle would seem to be absolutely incompatible with the candid, direct, spontaneous quality of ethnographic film. However, as Rey Chow points out, the two extremes are intimately linked in Chinese cinema, connected by the female body as an emblem of Chinese "primitivism"—sexualized, feminized, infantilized, oppressed, inarticulate, impotent, and backward (i.e., the marriage of Huanhuan and Dunzi). Although, as Chow notes, "primitivism" also has another side to it that connects the primitive with the primordial, the authentic, and the native, and thus with a certain type of Chinese chauvinism linked to the idea of China as the "central kingdom." From this perspective, the primitive manufacture of the sesame oil in *Women from the Lake of Scented Souls* guarantees its culinary "purity," and the authenticity of the primitive folk opera supersedes the vacuous reproducibility of KTV or the mechanical Western dance routine of the older women in *A Little Life Opera*.

However, the primitive in either sense of the term alienates the filmmaker from the subject of the work. Chow notes a tendency on the part of some artists and intellectuals to envision China "as if it were a foreign culture peopled with unfamiliar others."[23] For filmmakers, this creates a sort of cinematic schizophrenia with a conflict between the aesthetic and the ethnographic forming a schism within contemporary Chinese cinema: "Filmmaking itself becomes a space that is bifurcated between the art museum and the ethnological museum, a space that inevitably fetishizes and commodifies 'China' even while it performs the solemn task of establishing records of China's cultural violence."[24] Certainly, Li Hong, Allen Fong, and Xie Fei all come to the subject of Chinese women workers as

FIGURE 13. Still from *Out of Phoenix Bridge*. Unofficial women workers pose as part of the "official" economy of tourism as they have their picture taken under the portrait of Mao in Tian'anmen Square. (Courtesy of Women Make Movies.)

strangers. Through the voiceover narration, Li Hong periodically reminds the viewer of how alien the lives of the women from Phoenix Bridge seem to her; even though she lives so close to their hidden hu tong, she had no idea what the lives of these women migrant laborers were like until she began her video project. Allen Fong, from Hong Kong, uses Taiwanese talent to depict mainland women working in Fujian opera, and the lives of women in the countryside seem remote from Xie Fei's primary responsibilities as a film educator in Beijing. All three filmmakers, particularly Fong and Xie, balance their approach between the aesthetic and the ethnographic, between creating a captivating spectacle and detailing the daily inequities of working women's lives.

Thus, although all three films provide critical insight into conditions under which women labor in China today, they offer little to viewers interested in labor issues, political activism, or social change. In fact, to varying degrees, all three films remain ambivalent about the connection between women's oppression and the emergence of a newly stratified class system in China. Although *Out of Phoenix Bridge* comes the closest to articulating a critique of the exploitation of Chinese women's labor in the global system, all three films ultimately pull back from any direct condemnation of globalization, the dismantling of socialism, or the negative impact of consumerism and capitalism on China. Women may continue to serve as a general barometer of social ills, but they no longer act as models of social change as they did in the cinema under Mao. Cast adrift in the new economy, these women, however, do serve as cinematic reminders that class struggle, labor inequities, and gender inequalities continue to haunt China and give the dark side of global capitalism uniquely Chinese characteristics.

Interview with Allen Fong

You are such an established figure in Hong Kong film, particularly Hong Kong New Wave film, and so many of your films are considered classics—Father and Son *(1981)*, Ah Ying *(1983)*, Just Like Weather *(1986), and* Dancing Bull *(1990). How do you situate yourself?*

I am just doing alternative, not mainstream cinema. Actually, I am very interested in the performing arts. *Father and Son* is about cinema, *Ah Ying* is about theater, and *Dancing Bull* is about choreography. *A Little Life Opera* is about Chinese opera. I have been very interested in Cantonese opera ever since I followed my mother to the countryside and saw a performance as a kid. That actually inspired me to become an artist.

For *A Little Life Opera*, my producer asked, "Do you want to make a film in mainland China?" I said, "Of course!" He asked me, "Where?" I said, "Well, Fujian!"

Why Fujian?

During 1982, I went to Fujian for the first time with my scriptwriter, who is from Fujian, and we spent weeks and weeks talking to each other just to avoid the telephones and the expense of Hong Kong. We would lock ourselves into a hotel room (hotels were very cheap in those days) and try to grind something out on the script. Now, Fujian is like a second home. The producer loved the idea because the Fujian dialect is also spoken in Taiwan as well as Singapore, Malaysia, and Southeast Asia. So that was a commercial plus for the marketing of the film. The film was about opera, and I went back to Fujian and spent almost a year there. That was three years ago.

Opera is really the main character of the film. The structure is very thinly based on a love story. This always has been my style. I am more interested in the culture, the background, and the location—the relationship between Asia and the life of an artist. That is what I am mainly interested in all my films.

Could you talk about how you chose the opera performers for A Little Life Opera?

Actually, they are all from different companies. Some of them come from official companies, sponsored by the government, and some from private companies. In Fujian, there are still many opera companies. It is not true that only the elderly want to see Chinese opera. Ninety percent of the Chinese population is rural, and these farmers enjoy this kind of performance to celebrate birthdays, weddings, the construction of a new house, and other kinds of festivals. The government still uses opera for propaganda, too. They have operas that address the one-child policy and that sort of thing.

Stage opera is still very important. Fujian has a performing arts culture that is livelier than in any other part of the world, even the United States. Chinese opera is very down to earth—in tune with the people. It has standards, of course, but they are reasonable. Certainly, performances in Beijing are more serious. In the countryside, though, people want to tell jokes and have some fun for a night. The production values vary—whoever can pay more has a better show.

Has there been an opera revival because Fujian has been more prosperous lately?

Yes, the coastal towns are doing well. All China is rich at the moment, but not as rich as five years ago [1993]. The revival really took place about five years ago. If the business people are not willing to pay, then this kind of performance does not happen. In China now, business is wide open—official and unofficial—people are getting rich with privately owned companies.

Was there anything that frustrated you about working in the PRC?

Beijing demanded a Mandarin version of the film, and it cost me extra money to dub another version. For them to approve the film, they needed a Mandarin version.

Completely Mandarin version?

Completely!

In this version, you have Mandarin and the local dialect mixed together.

That is not good enough. They did not want Fujian dialect in there for business reasons. They wanted to sell the film to every province in China, so it had to be in Mandarin for release in the PRC. Of course, that is not the way to do it. Just try to imagine this film with no Fujian dialect. What happens?

The use of the dialect seems critical to me to understand the local culture. Could you talk a little about the town you depict in A Little Life Opera?

The place is called Shishi. " Rock Line" is the direct translation. It is very close to Taiwan. They watch Taiwan television more than mainland television. In their daily lives, there is a lot of influence from Taiwan and the West. The place is nicknamed "Little Hong Kong." There is a lot of smuggling, a lot of business, blue jeans, Madonna, even Kentucky Fried Chicken—a melting pot of East and West. Financially, it is very open with a lot of factories—mainly textile businesses. It is not the provincial China you usually see in films. This is modern China, I would say.

I got the idea for *A Little Life Opera* when I met a lot of businessmen to finance my film. Originally they were from an opera company, and they eventually became businessmen because of China's "open-door" policy. A lot of artists saw no future in what they were doing, so they became businessmen. After making money, they became involved in the arts again in some way. However, they would never become artists again full-time. They sponsor the arts, and they support the arts by going to see a film, a dance performance, or by visiting friends. They may continue to see a girlfriend involved in the arts. I think a lot of people would like to be artists, if given the chance, but fate intervenes.

Winston Chao, the film's lead, of course, started the other way around. He began in the business world as an airline steward, with some army background, and then became an actor. Like the character he plays in the film, he really understands both sides. So, I thought he could do the role.

Has the film been shown in the mainland yet?

No, not yet. It has not been released yet in Hong Kong or Taiwan either. I am showing it on the festival circuit right now—Hong Kong, Berlin, Switzerland, Tokyo, India, Singapore, and Vancouver.

When it opens to the public, I think the audiences in Fujian will love the film because it is about their own culture. I want to expose mainland audiences to a wider variety of films beyond Hollywood features. I think the film will be well received in Taiwan, too, because the two stars are well known there.

Can you talk more about working in the PRC?

Yes, there was an upside and a downside to working in Fujian. In the mainland, some people have more pride in filmmaking than in Hong Kong, particularly if they have worked in a specific location before. I worked with the Fujian studio. Unfortunately, they were not very professional. Some people thought of me as "another rich guy from Hong Kong." I can understand commercial work and their financial needs, but they tried to squeeze every cent out of me without working at a professional level of competence. They did not understand that I was doing a personal film, trying to make a statement. They saw me as a "bad guy" from Hong Kong. They were happy because they were well paid, but I was not happy with the difficulties they caused. I was not there to mess around.

When Hou Hsiao-hsien worked there, he brought everything from Taiwan. He brought every piece of equipment, every artist, everything, and he was five years ahead of me. At that time, foreign investment and foreign production were very welcome. Five years later, the studio was not so keen. If I do another film in the PRC, I would rather work with the Beijing Film Studio or with one of the television studios.

Working with the local actors was not difficult, though. I got there, I announced myself, and I said that I wanted to make a film. The local opera performers have a certain mystique, and the people have so much pride in them. The performers are dying to have exposure. I just had auditions, and I selected the right actors for the characters from my script. Five hundred people came to the audition. In Hong Kong, not even five would show up. I had a lot of choice, and I began to adjust my script to fit the available talent.

It was also very important for me to try to be friends with them—without their knowing it, of course. If they love tea, I would suggest that we have a tea ceremony one day. That is the culture of Fujian—the way you strike up a friendship. Whenever you have friends sit down, they are doing their best performances. They will not have inhibitions; they are not afraid of the camera. It becomes more like life, and less like acting. I met a very good friend through a producer, who is also a businessman. He is a factory owner in Fujian, and the film is actually his story. This is his way of paying back what he gained from the arts. By helping me, he could realize his own dreams once again. One day, we were having tea backstage. He was playing music, just like Winston Chao does in the film. He was so enjoying himself. He played the trumpet very well. That is what I enjoy about the process of filmmaking, what makes it so beautiful. Now, he is one of my best friends.

April 29, 1998

4   Gangland Taiwan in the Transnational Imagination: *Mahjong* and *Goodbye South Goodbye*

> For the gangster there is only the city; he must inhabit it in order to personify it: not the real city, but that dangerous and sad city of the imagination which is so much more important, which is the modern world. And the gangster—though there are real gangsters—is also, and primarily, a creature of the imagination. The real city, one might say, produces only criminals; the imaginary city produces the gangster: he is what we want to be and what we are afraid we may become.[1]
>
> —Robert Warshow

ROUGHLY TEN YEARS AFTER the lifting of forty years of martial law in the Republic of China (ROC) on Taiwan, Edward Yang and Hou Hsiao-hsien, the two most critically acclaimed auteurs of Taiwan's New Cinema, turn to the machinations of petty hoods to examine contemporary Taiwan in their features *Mahjong* (1996) and *Goodbye South Goodbye* (1996). Although Yang is known for his portraits of Taipei and Hou for his depictions of small-town life, both directors share a common concern for questions of Taiwanese identity and the place of that mercurial identity within the contemporary global sphere. In these two films, Yang and Hou use the margins of society to look at the core of Taiwan. Personal relationships become metaphors for alienation, deracination, rural angst, and urban decay. Although, as is typical of their respective oeuvres, Hou is more interested in the closed world of the petty rural gangster and Yang more concerned with the global dynamics of cosmopolitan capital, both directors examine common themes that expose the dialectics surrounding issues of global, local, class, ethnic, gender, and familial identities.

In both films, Taipei represents a city in crisis. It is a place where identities lose their stability and characters must grope for ways to cope within the ever-changing metropolis. Moving beyond the easy dichotomies of urban/rural, traditional/modern, local Chinese/global player, these films look at the way capital circulates within and outside the city, mapping the transnational links that money forges in some of the least likely places. By looking at the criminal subcultures depicted in *Mahjong* and *Goodbye South Goodbye*, and the way those traditional "secret societies" are played off against the allure of international youth subcultures, a better appreciation can develop of the way in which identity must be negotiated in contemporary Taiwan.

TAIWAN AND THE UNDERWORLD: LOCAL VARIATIONS AND TRANSNATIONAL CONNECTIONS

In *Flexible Citizenship*, Aihwa Ong points to the popularity of gangster and kung fu films within transnational Chinese communities. At a time when national identity may be uncertain, the political economy volatile, and personal relationships unsettled, the Chinese gangster films "are all about brotherhoods, hierarchized allegiances, and kinship loyalty, which are frequently ways of defending against the authority of the state and the uncertainties of society at large."[2] *Mahjong* and *Goodbye South Goodbye* play with these themes to use the criminal underworld as a metaphor for contemporary Taiwanese society. The petty gangsters that populate each film generally manage to survive, but not prosper, within an increasingly complicated, global economy that eludes them. Like Taiwan itself, the gangs have tremendous difficulty situating themselves between a mainland they need to exploit but cannot quite fathom, as both more bound to traditional business practices and endemic corruption than Taiwan and less amenable to the "guan xi" connections offered by their supposedly richer Taiwanese "brothers," and the Western world that promises the luxuries of consumer society without clarifying the route to the successful acquisition of these goods.

As Warshow pointed out when he first wrote about the gangster as a "tragic hero,"[3] the figure represents a cinematic embodiment of the tribulations of modern capitalism and the alienation of urban society. In the figure of the gangster, "the quality of irrational brutality and the quality of rational enterprise become one."[4] Rooted in the rural traditions of the "old country," the Hollywood gangster rises above his humble origins by taking a page from Horatio Alger or Andrew Carnegie and claws a path up through raw ambition.[5] The differences between the "legitimate" businessman and the gangster have less to do with the bald competitiveness of capitalism and more to do with the fact that marginal figures (like new immigrants) were less likely to have access to legal business endeavors. Just as capitalism exerts its force globally, the gangster continues to endure as the embodiment of the untenable dehumanizing effects of capitalism within world cinema.

However, to understand the environment depicted in *Mahjong* and *Goodbye South Goodbye*, the particular nature of criminal gangs in Taiwan and in Greater China must be taken into consideration. Secret societies, tongs, triads, and assorted clan groupings based on kinship or local affiliations have served various functions for the Chinese at home and abroad. In places like the United States, Canada, and Australia, which had anti-Asian exclusionary laws, the secret societies often helped new arrivals navigate in a politically and socially hostile environment. However, these societies also provided gambling, opium, and prostitutes to those inside and outside the Chinese community engaged in forced labor practices and other forms of exploitation. Within China, these societies sheltered political dissidents and fed the resistance against the Manchu-ruled Qing Dynasty. Many societies helped those displaced by rural famine or political unrest find employment and housing in urban centers like Shanghai or Hong Kong that were wholly or partially under the sovereignty of colonial governments, and, thus outside of Manchu control. Again, although many of these groups funded their anti-Manchu and benevolent activities by pooling the resources of their members, other groups involved themselves in loan sharking, protection syndicates, gambling, opium, and prostitution.

Given the political vacillations that form its history, with Hakka, Fukien (Fu-jian), Portuguese, Dutch, British, Americans, and Japanese attempting to claim it over the centuries, Taiwan has a long tradition of piracy, gangsters, and secret societies. In fact, many secret societies trace their roots to Koxinga, a Hokkien-speaking, Taiwan-based pirate, who succeeded in maintaining Ming Dynasty/Han Chinese sovereignty on Taiwan after the mainland fell to Manchu rule in 1644. In *Lords of the Rim*, Sterling Seagrave describes the transnational triad descendents of these Hokkien-speaking Ming loyalists, known as the Hung Gang as follows:

> Members of the Hung League spread down the coast and set up branch organizations throughout Asia and the Pacific, using the ancient symbolism of the triad, an equi-lateral triangle with sides representing Man, Heaven and Earth.... Native popula-tions and Western colonials were often terrified of the triads, attributing to them all manner of sinister murders, extortion, kidnapping, gold hoarding, drug smuggling, protection rackets, counterfeiting, and abduction of village girls for brothels. On the positive side, they provided expatriate members with the social services usually denied them because they were Chinese.[6]

Chiang Kai-shek's arrival in Taiwan strengthened many of these old associa-tions, linked to the powerful Shanghai underworld, and threw other secret societies into chaos. In his exposé of Chinese power politics, *The Soong Dynasty*, Sterling Seagrave documents Chiang Kai-shek's long association with the criminal under-world of Shanghai through the Green Gang, headed by Tu Yueh-sheng.[7] Son of a devout Buddhist, self-styled Confucian gentleman, and Christian convert, Chiang used his gangster associations to solidify his power through assassinations, in-timidation, and robbery. (Perhaps his biggest heist, orchestrated with Tu's help, was the "transfer" of the gold from the Bank of China in Shanghai to Taipei on the eve of his loss to Mao.) When Chiang established the Republic of China on Taiwan as a supposedly temporary base from which to launch a renewed assault on Mao's People's Republic of China, he brought his Kuomintang (KMT) supporters with him as well as their mainland underworld connections. Because Taiwan suffered under martial law until Chiang Kai-shek's son, Chiang Ching-kuo, lifted it in 1987, scholars, journalists, and filmmakers were forbidden to speak of these connections. Only after the end of martial law was Hou Hsiao-hsien able to chronicle this period and the impact the infusion of corrupt KMT officials and Shanghai gangsters had on postwar Taiwanese society in his epic film *City of Sadness* (1989).[8]

As the children of the KMT and their supporters came of age, many of them formed their own secret societies. The Bamboo Gang, responsible for the political assassination of dissident journalist Henry Liu in San Francisco in 1984, is per-haps the most notorious. Under Taiwanese-born, Western-educated President Lee Teng-hui, the KMT continued to rule Taiwan in the 1990s but with greater opposition from other political parties (e.g., Democratic Progressive Party, or DPP), that were no longer outlawed. With increased cross-straits contact after the 1987 lifting of the ban against travel to the People's Republic, Taiwan and the mainland were economically, socially, and culturally coming closer together at a time when calls for Taiwanese independence intensified and Taiwan continued to press for political recognition by the United Nations. Although the United States officially recognized Beijing as the capital of China in 1979, it continued to sell arms to Taiwan to stave off any forced unification of Taiwan with the mainland.

The year 1996, when both *Mahjong* and *Goodbye South Goodbye* were released, was an especially tense year for Taiwan.[9] In fact, both films refer to the economic recession, particularly the devaluation of real estate. In *Goodbye South Goodbye*, one of the gangsters has difficulty getting a decent price for a house he wants to sell, and in *Mahjong*, a shady businessman tries to get his mistress to take a devalued Taipei condominium off his hands in payment for a debt. In 1996, the ROC held its first direct presidential election, the PRC conducted a series of missile tests and war games in the Taiwan Straits, the mainland increased its rhetorical threats of direct military action against what it considered a wayward province, the economy suffered considerably from the loss of cross-straits trade, and criminal activity resulting from the poor economy as well as political violence surrounding the election increased considerably. Black gold,[10] as triad money is called, circulated throughout Taiwanese society. The triads continued to turn out the vote for the KMT, Lee was reelected, and secret societies prospered through government building contracts, crooked real estate deals and land speculation, and illegal activities.[11]

Although some secret societies have mainland KMT roots and others boast a local Taiwanese rural base, all maintain transnational connections to the Chinese diaspora worldwide as well as to criminal societies in Hong Kong and the PRC. The criminal subcultures mirror the larger Taiwanese society with its economic booms and busts; its dependence on the West, Japan, and the mainland; and its difficulties negotiating its own identity and maintaining its interests locally as well as globally.

Building on Pierre Bourdieu's *Distinction*,[12] Aihwa Ong looks at the transnational circulation of various forms of "capital," including economic, social, cultural, and symbolic, within Greater China in *Flexible Citizenship*. In brief, these various types of capital can be translated into what you have, who you know, what you know, and what you have to show for it. Although hard cash lies at the root of all forms of capital exchange, the conversion of social relations, cultural knowledge, or symbolic acts into cash, and vice versa, characterizes the way gangsters circulate within the business environment and build *guan xi* networks. Many aspects of the triad subculture, for example, harmonize with the aesthetics, morals, and mores of mainstream Chinese society. In fact, even though the triads by definition are outside the law and "decent" society, they take up the trappings of mainstream society, and sometimes seem to act as repositories of traditional culture assailed by Western influence. Their old-fashioned taste in dress, music, banqueting, and so on, symbolizes their commitment to what can be seen as Chinese, Confucian values in the face of rapid Westernization. Hiding violence, deceit, and lawlessness under the veneer of cultural capital allows the gangsters freer access to the world of legitimate business and government. It also helps mark off class distinctions within the triads, as gangsters take on European luxury goods such as Rolex watches and Mercedes or appreciation of expensive Chinese teas as indicators of success that have meaning within and outside the triad world.

However, the triads also have considerable cultural capital that falls completely outside legitimate society and should be called, following Sarah Thornton, "subcultural capital."[13] As it circulates throughout Asia and the Chinese diaspora more generally, this triad subcultural capital takes on the properties of what Mike Featherstone or Jan Nederveen Pieterse might refer to as "third cultures,"[14] providing a platform for common discourse and guan xi transnationally. Certain forms of tattoos, particular types of weapons, drug use, slang vocabulary associated with gang business, and so on, set the triads apart from the legitimate world in which they cannot succeed because of lack of education, family background, lower class status, or personal temperament. A gangster style may overlap with mainstream notions of taste, but it also flamboyantly distinguishes itself and provides a ready spectacle for dissemination through the cinema.

LOCAL/GLOBAL CRIMINALITY IN *MAHJONG* AND *GOODBYE SOUTH GOODBYE*

With their loose, episodic narratives, *Mahjong* and *Goodbye South Goodbye* are free to explore various types of gang activity in Taiwan in the mid-1990s without the constraints of a tight plot and strict causal structure. Both films deal with marginal elements of the criminal underworld where gangsters meet with youth, drug, and other subcultures as well as the world of big business and high-stakes politics. Unlike the Hong Kong gangster films by directors like John Woo and Tsui Hark, *Mahjong* and *Goodbye South Goodbye* do not focus on the gangster hero, brotherhood, martial prowess, and nostalgia for an imagined triad golden age of loyalty and righteousness. Rather, these two films deal with the place of criminality within international capitalism and government corruption, with the structures underpinning the gang's existence and with the pettiness of the gangster's schemes. In fact, these films depict the rituals, language, personal relations, and lifestyle of the gangsters in a detached, matter-of-fact way that underscores the vague line between the gang member and the legitimate citizen in contemporary Taiwan.

Although the focus is on the younger generation in each film, both *Mahjong* and *Goodbye South Goodbye* look at the present criminal subcultures within the context of Taiwan's historical triad society. The events in *Mahjong*, for example, are precipitated by Winston Chen (Zhang Guozhu), the father of the young leader of a group of petty criminals. Chen, who is absent throughout most of the film, must hide out from his mobster creditors to whom he owes several million dollars because of a scheme involving a chain of preschools that goes sour.[15] His seventeen-year-old son, Red Fish (Tang Congsheng), models himself after his father, whom he lionizes for his devotion to the profit motive and ambitious willingness to do anything to get ahead financially. As a form of high praise, he reminds his downtrodden father, "You're still the most shameless crook in this shameless country." Unknowingly, Red Fish has himself been put in jeopardy by his father's triad ties. To force Chen out of hiding, Chen's creditors plan to kidnap his son.

Kidnappings for ransom or for political purposes increased considerably in the 1990s. Highly political gang killings (one of a magistrate and his associates, another of a women's rights activist) monopolized the headlines. In 1995, a magistrate was sentenced to death for his involvement in the gangland murder of a casino operator.[16] In fact, the year after *Mahjong*'s release, the news coverage of the kidnapping and murder of Pai Hsiao-yen, the daughter of Taiwan TV personality Pai Ping-ping, and the subsequent crime spree and slipshod police manhunt eventually ending at the home of the outgoing South African diplomat, whose family was taken hostage by one of the original kidnappers, gripped the island. (Ironically, South Africa had severed its diplomatic ties with Taiwan that year in favor of recognizing the PRC.) The botched kidnapping in *Mahjong* bears an eerie resemblance to this subsequent tragedy with its quest for quick money, exploitation of a young girl, and senseless violence and morbidity.

A team of two gangsters tries to locate Chen's son, and *Mahjong* begins from the point of view of the younger of the two (Wang Bo-sen) on a moped following a pick-up truck through Taipei traffic at night. Dressed for business with a jacket and tie, he chats on his cell phone with his superior, preferring to talk about the abduction in terms of "accounts receivable" rather than blackmail. He speaks in Hokkien, signaling his status as part of a triad with roots that go back to pre-1945 society, perhaps more comfortable in the company of rural mobsters than the Mandarin-speaking urbanites he pursues.

However, just as Red Fish has no idea that his father's creditors are pursuing him, this gangster has no idea that the pick-up he follows is also involved in a scam. In this case, the driver slams into a pink Mercedes. Later, the Mercedes turns out to be part of a plot Red Fish has cooked up with his gang to swindle Jay (Zhao De), a well-to-do gay owner of a trendy hair salon, who employs one of the gang members, Hong Kong (Zhang Zhen), as a stylist. Through this connection, Red Fish has concocted a scheme to convince Jay that another gang member, Toothpaste (Wang Qizan), a.k.a. Little Buddha, has the power to predict the future and cure curses as a "feng shui master." In addition to extorting money from Jay, Red Fish plans to take advantage of the hair salon's wealthy clientele. After the other gang members ram into Jay's pink Mercedes, Little Buddha foretells that Jay's beloved car will be in an accident, and Jay later discovers the prediction to be true.

In *Mahjong*, the hunter and the prey cannot be distinguished, because each slips from one role to the other throughout the course of the film. While his father's mobster creditors pursue him, Red Fish has his eyes set on his own prey. With links to prostitution through an escort service operated by American expatriate Ginger (Diana Dupuis), Red Fish plans to entice Marthe (Virginie Ledoyen), a young Parisian in Taipei in search of her wayward British boyfriend, Markus (Nick Erickson), into prostitution. Rescuing Marthe from an unscrupulous Taipei cabdriver, Red Fish and a new gang member, Luen-Luen (Ke Yuluen), set Marthe up in a hotel. Because his father runs a rooming house for international students, mechanic Luen-Luen speaks English and is able to help Red Fish communicate with Marthe. After helping Marthe, Red Fish intends to return to show her how to pay off her debt by working for Ginger.

Later, the gang jokes about Marthe, saying she'll be like Chiang Kai-shek, the face on Taiwan's currency, enriching the gang brothers, that is, like money in the bank. As they plan to turn Marthe into cash, they also pay a fitting homage to the man who founded modern Taiwan on his connections with the triad under-world. Within the corrupt capitalist system, Marthe can easily be reduced to a commodity and given a clear cash value. As Tonglin Lu notes, this depiction of money characterizes Yang's oeuvre more generally:

> One of the dominant themes in Yang's films is how money, god of consumer society, has undermined and disrupted traditional Asian family structure—although the structure disrupted is shown in his films not to have much merit. If the modernization process has caused confusion among citizens in Taipei, returning to the past is definitely portrayed as not only impossible but also undesirable. Consequently, in Yang's films, Taipei often appears as a society cut off from its past but at the same time without a viable future.[17]

Red Fish's gang has a set routine for putting women into their debt. Self-styled gigolo Hong Kong seduces a woman, brings her back to the gang's communal flat, and asks her to prove her love for him by sleeping with all his gang brothers. Hong Kong tries this procedure with Markus's current girlfriend, Alison (Ivy Chen), a wealthy Chinese socialite. Angered by Marthe's appearance, Alison goes off with Hong Kong and sleeps with him, but the plan for her to sleep with the others is interrupted by a family emergency for Red Fish and Toothpaste's objection to kissing Alison, which he claims is bad luck.

Hong Kong's gigolo/pimping efforts receive another blow in another scam to take advantage of one of Red Fish's father's business partners, Mr. Chiu (Ku Pao-Ming), and his mistress, Angela (Wu Jiali). Under the mistaken impression that Angela had an exploitative affair with his father, Red Fish encourages Toothpaste and Hong Kong to team up to swindle them. Toothpaste tries to get Angela to pay him to exorcise her haunted apartment, and Hong Kong plans to seduce her away from Chiu. However, worldly Angela simply laughs at the young cons. When Hong Kong refuses to kiss her because of bad luck, she counters, "Every man who's kissed me now drives a Mercedes." Although Toothpaste continues to try to bilk Chiu and Angela for his feng shui sessions for the haunted apartment, Hong Kong has less luck. Already in trouble with Alison because of Angela, Hong Kong is humiliated further when he goes for a rendezvous with Angela and discovers he has been set up. Angela's friends arrive at the apartment and claim him as group property, saying, "Just feel you're part of the family—the three of us even share panties," and addressing him as "younger brother" in the process. After taunting him and force-feeding him, the "macho" Hong Kong vomits and doubles over in tears as the women laugh at him.

Winston Chen's gangster creditors do not fare any better. They mistakenly kidnap Luen-Luen and Marthe, thinking Luen-Luen is Chen's son when, as in

FIGURE 14. Still from *Mahjong*. Marthe (Virginie Ledoyen) and Luen-Luen (Ke Yu-luen) are kidnapped by mistake. (Courtesy of the Hong Kong Film Critics Society.)

Hitchcock's *North by Northwest* (1959), Luen-Luen answers a page for Red Fish in a restaurant under surveillance by the other hoods. However, Marthe manages to get the gun of the younger gangster who holds them at a construction site. They take him to the gang's apartment, beat and bind him, and trick the older gangster (Wu Nien-jen) into coming to the rescue. However, after disarming him, they return the gun to him and tell him to settle the account with Chen as he pleases. The entire group goes to Chen's hangout, but Chen and his mistress have committed double suicide. In a panic, the mobsters call the police for help.

Still hanging on to his hope for revenge against Angela, Red Fish meets with Chiu at Angela's apartment. Although Red Fish had assumed Angela to be in Chiu's debt, actually, to the contrary, Chiu needs Angela to agree to keep the apartment to clear a debt he has to her. Apparently, the feng shui scheme actually helped Angela continue to demand payment from Chiu, so, again, Red Fish has been foiled in his attempts to avenge the wrong she did his father years before. Angered by Chiu's pleas for his help, Red Fish begins to push Chiu around and pulls a gun on him. As Red Fish questions him, Chiu reveals that his current mistress Angela is not the same Angela that had been involved with his father, that Angela had moved to the United States years before. Frustrated and enraged, Red Fish empties the gun into Chiu, killing him. He points it at his own head but does not shoot, and he breaks down in tears and laughter instead.

The petty gangsters in *Goodbye South Goodbye* are just as feckless. Unlike the delinquent teenagers in *Mahjong*, however, they have more in common with the Hokkien-speaking mobster creditors in that film. Like the gangster duo in *Mahjong*, Kao (Jack Kao), Flathead (Giong Lim), and Pretzel (Annie Shizuka Inoh) inhabit a world closer to a more traditional rural Taiwan than to cosmopolitan Taipei. In *Goodbye South Goodbye*, the trio moves between Taipei and Chia Yi, a smaller city in the central part of the island, to engage in their criminal business enterprises. Rather than being involved in multimillion-dollar loans, the prostitution of Western women, schemes to defraud the very wealthy within a cosmopolitan environment in which English competes with Mandarin for business and social affairs, Kao, Flathead, and Pretzel live in a world that revolves around gambling houses, family-run restaurants, and schemes to defraud the government involving the transfer of ownership of farmland and livestock. Rather than trading in young French girls, these gangsters try to make a profit by marketing hogs.

Goodbye South Goodbye makes explicit the political corruption and exploitation of public funding that remain implicit in *Mahjong*. In *Mahjong*, for example, Marthe is nicknamed MARTA, for the subway system of Taipei, the first section of which opened in 1996 after a considerable delay caused by corruption and accidents. The endemic corruption that allows for Marthe's exploitation finds its natural correlative in the debacle of the metro transportation system. Marthe and Luen-Luen's kidnappers take them to a MARTA construction site as a hideaway, again implicitly underscoring the relationship between the triads, government contracts, and the construction industry.

In *Goodbye South Goodbye*, the gangsters manipulate the corrupt political system with ease, and many of their schemes revolve around exploiting existing government policies. For example, Taiwan has an elaborate system of rezoning land for residential, commercial, and industrial use. Thus farmers can profit from the sale of their ancestral land. This policy goes back to the economic planning of Chiang Kai-shek, who wanted to modernize the island, urbanize the population, and industrialize the economy. To do this, he encouraged the sale of farmland to the state for resale, urging farmers to invest that money in urban enterprises, and draining the countryside of potential dissidents with roots to pre-KMT Taiwanese society and its culture. In *Goodbye South Goodbye*, Flathead, a native of the rural area around Chia Yi, becomes involved in such a scheme when a member of his family agrees to sell their ancestral property. Flathead must agree to the removal and reinterment of his parents' remains. However, when he returns to Chia Yi to collect his share of the money, he finds that his brother has been swindled out of his allotment by a scheme to elevate his parents to divine status/nirvana in the afterlife that rested on the "donation" of his share to a temple. This use of religious beliefs and popular superstition to swindle money is similar to Toothpaste's/Little Buddha's shenanigans in *Mahjong*.

In the process, Flathead's share seems to have disappeared as well. When he goes to make inquiries of his uncle, his cousin, Ming (Ming Kao), a police officer, arrives and claims Flathead never demanded his share and is not entitled to it in any case because he looks like a punk. With a fellow officer, Ming beats up Flathead, handcuffs him, takes him to jail, and thrashes him mercilessly. The incident spirals

FIGURE 15. Still from *Goodbye South Goodbye*. Portrait of the gang. Big Brother Hsi (Hsiang Hsi) takes center stage with Kao (Jack Kao) on his left. (Courtesy of Wellspring.)

out of control when Flathead tries to locate a gun to revenge himself against his cousin. His cousin is tipped off, and Flathead again finds himself in prison.

At this point, Kao enlists the help of their boss, Hsi (Hsiang Hsi), to smooth things over by calling on the help of a politician with strong ties to both Hsi and the local police force. He arranges for Flathead's release as a personal favor to Hsi with the stipulation that Flathead leave town and be guaranteed not to cause further trouble. At the highest levels, no clear divisions exist between the gangsters and the government. Rather, all relationships become part of the same system of corruption and subject to extralegal authority.

In another scheme, Kao and his gang become involved in a plot to defraud the government by again manipulating its rezoning system. In this case, a pig farm, due to be rezoned, must sell its hogs. Instead of selling the pigs at cost, Kao plans, with one of his relatives, to convince the local farmers' cooperative to designate the pigs as stud hogs, requiring the government to buy the pigs at a considerably higher price. The farmers and the gangsters split the profits with the corrupt officials involved in the deal.

Although Kao and his crew seem to be preoccupied with local, rural land transfers and hog markets, they also represent a transnational gangster subculture with deep roots outside of Taiwan. Just as the criminal world in *Mahjong* revolves around the close association of Chinese criminals with Europeans and Americans, *Goodbye South Goodbye* portrays a gangster culture with international ties. Hsi's family has a home in Canada, a convenient escape from either a crackdown on the mob or the hard times of an economic recession in Taiwan. Kao's girlfriend Ying

(Kuei-ying Hsu) plans to join her sister in the United States to help in her real estate business. Also, Kao's yakuza-style Tokyo tattoos point to a connection with the Japanese underworld at some stage in his career.[18] Just as in the legitimate economy, Taiwan's long association with Japan as a former colonizer and current trading partner/regional competitor translates into strong gangland connections.

However, Kao's ambitions, along with his elderly father's, are directed toward the mainland, specifically the pre-1949 gangster mecca of Shanghai. Although he has seen many of his confederates lose their money in the mainland, Kao feels he can develop the right connections and make a killing in Shanghai with a restaurant or a disco. Like the American prostitute Ginger in *Mahjong*, who plans to expand her business across the straits, Kao sees a rapidly developing economy in the mainland ripe for exploitation.

Like many Taiwanese businessmen since the liberalization of trade restrictions after 1987, Kao sees greener pastures in the mainland, particularly in the booming city of Shanghai. For many in Kao's father's generation, Shanghai means a return home to what had been the cultural and economic center of the Chinese world before 1949. For the current generation, Shanghai's rapidly growing private economy promises easy profits for a city rediscovering consumer capitalism. The song "Shanghai Nights" accompanies a languid traveling shot over an art deco–inspired mural, which depicts circus acts and other types of entertainment that may have been enjoyed in one of Shanghai's famous amusement centers like Great World in the 1920s, 1930s, and early 1940s. The song's lyrics refer to Shanghai as a bustling, brightly lit, twenty-four-hour city with "no night" that has a bitter edge to it like a beautiful, unfaithful woman. A Chinese woman in a blonde wig sings the song soulfully into a handheld microphone, a youthful image of Western/Chinese hybridity that harkens back to Shanghai's colonial past. As in Wong's *Chungking Express* (see Chapter 2), the blonde wig embodies the contradictory status of contemporary Chinese, hiding behind the West, obscured by the West, able to appropriate the West, and be empowered by the West in the form of a particular type of femininity that also conjures up images of the past and fantasies of Hollywood glamour from Jean Harlow and Marilyn Monroe to Madonna.

The film cuts to an image of a watch through the distorted view of a crystal ball.[19] Kao's naked tattooed torso becomes part of the indistinct picture. He cleans marijuana, smokes it, and enjoys it with Ying as she plays with the crystal. The haziness of the future, the headiness of the marijuana, the inexorability of time, encapsulated in this image, become linked to song's romantic conception of Shanghai as Kao discusses his mainland business dreams with Ying.

Kao already has a deal percolating in Shenyang, Manchuria, in the industrial northeast of the People's Republic. Formerly known as Mukden, Shenyang, like Taipei, bears the physical marks of years of Japanese occupation in its architecture and industrial infrastructure dating from its days as part of Japanese-ruled Manchukuo. In fact, a 1931 explosion on a Japanese railway line in Mukden directly led to the Japanese military push into China. However, even with this shared history, business between Taiwan and Shenyang proves difficult. Kao's Shenyang deal goes sour, and he is forced to disassociate himself from his business contact.

Even though the Taiwanese businessman had mortgaged his house, he still could not come up with enough cash to place bribes at each level of the police force to do business in Shenyang. A power outage ends the scene with the hapless fellow, and business with the mainland seems to leave the most hardened Taiwanese gangsters in the dark.

GUAN XI: GANGSTERS AND CHINESE SOCIAL STRUCTURE

In *Goodbye South Goodbye*, Kao's elderly father tells a story about guan xi. Desperate to create guan xi in the mainland by giving gifts to people in authority, a family friend soon runs out of money, failing to establish business ties. Tenacious, the friend begins to make homemade sausages to give away. Gradually, news of the sausages spreads, and he begins to sell the sausages, making a fortune. Gift giving, almost magically, turns into capital.[20] However, guan xi transcends simple commercial relationships. Although necessary for successful business dealings, guan xi creates ties that bind people together for reasons other than material ambition or economic necessity. In *Flexible Citizenship*, Ong summaries the transnational nature of guan xi as follows:

> The guanxi institution, as invoked and practiced, is a mix of instrumentalism (fostering flexibility and the mobility of capital and personnel across political borders) and humanism ("helping out" relatives and hometown folk on the mainland). Although guanxi connections may be mixed with patriotic sentiment, overseas-Chinese investors are also moved by opportunities for mobilizing cheap labor in China's vast capitalist frontier. . . . It is probably not possible to disentangle nostalgic sentiment toward the homeland from the irresistible pull of flexible accumulation, but the logic of guanxi points to sending capital to China while shipping the family overseas.[21]

In many respects, *Mahjong* and *Goodbye South Goodbye* owe less to their plots for cinematic cohesiveness and much more to social institutions, like guan xi, used to structure the films. As Stephanie Donald points out, "The idea of guanxi can . . . work as an arcade, a visual metaphor that helps in imagining the transmittable secrets of cinematic space and time."[22] Relationships based on class, kinship, governmental organizations, economic ties, linguistic, regional, and sexual identities, as well as subcultural affiliations, provide the foundation for what appears on the screen. Guan xi gives shape to these relationships as a particularly Chinese system of mutual indebtedness, responsibility, and obligation. Literally meaning "connections," guan xi, as Mayfair Yang points out, can be subsumed under roughly four categories: "family and kinship, neighbors and native-place ties, non-kin relations of equivalent status, and non-kin superior-subordinate relations."[23] Although Yang's study focuses on guan xi in the People's Republic, many of the observations she makes are applicable to Chinese societies worldwide, including Taiwan.

Having guan xi can mean the difference between success and failure, alienation and personal belonging. In *Goodbye South Goodbye*, for example, Kao obsesses over having guan xi in the mainland. The Shenyang deal falls through because it was built on the assumption that guan xi existed with the city police force there and none did. However, though it is absolutely necessary for the success of criminal operations, guan xi forms a fundamental part of Chinese society that cannot be reduced to criminal activities or nefarious business dealings. Rather, *Mahjong* and *Goodbye South Goodbye* use guan xi as a way to highlight their use of these marginal criminal subcultures as a metaphor for wider corruption and more profound evils within contemporary Taiwanese society.

Based on Confucian precepts, the model for guan xi relationships comes from the traditional model for patriarchal family obligations with filial piety at the heart of those relationships. In *Mahjong* and *Goodbye South Goodbye*, both actual and fictive kinship relationships motivate most plot actions. Not only does the actual family serve as a model for the criminal gang, the interests of each become inextricably intertwined in each film.

As in Confucian society generally, the obligation of the son to the father provides the impetus for Kao's and Red Fish's principal actions in each film. Kao dreams of setting up a restaurant in Shanghai because his father desires it, even though his poor health and clear lack of success with his restaurant in Taipei does not seem to bode well for the endeavor. Similarly, Red Fish strives to live up to his father's reputation as an unscrupulous businessman. He adheres to his father's golden rule of business, "Tell them what they want and they'll kiss your ass." When Red Fish discovers that Angela had exploited his father, the son devotes himself to avenging his father's damaged machismo.

However, the very traditional foundation for Red Fish's behavior proves to be false, and, in fact, Edward Yang has called *Mahjong* "a post-Confucian outlook on the future."[24] Actually, Red Fish's father only exhibits a passing resemblance to his son's vision of him. Rather than relishing his role as a notorious scoundrel, Winston Chen prefers reading, listening to Western classical music, and conversing with his schoolteacher mistress in a modest but elegant apartment. He puts a stop to the criminal life he loathes by committing suicide.

In *Goodbye South Goodbye*, Kao is integrated into a complex extended family system in which he helps run the family restaurant with fictive family members like Flathead and Pretzel as well as actual blood relatives. All involved defer to him respectfully by referring to their relationship to him within the traditional Chinese family hierarchy in which the younger generation bows to the older and younger siblings must respect and obey older siblings. For some, he is uncle, for others, he is elder brother. These same terms are used within the fictive gangster family to delineate the hierarchical structure of the gang and the expectations of each member in relation to the other. Even Pretzel calls Kao elder brother, for example, particularly at times of crisis when she needs his help badly.

It is important to remember that blood ties do not necessarily take precedence over other forms of guan xi. In her study, Mayfair Yang quotes a common Chinese saying, "Distant relatives are not as dear as close neighbors."[25] Thus, Ming's betrayal of Flathead's trust in the family does not come as any particular shock to the community.

Flathead, residing primarily in Taipei, has become distant from Chia Yi, and his cousin has merely taken advantage of that distance to line his own pockets.

While proximity loosens some ties, it creates and strengthens others. Even non-Chinese, like Markus and Ginger in *Mahjong*, have little difficulty insinuating themselves into the system, and both are able to take advantage of guan xi to advance financially and socially in Taipei. Similarly, Red Fish expects Parisian Marthe to understand guan xi by osmosis and feel obligated to exchange her body for a place to stay and his protection as an "older brother"/pimp. Although she toys with the idea of prostituting herself, she does so because she wants to make Markus feel guilty, and she has no sense of face or the necessity of repaying a debt to Red Fish.

Although only seventeen, Red Fish clearly occupies the place of big brother in his gang. He orchestrates all the gang activities and plans ways to take advantage of the connections and talents of his "younger brothers," for example, Hong Kong's good looks and sexual prowess, Toothpaste's theatrical abilities and convincing pseudo-expertise in *feng shui*, and Luen-Luen's mechanical aptitude and ability to speak English. He solidifies gang ties through homosocial rituals like coerced group sex with gang members' girlfriends, so that heterosexual romance need not interfere with fraternal bonds. After Red Fish can no longer function as head, Toothpaste takes over with very little effort; having been initiated into the system, he knows how to recruit and retain others. However, Luen-Luen's departure from the gang makes a strong statement about the inevitable failure of guan xi to sustain Taiwanese society.

Kao serves a similar function as elder brother in *Goodbye South Goodbye*. Older and more experienced than Red Fish, his obligations run deeper and are more complex. He exists in a clearly defined and rigid hierarchical, criminal structure. Hsi, whose elaborate system of guan xi expands from Taiwan to the mainland and North America and from gambling dens to the halls of government, acts as *da ge*, the "big older brother," in the gang and Kao serves as his underling. However, as in most guan xi relationships, the interactions can be loose and inconsistent. Although a superior in the system, Hsi does not really function as a boss, rather Hsi and Kao have some common business ventures and a mutual system of protection in which Kao feels he can call on Hsi in times of crisis, expecting to access his mentor's guan xi in that way.

Kao has a more intimate relationship and more pressing sense of obligation to his underlings, Flathead and Pretzel, and his mistress, Ying. Although Ying drifts away from Kao during the course of the film, Kao, Flathead, and Pretzel remain a closely knit unit throughout most of *Goodbye South Goodbye*. Childlike and dependent, Flathead and Pretzel drain Kao's energy and resources. The explosive Flathead has a knack for fighting with other gang members and his blood relatives, requiring Kao to draw on his own guan xi reserves to get Flathead out of these jams. Pretzel runs up enormous debts, forcing Kao to find money to pay her creditors. The last words heard in the film come from Flathead who calls out for his "elder brother," after their car has fallen into a ditch. Although the reason for the crash never becomes apparent (Kao may have finally had a heart attack or died from exhaustion), Flathead's dependence on Kao and the guan xi system that links them persists to the bitter end.

Like Red Fish and his gang, Kao, Flathead, and Pretzel live communally, and all defer to Kao. When Kao sleeps, Flathead screens his calls. When Kao gets drunk, vomits, and has a crisis in confidence, Flathead and Pretzel rub his back, clean him up, and put him to bed. They listen and do not answer back when Kao criticizes them for their bad behavior. When Kao complains about the housekeeping in their apartment and Pretzel's habit of leaving the bathroom door open when she uses the toilet, Flathead and Pretzel listen sheepishly as he complains that they "mei you li mao" (that they have no manners, indicating a poor upbringing, and that they don't know how to behave), using language that a parent might use with a naughty child.

In fact, guan xi often involves knowledge of how to behave well in particular circumstances and in relation to others.[26] Performance is an essential part of any guan xi relationship, and verbal address, proxemics, deportment, eye contact, haptics, and other nonverbal modes of communication can be as important in establishing and maintaining the relationship as the rituals surrounding gift giving and banquets. As a consequence, guan xi interactions can be highly theatrical and rigidly stylized. Red Fish, for example, stands out as a guan xi master in *Mahjong*. When he first meets Chiu, for example, he behaves in a way that makes him a model of a younger man currying favor with an older, established businessman whom he feels can help further his ambitions. Red Fish knows how to perform this role so expertly that Chiu never suspects that Red Fish wants to establish the relationship to destroy rather than enhance Chiu's standing. Red Fish rushes after Chiu, follows slightly behind him, calls him *shu shu*/"uncle," and establishes a common bond with his father, Winston Chen, through reference to their membership at an exclusive golf club. Red Fish asks for Chiu's business card (a ritual more important in Asian social transactions than in the United States), and by the time Red Fish opens the door of Chiu's black sedan, he has insinuated himself into a guan xi relationship with Chiu as an elder obliged to help his younger colleague. In the process, Chiu expects to gain social standing by acquiring a new protégé. Red Fish expertly performs his role, and the fact that the relationship is based on a plot to destroy the elder man only underscores the power of role-playing in guan xi relationships that need not be based on any genuine feeling. All parties involved slide easily into these socially defined roles and success can be based more on the ability to perform them convincingly than on the sincerity of the players.[27] As Edward Yang notes, in reference to *Mahjong*, "Urban society is itself a stage."[28]

However, in *Mahjong* and *Goodbye South Goodbye*, global youth culture vies with the traditional obligations of the guan xi system in the lives of the films' characters. Flathead and Pretzel, for example, share a common youth culture with Red Fish, Toothpaste, Hong Kong, Luen-Luen, and Alison. They all have difficulty establishing and maintaining guan xi in the traditional way, and their failures point to the potential breakdown of the system. Only Toothpaste seems to maintain his gang, but with the significant loss of Luen-Luen and the gang's potential cash cow, Marthe, to the wider world of international youth culture.

SOCIAL RITUALS AND SUBCULTURE CLASHES

The clash of the traditional gangster subculture with international youth subcultures and the tensions between the rural and the urban, the traditional and the modern, an economy based on guan xi and one based on cash alone, can best be seen in the ways *Mahjong* and *Goodbye South Goodbye* present social rituals. Common acts become metaphors for more deeply rooted social crises based on Taiwan's continuing political and economic problems.

Although by their very definition subcultures distinguish themselves structurally from the mainstream culture because they transgress the boundaries of what most consider to be normal behavior in that society, the subcultural style associated with the criminal underworld in *Goodbye South Goodbye* and, to a lesser extent, *Mahjong* seems stuffy, ritualistic, and anachronistic. However, although the youth subcultures represented in each film seem more vital, they also appear to lack a sense of rebellion associated with the youth of a previous generation.

One of the principal locations in *Mahjong*, the Hard Rock Café, provides a case in point. The GenerAsian X teenagers, like Red Fish, Hong Kong, and Luen-Luen, who frequent this Taipei branch of a transnational chain, have a very different relationship to the American popular culture enshrined there than even slightly older patrons like Jay. Although rock and roll music came to Taiwan with American military groups in the 1950s as part of the United States' efforts to "contain" Communism during the Korean War and throughout the Cold War era, its associations with cultural imperialism were always tempered by the rebelliousness of its open expression of sexuality, youth identity, and antiestablishment sensibility.[29] When Jay points out the Beatles memorabilia on display, the camera pans across the wall of mementos, including an old electric guitar. Luen-Luen takes a look, but does not seem particularly impressed. The Beatles, Prince, and other American rock personalities form the backdrop for the sexual and business transactions that take place there. However, they are signs drained of their meaning, part of a culture of nostalgia that Fredric Jameson describes as a longing for images of an era that passed out of fashion before being experienced by those surrounded by the style in the present, postmodern moment.[30]

The rebellion of the past has become the status quo of the present. Ginger, in particular, represents this transition. Seeing her own youth in the rebellious, independent, passionate teenager Marthe, Ginger embodies the transition from adventure and sexual liberation, as a showgirl with magician David Copperfield's tour, to the "next international VP for Asia Tech." She proudly states that she's "corporate now." In between, she sold herself as a prostitute, and the foundation of her business remains in the sex industry. Sexual rebellion and female liberation are transformed into profit as youth enters the capitalist system. Youth culture becomes ossified, commodified, and drained of its original subcultural punch. However, even though Ginger sees herself in Marthe, *Mahjong* does not necessarily doom Marthe to Ginger's fate. Rather, the film holds out the possibility of hope for youth, even if the picture of those future possibilities remains indistinct.

Perhaps because of the casting of Giong Lim as Flathead and Annie Shizuka Inoh as Pretzel, both part of Asia's pop music scene, and Lim's orchestration of the punk-industrial soundtrack for the film, *Goodbye South Goodbye* provides a more concrete picture of GenerAsian X than *Mahjong* does. Even though the narrative privileges Kao as the film's protagonist, Flathead and Pretzel occupy the visual cynosure of the film because of their style of dress, gestures, and physical movements. In one scene, for example, Flathead and Pretzel help out at the Kao family restaurant. With a red filter and loud industrial punk drowning out all other sound, a handheld camera makes its way among the tables of the cramped restaurant, nearly empty of customers. The filter, music, and camera work give a visceral impression of altered consciousness, and the shot immerses the viewer in an atmosphere closer to a subcultural Rave than to the quotidian operation of a restaurant.

A young customer addresses the camera, and a reverse shot reveals that the camera had taken on Flathead's perspective. He removes his Walkman's earphones, and the punk music (which turns out to be diegetic) stops; the young customer repeats his order for a Coke. Flathead wears rose-tinted sunglasses (hence the red filter), a large red medallion around his neck, T-shirt, and plastic vest. Although through most of the film Flathead dresses as a slightly more colorful version of Kao in loud rayon Hawaiian print shirts and shorts, in this scene he takes on a more obviously punk style.

Flathead calls for Pretzel to bring a Coke. Obviously inebriated and sucking on a baby bottle, Pretzel looks like she has just come from a Rave, where ubiquitous pacifiers make a subcultural statement about youthful gratification. Having run out of Coke, Pretzel forces another canned drink on the young customer. He repeatedly says he does not want it, but Pretzel insists it is *zhen hao*/"really good." In a good-natured way, the young man finally accepts the can and tries to pass it on to one of his friends, who also refuses it. The young customers seem understanding of their equally young waiter and waitress; knowledge of youth culture appears to give them a mutual sympathy and familiarity that does not cross the generations but can clearly cross class divisions between staff and customer.

Flathead and Pretzel, in this case, are able to bank on what Sarah Thornton, in *Club Cultures: Music, Media and Subcultural Capital*, calls "subcultural capital" to stay afloat in a legitimate business world in which they have very little real investment. Unlike the gangster subculture that deals more directly in economic necessity, Flathead, Pretzel, Marthe, Red Fish, Toothpaste, and, to a lesser degree, Hong Kong and Luen-Luen enjoy a respite from the economic imperatives of the adult world. Although many work legitimately and all have their own schemes that ensure their survival, they also draw on blood kin and their gang associations to remain outside the more rigidly defined business world of competitive Taiwan. They can afford to drift because they are young in a way that Kao, for example, cannot.

In both *Mahjong* and *Goodbye South Goodbye*, youth culture creates communal spaces for associations that transcend class, ethnic, national, and gender divisions. Red Fish's gang's apartment and Luen-Luen's family rooming house, for example, host an array of young inhabitants from the extremely wealthy Red Fish to the working-class mechanic Luen-Luen, young women like Alison and Marthe come and go, and Chinese and non-Chinese youth live in the same space. Similarly, in *Goodbye South Goodbye*, even though Kao is clearly "big brother," the apartment is outfitted to reflect the tastes and interests of adolescents, with video games, a basketball hoop, punching bag, green sheets, and orange walls. Punk/electronica/industrial music plays more often than Mandarin or Hokkien pop tunes. The common idiom and style of global youth culture draw Marthe and Luen-Luen together and divide Flathead and Pretzel from Kao. Looking for lost car keys in the dark, Kao pulls out a cigarette lighter, while Flathead and Pretzel happen to have handy the neon-glow light novelties popular in youth clubs and at Raves.

For Flathead, the anarchistic aspects of the punk style violently alienate him from ritualized practices of the triads. For example, frustrated by his inability to gamble, Flathead sends a child's whirly-gig toy sailing onto the gaming table. A gangster's incapacity to appreciate gambling seems ludicrous in the context of Chinese society in which games of chance have a very traditional, quasi-religious function and long association with the triads. Earnings from gambling point to luck and prosperity in the future. Fortune-telling, cults of the Ts'ai (Cai) Sheng (prosperity god) and other deities, and other occult practices and superstitions surround the world of legal and illegal gambling in Taiwan. Kao and the other gangsters wear gold Rolex watches and Buddhist worry beads as they gamble, visually pointing to their actual and hopefully continued success as well as a blending of European luxury with traditional religious practices. Thus, Flathead's disruption borders on sacrilege.

Referring to the game of chance, *Mahjong*'s title alludes to the wildly popular international game, much like bridge played with tiles, which originated in China, that succinctly symbolizes the strategies, plots, coordinated efforts, competition, and chance encounters that structure the film's plot. The foreign students who live in Luen-Luen's father's rooming house enjoy playing the Chinese game next to a decoratively draped American flag, and mahjong represents the meeting of cultures across the gaming table. It also serves as an apt metaphor for the ways the film's characters bump against each other by chance and recombine like tiles on the mahjong table.

Driven from the gambling table in *Goodbye South Goodbye*, Flathead wanders over to sit with a group of gangsters drinking tea. Like gambling, tea drinking is a traditional Chinese activity, taken very seriously. In recent years, as Chinese tea parlors of various sorts have become more fashionable in Taiwan, tea connoisseurship has been associated with the triad lifestyle as a concrete expression of the gangster's appreciation of the rarefied, expensive, and traditionally Chinese commodity. Although not as strictly codified as the Japanese tea ceremony, Chinese tea drinking has its own rules of etiquette and ritualized routines. Particular practices of tea drinking are associated with Taiwan and Fujian, and the manner of drinking tea in *A Little Life Opera* is quite similar to the tea drinking in *Goodbye South Goodbye*. Drinking tea, the gangsters solidify their bond by talking about the aroma, flavor, and aftertaste of the award-winning green tea that one of the men has stolen. They show their appreciation of the Taiwanese tea by comparing it to some stale tea from the mainland they had drunk the day before. Flathead refuses the cup of tea he is offered, puts his feet up, begins to smoke a cigarette, and asks for a beer. Verbally, the older gangsters try to subordinate Flathead by discussing his nickname and physical features. Flathead explodes and pushes the tea off the table and into the face of one of the gangsters. From the smallest gesture of not knowing not to smoke when the others enjoy the aroma of the expensive tea to the audacity of picking a fight with the big brothers to whom he should show the utmost deference, Flathead shows that he has serious difficulties acclimating to the traditional Taiwanese triad world. His lifestyle and other subcultural affiliations draw him away from the underworld.

Unlike Flathead, Kao has a definite appreciation of triad style, and this subcultural knowledge helps him form new associations and expand his guan xi networks both vertically and horizontally. For example, he forms an immediate bond with his sister's moving man because both have an appreciation of tattooing. Although principally associated with Japanese yakuza in the Western imagination, specific types of tattoos physically mark the body's associations with particular places and sensibilities within the Chinese underworld as well. Kao, for example, is impressed that his new acquaintance can spot the difference between tattoos from Tokyo and Kyoto, and he is equally impressed by the mover's ability to tattoo his own body that shows a macho disregard for pain as well as his artistic temperament and connoisseurship, qualities prized within the traditional triad subculture.

However, even Kao sometimes has difficulty stomaching traditional rituals. A banquet to celebrate the pig deal that includes a series of toasts in which the revelers must drain their cups makes Kao vomit. Like tea drinking and gambling, banquets and karaoke singing parties form staple parts of the triad subculture as well as mainstream Chinese social interactions. Karaoke clubs that supply private rooms for loud, drunken singing, also provide excellent venues for secret business deals—both legitimate and criminal. In fact, *Goodbye South Goodbye*'s climax does not feature a shootout with the police or a kung fu fight among rival gangs, rather the film culminates with a meeting of the gangsters, cops, and politicians at a karaoke club.[31]

After performing a lugubrious ballad about lost love, the contemplation of suicide, violence, and romantic debts against the backdrop of TV monitors illustrating the song while displaying its lyrics, the singer, a corrupt politician dressed casually but conservatively in a sports coat, joins the assembled group. Still in jail, Flathead does not attend the gathering at which his freedom is negotiated at the expense of his permanent exile from his hometown of Chia Yi. Marginal to the triad world, Flathead's absence at this climactic moment underscores the fact that when the assembled party agrees, "We are all brothers," Flathead cannot join in the refrain. Flathead's personal style celebrates punk anarchy, far from the Chinese popular ballads that uphold traditional stoicism and

Confucian values within the karaoke club. Just as Luen-Luen and Marthe's kiss signifies an end to an anachronistic triad tradition in the face of contemporary global movements of youth and liberated women, Flathead's absence at the karaoke gathering absolutely severs him, and the generation he represents, from the traditional rituals of the past.

For Kao, Ying's decision to leave him and Taiwan/China for America signifies a similar break with Confucian values of patriarchal domination and Chinese chauvinism. For Luen-Luen and Ying, the future lies outside of Chinese tradition and within the globalized spaces of international youth culture and the Chinese diaspora. Ultimately, as they do in Hong Kong gangster films, the triads in *Mahjong* and *Goodbye South Goodbye* symbolize, in a contradictory fashion, nostalgia for traditional values as well as a condemnation of those values, a tenacious celebration of the daily joys of Chinese culture and a devaluation of its corruption, superstition, and senselessly strict hierarchy. They provide a tacit—but ambivalent—recognition that something essentially Chinese still functions within global consumer capitalism despite the pressures of American cultural imperialism.

TALES OF TWO CITIES (TAIPEI AND CHIA YI) AND TWO DIRECTORS (EDWARD YANG AND HOU HSIAO-HSIEN)

Although it may be tempting to look at *Mahjong* and *Goodbye South Goodbye* as films about the decay of traditional, primarily rural Chinese values and the triumph of a Western-inflected, global consumer culture, a closer look at the way the films portray urban space—from the global metropolis to the local backwater—reveals a more telling, contradictory picture of the uncertainties that plague contemporary Taiwan.

Edward Yang and Hou Hsiao-hsien have built their careers on chronicling Taiwanese society. Yang concentrates on portraits of the urban middle and upper classes, mainly the children of the KMT and their supporters who came to Taiwan after 1949; Hou bases his films in rural life, the world of primarily Hokkien speakers living in small towns or the countryside and often sets his narratives in Taiwan's immediate past. Educated in Taiwan, Hou seems most comfortable close to home, working within a Chinese environment. Yang, educated in the United States and residing there for a good portion of his adult life while working in the West Coast computer industry, speaks fluent English and has interests that go beyond the Greater Chinese social and cultural sphere.

However, despite these different approaches, Yang and Hou have quite a bit in common, as do their respective visions of Taiwan. Both came to Taiwan as children, their parents relocating after 1949. Both helped create the renaissance in Taiwanese film known as the Taiwan New Wave in the 1980s. Internationally acclaimed, award-winning filmmakers, they have worked together on a number of projects. Hou, for example, stars in Yang's *Taipei Story* (1985). Yang has worked with Hou's principal scriptwriter, Chu T'ien-wen (perhaps the most celebrated female scriptwriter working in the Chinese language today), and both have worked with writer-director-actor Wu Nien-jen in front of and behind the camera. (Wu plays the senior gangster in *Mahjong*.)

Born in 1947 in Guangdong, Hou spent most of his childhood in the relatively small town of Hualien. His autobiographical *The Time to Live and the Time to Die* (1985) deals with life in small-town Taiwan, and many of his other films, including *Dust in the Wind* (1986) and *Daughter of the Nile* (1987), deal with the tribulations of adjusting to urban life. Many of his films, including the ones just mentioned as well as *Summer at Old Grandpa's* (1984) and *Boys from Fengkuei* (1983), focus on youth, youth culture, and the perspective of the young.[32] Several of his films, including *City of Sadness* and *Good Men, Good Women* (1996), deal with marginal criminal figures, and Jack Kao, the lead in *Goodbye South Goodbye*, portrays petty gangsters in each of these films. (In *Good Men, Good Women*, in fact, he plays opposite Inoh.)

Just as the worlds of *City of Sadness, Good Men, Good Women*, and *Goodbye South Goodbye* bleed together though the characters portrayed by Kao, Yang's *Mahjong* also shares sundry characters with his previous *Confucian Confusion* (1994) and subsequent *Yi Yi* (2000), creating a portrait of Taiwan that unwinds and flows together like a Chinese hand scroll. Also born in 1947, but in Shanghai, Yang focuses on urban life in Taipei. However, like Hou, he has a commitment to youth culture and looking critically at Taiwan's past, as can be seen in films like *A Brighter Summer Day* (1991) that deals with displaced youth, the children of the KMT, coming of age violently in the 1960s.[33]

Moreover, both filmmakers enjoy the use of the long shot/long take technique to place their characters in particular environments, again underscoring the social dynamic at the root of their narratives. Throughout *Mahjong*, enclosed compositions give the impression that Taipei is a city of box-like rooms in constricting and monotonously designed buildings, where people must conform to the strictures established by a corrupt society with little room for escape.[34] Similarly, in *Goodbye South Goodbye*, the static camera puts Kao's gang's apartment in a closed frame that emphasizes the cramped quarters in which they live. However, the box in which they live cannot contain their rage and frustration, and, as a visual metaphor for their lives, taking a "flying leap" out the window and "beating their heads against the wall" seem to be the extreme alternatives available to these marginal characters. Both gangs share a common environment, visualized similarly in each film, of static, confined urban spaces in which options for the simplest physical movements are limited and relationships quickly reach their breaking points.

However, neither *Mahjong* nor *Goodbye South Goodbye* unfolds as a series of these static interior tableaux; rather, each film relies heavily on numerous traveling shots to give a sense of the mobility and volatility of contemporary Taiwan. By car, moped, motorcycle, train, and on foot, the characters move through the streets of Taipei and, in the case of *Goodbye South Goodbye*, Chia Yi and the Taiwanese countryside as well. Each film paints a portrait of the Taiwanese city as a blur of motion. In *Goodbye South Goodbye*, the use of filters, shots in tunnels and underpasses, and shifts from its industrial punk score to ambient sound give a surreal quality to the streets of Taipei. Similarly, *Mahjong*'s use of Taipei streets as sites

FIGURE 16. Still from *Goodbye South Goodbye*. Although on the move in the city, Flathead (Lim Goong) and Kao are boxed in behind the windshield of their car. (Courtesy of Wellspring.)

for planned vandalism, surveillance, and pervasive criminality gives the impression of a city on the brink of chaos. Appropriately, *Mahjong* ends with one of Taipei's night markets as the backdrop. While Luen-Luen and Marthe seem to rise above the twenty-four-hour commercialism of Taipei with their cross-cultural kiss, Taipei remains inexorably a city where relationships have their root in commerce and human ties stay bound to material ambitions.

Some of the Western characters in *Mahjong* express particularly telling opinions about Taipei. Although it is a cosmopolitan metropolis situated solidly within a global economy, Taipei continues to be a city considered open for exploitation by non-Asian interests. Referring to both America's imperial expansion West in the nineteenth century and more obliquely to the U.S. military presence in Taiwan beginning in the 1950s, Ginger talks about Taipei as analogous to the Wild West as she tries to recruit Marthe into prostitution by saying she seems like a "quick draw." British Markus looks at Taipei as an imperial outpost and sees himself in the role of a reinvented colonial merchant. He feels more comfortable in Taiwan than closer to home in the European Union center of Paris, because "everyone speaks English" in Taipei. Instead of struggling to establish himself in England or France, Markus comes to Taiwan equipped with the "superior" knowledge of his own native tongue. In a speech that could as easily be placed in the mouth of a British tycoon during the nineteenth-century Opium Wars and that bears a striking

FIGURE 17. Still from *Goodbye South Goodbye*. Flathead, Pretzel (Shizuka Inoh), and Kao are set loose as they cruise through the verdant countryside on their motorcycles. (Courtesy of Wellspring.)

resemblance to Queen Victoria's monologue in Xie Jin's *The Opium War* (see Chapter 2), Markus haughtily informs Marthe: "In ten years, this place will be the center of the world. The future of Western civilization lies right here. I'm so lucky to end up here, and I have no intension of telling anyone back home about it." For Markus, that center (a play on China as "Zhong Guo"—the "middle" or "central kingdom") is decidedly Western, English speaking, and commercially driven. Little has changed in Taiwan's long history of imperial conquest and foreign exploitation. Rather, a new generation from the West sees Taiwan in the same old light as a place for easy pickings, while the Chinese in Taiwan look for ways out—in the mainland, the United States, Canada, or elsewhere.

Trapped by its colonial history and a bitterly divisive political present, Taiwan has an uneasy relationship with global modernity. Although superficially at the center of modern capitalism with its pervasive cell phones, international restaurant chains like the Hard Rock Café and T.G.I. Friday's, its expensive European cars, highly educated, cosmopolitan populace, and easy associations of Westerners with Chinese, nothing functions properly. Cell phones create more miscommunication than genuine understanding, as can be seen when Kao's cell phone refuses to work on the train in the first scene of *Goodbye South Goodbye*.

Western food and fashions create a cultural vacuum like the empty TV screens that pop up within *Mahjong*'s mise-en-scène during the scenes at the Hard Rock Café. Although *Mahjong* may critique Markus's arrogant glee in being able to conduct his business affairs in English in Taipei, Marthe and Luen-Luen still need English to conduct their romantic affairs. If Western capitalism does not work, traditional Chinese relationships based on guan xi, female subordination, and

FIGURE 18. Still from *Goodbye South Goodbye*. In flowered shirt, Kao blends in with the rural scenery. (Courtesy of Wellspring.)

Confucian ethics also fail, and the promise of a genuine cultural hybridity remains equivocal.

In *Goodbye South Goodbye*, Chia Yi does provide an alternative to cosmopolitan Taipei—at least to a degree. An agricultural city, Chia Yi had been built up by the Japanese during their occupation of Taiwan, and it became known as a steam rail center. Economically sluggish, Chia Yi was downgraded politically under the KMT and only again became an official provincial center in 1982.[35] Although the city may be nondescript, the countryside surrounding it is breathtaking. As the camera travels in front of Flathead, Pretzel, and Kao on motorcycles going up a hill surrounded by the lush bamboo and fern forests of the countryside around Chia Yi, the dramatic difference between rural and urban Taiwan could not be more apparent. Rock music is on the soundtrack; the trio, wearing sunglasses, resembles the characters on the road in *Easy Rider* (1969). Like their 1960s American counterparts, this Taiwanese trio blends freedom from the confines of consumer society with a nostalgic communion with nature and impression of innocence despite their criminal connections. The characters in *Goodbye South Goodbye* live lives on the road very similar to those of the countercultural protagonists in *Easy Rider*. However, although both films celebrate the grandeur of the countryside and relish in the freedom from social constraints youth seem to enjoy, all the principal characters in both narratives end up in a ditch at the films' conclusions.

FIGURE 19. Still from *Goodbye South Goodbye*. Flathead, Pretzel, and Kao always seem to be on the wrong side of the tracks. (Courtesy of Wellspring.)

For Flathead, Pretzel, and Kao, saying goodbye to Chia Yi pushes them deeper into a Taiwan moving away from an agrarian past and into an urban present and an increasingly globalized future. Unlike Ying, who can adapt, learn English, and emigrate, Flathead, Pretzel, and Kao remain mired in a system of guan xi that should serve them but instead abandons them to their unhappy fate at the bottom of a ditch. Though young love seems to transcend the system in *Mahjong*, the teenagers' fate is far from certain as the lights of the night market insist on the commercial underpinnings of all relationships in contemporary Taipei. As a city perpetually under construction, corrupted by triad ties, Taipei represents the possibility of limitless public consumption within the transnational spaces of its restaurants, hotels, and shopping centers tempered by the fact that they are always "under development." As Zhang Yingjin points out in *Screening China*, these "postmodern liminal spaces" symbolize "despair and hope, destruction and re-generation, disappearance and reinscription—in short, a space beyond good and evil, beyond hatred and love, beyond any fixed meaning or signification."[36]

CONCLUSION

Though known for their very different approaches to Taiwan, Edward Yang and Hou Hsiao-hsien zero in on strikingly similar aspects of contemporary Taiwanese society in their cinematic portraits of the mid-1990s. Sensitive to the political and

FIGURE 20. Still from *Goodbye South Goodbye*. The end of the road for Flathead, Pretzel, and Kao. (Courtesy of Wellspring.)

economic trials of Taiwan, they focus on the margins of the triad subculture as it intersects with international youth subcultures to uncover the roots of the cultural crisis Taiwan faces. No easy answers surface, and the apparently simple conflicts between the rural and the urban, the traditional and the contemporary, guan xi and youth culture, the corrupt and the innocent, the criminal and the legal, the global and the local actually turn out to be inextricably intertwined in ways that make the contradictions of Taiwanese society difficult to fathom.

In his analysis of Yang's *The Terrorizer* in "Remapping Taipei,"[37] Fredric Jameson points to the petit bourgeois managerial bureaucrat as emblematic of the limits Taiwan faces in a world economy where it must function as the perennial middleman, always lagging behind the stronger economies of Japan and the West, forever dependent on the global corporate system in which it plays a comparatively minor role. In *Mahjong* and *Goodbye South Goodbye*, the petty gangster fulfills that same allegorical function. Trapped by rituals and practices associated with the past, the gangster cannot extricate himself from the system that promises prosperity and cannot deliver it in an increasingly complex global economy. The uncertain fates of the characters in *Mahjong* and *Goodbye South Goodbye* parallel Taiwan's uncertain future as a global center of international commerce, a devalued province of an increasingly powerful mainland, an independent state with an identity that distinguishes it from the rest of China, a vital part of a more diffuse global China with borders that extend beyond both the PRC and the ROC, or an increasingly marginal island with decreasing strategic importance and an outward-bound, educated bourgeoisie that prefers to live abroad. Whether mahjong continues to fascinate a fickle West hungry for novelty or whether the south can ever be bid farewell forever remain open questions as Taiwan continues to negotiate its identity in an uncertain world.

Interview with Edward Yang

Could you talk a little bit about your inspiration for Confucian Confusion *and* Mahjong? *Did you conceive of them as part of the same project?*

I think *Confucian Confusion* and *Mahjong* belong to one period in my career. At the time, I sensed a big change in Taiwan. I noticed corruption in the society, and I was very concerned about the younger generation. *Mahjong* and *Confucian Confusion* tried to build a dialogue with the younger generation, but as it turned out, the media were part of that corruption, and that dialogue did not happen. In fact, the media portrayed the two films in very different ways than I envisioned.

In the late 1980s and early 1990s, Taiwan actually had a very vibrant economy. This was because of the confidence of my generation in Taiwan. Virtually all of my schoolmates owned computer companies, and that was the time when the semi-conductor business and computer manufacturing were really taking off in Taiwan. The future was very bright in the '80s. However, with the liberalization of Taiwan at the same time, the government had to learn to exert even greater control over the media. They realized that if they still had control of the media, they could control the way people were informed. The press should promote democracy, free speech. However, the government was trying to silence criticism. Actually, criticism or freedom of speech is always a negative thing within the Confucian value system. I made *Confucian Confusion* to create a dialogue about free speech with the younger generation. To accomplish this, I decided to make the film a very light comedy and cast all new actors and actresses.

Can you describe how things have changed for filmmakers since the 1980s?

In the '80s, we tried very hard, and eventually we succeeded in building this subsidy program for filmmakers, especially younger filmmakers, upstart film-makers. However, soon this system was used to replace censorship. Before the end of martial law, the government could put people in jail if they expressed views against the KMT. After liberalization, the government suddenly realized the power of money. With the subsidy program, officials can select filmmakers who are saying politically correct things by giving them money. If they do not say politically correct things, the filmmakers do not get money. Lack of funding can be a worse punishment than prison.

That is the American way—money determines access to the media.

In America, there is one crucial difference. In American society, there still is the independent justice system. There is none in a Confucian society like Taiwan.

Also, if you are a media mogul, if you own all the media, the cable stations and so forth, you side with authority, because that is where the money is. You tell your reporters not to say certain things. That is what happened in the '90s. All the media, especially American media, were trying to hype Taiwan as a democratic society. What kind of democracy do you have when people are not fully informed? You make wrong decisions.

At least I tried to engage the younger generation and to alert them to the fact that they have to think about these kinds of things and be aware of these issues. For example, Red Fish in *Mahjong* thinks about money from a very early age. He only wants to go for "Chiang Kai-shek" because his face is printed on all the banknotes. Money is the only thing Red Fish lives for and the only objective the kid Red Fish has—go for the money, go for the banknotes. Maybe Chiang Kai-shek would regret that his face is shown all over the place, who knows?

Red Fish's role model is his father, because his father knows how to make money. All of a sudden, his father's conscience starts to surface, and suddenly Red Fish is lost. If money is not what his father wanted, then what was it? Why did his father have to kill himself? That is why, in the climactic scene, Red Fish just takes out a gun and shoots the other guy without even thinking. His own life is so frustrating. After the film, I felt I had done enough; I said what I wanted to say.

When *Mahjong* came out, the press was not interested in social criticism. They accused me of trying to lecture the public. They painted a very negative picture, since they are negative about anybody who has a conscience. The media do not want the filmmaker's conscience to alert people to the fact that they are doing the wrong things. Afterward, I thought I had done my share for society, now I am just going to do my own thing. I decided to focus on the regular things in life—the simple things in life.

What is the situation like with the distribution of your films in Taiwan?

There is really no distribution available in Taiwan for local people to see locally made films. Although there was hope in the '80s, in the '90s, it has been very depressing. Everything revolves around chasing a few bucks. Not just films, but music, books, other publications, and so forth have been in decline in the last ten years.

How do you think youth culture has changed?

America provides the world's pop culture for teenagers. The Japanese are in the habit of copying what is happening in America, and they make it their own. Taiwan is heavily influenced by America and Japan. Hong Kong was much different because of the British influence under colonial rule. However, the difference is not that great now, and Hong Kong has more American and Japanese influence, increasingly like Taiwan.

Fredric Jameson's essay on your film The Terrorizer *has had an enormous impact on film scholarship. Do you have any thoughts on his use of postmodernism to discuss your film?*

I am not a philosophy scholar, and I really am not aware of postmodernism, except perhaps architecturally. I understand postmodernism as an architectural style.

Perhaps the actions I have been taking for the last twenty years reflect what postmodernism is expressing. I think it just happened that I became part of the phenomena of postmodernism . . . I did not do it intentionally.

People have more things in common than otherwise, so, before we begin to discover the interesting differences we have or the subtle differences we have among ourselves, we should build on the understanding that we share so many things in common, the universal elements of humanity. This is really the reason why I do not go into the countryside and look for something ethnic or exotic to show to tourists. That is not my way of doing things. I like to look at facts. I want to understand reality as much as possible, because I have confidence that somewhere in it there is an interesting story. Perhaps Jameson is affected by my work; maybe I was that trailblazer, the pioneer? I dig out things and then show them to people, and maybe philosophers can base their theories on some of my work.

October 4, 2000

5 The Postmodern Condition in Singapore: *Mee Pok Man* and *Twelve Storeys*

SINGAPORE BALANCES THE PROCESS of nation building it has undertaken since becoming an autonomous state in 1965 with the important transnational role the port plays in global flows of capital, commodities, and labor.[1] The island nation, therefore, must be staunchly anti-imperialist and chauvinistically "pan-Asian," while still being open to Westernized consumer culture within the global marketplace in which it has been, until the regional crash in 1997, enormously successful. The government officially calls for adherence to "Asian values,"[2] principally based on a Chinese understanding of Confucian morals. In fact, the city-state officially decries the decadence, materialism, individualism, and moral bankruptcy of Western consumer culture, a conception primarily drawn from an American model based on Hollywood movies, Disneyland, and McDonald's fast food restaurants. However, capitalism is encouraged, material success lauded, and participation in the international marketplace celebrated.

The Singapore film industry builds itself up on the foundation of what had been a thriving colonial business[3] to situate itself in the global arena of the international art film and Chinese transnational cinema culture,[4] while still appealing to a domestic market hungry for local images of the country's unique cultural mélange. As a global cinema with a local flavor, it competes with Hollywood and Hong Kong for the domination of the country's screens. Although dormant for many years, the industry has experienced a minor renaissance in the 1990s.

One director, Eric Khoo, has been credited with single-handedly reviving Singapore's sluggish film industry with two internationally recognized features, *Mee Pok Man* (1995) and *Twelve Storeys* (1997).[5] Khoo shot films as a child and went on to study film production in Australia. An award-winning short filmmaker, Khoo has also worked in music videos, commercials, and series television in Singapore. With keen observational skills and a very dark sense of humor, Khoo paints a portrait of the city-state of Singapore as a global society wrestling with the postmodern condition.[6] To this end, Khoo juxtaposes the public, global "face" of Singapore as an ultramodern, hygienic, orderly, rational, Confucian nation-state with the underbelly of Singapore's colonial past, transnational sex trade, urban blight, racism, political oppression, and economic inequities. This chapter looks at Khoo's two critically acclaimed features, *Mee Pok Man* and *Twelve Storeys*, in relation to the malleability and uncertainty of Singapore's identity within global postmodernity.

The Postmodern Condition in Singapore

EXPOSING CONTRADICTIONS

Khoo has a succinct way of exposing and concretizing the contradictions at the root of contemporary Singaporean society. Toward the end of *Twelve Storeys*, for example, Khoo introduces the character of Eddy (Ronald Toh Chee Kong), who comes to pick up his teenage, GenerAsian X girlfriend Trixie (Lum May Yee). (For more on GenerAsian X, see chapters 4 and 7.) To go off on his date, he must first win the approval of Trixie's older brother, Meng (Koh Bon Pin). Eddy and Meng, of course, are polar opposites, each symbolizing extremes within Singaporean society. The bespectacled Meng is the poster boy for Singapore—a schoolteacher, proud of his academic accomplishments and compulsory military service. He wears the casual but sober short shirt sleeves characteristic of the ruling People's Action Party (PAP) or T-shirts with government slogans.[7] He does calisthenics in accordance with government directives; can spout statistics on health, education, and social welfare in Singapore; believes in the campaign to increase "graciousness" in the society; and takes his role as elder brother seriously and keeps his younger siblings in order while their parents are away.

Eddy, on the other hand, has difficulty remembering how he scored on his school exams. He deals in industrial parts and prides himself on his ability to get his international clientele what they want—namely, attractive women. He speaks Singlish as opposed to Meng's more proper English.[8] Eddy drives a flashy car; Meng has no car. Unlike Meng, Eddy wears gaudy, tasteless plaid trousers and buckskin loafers. Meng looks on uncomfortably as the uncouth Eddy uses a manicured pinky nail to dig wax out of his ear canal.[9]

Meng epitomizes what Singapore struggles to represent to the world—filial piety, Confucian virtue, cleanliness, orderliness, good manners, academic achievement, and sexual reserve. Eddy embodies the other side of Singapore—mercantilism, business savvy over academic acuity, the ability to play the middleman, sexual license, earthiness, and the flamboyant display of the good life through women, dress, leisure activities, and mode of transportation. Meng attempts to be modern Singapore, confident that an upgraded government flat, a good education, and the possibility of buying a car will make him happy. Eddy represents Singapore's actual postmodern condition. His ability to thrive in an international market for spare parts puts him within the old order of Singapore's legacy as a colonial port, within an economy that does not produce but repackages and recirculates, and that is very much at ease with the transnational flow of people and goods. Positioning him somewhere between a traditional Chinese and a postcolonial Singaporean identity, Eddy's Singlish enables him to do business in the transnational marketplace with Americans as easily as the Japanese or Koreans he recognizes as wanting the same thing. His relaxed attitude toward sex permits him to take advantage of postfeminist women like Trixie, who are freed from commitment to traditional marriage and family and able to survive independently in newly available careers or within the ever-expanding service sector without challenging male domination in more fundamental ways. Moreover, Eddy can also luxuriate in the port's historical institution of prostitution. Meng berates Eddy for being a pimp; however, Eddy claims he is simply a good capitalist, just giving the customer what he wants.

It is important to keep in mind that Eddy and Meng do not represent simple binary oppositions like past/future, modern/traditional, global/local, Chinese/ Singaporean, national/transnational, or conservative/progressive. Each contains aspects of the other. Eddy's ability to make cash out of trash puts him at the forefront of the postindustrial economy as well as linking him to Singapore's colonial past. Meng's ardent patriotism allows him to deplore British colonialism and celebrate the benefits of proper English diction and traditional British reserve and etiquette. The sex trade is as much a part of the old society as the contemporary global economy.

Meng and Eddy seem at odds, but when taken together as two sides of a single Singaporean coin, they present a picture of how Singapore functions as the embodiment of the dream of modern rationality coupled to capitalism, consumerism, the legacy of colonialism, nationalism, sexism, and class stratification. Within the narrative structure of *Twelve Storeys*, their interests coalesce within the figure of Trixie, whom Eddy calls a "hot babe." Eddy and the repressed, incestuous Meng both desire Trixie. Just as Singapore needs women's labor in the official sectors of the offices and shops as well as the unofficial sector of the sex trade, Eddy needs Trixie on his arm as a symbol of the achievements of capitalism. Similarly, Meng needs Trixie to be a "good girl," a virgin before marriage, a filial contributor to the patriarchal household, and eventually "pear-shaped" after marriage and child-bearing like "all Chinese women."

The nubile Trixie, like Singapore itself, has difficulty being both the virgin and the whore within the national and transnational economies. Trixie's own desires seem far less grandiose than either Eddy's or Meng's. Trixie wants to quit school, enjoy going to the trendy nightclub Zouk's, work at the mainstream department store Metro, read international glamour magazines, have sex when she likes, and go to the movies with her boyfriend. She seems to have genuine affection for her square older brother and her trendy younger one. Speaking *Singlish* and wearing mini-skirts and go-go boots, she functions less as a marker of national identity, economic mobility, or patriarchal power, and more as an emblem of a hybridized, transnational, GenerAsian X youth culture, taking Singapore with her out of a patriarchal past and into a postmodern present. She literally embodies the contradictions of Singaporean capitalism that measure success in material terms while condemning Western consumerism. Her existence and destruction mark a moment of crisis in the film and, perhaps, in the society. Trixie represents a youthful, female desire not beholden to traditional notions of national, class, ethnic, or gender identity, and this desire takes on an existence beyond her generation and gender as a symbol of a Singaporean identity somehow out of control and in crisis.

The triangular relationship, established by Eddy, Meng, and Trixie, repeats itself in several permutations in both *Mee Pok Man* and *Twelve Storeys*, exposing contradictions that stand unresolved even as the narratives reach their own conclusions. In *Mee Pok Man*, the unnamed, simple-minded *mee pok* man (Joe Ng) wins possession of the prostitute Bunny (Michelle Goh) from her pimp, Mike Kor

(Kay Tong Lim), and her British boyfriend, Jonathan Reese (David Brazil), even though the mee pok man ends up with only her decaying corpse for company. In *Twelve Storeys*, in addition to Meng and Eddy's tussle over Trixie, Ah Gu (Jack Neo) struggles for possession of his mainland Chinese bride, Lili (Chuan Yi Fong), with a string of off-screen suitors. San San (Lucilla Teoh) must endure her mother (Lok Yee Loy), who harangues her about her inability to attract a suitable mate and throws up her old charge Rachel (Neo Swee Lin) as the ideal woman who has found an overseas husband and gone to live in America.

Like Lili and Trixie, San San does not fit in with traditional patriarchal expectations, and the patriarchy in crisis is also blamed for the unnamed suicide's (Ritz Lim) demise, because a woman is assumed to have "driven him to it."[10] In each case, sexual and familial relations indicate a more general social malaise, and given the Confucian link between the health of the family and the well-being of the kingdom, the fact that these dysfunctional interpersonal relationships point to larger problems within the nation and beyond seems logical. [11]

POSTMODERN SPACES

Visually, Khoo's postmodern critique of Singapore's modernist project of nation building can be seen clearly in the way in which he uses space, particularly Singapore's distinctive architectural spaces, in *Mee Pok Man* and *Twelve Storeys*. In *The Condition of Postmodernity*, David Harvey distinguishes between modernist and postmodernist architecture as follows:

> In the field of architecture and urban design, I take postmodernism broadly to signify a break with the modernist idea that planning and development should focus on large-scale, metropolitan-wide, technologically rational and efficient urban *plans*, backed by absolutely no-frills architecture (the austere "functionalist" surfaces of "international style" modernism). Postmodernism cultivates, instead, a conception of the urban fabric as necessarily fragmented, a "palimpsest" of past forms superimposed upon each other, and a "collage" of current uses, many of which may be ephemeral. Since the metropolis is impossible to command except in bits and pieces, urban *design* (and note postmodernists design rather than plan) simply aims to be sensitive to vernacular traditions, local histories, particular wants, needs, and fancies, thus generating specialized, even highly customized architectural forms that may range from intimate, personalized spaces, through traditional monumentality, to the gaiety of spectacle.[12]

Khoo most commonly sets his narratives in the two urban spaces that most typify Singapore—the Housing and Development Board (HDB) block and the hawkers' stalls of the open-air food courts that often line the bases of the HDB apartments. The outdoor food stalls hark back to the colonial period and the lines of shop houses that can still be found in some of the shrinking older quarters of Singapore. The shop houses consist of three basic parts: a downstairs shop, upstairs living quarters, and an overhang that forms an arcade-like shelter for those walking from shop to shop and protects customers from intense tropical sun and frequent rain. Crowded together, the shops and food stalls form a marketplace and public forum for shopping, eating, chatting, and general socializing. These spaces exist somewhere between the colonial marketplace and postmodern shopping malls.

The HDB apartment blocks are strictly within the modernist tradition of urban planning. The buildings, which look like high-rise public housing found in any metropolitan setting, give the Singaporean skyline its distinctively monotonous and uniform quality. The majority of those living in these housing projects, however, own their apartments; most Singaporeans live in these buildings and thus enjoy a common standard of housing determined by the government. Indeed, simply by depicting housing in a particular way, Khoo implicitly critiques the Singapore government (dominated since independence in 1965 by the PAP, headed by Senior Minister Lee Kuan Yew). Audrey Wong describes Khoo's "HDB Filmscape" as follows:

> The minute, hidden tragedies of daily life in the orderly blocks of HDB flats are fleshed out in Khoo's feature films. Within the cramped flats where the majority of Singapore's population lives, stories of thwarted desire, love, hate, and conflict are played out. In *Mee Pok Man*, the climax, horror and sadness of the love story takes place within the dull confines of the *mee pok* man's small, plainly furnished flat as he props the decaying body of Bunny the prostitute at the dining table in the kitchen. . . .
>
> The claustrophobic spaces of HDB flats also intensify the hate and heartache. In *12 Storeys*, San San is tormented by her mother's constant nagging—and browbeaten into silent submission because she is unable to escape from her mother in such a small living space. The close proximity in which Trixie and Meng live throws into sharp relief Meng's hidden desire for his sister. He wakes her up in the mornings when he is given a good view of her in bed, and her underwear hangs openly up to dry in the kitchen. These things give those of us who are familiar with such living spaces a shock of recognition. We realize that there may be small dramas in our lives which may become volcanic as well.[13]

In *Twelve Storeys*, Khoo begins his depiction of these housing estates with a series of abstracted views of the buildings' exteriors. The spaces unfold for the camera like the prisoners' cells on view in the panopticon Michel Foucault describes in *Discipline and Punish*.[14] In the opening montage, Khoo offers a glance at the range of ethnicities (Chinese, Malay, Indian), generations (infants to grandparents), and family arrangements (singles to extended families) that inhabit these spaces. This slice of life in the HDB block shows that the organization of the architectural space defines these people's lives in important ways. They live in close proximity, but they do not operate as a cohesive community. The concrete walls of the apartments separate people. The cramped spaces within the apartments work against healthy interpersonal relationships and promote further isolation and atomization. Most of the shots isolate individuals in the frame, show the lack of communication among family members involved in the electronically mediated spaces of the TV or computer screen, or show the separation of ethnic/racial communities within housing that must meet various racial/ethnic quotas to ensure against the ghettoization of any given group[15] and the possibility of race riots or political uprisings based on race or ethnicity.

The architectural design of the HDB flats defines key aspects of the narrative in many other important ways. For example, to be more efficient, the elevators in

HDB buildings do not stop on every floor. In the case of the housing estate in *Twelve Storeys*, the elevators stop at one, six, and eleven; thus, the inhabitants of the twelfth floor are those just unlucky enough to miss the convenience of an elevator stop by one floor, so they have to trudge up one extra flight to their homes. Thus, the film's title points to those within the society who seem to just miss the Singaporean ideal. They are off a floor, out of pace, and unable to conform to the rest of the society.[16]

The building also provides fuel for Beijing-born Lili's fiery temper as she verbally assaults HDB housing standards as an indirect attack on the Singaporean husband she despises. In one of her heated tirades, she complains about the filthy conditions in the HDB block by noting the infestation of mosquitoes in the building as well as the necessity for urine detectors in the elevators that simply moved the miscreants to the building's corridors to relieve themselves. She admits that the public toilets in her hometown of Beijing are filthy but claims never to have heard of elevators being used for urinals.

Like *Twelve Storeys*, *Mee Pok Man* begins with a montage that presents a range of people within a characteristically Singaporean space. The focus here, however, is on the hawkers' open-air food court rather than the HDB apartments. Just as *Twelve Storeys* connects the ultramodern HDB estates with base bodily functions, *Mee Pok Man* links the hawker stalls with food and sex. The rapid montage, set to a driving hard-core punk beat,[17] intercuts shots of men and women eating noodles lustily; close-up fragments of nude women's breasts, buttocks, and pubic areas; noodles being cooked in a wok; mounds of food on display; hanging meat; close-ups of flies alighting on piles of refuse; and more noodles and ribs devoured by Asian and white clientele. The neon light of the streets and the harsh fluorescents in the stalls give the scene a distinctly unappealing quality. Seedy hotels and a Shell station frame the hawkers' food court between the official economy of transnational capitalism (e.g., Singapore's position as one of the leading centers for oil refining situated on the shipping lanes between the Persian Gulf and East Asia) and the other, unofficial, transnational economy of the sex trade. The proximity of the Shell station to the world of the food hawkers and prostitutes inexorably ties these Singaporean businesses together, tacitly commenting on the links between the official face and hidden realities of the nation.

The tables at the hawkers' stalls in both *Mee Pok Man* and *Twelve Storeys* provide rare public spaces in which customers can indulge in their vices (e.g., pick up prostitutes, gamble on the lottery, drink liquor), and also speak their minds (e.g., talk about recent news items like the Flor Contemplacion execution and the Michael Fay caning). Part of the street culture and "informal" service economy of prostitution and an official part of the legitimate economy of business owners and entrepreneurs, hawkers, like the eponymous mee pok man and the tofu vendor Ah Gu in *Twelve Storeys*, eke out an existence that embodies the contradictions of Singapore's economy. The hawker courts are both marginal to the operation of the country and central to an understanding of its culture. Like mee pok itself, they are hybrid entities that bring together the various ethnicities and food preferences of the nation. Unlike the atomized HDB flats, the food courts open up spaces for a potential mixing of

FIGURE 21. Still from *Mee Pok Man*. Food hawkers and prostitutes share the same space, linking the "official" and "unofficial" economies together. (Courtesy of Eric Khoo, Zhao Wei Productions.)

languages, foods, ethnicities, and classes; however, this space also allows for pimps, hooligans, and the detritus of society to operate in the open air.

In both films, Khoo works well with the global/local spaces that characterize Singapore. Although the urban flats, food courts, office buildings, public mass transit, and shopping districts decorated for Christmas can be found in most of the world's large, metropolitan cities,[18] Khoo maintains a very local understanding of the way these transnational spaces take on a peculiarly Singaporean form. Ironically, the global force of modernity allows for the circulation of capital and people, which makes the local so important for Singaporean industries like tourism. As Mike Featherstone points out in *Undoing Culture: Globalization, Postmodernism and Identity*, the local takes on a new significance in the global postmodern environment: "With postmodernism, there is a re-emergence of the vernacular, of representational forms, with the use of pastiche and playful collaging of styles and traditions. In short, there is a return to local cultures in the plural, the fact that they can be placed alongside each other without hierarchal distinction."[19]

Khoo visualizes the "messiness" of postmodern spaces set against the imposed order and belief in rationality epitomized by high modernist architecture. The hygienic orderliness of Singapore's Orchard Road shopping district, downtown financial center, efficient rapid transit, and HDB flats hide the irrational, chaotic, and uncontrollable. In Khoo's oeuvre, the pick-up bars, hawkers' stalls, and vomit-strewn toilets in the Singaporean cityscape get more than equal exposure.

THE POLITICS OF LANGUAGE

One of the most strikingly hybridized characteristics of *Mee Pok Man* and *Twelve Storeys* is the use of language. Since splitting from Malaysia in 1965 to establish itself as an autonomous nation, Singapore's government has tried to create a national culture that would maintain multiculturalism as an official policy. In "Contending with Primordialism" Wee points out that nationalism, multiculturalism, and modernity formed the foundation for Singapore's creation under Lee Kuan Yew:

> Since there was no one racial identity—and thus no single "nation"—upon which safely to erect a national identity, Lee and his colleagues aimed to make industrial modernity the metanarrative which would frame Singapore's national identity, and to create a remarkable "Global City" which, because of its trading links, would escape the restraints placed upon it by history and geography. The "national" as a category was not to be jettisoned but to be renovated so that Singapore's racial and cultural difference would be contained and to some extent homogenized for the leap into modernity. The people of Singapore would have to adapt their ways of life to fit the new state.[20]

Rather than choosing a single language that might alienate the majority Han Chinese, the Malays, who make up the majority of the neighboring populations of Malaysia and Indonesia, the South Asians, who have been an important economic force as merchants, laborers, and government officials since the British colonial administration, or the very marginal Eurasians (a rather malleable classification that seems to include biracial individuals as well as people of various racial and national groups who do not fit in the other three categories), who maintain important economic and cultural ties to the West, Singapore chose a limited form of multiculturalism. Thus Singapore has four official languages (English, Mandarin, Malay/Bahasa, and Tamil). Although English is the primary medium of commerce and instruction, the three other "mother" tongues can also be used to conduct "official" business and must be included in the curriculum at government schools. Although this may seem like a logical path to multiculturalism, the irony of the situation lies in the fact that the preponderance of the majority Chinese population does not consider Mandarin its native dialect. Hokkien (spoken by the majority population on Taiwan and by mainlanders across the Taiwan Straits), Cantonese (spoken by the majority in Hong Kong and by most in Guangdong Province in the PRC), and the Shanghai dialect, among others, are very much in use unofficially in Singapore. As the official language of both Taiwan and the People's Republic,

Mandarin makes sense as a medium of education and commerce, but the concomitant drive to eliminate the other dialects has also inhibited free expression in Singapore. For a time, Cantonese opera, Hokkien puppet shows, and other entertainments were banned, and Cantonese films from Hong Kong are dubbed in Mandarin before exhibition in Singapore.[21] A similar irony exists for the Indian community. Although the majority in Singapore comes from Tamil-speaking southern India, Hindi, the Indian nation's "official" language, may seem more attractive to some as a medium of commerce and education.

In *Mee Pok Man* and *Twelve Storeys*, Khoo concentrates on the Chinese majority. The Malay and Indian Singaporeans provide a backdrop, much as they do in the nation at large. Meng, for example, has a brief exchange with a neighbor in Bahasa that only reinforces Meng's privileged position as an educator in the community.

However, Khoo does not attempt to forward the Chinese as the unified face of Singapore. Mandarin divides as much as it unifies the Chinese community within Singapore as well as Singaporean Chinese within the rest of the Greater China global sphere. Although Singapore's government has attempted to forward Mandarin as a unifying force among the Chinese globally and Confucianism as an orthodoxy so that "Chinese" values (e.g., filial piety, patriarchy, and authoritarian hierarchical order) could stand for Asia and against the West, Khoo remains suspicious of the role Singapore has fashioned for itself in Asia.

For Khoo, Singapore, as represented by the Chinese community in his films, is fragmented, without a coherent sense of identity, or unambiguous means of self-articulation. Mandarin competes with Singlish, Hokkien, and Cantonese as the favored means of expression. In fact, narrative points are often made through changes in dialect. The switch from the strident Cantonese of San San's mother to San San's halting Mandarin to communicate with Rachel speaks volumes about the social gulf between the two women. Similarly, Trixie and her younger brother's Singlish forms a wall between them and Meng who sticks with proper English. Bunny, too, sets herself apart by speaking the transnational languages of Mandarin and English, hoping to escape the constraints of Singaporean society, ironically through mastery of two of its official tongues. When Hokkien is spoken freely in the hawker stalls, the mood relaxes, plot development slows, and social commentary can be inserted.

Khoo's self-conscious use of dialects situates his features within a uniquely local culture in Singapore. Unlike the Shaw Brothers' use of Mandarin to establish a transnational Chinese audience for their films throughout the Chinese diaspora by celebrating a golden age of the Han Chinese by creating an imaginatively unified audience through the modern mass medium of the motion picture, Khoo creates a very different, hybrid discourse. The address may still be primarily to a global Chinese audience, but it does not disguise its cosmopolitan, Singaporean origins. Khoo uses language much the same way that Wong Kar-Wai uses Mandarin, Japanese, Cantonese, and English in *Chungking Express* to depict a very particular, local environment marked by its cosmopolitan hybridity. Rather than use English or Mandarin to appeal to broad segments of the audience, or use Cantonese or Hokkien exclusively to make a statement against U.S. cultural imperialism experienced through the use of English or the pressing political hegemony of the "official" Mandarin-speaking governments of the People's Republic or Singapore, Khoo and Wong prefer creating films that cross linguistic boundaries more fluidly but also more self-consciously. Language becomes opaque, and it presents an implicit critique of the unified nation and the cohesive self within the transnational, postmodern, postcolonial city.

POSTMODERN STYLE

The relationship between allegory and postmodern style finds a particularly welcome meeting ground in the work of Eric Khoo. Like many of his contemporaries, Khoo draws on a tradition of allegory within Chinese discourse to circumvent political restrictions and weds it to a contemporary taste for displacement and slippage within texts. Although visual style, dramatic interest, and narrative pleasures may overwhelm other readings, these allegorical interpretations are still available.

Mee Pok Man and *Twelve Storeys* slide between being part of the circulation of images characteristic of postmodern consumerism and critiquing that image market. Both films travel as commodities while also being self-consciously critical of the marketplace. Resuscitating the idea of a "national" cinema by presenting a vision unique to Singapore, Khoo frustrates any fantasy of nation building by systematically underscoring the mistakes and excesses of Singapore's government from education and housing to law enforcement.

Mee Pok Man and *Twelve Storeys* situate themselves within the spectacle of everyday life. Radio and TV broadcasts, cartoon characters, internationally recognized brand names, and other images of global consumer culture saturate the mise-en-scène and soundtrack. *Twelve Storeys* (and *Mee Pok Man*, to a lesser degree) relies on a televisual aesthetic that privileges the surface flow of images over meaning.[22] Channel surfing, particularly in *Twelve Storeys*, dominates the film's aesthetic as it cuts among its various plotlines, often paralleled by characters clicking through the available images from Hong Kong films to TV commercials on Singapore's government-run television. Moreover, *Twelve Storeys'* televisual style makes it "look" like Singapore, because the HDB flats illuminated from within look like television monitors and images of HDB interiors abound on Singaporean TV in popular series, like *Under One Roof.*[23] Shot on Super 16 in the ratio that replicates the shape of the television box, *Twelve Storeys'* reliance on talking heads places it squarely within a televisual sense of space. San San's mother's direct address to the camera mirrors the parade of talking heads that cross international TV broadcasts of everything from news stories to soap operas. The confined frame, the camera's close proximity to its subjects, and intense scrutiny of the close-up bring to the fore the film's critique of the claustrophobia and insularity of the HDB flat and, by extension, Singaporean society.

The mass media pervade this cloistered world but fail to offer any outlet. Rather, mass (mis)communication is revealed to be woefully inadequate to provide a forum for public discourse for its audience. *Twelve Storeys*, for example, includes an upbeat radio DJ who comments on the weather (which is usually monotonously hot and humid) as Meng gleefully goes through his morning calisthenics and San San rather gloomily looks on. The public "face" of the radio broadcast is greatly at odds with the lives of the characters in the film. Similarly, in *Mee Pok Man*, the pleas of Xiao Ming, a suicidal student in the midst of the viciously competitive "examination hell" that sweeps the country every year and can determine the job prospects of many at a very young age, contrast with the flippancy of the female DJ to whom he confides.

As direct interpersonal communication shuts down, mediated communication attempts to fill the gap. In the opening montage of *Twelve Storeys*, a teenager pulls away from a grandparent to pursue a conversation with a stranger on the Internet. Playing with his portable game system and listening to punk music, Bunny's younger brother only begins to hear her voice through her diaries after she is dead. Meng serves as a ventriloquist's dummy for government propaganda on topics as wide ranging as eating breakfast to boost productivity, the AIDS crisis, and improving the quality of life by being gracious. Ah Gu tries to fashion a sense of Asian masculinity by watching soap operas, happy family TV commercials, and Bruce Lee movies. Jonathan criticizes Bunny for casting herself in the Julia Roberts role in *Pretty Woman* (1990), and *Twelve Storeys*' unnamed ghost positions himself in relation to GI Joe action figures and Japanese anime.

Khoo's films exist on the borders between the high-art world of the international art film and the low pop-cultural environment of the B-grade exploitation film, the TV soap opera, and the cartoon. As such, the films contain enormous narrative gaps and inconsistencies of tone. Khoo does not assume a unified viewership, and he attempts to communicate with local teenagers in Singapore, art film aficionados internationally, and the mixed audience for Chinese films globally.

To this end, Khoo draws broadly from an international lexicon of film style. The voyeuristic aspects of *Mee Pok Man* and *Twelve Storeys* refer to Hitchcock's films. *Twelve Storey*'s setting in an apartment block conjures up *Rear Window* (1954) in particular. The corpse at the center of *Mee Pok Man* links it to *Psycho* (1960), and the plot mirrors any number of films dealing with the attempted rescue of fallen women, most notably John Ford's *The Searchers* (1956) and Martin Scorsese's *Taxi Driver* (1976),[24] as well as lighter fare like *Pretty Woman*. The specifically Asian setting of *Mee Pok Man* links it to films like *The World of Suzie Wong* (1960), *Saint Jack* (1979), and a host of others that have exploited Asian street life to both profit from and condemn white men's lascivious interests in the "Orient." Khoo connects with Asian popular culture as well through Hello Kitty, Bruce Lee, and references to Hong Kong romances like Stanley Kwan's *Rouge* (1987).

Khoo also takes up New Wave counter-cinema stylistics to create a sense of alienation, disaffection, and angst, placing his work in conversation with contemporary international art cinema. Like his New Wave cohorts, he reflects on his own place in the image market. Not only does GI Joe pop up throughout his oeuvre, animated cartoons and popular music become reoccurring motifs. More directly, Mike Kor reappears in *Twelve Storeys* to comment on the loss of Bunny to the mee pok man in the earlier feature, forming a bridge across his works to reward the cognoscenti.

Although the hybridity and "double consciousness" of the postmodern condition may be a novelty for the white European male whose unified Cartesian ego dominated the globe for so many years, the pastiche and schizophrenia that characterize postmodern consumer culture for Fredric Jameson has long been a part of the colonial and postcolonial condition.[25] The malleability, heterodoxy, hybridity, and playfulness that characterize postmodern stylistics serve Khoo, and many other filmmakers in similar circumstances, well. Postmodernism maximizes viewer pleasure by structuring various shifting points of identification within its ironic, ambiguous, contradictory, and, generally, mysterious texts.

For commercial Hollywood, postmodernism cannibalizes film history, rewards intertextual knowledge, plays with political critique, and promises both resistance to and nostalgia for the status quo. For Khoo, and other filmmakers within and outside of the Chinese diaspora, who often work under the weight of official censorship, pressure to excel in international film festivals and the economic constraints of the cinematic marketplace, postmodernism satisfies an even wider range of needs. For example, the loose construction of the narratives, the lack of linearity and causality, the fragmentation of space, and the uncertainty of time all lend themselves to working with censors while still offering audiences sex, violence, and topical commentary on current events.

In *Twelve Storeys*, for example, Khoo alludes to two of the most sensitive media events involving Singapore in the international press in recent years; however, he refers to these events playfully and in passing, during a conversation among friends in the hawkers' food court. Without mentioning Flor Contemplacion by name, the friends agree that being a Filipino is great because the Philippine people treat murderers as heroes, alluding to the throngs that gathered when Contemplacion's executed body was repatriated for burial. The conversation continues with a reference to "My Café." At first, the other fellows cannot understand what their friend is talking about, until they realize he means Michael Fay, the American boy who confessed to vandalism and was sentenced to a caning in 1994. After U.S. President Bill Clinton asked for clemency, the number of strokes was reduced, but the international press still had a field day with accusations of Singaporean barbarism. All agree that being an American is also wonderful because the president even comes to the aid of hooligans. The playfulness of the scene hides the more subversive ways in which it can be read. Although it can be interpreted as satirizing the international press for making two isolated incidents stand for the excesses of an entire nation, the scene can also be seen as a knowing critique of what the Singaporean media cannot say because of censorship, for example, that innocent people may be executed and teenagers beaten under draconian laws that are out of step with international standards for human rights. Furthermore, it indirectly critiques a system in which the "average" Singaporean is so out of touch with international sentiment as to fail to question Contemplacion's guilt or the excessiveness of Fay's sentence.

However, beyond the ambiguity at the heart of the exchange, the scene itself is expendable. Like many of the incidents in *Mee Pok Man* and *Twelve Storeys*, this scene does nothing to further the plot or provide insight into the character of one of the film's protagonists. Rather, only loosely motivated by the narrative, the scene allows for a potential moment of resistance or critical observation that can be easily dismissed as mere play or eliminated altogether if the censors demand it. *Mee Pok Man* and *Twelve Storeys* offer fragmented, localized, and isolated points of resistance rather than call for any revolutionary change. Belief in universal emancipation gives way to poking fun at the PAP's campaign to get Singaporeans to smile or critiquing the obviously excessive aspects of capitalist consumerism in the institution of prostitution.

In fact, Khoo tries very hard to work within a system that had recently changed to broaden what was permissible on Singaporean screens. Certainly, *Mee Pok Man* could not have been made before 1991, when a ratings system was introduced to allow for the exhibition of films restricted to adult audiences. Modeled on Hong Kong's Category III films, *Mee Pok Man* addresses an adult audience interested in lurid sexuality and a violent underworld while obliquely critiquing the status quo and offering an "artistry" that gives it what U.S. courts have termed "redeeming social value." With *Twelve Storeys*, Khoo wanted to break out of this R(A) ghetto to converse with his preferred audience of GenerAsian X Singaporeans (see interview with Khoo following this chapter), and the film's multiple plots, unrelated incidents, and mercurial characterizations are made to order for a film in which violent incidents (e.g., Meng's likely rape and murder of his sister, Trixie) or sensitive issues (e.g., relations between the Chinese and their Malay and Indian neighbors) would need to be reworked throughout the course of the project. Khoo won the battle for his young, local audience with this hip mix of angst, punk music, and sexy young performers. However, it did not fit as easily into the international art film market as *Mee Pok Man* did with its affinities to Asian soft-core porn and titillating exposés of the Asian sex industry. Still, *Twelve Storeys* did compete at Cannes and was picked up for distribution by Hong Kong's EDKO Film and the local Golden Village Entertainment Company.[26] Khoo has managed to find a domestic, regional, and international market with a postmodern style that travels easily within global film culture.

THE TRAFFIC IN WOMEN

Mee Pok Man and *Twelve Storeys* rely on the circulation of images of women within a libidinal economy linked to the global sex trade as well as the transnational market for female domestic workers. Desire fuels this economy, and the women travel to fulfill the dreams of men who expect the sensual but submissive Asian prostitute or the equally docile, loyal domestic servant. In *Twelve Storeys*, the opening montage introduces the image of the Singapore Airlines stewardess, an emblem of Singaporean national industry, dressed in distinctive batik, who travels the globe to promote the nation as a sensual servant.[27] Just as oil passes through the centrally located port of Singapore, women circulate within the marginal service economies as prostitutes, brides, and maids. In Khoo's films, this libidinal economy intersects with and stands in for the broader Singaporean economy. Prostitution becomes a metaphor for the dubious underpinnings of capitalism. Women, like goods, circulate to enrich men, and Singapore's economy enriches some at the expense of others.

Mee Pok Man, for example, offers both a detailed account of the sex trade and a more general appraisal of the effects of capitalism and the legacy of colonialism.[28] The film begins in a public lavatory. One of Bunny's fellow prostitutes has presumably just finished shooting up drugs as she slowly gets up from the floor next to the toilet. Khoo immediately links the sex and drug trades together. Given that the penalty for drug trafficking in Singapore is death, Khoo soberly places the sex trade in the same category as the violently suppressed narcotics business. Defining itself against Peter Bogdanovich's *Saint Jack* (1979),[29] which romanticized Singapore's sex trade, and Yang Fan/Yonfan's *Bugis Street* (1994), which looked at the world of transvestites and transsexuals in Singapore from a gentler perspective, *Mee Pok Man* does not shy away from showing the toll prostitution takes on the women involved in Singapore's sex industry. Throughout the film, the pimps, taxi drivers, and clients talk casually about their whores. Nationality is often used as a marker of sexual desirability as men talk about the relative merits of prostitutes from Indonesia, Thailand, the Philippines, and Russia, in relation to the Chinese, Malay, and Indian women native to Singapore.

Ironically, within the transnational sex industry, Bunny finds herself inextricably rooted in Singapore. Jonathan, a photographer and "professional" voyeur, enjoys his base in Singapore and has no plans to take Bunny away. He is one of those transnational professionals who benefits enormously from his expatriate position in Singapore. He can come and go as he pleases, enjoy his penchant for Asian women, and be free from any stigma, competition, or expectation for a more settled, married existence he may find in London. Despite Jonathan's refusal, Bunny insists on living out the fantasy that he is her white knight who will take her away from the world of prostitution. However, Bunny does not enjoy the same fate as Suzie (Nancy Kwan) in *The World of Suzie Wong* or any of the number of other Asian prostitutes saved by white men in Hollywood films.[30] When Bunny gets up enough courage to leave Mike Kor, she does not fall into the arms of her white savior, but instead ends up near death in the gutter from a hit and run.

As soon as Bunny is knocked unconscious and thereby silenced, her subjective voice is finally heard. Her younger brother has found, along with birth control pills, the pager she carries to communicate with her pimp, a well-marked map of Europe, and Bunny's diaries. As he reads the diaries, Bunny's voiceover and inserts of the written text reveal her perspective on her profession. The diaries follow a reverse chronology so that Bunny's immediate past gives way to a change in her voice that indicates the transition to her childhood. Ironically, as her brother learns more about what led Bunny to prostitution and as her voice becomes more childlike and innocent, her body decays in the mee pok man's apartment.

The segment devoted to Jonathan picking up a prostitute to succeed Bunny is particularly telling. While Bunny's diary talks of meeting Mr. Right, Jonathan walks down an arcade with a display of photographs of Asian women. He enters a disco and tells the hostess he is from England, wants a girl who speaks English, and prefers to look around on his own. Jonathan seems to know the routine well, and this sequence, reminiscent of Godard's *Vivre sa vie* (1962), takes the viewer through a step-by-step explication of the procedure involved in procuring a whore in Singapore. Jonathan sits down and begins to chat with one of the women. He uses his photography as a means to pick up the girl. When he tells the young woman that she is photogenic and has unusual looks, she replies that her mother was Eurasian (adding that she never knew her father), but she cannot be a model because she is too short. She readily agrees to pose for Jonathan on the condition he buys her a drink first.

All of the basic elements of the global sex trade are found in this sequence: the use of Asian women's images as enticements; the sale of the exoticism of the women to white men intent on continuing a fantasy of colonial domination in a postcolonial situation; the importance of a postcolonial hybridity to these trans-actions that need to take place in English with women who are Western enough to understand how to fulfill Eurocentric male fantasies; the promise of a return to absolute male sovereignty in a land where feminism does not exist; the bar as a marketplace for Asian women; the meeting of the legitimate and unofficial economies in the bar that uses the women to push the sale of liquor; the symbiotic relationship between bar owners, hostesses, and pimps in exploiting the women at several points in the transaction; the emphasis on the marketability of the image in this exchange between photographer and potential model; and the importance of capturing and using these women and their images in transnational exchanges that bring capital into related industries ranging from pornography to travel and tourism.

In addition to circulating as prostitutes, women also act as domestic laborers in Khoo's features. Although not treated in detail like prostitution, the maid trade does appear and parallels the transnational trafficking in sex. Even though space is severely limited in the preponderance of Singaporean homes, the maid (almost always a foreign national, typically a Filipina) is a common fixture in many households. A holdover from colonialism, when an Asian maid (usually a Chinese *amah*) indicated a standard of living above what could be expected in England for many in the middle ranks of the colonial administration, the maid also indicated a higher class standing for wealthier Asian families. Although small apartments require little maintenance, the increase in households with two working parents, lack of day care, and the expectation that the elderly be cared for in the home make the added expense of a maid seem like less of a burden. Many larger flats have small separate rooms off the kitchen expressly for the maid, and some even have separate maid entrances.

Although in the past maids generally came from poorer areas of China or occasionally were poorer or unmarriageable female relations, most maids in Singapore (and, for similar reasons, in Hong Kong) are from the Philippines.[31] Because of the close control Singapore's government exercises on the ethnic balance of the nation, maids are chosen for their inability to assimilate easily into Singaporean society. However, maids must be able to communicate with em-ployers and must come from a country close enough to make travel relatively

FigURE 22. Still from *Twelve Storeys*. San San's mother, a retired amah. (Courtesy of Eric Khoo, Zhao Wei Productions.)

inexpensive and poor enough to make the wages offered seem attractive. In all cases, the Filipinas fit the bill. As Tagalog-speaking Catholics, the Filipinas are different enough to make them less attractive as potential wives; however, they speak English, because of the American colonial legacy in the Philippines, and therefore can communicate in the common language of commerce and public transactions. Also, because their culture and language is closely linked to Malaysia and Indonesia, they tend to be able to cook food palatable to most Singaporeans. As the dialogue between the two Filipina maids in *Twelve Storeys* indicates, maids often have children back home and are thus even less likely to plan on taking up long-term residence in Singapore. Large numbers of Indian, Malaysian, Indonesian, or Chinese maids, on the other hand, would threaten the ethnic balance of the country and may lead to racial unrest.

However, the existence of a maid of any national origin in cramped quarters carries its own set of social problems. Although Flor Contemplacion is only mentioned in passing in *Twelve Storeys*, her tragedy resonates throughout the film.[32] Convicted of killing a fellow Filipina maid and a young boy in her care, Contemplacion was executed in 1995 after Philippine President Fidel Ramos failed to persuade the Singaporean government to grant a stay of execution. The story shades the way in which Rachel's Philippine maid is viewed as well as the way in which San San and her mother are depicted.

Like Contemplacion, Rachel's maid must leave her family behind in the Philippines while she raises another woman's son. The warmth and affection of the relationship between the boy and the maid is indicated as they hold hands in the back seat while Rachel drives the car on their visit to San San. However, the alienation of the maid's mother from her own child is illustrated by San San's strained relationship with her mother, who favored her charge Rachel over San San while in service. Although how the sharp-tongued Cantonese maid found her way into Rachel's family's service is not explained, it seems to represent an earlier moment of the transnational circulation of labor, when during the colonial period, Chinese coolie/*ku li* (bitter labor) workers poured into Singapore to satisfy the demand for cheap labor.[33] In their essay, "Contemporary Singapore Filmmaking," Tan See-Kam, Michael Lee, and Annette Aw make a compelling case that San San's adoptive amah mother may indeed be part of a lesbian sisterhood of domestic workers who fled China to escape not only poverty but also the constraints of arranged, forced, heterosexual unions.

Rachel herself represents another aspect of diasporic displacement, because she endured an unhappy marriage to an overseas Chinese in the United States. Like the Philippine maids and the Southeast Asian prostitutes, she went abroad hoping to better herself financially or escape the confines of a closed society and encountered instead a man who, as she confides to San San, tried to treat her like a servant because of a mother that spoiled him when he was young. Like Bunny, Rachel unrealistically expects comfort, wealth, security, and liberation in the West through a liaison with a foreign man, whereas the men abroad expect Asian women to be happy in domestic bondage. The fact that Rachel ends up back in Singapore after the divorce provides a tacit commentary on fantasies of life in the West. In "Sex Machine: Global Hypermasculinity and Images of the Asian Woman in Modernity," L. H. M. Ling summarizes the conundrum for women in postcolonial Asia as follows:

> To the white master, she is a potential ally as well as a handy maid. To the Asian male Other, she vacillates from sublime mother to the white man's profane whore. Yet, the Asian female also fulfills a common function for both. Her image embodies profits and fantasy, markets and sovereignty, globalism and colonialism, East and West.[34]

THE CHINA BRIDE

As a bride, Rachel joins the ranks of women who have left Asia through marriage. In Taiwan, Hong Kong, as well as Singapore and throughout the Chinese diaspora, mainland Chinese women have filled this gap in potential brides. With the exponential increase in travel to and from the People's Republic of China since the end of the Cultural Revolution and institution of economic reforms under Deng Xiaoping, marriages between Chinese women and so-called overseas or diasporan Chinese have been on the increase. The China bride, in fact, has become a fixture in a range of comedies and romantic melodramas from Taiwan,[35] Hong Kong, and other parts of the Greater China cultural sphere. *Twelve Storeys*, along with films like *The Wedding Banquet* (1993), produces a portrait of this new cinematic type.

In certain respects, Ah Gu's desire for mainland women parallels Jonathan's lust for Asian women. Like Jonathan, Ah Gu looks for the perfect woman (i.e., conventionally attractive, feminine, submissive, domestic, and undemanding) in a location that is supposedly economically, socially, and culturally inferior. As the "stronger," more "modern" (i.e., more masculine and potent) West sees itself as naturally superior to a feminized Asia, the nation of Singapore (represented by Ah Gu) sees itself as superior to the more rural, traditional, and "backward" mainland. However, the China bride (much like Bunny) usually has a very different appreciation of her relationship to the Western or overseas Chinese male. Lili, for example, sees herself in control of the relationship because of her sexual desirability. In this respect, Lili fares better than Bunny, and Ah Gu feels he has a real treasure in the physically attractive Lili. Much like Meng, Ah Gu has a genuine belief in the Confucian patriarchy, and he takes his obligation to have children quite seriously. Although he may fraternize with the other hawkers, he spends the preponderance of his time in his flat trying to convince Lili to have sex with him.

Lili, on the other hand, has no illusions about her relationship with Ah Gu, which she sums up as economic and gender inequality in action: "Because we people from China are poor, you think you can push us around. . . . You married me because you needed a toy, and I happen to be a pretty and cheap toy." Lili compares herself to other commodities made in China, and she clearly articulates the disadvantage she experiences as coming from the mainland. However, she also attempts to take advantage of that unequal relationship as best she can. She married to better herself socially and economically. When she met Ah Gu in Beijing, she expected a thriving businessman with a good home and car, not a struggling hawker with a cramped flat and nearly defunct auto. After decades of anti-Confucian campaigns, integration into the labor force, and government-sanctioned women's liberation, Lili and her mainland Chinese sisters have little commitment to Confucian values beyond the desire for the material prosperity and security promised by a strong, affluent patriarch.

Although the liberated Lili with her string of male admirers and penchant for the latest couture may have little in common with the traditional Chinese bride, Ah Gu also falls short as an icon of Singapore's prosperity and modernity. Actually, Ah Gu, with his buckteeth (which can be read as "poor," because he does not have the money for orthodontics) and T-shirt (which can be read as "uncouth" and "working class"), has more in common with the vision of the mainland held by the Chinese abroad. Lili, on the contrary, appears as the Westernized, independent, untrustworthy, liberated woman that has soured the pool of available mates for overseas Chinese men and for whom a mainland bride should provide a cure.

Twelve Storeys devotes considerable screen time to establishing Lili as a selfish, materialistic shrew and Ah Gu as the ridiculous, masochistic, hen-pecked cuckold. Even when the couple appears in public holding hands to present the proper face to their relationship, Ah Gu's cronies intuitively know the real situation and comment that Lili will divorce as soon as she acquires permanent residence status and no longer needs Ah Gu to live and work in Singapore legally.

However, *Twelve Storeys* does not permit a simple, one-dimensional interpretation of the mainland Chinese gold digger to go uncontested. Rather, the film presents its final view of Lili at the edge of her bed with Ah Gu loudly snoring in the background. She takes out a photograph of herself in front of the Tian'anmen gate in Beijing next to a young man, wearing a red star on his cap, under the portrait of Chairman Mao. She weeps. Like many of the unexplained images and narrative fissures in *Twelve Storeys* and *Mee Pok Man*, this image resonates far beyond anything even remotely hinted at in the narrative. Although a romantic interest may be assumed between Lili and the young man, nothing is stated. The sunny day and dispositions of the couple in the photograph point to happier times; however, the sheer volume in the composition devoted to Mao and the gate may conjure up the carefully censored news items involving Tian'anmen in 1989.[36] Questions surrounding why Lili needed to leave Beijing become more complicated, and affairs of the heart and pocketbook take on an implicitly political dimension.

This image may conjure up a range of emotions and thoughts in Singapore. Very simply, it could be read as a direct confirmation that Lili's true love is not Ah Gu, and her heart is miles away. Another interpretation could take the allegorical significance of that a step further by confirming the suspicion that mainland émigrés really do not owe allegiance to Singapore but continue to picture themselves in the People's Republic.

However, given *Twelve Storeys*' critique of Singaporean society generally, other possibilities seem as likely. Lee Kuan Yew, throughout his political career, has had a love-hate relationship with the People's Republic and with Communism. Stan Stesser, for example, notes that Singapore's "authoritarian government functions in many ways like that of a Communist state yet is dedicated wholeheartedly to the pursuit of capitalism."[37] When Lee's PAP,[38] came to power on a vehemently anticolonial platform, the government modeled itself on many aspects of socialism while viciously suppressing the Communist Party out of a dual fear of losing Western capital pouring in from the multinationals and of coming too closely under the control of mainland China. Lee carefully positioned newly independent Singapore between capitalism and communism by reviving a Confucian trust in authority and obligation. After the end of the Cultural Revolution and the death of Mao, Singapore, Japan, and most of the West warmed toward the reformers in the People's Republic. These countries coveted the gigantic market potential and cheap labor of the mainland.

The relationship, like Ah Gu and Lili's marriage, however, has not been totally blissful. The image of Mao and the Tian'anmen gate conjures up, particularly after 1989, feelings of loss, terror, and confusion, that link Mao, Deng Xiaoping (a close personal and political ally of Lee), and Lee Kuan Yew together. The photo seems to be nostalgic, alluding to both the romance of halcyon youth and the stability of a potent political authority. However, this double loss of love and political certainty also seems tainted by Singapore's own record of political oppression indirectly linked to the bloody events in Beijing. Personal sentiments and governmental actions become intertwined, and political uncertainty is associated with the decay of the patriarchy, the unhappy consequences of women's independence, and a deterioration of the Confucian order.

Within the postfeminist universe of *Mee Pok Man* and *Twelve Storeys*, the economic liberation of women; their increasing ability to move away from the familial sphere of father, elder brother, and husband; and their expression of personal desire does not equal freedom from patriarchal restraint.[39] Meng and Bunny fall victim to the last desperate gasps of the sexual excesses of the patriarchy. Lili suffocates in a marriage of convenience, and San San does not stand a chance in a system in which physical appearance means everything. Although a feminist modernity may have promised equality within the public and domestic spheres, Khoo's films underscore the dissipation of the opposing promises of the Confucian patriarchy and the international women's movement. Both fail the films' struggling female characters, just as the promise of modernity is revealed as a sham for the nation as a whole.

Chinese Ghost Stories

Ghosts, apparitions, and visions of various sorts are common in the Khoo universe, as they are in many other postmodern fictions (e.g., David Lynch's *Twin Peaks*, 1990). Many Western filmgoers are more familiar with the cinematic ghosts found in Hong Kong popular films like the Tsui Hark–produced *A Chinese Ghost Story* series (1987–91; animated version, 1997) and Stanley Kwan's *Rouge* (a clip of which is included in *Twelve Storeys*). However, Khoo's ghosts operate somewhat differently as part of the quotidian lives of the characters in *Mee Pok Man* and *Twelve Storeys*. The ghost is a familiar figure (e.g., a loved one) who becomes transformed by death into something ghastly (e.g., a corpse). After Bunny's death, for example, the mee pok man transforms her from a flashy prostitute by replacing her scanty black evening dress with a housedress he has fashioned from the apartment's curtains. Domesticated, Bunny is relegated to the kitchen, permanently immobile, and totally under a man's tutelage; however, because Bunny is a corpse, the mee pok man's necrophilia takes his desire to possess her into the realm of the grotesque. The patriarchal impulse to rescue the fallen woman and reinsert her into an idealized, male-dominated domestic sphere becomes a perverse vision of desire out of control.

As the interior and the exterior psyche dissolve in what Jameson has labeled the schizophrenia characteristic of postmodern existence, ghosts and other liminal figures insinuate themselves into the daily lives of the characters inhabiting an otherwise conventionally realist diegetic universe. As the generic breakdown of postmodern texts enables the merger of horror, science fiction, comedy, romance, soft-core pornography, gore, and the domestic melodrama in Khoo's fiction, the psychic fragmentation of the postmodern subject makes the appearance of ghosts and other supernatural and/or delusional visions unremarkable.

These visions make any feeling of a common reality problematic. Who sees what and when becomes questionable, and Khoo casts the viewer adrift in a world in which vision veers far from truth or certainty. This is particularly striking in the case of San San and her mother in *Twelve Storeys*. *Twelve Storeys* takes place during the course of a single day within the immediate vicinity of a single apartment block. As the narrative enfolds, San San calls her mother's old charge, Rachel, to give her a package her mother willed to her. Although the mother has been sitting in the flat up to this point, San San's call to Rachel breaks the spell, and it becomes clear that San San's mother has been dead the entire time. What had been taken for granted about the abusive relationship between mother and daughter now comes into question. Is San San's mother's haranguing really San San's own voice of inadequacy and regret? Was the mother really this bad, or is San San exaggerating her abuse? Does Rachel have a point when she says that San San's mother was a *hao ren*, a good person?

Some of these narrative lacunae can be explained by referring to Chinese ghost stories and lore surrounding the dead, whereas other aspects remain unexplained idiosyncrasies of these two films. For example, from a Western perspective, the ghost of the young man who committed suicide, the ghost of the mee pok man's father, and the ghost of San San's mother would all operate on the same supernatural plane, and they would be assumed to be malevolent until proven conclusively otherwise. However, within Chinese mythology, the spirits of ancestors (e.g., San San's mother, mee pok man's father) would be perceived of as qualitatively different from the ghost of the young suicide victim. In fact, the English word *ghost* really is not appropriate to the position these spirits occupy as ancestors, whereas the distance implied by the word *ancestor* in English does not really fit the intimate link these spirits have to their progeny.[40] According to Chinese cosmology, dead or alive, ancestors are ancestors and should be accorded filial respect. They can still take an active interest in their descendents' lives and must be given the same attention granted to them while they were still among the living.

Although it may seem peculiar from a Western perspective and a little old-fashioned in Chinese thinking, the mee pok man's daily breakfast ritual of offering an egg and a lit cigarette to the photographic portrait of his stern father exists within the realm of proper filial obeisance. When the mee pok man's father's ghost pays a visit and sits in the kitchen chair recently occupied by Bunny's corpse, he seems to be taking account of what is going on under his roof, because the mee pok man's affair with a corpse will produce no progeny. Similarly, San San's mother's spirit seems out of line with her continuous harangues; however, she does seem to have a point when her own inability to raise a daughter suitable for marriage is taken into account. This is a black mark against any spirit given the task of producing sons to carry on a family name and, if that proves impossible, at least seeing to it that a daughter will be dutiful and fit to move into another household.

When looked at from this perspective, any sympathy for the mee pok man or San San must be linked to their potential rebellion against Confucian authority. The possibility emerges that the mee pok man may be perfectly happy with an unproductive corpse and that San San may want to escape the confines of the patriarchy. However, the mee pok man may simply be a tragic victim of fate and star-crossed romance, and San San may be suicidal because she cannot live up to her mother's expectations. The narrative provides both options, and it is impossible to determine if the conservative or the transgressive reading is favored.

This becomes even more apparent when San San's mother and the mee pok man's father are contrasted with the young suicide. Of all the supernatural entities that people these two films, this suicide is the only one that would be considered a genuine ghost within Chinese cosmology. Because he died without progeny and visits living beings with whom he has no blood relation, he must be classified differently from the others who have the parental authority to haunt their children. The young man represents the type of spirit that can cause the most trouble. Always hungry because they do not have progeny to feed them as the mee pok man dutifully offers food to his dead father, these rogue ghosts can bother the living if they are not occasionally appeased by the odd offering at the roadside or during the annual Hungry Ghost Festival.

However, in *Twelve Storeys*, this unnamed ghost brings with his unmotivated suicide a number of issues that resonate within Chinese cosmology in ways that differ dramatically from Western traditions. Historically, suicides in Chinese culture have been identified with public acts of defiance and protest. Women forced into unwanted, arranged marriages or victims of domestic abuse saw suicide as not only a personal way out of an impossible situation but a public statement against the excesses of the patriarchal system. Certainly, the best-known suicide in Chinese history involves the patriot Qu Yuan, who threw himself into a river because he was so frustrated with the poor government of his ruler. The annual Dragon Boat Festival celebrates this act as dragon boats symbolically race to save his body from hungry fish and *zong zi* (wrapped packages of glutinous rice) thrown into the river appease sea creatures that would otherwise nibble on his corpse.

Like Qu Yuan, Khoo's unnamed suicide seems to be generally fed up with Singaporean society. The young man's mother and Meng speculate that romantic difficulties are behind his drastic act. However, the film remains silent on the exact motivation, allowing the suicide to be caused by everything generally and/or nothing at all in particular. It can be interpreted as a nihilistic act of self-destruction or as the ultimate critique of a corrupt society. Like the hard-core punk music the young man listens to before he dies, the roots of his malaise may be a very personal self-destructive impulse or a very political, public rebellion against a society that gave him few options.

Extratextually, the ghost is linked to Khoo himself. Like Khoo, the ghost surrounds himself with GI Joe dolls (alluding to Khoo's early short *Barbie Digs Joe*, 1990) and the shots of comic books and cartoon characters like Mickey Mouse seem to allude to Khoo's own penchant for animation. Like Khoo, who comes from a privileged family of well-to-do hoteliers, the young man is an outsider in the building, a new arrival whose wealthy family purchased the flat to appease their son's desire for his own apartment. However, the suicide is also the consummate insider, able to penetrate into every crevice. Like Khoo, the ghost remains a mute presence that simply uses his eyes, as Khoo uses his camera, to point to and point out what must be assumed to be most abominable. The ghost, like the filmmaker, is the ultimate voyeur, privy to the private lives of the characters he scrutinizes. Given the censorship regulations governing filmmaking in Singapore, Khoo and his suicidal avatar must remain mute. Critique lies in what is only glimpsed, the liminal, the proper realm of the ghost.

Just as the viewer may speculate on the symbolic significance of the suicide in relation to Qu Yuan or Eric Khoo, the young man becomes an object of intense speculation in the narrative. Following the folk superstition that sees a link between sudden death and the ability to predict the future, a taxi driver quickly jots down all the numbers associated with the fresh corpse. As he chats with his cronies at an outdoor food stall, he decides to play the number of the floor from which the young man jumped and his age. They all agree to exorcise his ghost after they hit the lottery jackpot. The folk behaviors surrounding the young man's death may seem odd to those outside Chinese society; however, stories of taxi drivers and truckers winning big with numbers based on the license plates of cars involved in fatal crashes are the stuff of urban legends throughout the Chinese diaspora.

It is important to note, too, that speculation on the suicide brings diverse characters together as a community. The fact that so many of the characters in the film find the suicide fascinating, and beyond that somehow identify with the young man's desire to die, seems to move this speculation beyond the narrative exigency, which attempts to link three separate plotlines into a single narrative and into the realm of social critique. For example, Meng discusses the suicide with Trixie and their younger brother Tee (Roderick Lim) by referring to government statistics, but Tee identifies silently with the young suicide to the point of lying down in the blood stain left after the corpse is removed. Ah Gu literally speculates on the death by arranging with the taxi driver and his cronies to purchase the lottery ticket. The young man's parents are left to speculate as to the reasons behind the suicide because his father insists he was a good son who "knew how to make money," thus, with no reason to feel out of step within Singapore's booming and often cutthroat economy. The viewer, too, can join this fictional community and be drawn into that mechanism of the discourse that invites speculation and critical thought beyond that which is actually directly expressed within the narrative. However, the fictional world of ghosts also safely distances the viewer from any danger that too sharp a critique may evoke.

Twelve Storeys ends with an extreme close-up of San San's eye intercut with the abstract pattern of the HDB building. A blank screen with the child Bunny's voice promising to listen to teacher and do better in school concludes *Mee Pok Man*. In both cases, these endings say more by eerie implication than by actual articulation. San San merges with the HDB flat as the stricken soul of Singapore, still on the verge of suicide, and the child Bunny pathetically places her faith in the educational system that tragically failed her. The housing project and the school represent two of the principal institutions of governmental control over the lives of Singaporeans, and these films' implicit critique of the failure of the promise of modernity embodied by those institutions haunts the final moments of these films like a ghost.

CONCLUSION

Like Singapore itself, Khoo's films seem positioned on the crossroads of global traffic in people, images, cultures, and capital. They thrive on the indeterminacy of the postmodern condition and the hybridity of postcolonialism. His films are local favorites and the emblem of an emerging national cinema while they vigorously critique the very foundations of that PAP-defined identity. While laying claim to a peculiar local Singaporean flavor, they are also transnational products able to appeal to Western tastes for the exotic and a Chinese diasporic sense of connection though language, ethnicity, and a common history. They acknowledge resistance, embodied by hip representatives of GenerAsian X, but playfully pull back from any direct commitment to social or political change. By delving into the depths of Singapore's postmodern condition, Khoo's features find themselves in the thick of a global film culture that thrives on instantaneous images, ephemeral style, indeterminate meanings, dark humor, impenetrable surfaces, self-referentiality, and intertextuality where Singapore's marginal postcolonial position takes center stage in current cinematic practice.

Interview with Eric Khoo

How did you get involved in filmmaking?

Actually, it has a lot to do with my mother. When I was a little boy, she would bring me to the cinema, and that got me hooked, probably around the age of three. When I first started shooting, it was with her camera, a little Super 8 Canon camera. I was probably about eight years old, and I did a lot of stop-motion films with GI Joe and Barbie dolls. As a little boy I also drew a lot, so it was another way of getting my stories across.

When I was about thirteen, I had dreams of being a filmmaker. I wanted very much to do a full-length film before I was thirty years old. I studied at the City Art Institute in Sydney, which is in New South Wales, and I got my bachelor of arts degree in cinematography there. I had to come back to Singapore for my national service [all young men in Singapore must perform some sort of national service—typically, a stint in the army], which was two and a half years. After that, I thought about going to Columbia University to get a graduate degree in film directing. I was accepted to Columbia, but my parents were not too keen on the idea.

I started by doing corporate videos for TVCs [Singapore's television corpo-ration], and, in my free time, I began making short films. I have to thank the Singapore International Film Festival, because, around 1990, the festival started the short film competition section. I submitted a little work called *August,* and it won the top prize that year. Every year I submitted entries into the short film category, and I won quite a few awards. My films started taking off from there to go to international festivals around the world. The first one was Hawaii with *Barbie Digs Joe.*

When I ultimately did my full-length feature *Mee Pok Man*, the festival circuits were already quite familiar with my name because of my short films. Because of this, my first feature was programmed in over thirty film festivals. After *Mee Pok Man*, Brink Creative and Springroll, a subsidiary of Pony Canyon, approached me. Under Pony Canyon, Jimmy Wee had been pushing for local music to succeed in Singapore. James Toh, one of the directors of Brink, wanted very much to produce Chinese plays and journey into film production. Therefore, I had financing, but no script. I struggled for a couple of months trying to think of ideas. At the end of 1995, I had this idea about doing a film that would happen within the course of a day and within a block. It took about nine months to come up with a satisfying draft. James Toh was really on board for the script. He wrote a lot of creative short essays while he was in school. He passed me a few of his short stories, and I was really very impressed.

It was very interesting how we got the ideas for *Twelve Storeys*. We were constantly reading the *Straits Times*, and we got a lot of information from their

FIGURE 23. Photo of director Eric Khoo. (Courtesy of Eric Khoo, Zhao Wei Productions.)

statistics, and we threw into the film things that young Singaporeans did not know about especially their history. We gave the actors a lot of freedom during the preproduction rehearsals. We used a VHS camera to record what they were doing. Because there are three story lines, the actors only read their parts, their stories. During rehearsals, they came up with a lot of lines that were just so amazing that we eventually put those lines from rehearsal into the script. I did say to them, if possible, I did not want any improvisations during shooting, because we were working with a shoestring budget of $300,000 Singapore dollars. Once you start making mistakes and the camera starts chewing up the film stock, you are dead. Our shooting ratio was about three to one, and we had calculated for six to one, so I was very pleased. We shot it within fifteen days.

When you go into an area of about 750 square feet with ten people and lights, it is a squeeze. That was one of the reasons why we decided to shoot on Super 16 mm, which uses a smaller format camera. I was very interested in the framing of the film. I wanted a lot of talking heads. I suggested that, for the brother/sister story, we employ two cameras, so that their scenes could be filmed in one or two takes. In fact, quite a few of the scenes were done in just one take. For example, the brother and the sister's big confrontation scene was done in just one take, but with two cameras.

How does Twelve Storeys *differ from* Mee Pok Man*? Did you conceive of it for a different audience?*

Twelve Storeys is more satiric. It is a very black comedy. *Mee Pok Man* is really a love story about two main protagonists, and you really get under their skin. However, the last half hour with the corpse in the apartment turning blue does offend people. These things do happen, though. I know this social worker. She goes from home to home on a weekly basis just to make sure that families are surviving, and she gives them food or whatever. On one visit to an elderly couple's home, she got out of the lift, and she smelled this horrendous stench. The main door was ajar, and there was this lady sitting on the bed with her dead husband who had passed away four days before. She said he was as blue as the blue corpse in the film.

More recently, in a newspaper, I read about this lady in Hong Kong who kept her husband for three years. She threatened her kids, so they just kept quiet. For me, that is the ultimate love. It is definitely a very strange sort of thing to want to keep a corpse. If you cannot let that go, you must be really madly in love.

How did you do the research for Mee Pok Man?

I was supposed to illustrate these horror short stories done by a friend, Damien Sin—really gruesome, horrible, wonderful stuff. I kept thinking of one particular story that was in his anthology series, "One Last Cold Kiss." It was about a mortuary attendant who falls in love with a fresh corpse, brings it back home, and has a relationship with it. I thought why not use that as an idea and make it more local. So, I have a food vendor fall in love with a prostitute. I decided to call it *Mee Pok Man*, because mee pok is a flat noodle that I like a lot. He has been in love with her ever since he was a child, and she does not know that. Within a week, we had the first draft. Second week, the script was completed, and, the third week, we did the rehearsals. It just happened very quickly.

How did you get the idea of constructing the character of Bunny through her diaries?

When you look at a prostitute you think of her as once having been a baby, having been a virgin, and now she is what she is. A lot of girls here want to escape, go to the West, and have a better life. They are dreamers. Although Bunny has made sure that her family has food on the table, she has her own aspirations. She wants to date a Westerner in order to escape. Rather than to say prostitutes are the scum of the Earth, I wanted to show that they can be good people, too. They feel, and they love. To me, the mee pok man is someone who is very rare in this society, because you no longer find people who care so much and in such a sincere manner. Most people are just really in the game for selfish reasons. Here are two people that nobody cares about, but, to me, they are very real and good. In that sense, they may be kindred souls.

Twelve Storeys is about Singapore's grass roots. Eighty percent of Singaporeans live in the satellite towns. We wanted to capture a block that was built in the late '60s, early '70s. If you really want to talk about Singapore, you need to focus on the "heartlands" in the Housing Development Board (HDB) flats. I think some viewers see the film and say, "Finally, my living room is up on screen."

In the case of *Twelve Storeys*, we had a lot of different characters. We thought it would be interesting to have very different types of characters and to have the pacing much faster than *Mee Pok Man*. Also, the framing is different because of the number of cuts.

Mee Pok Man got the RA rating, but I was worried that we would have to make deletions. Fortunately, there were no cuts. After that, I wanted to do something that was going to get the PG rating. We went to visit the Board of Film Censors [BFC]. Initially, we told them what we had in mind, and, when we were doing the script, we were also censoring ourselves to a certain degree. When we finally finished *Twelve Storeys*, we had the rough cut on video, and I submitted it to the BFC, and I told them I wanted to send it to Australia for the negative cut. They told me it will be RA with no deletions, PG with deletions. Basically, they did not like one scene with these tough guys talking in a coffee shop. It was only thirty seconds, and it did not really hurt the film if we took it out, so we cut it out. After some discussions they let me keep the other scenes they initially objected to. We wanted it to be PG because, since it was a film about a block, we wanted to try and play the satellite towns, and those halls cannot show RA films. We wanted teenagers and students to be able to see it in Singapore.

In this film, I felt for the characters. Maybe some translate better to a Western market audience than others. The only place I saw it abroad was Cannes, and I was happy with the audience reaction. There were two screenings, which were full. I was very surprised because they laughed at parts that I wanted them to laugh at, and it was all with just subtitles. So, that was good. I have been overwhelmed by the positive reaction of people who have seen it so far.

I think that the press has also given the film a lot of attention. So much so, the film is still packing the halls. In our first week, we had maximum screenings of about five screening times per hall. Because of all the prior commitments that had been made to 20th Century Fox and Columbia, we were only given that one week. The next week our halls fell from five screens to maybe two or one at a three o'clock slot, but it had to be done this way. It is sad, because, when you look at the numbers, the first week was very big, but, by slashing down the halls the following week, attendance numbers were cut in half. Because of this, I feel the film didn't do as well as it could have.

If your budget is over a million, it is very difficult to recoup. With $300,000, it is okay. Also, we are trying to get French, British, and Japanese distribution. Television and video have been confirmed for Singapore. I am also thinking about the U.S. markets, particularly Chinatowns, and maybe straight to video. I do not really want this to go to the art house cinemas in the U.S., because small fringe movies hardly make a cent. I think that this one has a broader appeal if you are an Asian living abroad, because you will be able to understand English, Mandarin, and some of the Chinese dialects. Australia is another market that I am thinking about. There is also interest in trying to distribute the film in Taiwan, Hong Kong, and Malaysia.

I think it is really what is in the contract that matters. Miramax, for instance, bought Ann Hui's *Summer Snow*. They acquired the rights a year and a half or two years ago, and they have not released it, because, when they did their homework, they realized that by spending so much on advertising they will end up in the red. That film will never see the light of day. America is a difficult market to penetrate. Zhang Yimou's *Shanghai Triad* and Chen Kaige's *Temptress Moon* did not do well at all.

Why do you think that is the case?

The U.S. film [industry] is taking over—better effects, better entertainment value for the same price ticket. After a while you cannot fool the locals anymore. The U.S. films are going to reign supreme. In America, action-packed films or very subtle films with tiny budgets, like *Sling Blade* [1996], *Lone Star* [1996], or *Fargo* [1996] see a profit.

With those factors in mind when doing *Twelve Storeys*, we tried to have as tight a budget as possible. We hope to recoup domestically, because it is not certain where else it can be sold. France and Japan are really a bonus. Given this, I think Singapore can carry on making two or three films a year at most, and I believe those films will be good films. Still, this is definitely not what the Economic Development Board [EDB] had in mind when they were trying to woo over the Hong Kong film business because of 1997. The Hong Kongers were a lot smarter; they went to China.

Do you think that your production company, Zhao Wei, will become more of a production house? Or do you think it will produce only your films?

I would eventually like to produce films. I might do one more full-length feature, then, I would like to be like George Lucas and just produce. I feel that we do have a lot of talented people in Singapore. If given the opportunity and some guidance, they will be able to do something. Right now, I have a few people in mind that I would definitely like to work with as young film directors. I think they can definitely go far. One of the hardest things is getting a good script that the director is comfortable with. A lot of our young filmmakers are also writers. It is an added plus, because they know exactly what they want. Some of the new, young students, who submitted their works to the short film competition this year are very good.

I think we are still lacking a bit in technical expertise, however. There are only about ten people who can fully operate a 35mm camera in Singapore. Lighting is another issue, since many of the directors of photography work in television or still photography.

How do you place your films within the context of Asian film in general?

My first two features are very Singaporean. They are about urban survival. When you look at *Twelve Storeys,* for example, you would not feel that it is a Hong Kong film. Language is very important. In *Mee Pok Man*, we threw in lots of dialects because that is really how Singaporeans speak. Some gestures also are distinctly Singaporean. Still, we do not really have much of a culture because the country is very young. We are really a youthful, pop-culture city. I do not think Asian values are really here at all. I think we just want to have fun and it shows, given the number of entertainment areas here.

When I was doing *Mee Pok Man*, one of my brothers-in-law, who is Swiss-French, was here to stay for a couple of months. He knows Orchard Road and the downtown area. I needed a driver, so I asked him to help me out. For a couple of nights, he drove us to all the areas that we were shooting in, and he could not believe that these places existed in Singapore.

Would you call your films political?

The *Asian Wall Street Journal* calls *Twelve Storeys* a "political film," and I said, "No, it's not. It's just a slice of life." I want to make films you can go and experience, and maybe go home and try to think a bit more about it. I do not want to do something that is just totally black or white. I like to have a lot of gray area, and, then, you can work it out yourself, and it is up to your own interpretation. I am interested in human beings and how they try to communicate.

What type of government support exists to encourage filmmaking in Singapore?

The National Arts Council [NAC] has been in existence for many years. However, they only recently began to view film as an art form. That is a good step forward. We also asked them to create a film commission here, but I think they are not that keen on it right now. (The Singapore Film Commission was set up in 1998 and became part of the Media Development Authority in 2003). The problem with making films is that it costs a lot of money. Theater, for example, is less expensive. For the last fifteen years [prior to mid-1997], stage plays have had a lot of government support. Eventually, they may help film a little more. I feel that film is more important than the theater because it can travel a lot further. It is the mass medium of this century.

Do you see yourself working in television more in the future?

If given the right budget, I would tackle television. Television reaches out to a lot of people, and I do want to communicate. I love *The Twilight Zone* [1959–65]—the black and white television show. It was on television here for the last couple of months, so I have been recording every episode. It is just incredible. Good story, good lighting—all done within twenty-four minutes.

Do you have any ambitions to make any films outside of Singapore?

If there is an opportunity and if I like the script, I will consider it. I was offered a project in China, but I do not know enough about China, and I would not take the risk.

I think that for anyone who wants to make films it is a struggle anywhere; you have to believe in yourself.

July 3, 1997

II. Identities in Question: The Chinese Diaspora

6 Transnational Cinema and Hybrid Identities: *To Liv(e)* and *Crossings*

BORN IN MAINLAND CHINA, bred in Macao, educated in Hong Kong and the United States, Evans Chan, currently based in New York City, makes independent narrative films primarily for a Hong Kong, overseas Chinese, "Greater China" audience. Chan's films straddle the gulf between the international art film circuit and Hong Kong commercial cinema, attracting art film viewers worldwide.[1] Because of his particular position in global film culture, Chan's first two features, *To Liv(e)* (1991) and *Crossings* (1994), have been able to openly address issues that find only a marginal voice in the mainstream cinema of Hong Kong and the United States.

In *To Liv(e)*, Rubie (Lindzay Chan) lives in Hong Kong with her artist boyfriend, John (Fung Kin Chung). In December 1989, Rubie becomes angered by a statement made by Liv Ullmann about the inhumane treatment of Vietnamese refugees by the Hong Kong authorities.[2] In the wake of the events in Beijing that June, Rubie questions Ullmann's timing in a letter she composes and addresses to the Scandinavian actress. Passages from the letter punctuate the rest of the film as Rubie must decide, along with members of her family and circle of Hong Kong friends, whether to stay or leave Hong Kong before July 1, 1997.

Rubie's brother Tony (Wong Yiu-Ming) prepares to immigrate to Australia with his fiancée, Teresa (Josephine Ku). Teresa, however, has mixed feelings about the departure and about her relationship with Tony. Older, divorced, and estranged from her son, Teresa is prone to morbid thoughts and depression. Because Tony and Rubie's parents dislike her, Teresa fears losing the younger Tony to another woman. The stormy relationship comes to a head when Tony threatens suicide after a jealous scene at a party.

Crossings also deals with questions of immigration; however, in this film, the narrative focuses on the plight of the Hong Kong émigrés in New York City.[3] In this case, a red shoe, symbol of romantic happiness and the joys of marriage in traditional Chinese lore, is all that remains of Mo-Yung (Anita Yuen), a victim of a stalker's violence on a subway platform. Mo-Yung had come to New York, against her parents' wishes and illegally, to pursue her boyfriend, Benny (Simon Yam). She thinks Benny is a photographer, but he is actually an international drug smuggler. Pursuing Benny, Mo-Yung rubs against the seamy elements of New York as she unsuspectingly plays cat-and-mouse with a shipment of Benny's contraband. In "Small Triumphs: The New Asian Woman in American Cinema," Marina Heung notes:

FIGURE 24. Still from *To Liv(e)*. Rubie (Lindzay Chan) and her artist boyfriend John (Fung Kin Chung) look toward an uncertain future in Hong Kong. (Courtesy of Evans Chan, Riverdrive Productions.)

> Mo-yung's arrival embroils her in a nexus of sexual and racial tensions emblematic of life in contemporary America. For her, New York is an ominous place charged with the swirl of political cross-currents to which she is oblivious. Mo-yung's sojourn ultimately makes her an unwitting victim of a drama driven by the impersonal forces of racial and gender bias.[4]

Rubie (Lindzay Chan), in this narrative a social worker in New York, befriends Mo-Yung. Joey (Ted Brunetti), a psychotic schoolteacher with a fetish for Asian women, stalks Rubie, whom he has seen as a community spokeswoman on television. Mistaking Mo-Yung for Rubie, he kills Mo-Yung.

DETERMINING INDETERMINACY

With one foot in the United States and the other in Hong Kong, Chan can freely address topics as diverse as Hong Kong's return to China, the legacy of June 4 in Tian'anmen Square, the role of women in the world economy (in both the official financial system and the informal sector, which can include prostitutes and traffickers in narcotics), and the processes of immigration and dispersal involving the Chinese globally in his films. Although fears of censorship arising from Hong

FIGURE 25. Still from *To Liv(e)*. Rubie with her brother, Tony (Wong Yiu-Ming). (Photos this page courtesy of Evans Chan, Riverdrive Productions.)

FIGURE 26. Still from *To Liv(e)*. Involved with an older woman, Tony has trouble coming to grips with his future.

Kong's laws and the unofficial censorship of the marketplace in the United States place a boundary around what can and cannot be said in the cinema, Chan, with his transnational production team, manages to seriously explore controversial topics. In this way, Chan creates a transnational, transcultural discourse through the medium of the motion picture, pointing to a new type of cultural sphere that moves through and beyond Greater China.[5]

In *The Geopolitical Aesthetic: Cinema and Space in the World System*, Fredric Jameson notes that Edward Yang's *Terrorizer* (1986) is poised between the modern and the postmodern:

> What we must admire, therefore, is the way in which the filmmaker has arranged for these two powerful interpretative temptations—the modern and the postmodern, subjectivity and textuality—to neutralize each other, to hold each other in one long suspension in such a way that the film can exploit and draw on the benefits of both, without having to commit itself to either as some definitive reading, or as some definitive formal and stylistic category. Besides Edward Yang's evident personal mastery, the possibility of this kind of mutually reinforcing suspension may owe something to the situation of Third-World cinema itself, in traditions in which neither modernist nor postmodern impulses are internally generated, so that both arrive in the field of production with a certain chronological simultaneity in full post-war modernization.[6]

To Liv(e) and *Crossings* can also be seen as works suspended between the modern and the postmodern; indeed, their textual strategies rely on this deeply rooted indeterminacy to explore people and issues that are themselves difficult to pin down.

Like Yang, Chan is profoundly influenced by European cinema. The English title, *To Liv(e)*, for example, conjures up both Godard and Gorin's *Letter to Jane* (1972) as well as Ingmar Bergman's many works with Liv Ullmann. Chan characterizes the film as "inevitably a response to both Bergman and Godard."[7] In her insightful essay on the film, "The Aesthetics of Protest: Evans Chan's *To Liv(e)*," Patricia Brett Erens outlines the various ways in which the film draws on Godard.[8] Erens observes that *To Liv(e)* favors an aesthetic sensibility rooted in a Brechtian tradition of dramatic distance and political engagement.

Peter Wollen's approach to Godard's political films as "counter-cinema" can be used here to elucidate this legacy in both *To Liv(e)* and *Crossings*.[9] *To Liv(e)* is organized around a series of letters addressed to Liv Ullmann. The impact of Godard is clearly apparent in the scene in which Rubie reads her first letter to Liv. Over a shot of boats used as a transitional device, the tinny, hollow sound of a recording of Cui Jian's "Nothing to My Name" comes up on the soundtrack. The camera pans across an audience; Rubie is seated in the auditorium. A dance performance, "Exhausted Silkworms," inspired by the events of June 4 takes place on stage. Three male dancers, dressed simply in white shirts and black pants, tear their clothes to form gags and later nooses. One dancer pulls a red scarf out of his shirt like spurting blood. As "Nothing to My Name" ends, one dancer falls, as if shot. Suspended for a moment with a freeze frame, he finally lands on the ground, as the audience applauds.

FIGURE 27. Still from *Crossings*. Mo-Yung (Anita Yuen) finds herself alone, searching for her missing boyfriend. (Courtesy of Evans Chan, Riverdrive Productions.)

As the dancers perform, Rubie's voiceover address to Liv Ullmann (and, through her, to the world at large) adds another dimension to both Cui Jian's rock music, which says nothing explicit about "democracy" or politics at all (for more on Cui Jian and Tian'anmen Square, see Chapter 9), and to the performers' reenactment of the Tian'anmen demonstration and its suppression. As the dancers act out this violence, accompanied by Cui Jian's harsh and direct vocals, Rubie likens Liv Ullmann to a respected, distant portrait that comes to life and slaps her in the face with accusations of cruelty and indifference. Rubie not only complains of Ullmann's ignorance about the Hong Kong situation that her statement about the Vietnamese displays but also questions her timing. Speaking just months after Tian'anmen, an event that was taken by many in Hong Kong as a barometer of what to expect after 1997, Rubie reminds Ullmann that the population of Hong Kong may soon find themselves in the same boat, so to speak, as the Vietnamese.

In this scene, two visual planes collide. One features Rubie as the originator of the letter. Close-ups of her face accompany the voiceover presentation of the contents of the letter, grounding the letter in the person of Rubie as a fictional character. The other visual plane, using the same images, features Rubie as a spectator, clearly moved by the dance performance. There are also two audio planes: Cui Jian's music and the sounds of the auditorium on one plane, and Rubie's voiceover letter to Liv on the other. In this fragmented presentation of narrative information, all the elements of counter-cinema come into play. Narrative intransitivity comes to the fore in the casual introduction of an evening at the

FIGURE 28. Still from *To Liv(e)*. Teresa (Josephine Ku) and Tony. (Courtesy of Evans Chan, Riverdrive Productions.)

theater for Rubie's character; time is thrown out of synch because Rubie writes the letter heard in the voiceover at another time and in another place away from the theater. There is an estrangement from the character of Rubie as she becomes a mouthpiece for the people of Hong Kong, addressing an actual person about actual events, in addition to being a fictional character involved in other plot developments. Her address is not to other fictional characters, but to Liv, and to the world at large represented by the film audience. Foregrounding occurs as the film spectators are invited to see themselves as witnesses to the dance performance, and, by extension, the events in Tian'anmen, and think of themselves, with Rubie, as something more than spectators. Watching Rubie look at a political work of art foregrounds *To Liv(e)*'s own status as a similar work of political commentary.

The diegesis splits, featuring a self-contained performance piece within the film. Aperture encourages engagement, because an understanding of the references in the dance depends on a familiarity with the mass media spectacle of June 4, including photos of the demonstrators standing together in the square, Cui Jian's presence, and so on. The unpleasure of the breaking of classical conventions is self-evident, as is the nonfictional basis of the entire scene as a commentary on actual events—the expulsion of the Vietnamese, Ullmann's trip to Hong Kong and public condemnation of Hong Kong's action, the events of June 4 in Tian'anmen, and so on. Fictional and nonfictional realms overlap.

FIGURE 29. Still from *To Liv(e)*. Tony's fiancée, Teresa, wrestles with her own demons and doubts about their engagement. (Courtesy of Evans Chan, Riverdrive Productions.)

However, it would be wrong to conclude that *To Liv(e)* is simply an imitation of Godard. Another element in the scene takes the film in a radically different direction. While Rubie is presented as an agent addressing Ullmann, a spokesperson for Hong Kong, and a spectator of a dance piece (and, by extension, a political event), she is also depicted as distracted. Near the beginning of the scene, she looks at her watch and looks around the auditorium. In fact, Rubie is waiting for her brother, Tony. Rubie's relationship with her brother, his fiancée, and her family propels the film into another, totally different arena, that is, the realm of the love story and family melodrama. Rubie may be the voice of Hong Kong, but she also plays the roles of daughter, sister, lover, and friend in other parts of the narrative. Her distraction as a character points to a more general "distraction" found within the narrative itself. To echo Jameson, the "textuality" of counter-cinema meets the "subjectivity" of the melodrama, the "woman's film," and the love story.

There is a similar sense of distraction in *Crossings*. Although less directly indebted to the European New Wave, *Crossings* still bears the marks of cinematic modernism. Again, fiction and nonfiction overlap as actual footage of Tian'anmen 1989 is cut into newscasts in which fictional characters appear. Dance presentations divide the diegesis further into self-contained narrative realms. Characters function as mouthpieces for policies or ideas as well as fictional creations involved in the plot. Rubie (again played by Lindzay Chan) reappears to serve this function, turning up on New York TV as the public voice of the Chinatown community and, through voiceover excerpts from a diary, as the personal voice of the Hong Kong emigrant. However, although *To Liv(e)* has more clearly demarcated divisions between the various layers of the discourse, *Crossings,* closer to Yang's *Terrorizer* and other works of the Taiwanese and Hong Kong New Wave, experiments with time and space to a much larger degree. Distraction, in fact, becomes disorientation, because it is often difficult to know whether the location is New York or Hong Kong.

In one scene, for example, Mo-Yung has just finished a meeting with Rubie in Central Park. She walks past a shop window displaying a model airliner. The film cuts to a shot of clouds passing over the moon, followed by a graphic match on a toilet bowl. Mo-Yung is vomiting (an indication she may be pregnant). Members of her family come back from a shopping trip and smell the vomit. In this case, the transition from New York City to Hong Kong and earlier story events is quite abrupt. The shot in the bathroom offers no clue to Mo-Yung's whereabouts. Rather, this disorienting presentation of time and place mirrors the contemporary experience of immigration.

Unlike previous generations of explorers, pilgrims, colonialists, pirates, and other travelers, contemporary wanderers journey according to a different set of rules and restrictions. Jet travel condenses the time and space between New York and Hong Kong. If the spectator is confused following the character's disorientation, then the fictional world simply reflects a postmodern experience of time and space.

Here, Jameson's difficulty with Yang's *Terrorizer* as both modern and postmodern begins to make sense for *To Liv(e)* and *Crossings* as well. Although both have elements of counter-cinema and fit within the generic parameters of Hong Kong commercial film as love stories, crime stories, and melodramas, they seem to be doing something that adds up to more than just the sum of these modernist and commercial parts. They have a "schizophrenic" quality that can be seen in their titles. The English title, *To Liv(e)*, is a deconstructed play on words referring to Liv Ullmann, *Letter to Jane,* and a heartfelt desire for the people of Hong Kong to somehow endure and "to live." The title in Chinese, roughly translated as *Love Songs from a Floating World*, refers to the other face of the film that deals with romantic relationships and a Chinese tradition of misdirected and/or impossible love.

Crossings provides a similar case in point. The English title conjures up images of immigration, exile, nomadism, the modern metropolis as a crossroads, whereas the Chinese title, *Wrong Love*, refers to unhappy affairs of the heart. As the titles imply, these polyglot films offer a multiple address and potentially a multiple interpretation or at least a divided ordering of narrative hierarchies, for the English-speaking audience at festivals and art cinemas globally, for the expanding circle of Asian American film spectators, and for the Chinese-speaking audience looking at the films in relation to the standard Hong Kong commercial product.

However, another possible address needs to be taken into consideration as well. Rather than operating dialectically between the art film and the commercial love story, between English and Chinese, the films can be taken as palimpsests in which the elements superimpose, obscuring meaning for some, illuminating a different kind of meaning for others. A new meaning is not created through the clash of contradictory discourses, as can be seen in the work of Godard. Rather, layers sit on top of one another, some (almost) postcolonial in English, some diasporic with an American accent, some (almost) postsocialist in Chinese, some modern and part of the tail end of an international New Wave, others postmodern and part of contemporary global cinema culture.

Although *To Liv(e)* and *Crossings* are quite different, more than a single director links the works together. Taken as a set, they comment on certain common themes (e.g., Hong Kong 1997, immigration, changing family and social relationships in "Greater China," etc.) from two different temporal and spatial perspectives. *To Liv(e)* primarily looks at the edginess of Hong Kong residents who are able to leave but may or may not actually emigrate before July 1997. *Crossings* looks primarily at newly transplanted Hong Kong émigrés in New York City, that is, at immigration as a fait accompli rather than as a possibility. Two anchors hold these films together. One is a contemplation of June 4 in Tian'anmen Square, and the other is Rubie. The first represents a common location away from Hong Kong at a specific point in time that galvanized the world's attention. The other represents a particular face and voice that embody the sociopolitical as well as the personal psychological issues addressed by both films. Both Tian'anmen and Rubie are difficult to pin down, and the indeterminacy of both forms the heart of both of these films.

BETWEEN TIAN'ANMEN AND TIMES SQUARE

The problem of location, in every sense of the word, structures the narratives in *To Liv(e)* and *Crossings*.[10] As Rey Chow points out in her work on contemporary Chinese culture, looking for an "authentic" voice or a "native" position presupposes an Orientalist belief in a pure and distinct other and represents a desire on the part of the critic rather than the true nature of anything or anyone that actually exists.[11] In *To Liv(e)* and *Crossings*, characters move around Hong Kong and New York City and talk about places as diverse as Australia, Canada, Scandinavia, Italy, and South Africa. However, the films inevitably come back to Beijing, specifically to Tian'anmen, as a starting point, although the characters never physically journey to mainland China on screen. Footage and still photos of the spring 1989 demonstrations appear, but no plot action occurs in Beijing. Indeed, very little is said about the demonstrations at all. Rather, Tian'anmen anchors the slippery nature of the films' characters as well as the slippery identities those characters represent as citizens of Hong Kong or as immigrants elsewhere.

One scene in *To Liv(e)* brings to the fore this question of identity in relation to Tian'anmen. Rubie and her activist friend Trini have a snack in a Hong Kong noodle house after seeing an antinuclear performance. The scene begins as Trini talks about her family, resettled in England, and her white British husband. She is not keen to immigrate to England, however, because of the treatment she received from the British embassy while in Beijing during the demonstrations. At one point, she contacted the embassy to help some Hong Kong students escape arrest as counterrevolutionaries. The reply from the embassy was: "This should teach them a lesson. They should have thought twice before interfering with other people's business." On another occasion, Trini contacted the embassy for an escort to the airport. Her request was denied by the same staff member because her party was traveling on documents issued by the PRC government, implying that the bearers were considered Chinese citizens. Trini sums up the situation as follows:

> The first time he denied us help was because we're non-Chinese and he advised us to "think twice before interfering with other people's business." The second time he refused to help was because we are Chinese. We're Chinese subjects travelling with our *re-entry* permit. Either way we lose! What does he want us to be? My conclusion is we're not British *subjects*. We're probably British *objects*—to be freely disposed of.[12]

In *To Liv(e)*, Tian'anmen is filtered through the experiences of a number of characters who are all positioned as spectators. Rubie watches in the audience as dancers perform "Exhausted Silkworms" about the events in Tian'anmen. The newsreel footage of Hong Kong demonstrations in support of the Tian'anmen protesters illustrates one of Rubie's letters. She listens as Trini, acting as an activist/journalist during the demonstrations, finally concludes that she was an outsider in Tian'anmen, a spectator rather than a participant. Trini notes, "We're only onlookers. There's no question about that." Rubie also listens as Elsie Tu, a white resident of Hong Kong who is a former missionary and social activist (playing herself), describes her reaction:

> The Tian'anmen Massacre has thrown everything into a dilemma for me. On the one hand, I can't be disloyal to China. On the other hand, I can't accept what happened. I wonder, am I going to see the people I've been living with all my life be massacred if they speak up? In any case, I do plan to stay in Hong Kong till the end. ... I've devoted all my life trying to make Hong Kong a better place and I, too, would like to know what happens here after 1997.[13]

Rubie, Elsie Tu, and Trini are all caught up in the problem of location. Neither Chinese nor British, they are activists and onlookers uncertain of what they can or should be doing to help themselves and, by extension, Hong Kong.

In *Crossings*, the use of Tian'anmen as a point from which identity may or may not be determined continues. Here the shift is from Hong Kong to New York's Chinatown community. During the credit sequence, Rubie appears on a TV news segment discussing apathy in the Chinese community on the anniversary of June 4. Introduced by an image of the Goddess of Democracy, a woman newscaster appears on screen and remarks: "Almost five years after the Tian'anmen Square Massacre, amnesia seems to have set in New York's Chinatown. Is the United States foreign policy toward China still obsessively based on a tragedy that has no bearing on today's reality?" Rubie appears as an expert to answer this question. However, her reply is nonresponsive: "I feel that China and America are intimately connected." She continues as an off-screen voice: "Did you know the boots Chinese soldiers wore to put down the demonstrators were made in America and the gloves American medics wear to protect themselves from AIDS are made in China?"

Here, America is brought into the equation and implicated in the Tian'anmen events. However, the connection, like the connection of Rubie to the students and other demonstrators with whom she empathizes, remains vague. As Rubie comments on the anniversary of Tian'anmen off-screen, another character, the psychotic American, Joey, laughs hysterically on screen, enjoying a joke with some imaginary cronies. Rubie's observations on the political dimensions of the global economy are ironically juxtaposed with Joey's lunatic obsessions with Asia and Asian women.

At this point, Tian'anmen comes closer to another square, Times Square, as the center for New York's sex trade. In fact, Times Square takes up as a spatial reference where Tian'anmen leaves off. Painter John (Fung Kin Chung), Rubie's boyfriend in *To Liv(e)*, laughingly mentions that he can always work as a street artist in Times Square, like his mainland counterparts. Indeed, struggling Chinese painters can be found on the streets of New York, Paris, and other cities, trying to eke out a living painting portraits and caricatures of tourists. John fears, though, that he is not as tough as these other artists. Later a shot of Times Square appears in *Crossings*, but no artists are present. In this scene, Rubie compares New York to Chang An (Xi'an) during the Tang Dynasty as a crossroads of civilizations. From the Goddess of Democracy to the Statute of Liberty, from Tian'anmen to Times Square, the "crossroads" of China and America, specifically New York, point to an unsettling dislocation.

FROM ORGANIC TO DIASPORIC INTELLECTUAL

Contrasting the traditional with the organic intellectual, Antonio Gramsci saw the former as educated to maintain the status quo of the powers ascendant at that time, whereas the organic intellectual rose from the ranks of the subaltern classes to act as a spokesperson for their concerns and empower them with a voice in the larger body politic.[14] The idea of the organic intellectual has been influential in the thinking of many theorists since Gramsci. More recently, another view of public intellectuals has become current, that is, the "diasporic" intellectual. Unlike the organic intellectual who remains rooted in the community from which he or she emerged, the diasporic intellectual moves between nations, cultures, languages, and other "positions." Indeed, the position and the location of the diasporic intellectual are often difficult to pin down. From the scattering of the Frankfurt School, to the postcoloniality of Edward Said,[15] Gayatri Spivak,[16] and Homi Bhabha,[17] to the writings of Stuart Hall in cultural studies,[18] the diasporic intellectual works from the perspective of exile and/or immigration, from the pain as well as the freedom of displacement.

In the character of Rubie, *To Liv(e)* and *Crossings* create a fictional representation of the process of transformation of a concerned, educated, organic intellectual into a diasporic intellectual. Like activist Elsie Tu, who appears in *To Liv(e)* as the disillusioned British missionary/housewife turned urban activist, Rubie in *Crossings* leaves behind her roots in Hong Kong to take up the role of community activist and spokeswoman in New York City. In this way, the character of Rubie acts as the other bridge that links *To Liv(e)* and *Crossings*. Although it is never made explicit that a single, unified Rubie is exactly the same character in both films, the two Rubies clearly function in the same way in both works and in most ways can be taken as a single character.

However, the convergence of the two Rubies does not belie the fact that the character is presented as a conflicted, often contradictory presence in each film. Her roots, for example, are found among the poorer quarters of Hong Kong society. During a scene depicting a rather uncomfortable family gathering, her father digresses on the family history as squatters selling groceries, moving from one temporary housing development to another, threatened by floods and ravaged by fire, and exploited by corrupt officials demanding kickbacks for a business license. The family is taken under the wing of Elsie Tu, who uses her influence to set them up in a legitimate shop.

From these lower middle-class, small merchant roots, the children emerge as full-fledged members of Hong Kong's professional/intellectual sector. Rubie is a journalist who becomes a community activist/social worker in New York. Tony is a highly skilled radiologist, and the eldest brother has successfully established himself in Canada. Unlike their parents, the children have the education and skills to move outside a Chinese environment into a global, English-based, diasporic community of postcolonial professionals and intellectuals plying their trades along the path of the former British Empire—from Canada to Australia, the United States, and South Africa. They come from an impoverished China, but they now move in other circles. Ironically, it is the experience of colonialism (here embodied by the personal patronage of former British missionary Elsie Tu) that makes this movement and this upward mobility possible.

At one point, Rubie pays a visit to her family home and shop. It is filled with the details of a marginal small merchant's existence, including the outdoor tables, the bare floor of the main living room, the worn table used as part of the elevated family shrine, the special, round tabletop brought in for the family gathering, and the padded, old-fashioned vest and trousers worn by her mother. It becomes clear Rubie has not always led a solidly bourgeois existence. It may seem that the casting of Eurasian actress Lindzay Chan in this role and the inclusion of her reading from the lengthy series of letters to Liv in English contradicts this picture of Rubie's humble origins. Not only does this contradiction alienate the spectator from the character, it also serves to highlight the indeterminate identity and position of the people of Hong Kong as Chinese British subjects, as educated and superstitious, as Western and Asian, as poor and struggling and established and well-to-do.

Rubie speaks in two voices—in fluent Cantonese and impeccable British-accented English. Like Hong Kong itself, sometimes she looks Western, British, and white and sometimes she looks Chinese and Asian. For example, in *To Liv(e)*, she reads several of her letters directly addressing the camera in medium shots, seated against a British Union Jack, the American stars and stripes, and the flag of the People's Republic of China. Interestingly, when she is shot in front of the Chinese flag, the lighting of her hair accentuates its reddish highlights. The light allows her to blend in with the flag at the same time that it emphasizes her distinctiveness as a Eurasian performer. Rubie sometimes plays the role of a British subject, the role of an ethnic Chinese, the role of an Asian American immigrant, and, most important, the role of a character of an indeterminate identity.

In *Crossings,* Rubie tells another story about her origins. She explains her features as a throwback to the Tang Dynasty, when she must have had some European ancestor from exchanges along the Silk Route. The fact that Rubie's ethnic and cultural hybridity needs to be explained at all is itself telling. Addressing the reception of *To Liv(e),* Evans Chan has commented on critics who demand an "authentic" Hong Kong subject:

> One controversial issue the film does occasion seems to be the establishment of "the (post-)colonial subject," hence the problematic status of the letters which are written in English. ... I can understand the film's identity being characterized as schizophrenic, however, the notion that English is alien to the film's yet-to-be-post colonial identity is curious. After all, English is still primarily the official language of Hong Kong, where three major English dailies and two English TV channels permeate the everyday life of the educated class. Legal proceedings are conducted in English and Chinese politicians make speeches in English at the Legislative Council. If an average Hong Kong citizen speaks little English, that proves how linguistic schizophrenia may turn out to be a colonial legacy that will take some time, provided the will, to eradicate ... .
>
> That Hong Kong is a linguistically hybridized being is a fact that the film is not obliged to transcend.[19]

In English and Chinese, Rubie functions as the voice of Hong Kong, expressing, through her letters in *To Liv(e)* and her diary and appearances on the TV news as an "expert" insider in *Crossings,* the hopes and fears of her community. Her identity and the identity of that community may be difficult to pin down as they slip among Britain, America, Hong Kong, and China, between the lower small merchant classes and the upwardly mobile professionals, between a "traditional" older generation and a more urbane younger one. Rubie, however, manages to embody this cacophony of "voices."

Rubie is more than a mouth, however; she is also an ear. Throughout *To Liv(e),* the ear appears again and again as a motif associated with both Hong Kong as a place and Rubie as a character. Near the end of the film, the painting John has been working on throughout is revealed to be a picture of an ear. To break the tension of her brother's departure, John orchestrates a Vincent Van Gogh practical joke with a bloody cloth over the side of his face and a fake severed ear. Still unsteady from having just prevented her brother's attempted suicide, Rubie faints at the sight of the phony severed ear and falls into a dream in which the ear reappears.

In her last letter to Liv, Rubie refers to George Bernard Shaw's trip to Hong Kong in 1933: "Hong Kong 1933 didn't seem to exist for Bernard Shaw, except as a bad ear messed up by the British for communication with China. And an imperfect ear we've always been—as a bastardized link between a China weighed down by tradition and the clamorous demands of modernity."[20] Throughout both films, Rubie is this same kind of bastardized ear, understanding English (and, through that, the

FIGURE 30. Still from *To Liv(e)*. Having just prevented Tony's suicide, Rubie faints and begins to dream. (Photos this page courtesy of Evans Chan, Riverdrive Productions.)

FIGURE 31. Still from *To Liv(e)*. Images of severed ears appear in her dream.

perspectives of the British, American, and international communities represented by Liv Ullmann) and Chinese (through Cantonese, she understands the Hong Kong Chinese and, through Mandarin, she understands the Greater China community). Her trained, cultivated ear can appreciate experimental satiric theater as well as Italo Calvino and the films of Ingmar Bergman. Like the organic intellectual, she can "hear" the marginalized and dispossessed as well as the bourgeoisie. Like the diasporic intellectual, she can hear the subtleties of the official and unofficial proclamations of various national governments and other state institutions.

Indeed, Rubie moves in a social world that is marked by cultural and linguistic hybridity. This floating world of transnational, petit-bourgeois labor includes artists, professionals, activists, and journalists, among others, who are young, educated, culturally astute, and mobile. In both *To Liv(e)* and *Crossings*, Rubie's circle is rich in characters who are involved in a variety of artistic and intellectual endeavors.[21] Again, like Bergman and Godard, Chan favors educated, thoughtful, cultured protagonists. In *To Liv(e)*, Rubie's boyfriend, John, busily works on his paintings and reads to Tony from Calvino's *Invisible Cities*; Rubie attends experimental dance performances ("Exhausted Silkworms" on Tian'anmen and "Nuclear Goddess" on Daya Bay, China's nuclear power plant, constructed in suspiciously close proximity to Hong Kong); Teresa relaxes as an experimental video piece plays on her TV; Rubie quotes George Bernard Shaw and *The New York Times* in her letters to Liv.

This world is not only cultured but cosmopolitan, and Rubie's friends and relatives are part of a global society. In addition to Rubie's elder brother in Canada and younger brother on his way to Australia, Rubie's circle includes interracial couples (e.g., Chris and Leanne, Trini and her husband), expatriates like Elsie Tu, overseas Chinese like Tony's old flame Michelle on a trip back from the United States, and many others.

Crossings extends Rubie's circle even more. Again, Rubie functions as a bridge between various groups. She befriends Mo-Yung, who is an illegal visitor to New York. In this case, Mo-Yung acts as a fulcrum with Rubie on one side of the scale and Mo-Yung's gangster boyfriend, Benny, on the other side. Rubie and Benny battle over Mo-Yung. Rubie tries to divorce her from her destructive relationship with Benny, and Benny tries to find Mo-Yung either to use her to get to a cache of drugs or to take possession of her heart.

Artists, writers, and filmmakers have a long history of using criminals and gangsters as more than objects for social or psychological studies. Petty gangsters can serve as cinematic alter egos, articulating more than the concerns of petty hoods. The character of Benny is crafted in this tradition. It is difficult to tell whether Benny is a drug trafficker and pimp masquerading as a fine arts photographer or a sensitive artist doing a photo essay, "Countdown to 1997," who toys with a gangster identity. The photographs Mo-Yung spreads on her bed are as concrete as the drugs Benny's other girlfriend, Mabel, cleans on their dining room table. Both serve as visual manifestations of Benny's character, although it must be granted that the white powder carries more narrative weight than the photographs.

Since the silent era, the gangster has been used in film to concretize and contemplate economic relations. He is an outsider who serves as a mirror for the society he haunts. Like the intellectual, he has been produced by a certain milieu, but he is deviant, an implicit critic of the society that produced him. More recently, the gangster increasingly functions as an emblem of transnational economic relations as seen in Yang's *Mahjong* and Hou's *Goodbye South Goodbye*, discussed in Chapter 4. In *Crossings*, the comment is made that Marco Polo brought two elements of Chinese culture to Italy—pasta and the Mafia. Both food and crime continue to cross borders to exert their influence transnationally. The gangster is a sinister citizen of the world. He has become part of the Chinese diaspora—along with intellectuals, legitimate merchants and businesspeople, students, skilled workers, and professionals.

Benny is a hybrid, a gangster-intellectual. Like Rubie, he has humble roots in Hong Kong's underclasses; however, he transcends his origins through the drug trade rather than through painting like John, the medical profession like Tony, or journalism/social work like Rubie. He is a fitting object for Mo-Yung's wrong love, because the uncertainty of his relationship to her finally comes out on the side of genuine emotion. After using her to smuggle drugs and denying any feelings for her to Mabel, he gives up his freedom and takes a police bullet in the back when he realizes Mo-Yung is having a miscarriage because of his reckless attempt to escape from the law. More than the tenderness in his relationship with Mo-Yung elevates him within the narrative, however. *Crossings* portrays Benny as a pensive gangster who can appreciate African traditional art, has a certain flair for fashion, and looks at his trade in historical terms as a response to the British push to sell opium in China that occasioned the Opium Wars. Because America supposedly encouraged the trade further through its involvement in the politics of the Golden Triangle, Benny justifies his trade as a political act of resistance—getting back at American imperialists by poisoning the population through drugs. When Rubie meets Benny in prison, however, he has again taken on the persona of the hardened criminal, the face he used in his interactions with Mabel. Aside from a few brief moments with Mo-Yung, Benny never manages to voice a substantial social critique.

The character of Mo-Yung comes a bit closer. Unlike Benny, Rubie, and her relatives, Mo-Yung was born in Suzhou, in mainland China, into an educated family, descended from unassimilated non-Han invaders centuries ago. Her father, an engineer, was forced to kneel on broken glass during the Cultural Revolution. Taking the family away from the excesses of Chinese politics in the 1960s and early 1970s, Mo-Yung's family found itself downwardly mobile in Hong Kong, her father finding work as a carpenter. Mo-Yung's name marks her as a mainlander, specifically from Suzhou. When she asked to change it as an adolescent, her father questioned her desire: "Are you so eager to conform? To assimilate?" Thus, even in Hong Kong, where she grew up, Mo-Yung is an outsider.

The fact that she will leave Hong Kong is taken as a given by most in the film. Her family pushes her to marry a Canadian immigrant to provide another escape from the People's Republic after 1997. She has already rejected a plan to emigrate

FIGURE 32. Still from *To Liv(e)*. Performance of "Nuclear Goddess" to protest the Daya Bay nuclear power plant project across the border from Hong Kong in the People's Republic. (Courtesy of Evans Chan, Riverdrive Productions.)

as a nurse, because she fears that as a foreign nurse, she would be required to work exclusively with AIDS patients, under conditions she fears would not preclude her being infected. Finally, following Benny, Mo-Yung becomes an illegal alien in New York, sucked into his world of transnational trafficking in drugs and prostitutes. Mo-Yung, then, is left to drift in New York until she meets her tragic end.

As in *To Liv(e)*, the voice in *Crossings* is given to Rubie. Divorced now (presumably from John) and with a child left in Hong Kong, Rubie has been severed from her roots in Hong Kong's lower middle classes to find herself administering to a similar community of overseas Chinese in New York. At one extreme, in her work in a community clinic, Rubie sees illegal immigrant women brought in to work in the sex industry in New York, including some infected with AIDS. She also becomes involved in the edges of the illegal drug trade through her relationship with Mo-Yung. At the other extreme, Rubie moves in a very different social sphere represented by one of her close male friends, a Mandarin speaker, who is part of the New York avant-garde arts community. This character is gay and has a white boyfriend. He does experimental dance dressed as a female character from Beijing opera to a pop music beat in a disco frequented by Asian transvestites. He speaks in Mandarin, she responds in Cantonese, and both translate for the American boyfriend in English.

These divergent cultural spheres overlap throughout the film, and come together most dramatically at Mo-Yung's funeral. In this scene, the dancer performs

FIGURE 33. Still from *Crossings*. Benny (Simon Yam) is a fitting object of Mo-Yung's "wrong love." (Courtesy of Evans Chan, Riverdrive Productions.)

a piece in which his defiantly thrown-back shoulders, high aerial kicks, and simple male attire work in concert with wreaths denouncing violence against Asians from various community groups. Looking at this scene in conjunction with the scene featuring a similar dance performance, "Exhausted Silkworms," in *To Liv(e)*, underscores the two extremes used to position the characters and events in both films. "Exhausted Silkworms" reenacts the violence of Tian'anmen, and the funeral performance memorializes Mo-Yung not as a victim of wrong love but as a victim of random anti-Asian violence in the United States, a different sort of "wrong love" that enables Joey to brutalize Asian women.

Here the position of the global Hong Kong community hits two violent terminal points: one in the political fear prompted by the suppression of the 1989 Tian'anmen demonstrations and the other in the social fear of racial violence in New York City. Caught between these two extremes, Rubie tries to sort out her own position and identity. At one point in *Crossings*, Rubie is on an elevated train platform, putting on lipstick. Taking the position of a stalker, the hand-held camera moves in on Rubie. When she is framed in a close-up, Rubie turns and runs. The camera then turns to reveal Joey, who addresses the camera directly, "Blood must flow. What if I push you on the tracks?" The film cuts away to a street person screaming on the sidewalk as the elevated train screeches in the background. A frightened Rubie is shown escaping on the train; a musical bridge connects this scene with a scene of Rubie writing in her journal in her apartment. She recalls a similar incident that happened the week before. The flashback shows Rubie reading the paper on the elevated platform. In this case, rather than taking the point

FIGURE 34. Still from *Crossings*.
Two outsiders, Mo-Yung and Rubie
(Lindzay Chan), share a moment in
Central Park. (Courtesy of Evans
Chan, Riverdrive Productions.)

of view of the stalker, the camera takes Rubie's perspective as an African American man directly confronts the camera (i.e., Rubie) and lashes out at her, "Man, I hate you Japs." He rambles on incoherently about a blood reckoning to be paid. Back at her apartment, Rubie continues in her diary: "Would it have helped if I'd told him I'm not Japanese, but a Chinese from the British Crown Colony of Hong Kong? Where would I have felt protected? Britain? China?"

While the cosmopolitan world of Hong Kong or New York promises a certain freedom associated with the hybridity of the metropolitan experience, it also represents a world in which identity is cast adrift, and there is no safe haven. Joey's psychosis, which these parallel scenes show is not uncommon, revolves around a misrecognition of the Asian woman that operates on several levels. Joey stalks Rubie, but under the assumption that any Asian woman would satisfy his blood lust, he kills Mo-Yung. Joey is driven into this delirium by an encounter with an Asian transvestite, whom, in *M. Butterfly* fashion, he mistakes for a woman. Indeed, Joey mistakes all the Asian women he encounters, from his prostitute girlfriend in Thailand to the newly arrived mainland Chinese prostitute he visits in a New York massage parlor, for his "dream girl," that is, submissive, compliant, subservient, and posing no threat to his own uncertain sexuality. In his delirium, Joey even mistakes Mo-Yung for a dummy, raving happily about passing the test to

FIGURE 35. Still from *Crossings*. Even though Rubie and Mo-Yung grow close, Mo-Yung does not take her friend's advice. (Courtesy of Evans Chan, Riverdrive Productions.)

see if he could tell the difference between a real person and a mannequin. His racism levels all distinctions, turning all Asian women into objects. When Joey's sister tries to explain her brother's mental illness to Rubie at Mo-Yung's funeral, Rubie's only response is, "It could have been me! Don't you see, your brother was stalking me! It could have been me." Between Trini's analysis of her position as a British object in *To Liv(e)* and Joey's interchangeability of Asian women as objects in *Crossings*, the voice of the diasporic intellectual becomes silent. If Rubie's role as an intellectual is to listen and speak for her constituency, she ends up silent between two worlds marked by violence.

Ironically, Joey does not inhabit a world totally dissimilar to Rubie's. As a public schoolteacher in New York, he is, like Rubie, part of a class of educators, social workers, media artists, and so on, who can be loosely grouped as intellectuals. He has a secure job; the principal of the school laments the fact she cannot fire him, even though he alternately brutalizes and ignores his students, because he has tenure and is "competent until proven incompetent, sane until proven insane." He has disposable income to travel to Thailand. Also, like Rubie, he seems to be upwardly mobile, living with a sister whose accent and demeanor point to working-class roots. However, if Benny represents the intellectual as gangster and Joey represents the intellectual as madman, Rubie represents the intellectual as something different—as a woman within the diaspora.

FIGURE 36. Still from *Crossings*. Mo-Yung remains alone. (Courtesy of Evans Chan, Riverdrive Productions.)

THE EAR IS ATTACHED TO A WOMAN

Rubie functions in both films as a public, intellectual ear that is able to hear and validate the various voices she represents. However, she also serves as a private, personal ear. Rubie listens to an array of personal problems voiced by those in her circle of family, friends, and acquaintances. With few exceptions, both films' characters talk to Rubie, and Rubie listens and processes her thoughts in her letters to Liv in *To Liv(e)* and in her diary in *Crossings*. As this narrative ear, Rubie holds the plots of both films together, giving them a structure, logic, and certain order.

Many directors are known for establishing ongoing relationships with actresses who represent the filmmakers' concerns and provide entry into other realms involving women, the female psyche, and issues concerning feminine subjectivity. Bergman's relationship with Liv Ullmann comes immediately to mind. In his films, Chan develops a rapport with Lindzay Chan that allows him to explore not only issues of cultural hybridity but also topics involving women and their concerns. Moving from the textuality of the political discourses of the films to the subjectivity of the "women's film," *To Liv(e)* and *Crossings*, in their stylistic and generic hybridity, highlight issues that go beyond newspaper headlines and

FIGURE 37. Still from *Crossings*. Mo-Yung has a change of mood as the camera moves from the exterior...(Courtesy of Evans Chan, Riverdrive Productions.)

immigration statistics. Although Chan employs a Brechtian/Godardian alienation from his characters, using them as types to illustrate particular points, he also presents these characters in more naturalistic ways, underscoring their individuality, allowing them to speak as distinct entities as well as representatives of ideological positions and abstract social categories.

To illustrate this point, it might be instructive to look at two parallel scenes, one from *To Liv(e)* and the other from *Crossings*. Both scenes involve Rubie having a tête-à-tête with another woman. Each scene points to the intimacy between the women. Each features a discussion of the situation of women drifting between countries, roles, and emotions, adding to narrative information, but also standing alone as discourses separate from the public pronouncements of Rubie's letters or her appearances on American television.

In *To Liv(e)*, Rubie meets with her brother's fiancée, Teresa, at Victoria Peak, overlooking the Hong Kong skyline. The two are seated near a ledge, on opposite sides of the frame, with the cityscape between them. Teresa voices her concerns about going to Australia. She also talks about her divorce and difficulties maintaining a relationship with her son studying in the United Kingdom. On a short visit to Hong Kong, the son went shopping with his father rather than taking time

FIGURE 38. Still from
Crossings. . . . To the interior of the
café near Times Square where she
meets Rubie. (Courtesy of Evans
Chan, Riverdrive Productions.)

to see his mother. Because of her divorce and the death of her own mother, Teresa
feels adrift emotionally. Rubie listens and sympathizes with Teresa. The sounds of
the city below can be heard throughout the scene. Rubie moves from her position
screen right to sit close to Teresa; the camera slowly moves in to frame them
together on the ledge. When Rubie tries to reassure Teresa that there will be plenty
of Hong Kong emigrants to befriend in Australia, Teresa counters that she and
Tony want to escape Hong Kong to get away from its people (i.e., Tony and
Rubie's parents, who disapprove of a union between a younger man and a divorced, older woman). The camera moves out again, to show Rubie and Teresa in
relation to the city, as the two embrace each other at the scene's conclusion.

In *Crossings*, Rubie meets Mo-Yung in a café near Times Square. The camera is
positioned outside as the scene begins, then moves inside to frame Rubie and Mo-
Yung silhouetted against the café's window as the traffic of New York passes by
outside. Throughout the scene, the camera moves between the two women, using a
vase with dried flowers on the table as a pivotal point. Mo-Yung talks about
coming from Suzhou; Rubie talks about her features and an imagined Silk Route
ancestor. Both laugh that they are "two barbarians invading New York."

The camera cuts away to a shot of Mo-Yung, framed through the café's window,
and the mood changes. The two begin to wonder about a missing acquaintance,
Carmen, who had also been involved with Benny. Rubie fills Mo-Yung in on her

FIGURE 39. Still from *To Liv(e)*. Rubie's vision of Tony and Teresa's self-destructive romance. (Photos this page courtesy of Evans Chan, Riverdrive Productions.)

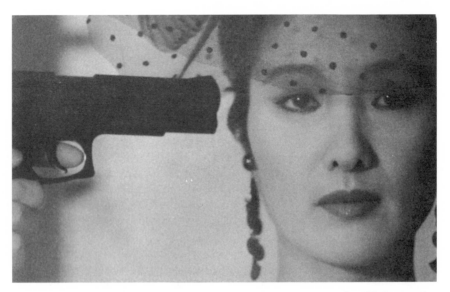

FIGURE 40. Still from *To Liv(e)*. In Rubie's dream, Teresa appears to be oblivious to the fact that she is under the gun.

own situation and her desire to get a green card and open America as a possibility for her son. Mo-Yung asks, "What if your son doesn't like America and blames you?" When Rubie replies that he can always go back, Mo-Yung counters, "Do you think you can re-create the past just like that?" The scene ends on a close shot of Mo-Yung putting out her cigarette in an ashtray near the dried flowers, flanked by the empty coffee cups.

These two scenes highlight elements that move the narratives into the realm of the women's film. The emphasis is placed on the relationship between women, their solidarity in the face of the trials of immigration as well as in the face of changing sexual mores and family relationships. Here, as friends, mothers, lovers, ex-wives, fiancées, and confidantes, Rubie, Teresa, and Mo-Yung illustrate the personal dimension of the political concerns of 1997. Women experience a different type of crossing than men. Traditional roles for women dissolve in the diaspora. Families become unhinged, scattered; romantic relationships become more fleeting. Cast adrift by a desire to escape from rigid families, ex-husbands, and the feeling of being alienated from the traditional world in which they were born and bred, these women move off to Australia and New York with a distinctive sense of loss, particular fears, and for reasons that go far beyond the political dynamics of 1997. Following Rubie as the ear, the camera in both scenes invites the spectator to share these intimate moments.

These two scenes are not unique in either *To Liv(e)* or *Crossings*. Rather, they form part of a pattern of scenes in which women's issues are voiced and Rubie listens to her girlfriends' concerns. In *To Liv(e)*, for example, Teresa will only discuss her fears of death and abandonment with Rubie; Tony must eavesdrop outside the bedroom door. In *Crossings*, female characters as diverse as the unnamed, unseen AIDS-infected prostitute at the clinic, Joey's sister, and a next-door neighbor seek out Rubie as an ear for their stories. Mo-Yung tells the story of her family to Rubie rather than Benny. These acts of speaking and listening among the female characters propel both films out from the orbits of the political essay or the crime story. Like the in-between, transnational, transcultural characters they depict,[22] *To Liv(e)* and *Crossings* also defy easy classification. However, although identities may be uncertain and fluctuating, the issues these characters embody remain concrete and disturbingly fixed.

ENDINGS

To Liv(e) concludes with cautious optimism on two fronts. In her last letter to Liv Ullmann, Rubie ends with the hope that China, Vietnam, and by extension Hong Kong will improve their respective situations so that all, including Rubie and Liv, will be able to meet as friends. Rubie concludes the film on a note of good humor. In fact, she signs her letter, "Love, Rubie." The last image of the film shows Tony and Teresa, saved from near suicide and break-up, alighting from their taxi at the airport, baggage in hand, on their way to Australia.

Crossings, on the other hand, ends on a pessimistic note. Rubie burns incense in memory of Mo-Yung on the subway platform where she was murdered. The last shot shows a graveyard in Hong Kong. Earlier, Benny and Mo-Yung had had a tryst near that graveyard, and Benny told the story of his mother being buried there after working herself to death to support the family. Rubie has promised to return Mo-Yung's bones to Hong Kong, presumably to that same cemetery.

Whereas *To Liv(e)* ends with death averted and hope in the future, *Crossings* concludes with the finality of death and the uncertainty of Rubie's future. She returns to Hong Kong with Mo-Yung's bones, but it is not certain whether she will return to New York, stay in Hong Kong, or go elsewhere. Because after death even bones continue to drift between continents, Rubie's continued crossings between roles and professions, between nation-states, and between Asia and the West also seem to be one of the few certainties in a very uncertain, fictional world. The fact that global filmmakers themselves continue to drift and make films about this floating world of displacement and hybridity also seems certain. To bring the film's pessimism back around to a more hopeful note, we might consider the following from Homi Bhabha's "DissemiNation: Time, Narrative and the Margins of the Modern Nation": "For it is by living on the borderline of history and language, on the limits of race and gender, that we are in a position to translate the differences between them into a kind of solidarity."[23]

Interview with Evans Chan

Before we discuss Crossings *and* To Liv(e), *could you tell me a little bit about your current [1998] project?*

I'm working on a documentary entitled *Journey to Beijing*. The film follows a group of walkers who engage in a four-month trek beginning in mid-February from Hong Kong to Beijing, reaching their destination about a week before the July 1 handover of Hong Kong by Britain to China. The purpose of their walk is to raise educational funds for China's impoverished rural children. Even though the group—Sowers' Action—has denied that there is any political intent behind the walk, I find the timing of this philanthropic enterprise very intriguing.

I'm not following them all the way, though. Instead, I'm making several filming trips to break their route into different sections. They make school visits at the Guangdong border. They stop by the Yellow River. Then they pass through Shaoshan, the birthplace of Mao. They'll arrive in Beijing and walk from Tian-'anmen Square to the Great Wall. These are significant markers and pointers that allow me to meditate on Hong Kong's own journey to Beijing that will result in decolonization, or reunification, in July. Back in Hong Kong, I'm interviewing representatives from different segments of society: from democratic politician Martin Lee to gay rights activist Julian Chan, who'll offer their perspectives on Hong Kong at this historical moment of transformation. Essentially, the walk provides me with a framework to do a countdown journal of Hong Kong up to the handover.

Hong Kong's current situation is overwhelmingly complex and amorphous. Yet just to film a current affairs kind of documentary doesn't interest me. All the news media are doing that. So I am trying to distill this closing chapter of Hong Kong's colonial history, the final leg of its "homecoming" journey, through a walk for charity, which is the most patriotic, forward-looking attitude one can find. Yet it is far from being typical. You can't say it's being shared by everyone in Hong Kong, hence my inclusion of other viewpoints.

When you work on a project like this, you always have to cope with the changing nature of current events. For example, while I was making *To Liv(e)*, I had this nagging feeling that the moment I finished the film it would become dated. However, I hope there are elements of this documentary that will transcend the timeframe. Isak Dinesen wrote a piece about the First World War in which she said, what will survive in times of chaos is what is human. I hope that I have taken in enough elements to make *Journey to Beijing* a human document.

In the course of making films on Hong Kong before 1997, has your perspective on the handover in relation to suppression of the 1989 demonstrations in Tian'anmen changed at all?

I don't think my views have changed significantly. The post-Tian'anmen drama is still unfolding historically, and the June 4 trauma is still part of the collective psyche of Hong Kong, or China itself. The historical condition, namely, the tension between the developing economic and political realms that resulted in the crackdown remains unresolved and potentially could produce a similar situation again. That is why the people of Hong Kong are worried about the handover. And people's lives are directly impacted. You call tell by the massive waves of post-June 4 immigration and the compulsion to obtain foreign passports as safety hedges.

By sheer chance, I stumbled into Beijing during the democratic uprising in late May of 1989, and I was in Hangzhou when the Tian'anmen Massacre happened. Starting in March, I had been traveling through China—from Guangxi to the Silk Route, then to Shanghai and Beijing. Along the way, I was stunned by the widespread anger among my compatriots. They were furious at the corruption among the ruling class—those *guan daos*, officials-cheats, as they called them. When the news about the massacre broke out in the form of huge banners written in black ink covering the town-square buildings in Hangzhou, I felt painfully powerless. I was approached by some weeping students, who were trying to communicate to me about their worries for their friends in Beijing, as though I could help. I left China, along with other foreign tourists, in a convoy and in tears. Until then, I didn't take 1997 seriously. I had been living in the U.S. for a few years and I already had my green card. But all of a sudden, I felt that part of my cultural roots, which are in Hong Kong, could be destroyed. That was one important push for me to create *To Liv(e)* and begin making movies. The Chinese government was calling on people to forget the whole thing and move on. But how? They call it the June 4 "complex." You know, there is this Dragon Boat Festival, which commemorates Qu Yuan, the poet governor who drowned himself to make an impression on the emperor—to wake him up, so to speak. Qu Yuan committed suicide in the hope that he would have some impact on the political scene of the day. Since then, we've had the Dragon Boat Festival for almost two millennia now. Has anybody ever talked about a "Dragon Boat complex," dismissing it as irrational and banning the dragon boat race? That the Tian'anmen demonstrations are still being labeled as "irrational" in Hong Kong and "counterrevolutionary" in China only reflects the authorities' insecurity and unwillingness to own up to history. Why don't they create a formal channel for mourning the massacre, recognize it as an unnecessary mistake and give the tragedy its proper place in political discourse? Is that giving away too much to the people? Should that be a concern of a mature, dignified nation? Hence, we are left with no choice but to be caught up in an ongoing struggle involving how history and collective memories are being shaped and written. In *To Liv(e)* and *Crossings*, I'm looking at the incident's impact on some individual lives.

Could you tell me a little bit about the inspiration for Crossings?

Crossings was inspired by an actual incident that happened in the early 1980s, when I was freelancing for a Chinatown newspaper. This white man pushed an Asian woman off a subway platform, and then jumped up and down in ecstasy. The woman's stranded red shoe, left on the platform, was part of the true story. Some people said that I was making a dig at the *Wizard of Oz*. That's not true. I just thought that that lonesome, pathetic red shoe says so much about human passion, which may or may not be misguided. The real-life victim was a garment factory worker, a new immigrant woman, married, with a child, who arrived in the U.S. not long before the incident. I felt that somehow there seemed to be an imbalance between the assailant's story and the victim's tale. For me to follow the victim's story, I would be going in a very different direction, meaning that I might be focusing on the new immigrant community from mainland China, of working-class background; it would have to be about their daily struggles and dreary livelihood. Somehow, that seemed at odds with the image of the red shoe. By the time I came to conceive *Crossings*, the exodus from Hong Kong was something that was haunting me, so I wanted to find a Hong Kong woman's story to counter the assailant's insane behavior. And I came up with this idea about a headstrong woman's search for love ending on the subway tracks of New York. My co-writer Joyce Chan made Mo-Yung, the protagonist, a younger woman than I originally intended. The film became her poignant passage into womanhood—and death.

Crossings has Rubie's story, continued from *To Liv(e)*, as well. Rubie might be somewhat larger than life in *To Liv(e)*—more of an intellectual than is ordinarily found in the daily life of Hong Kong. At any rate, Rubie is a highly competent, intelligent woman, and I felt that her story didn't end in *To Liv(e)*. Presumably what happened to her between *To Liv(e)* and *Crossings* is this—she had a divorce, became a mother. Like some Hong Kong parents, Rubie also decided to obtain a foreign passport for her child. (As a matter of fact, the elderly mother of Thomas Chow, my assistant director for *Crossings*, was then living alone in New York hoping to get her citizenship for Thomas's benefit. There are lots of stories like that.) I thought with someone with Rubie's resources would fit in well in China-town, where she could work in the community helping people. That's how we meet her in *Crossings*. During my years working in New York's Chinatown, I know quite a few people who are very motivated, very warm, idealistic, Chinese or Asian American, working in the community for the advancement of their own people. It's a pity that they are not represented very often in Asian American movies. Rubie echoed some of these kind-hearted people that I know in New York whom I wanted to show on screen.

The character of Rubie essentially emerges out of a group of artists and in-tellectuals I know in Hong Kong. While there isn't a big bohemian, intellectual circle in Hong Kong, there definitely is an arts scene. Artists and intellectuals are there, and they are the people that I knew during my university days. That's the milieu I created in *To Liv(e)*. In fact, I wrote *Dream Tenants*, a novel about bohemian life in Hong Kong that was serialized in a newspaper, long before I made my first film. As an aside, lately I've been strongly tempted to write a novel, drawing upon my personal background—with the protagonist as a child in Macao, spending his early years in Hong Kong, and then moving to New York in the 1980s. I am afraid of losing touch with the material if I don't do it soon. My mother died from breast cancer last year [1996], and my father also had a close brush with cancer.

While I've been making movies—maybe sparingly—I've never stopped considering myself a writer. Making independent films is very difficult in Hong Kong. In fact, intellectual cinema is difficult worldwide. The kind of art film with an essayist bent, championed by Godard, Marker, and Kluge, more allied to high modernism than postmodernism, is particularly difficult. It is as though that's part of the backlash against the '60s, against serious, demanding art. There never was such a tradition in Hong Kong and Chinese cinema, and understandably there is a lot of resistance. Filmmaking simply is not easy. Period. Still, that's its seductive challenge—it's like waging a battle against the world. The completion of a film always brings a certain conquest-like satisfaction. (That's why it is so easily corrupted, because film is an art form that flies too close to money and power, especially now, more than ever.) Yet I started out as a writer/critic, and over the years, writing, as much as filmmaking, has been an important outlet of mine. It's something that I can always do without relying too much on external resources, and I am glad that I can write. I've seen enough frustrated, embittered filmmakers waiting for their next chance, next project. I guess, to survive as a creative artist, one has to look at all the options. However, it may be that, because I write, I can't become as good a filmmaker as I might be, or vice versa.

Do you see yourself as a Hong Kong filmmaker or do you identify more with Asian American or American indie cinema?

Despite some doses of U.S. funding now and then, money for my films still comes mostly from Hong Kong, so that is the umbilical cord. The films get distributed in Hong Kong, then they play elsewhere. In that sense, I am luckier than some American independents who make a movie that may be shown only a few times at some film festivals, then disappear. I mean a work has to find its place in the world somewhere, or else it is as though it's never been made. There is simply no way to preserve them. Luckily I can still use Hong Kong as a base, where some kind of distribution is always available. On the other hand, it is also a double bind, since my films have always had a classification problem. When I first held a press screening in Hong Kong for the local papers, these entertainment reporters came out of the screening room, and one person asked me, "So, what is this? Is this an American film? Or is it a Hong Kong film? What is it?" I said, "Well, maybe it's both." If I had not lived in New York all these years, I would not have been able to make *To Liv(e)* to begin with. The independent scene in New York had inspired me, or else I wouldn't have considered filmmaking within the realm of possibility for my development as an artist. So I did derive my model from American cinema. On the other hand, the Hong Kong film industry is still one of the strongest in the world, and I still have enough Hong Kong ties to make that work for me. How well it works for me is another story, and whether that will turn against me is also another story.

For example, the full version of *Crossings* has not been really seen in Hong Kong. I was under so much pressure from the distributor when I was completing it, coupled with this disastrous chapter of my life—I mean, my parents' cancers began around that time—so I was too weak, too vulnerable, to really fight for the integrity of the film. While *Crossings* employs a thriller-melodramatic vehicle, it is in fact a highly serious work, though its serious strands are hidden. *To Liv(e)* is clearly an art film, an intellectual film, but *Crossings* goes into genre cinema in order to reinvent it from within. That intention seems lost on the Hong Kong critics, and I may be partly responsible because I didn't fight hard enough to include the crucial scenes. At any rate, the film might be too gloomy for Hong Kong to take at that time. Because of this, I do not feel that *Crossings* had a successful reception, either in Hong Kong or overseas. Despite some initial re-sistance, *To Liv(e)* seemed to find a more favorable critical environment.

Could you comment on the depiction of women in your films?

In *To Liv(e)*, there are two principal female characters, Josephine Koo as Teresa and Lindzay Chan as Rubie; and, in *Crossings*, Anita Yuan as Mo-Yung and Lindzay Chan again as Rubie. For me, those pairs vaguely represent "sense and sensibility." Many directors are drawn to women's stories because women are supposed to be sensitive, more vulnerable, and emotionally more expressive than men. In both *To Liv(e)* and *Crossings*, one of the female characters' life is ruled by emotions. Teresa, Josephine Koo's character, for example, is very self-destructive because of the situation of her relationship. In *Crossings*, Mo-Yung definitely pawns her life for romance. Sexuality exerts a powerful pull in people's life. It goes beyond all bounds, and it is potentially lethal.

Rubie is the one who is always responsive to others' needs and to the world. She is somewhat more detached, more sober, and more in control. But that doesn't mean she isn't grinding her teeth often. Maybe because she lives more than just for herself, she is capable of keeping that at arm's length—keeping that fatal assault of one's sexuality under control. Maybe for her, to live and to love is also about *how* to live and *how* to love. So she is the survivor, and not just in *Crossings*. Rubie survives across the border of countries and languages. However, she also under-stands the horrendous power of sexuality and the extraordinary force of circum-stances, and she extends her helping hands to other people, including vulnerable women in each film.

The ending of To Liv(e) *seems so much more optimistic about the future than the ending of* Crossings. *Does that reflect your feelings about the future of Hong Kong?*

I don't think it is so much about the future of Hong Kong. I think it is the future of the Chinese diaspora. It may simply reflect my mood at the time. There were many deaths around me when I made *Crossings*. Also, the original incident is inherently depressing. You know, just as in my film, the real-life assailant actually claimed that his victim didn't exist. I find that extremely shocking. She really is murdered twice. The first time her life is taken, and the second time her very existence is denied. *Crossings* has a very tragic dimension, and the film is practically staring into a void. Without Tian'anmen, Mo-Yung's family wouldn't have put so much pressure on her to marry someone abroad; without love, she wouldn't have come to New York; without her encounter with Rubie and finally Joey, she might have lived.

Crossings looks at death and destiny. People tend to gripe about fate, they live in denial of death, yet fearful of the threat of nonexistence. Yet fate is inexplicable, in its way beyond reproach; and it is memory that ultimately testifies to human lives. The final home for the dead, be they in New York or Tian'anmen, is always human memories. For Mo-Yung, she'll live on, at least in Rubie's mind, in her melancholic acceptance of the absurdity of human existence. Through Rubie's character I also tried to convey some sense of endurance. I'm a student of Nietzsche; I believe there is always some joy, some glimmer of hope recoupable from the void.

I have this idea of returning to Rubie's story again in the future, if I can continue to make movies. But what the story would be I don't yet have a clue. Maybe it should take place in Hong Kong again, or even somewhere in China. The fate of Rubie, like Hong Kong's apprehensive journeying back to the motherland, like China's rocky journeying into modernity and postmodernity, remains a mystery.

June 4, 1997

7   Gender and Generation in Clara Law's Migration Trilogy: *Farewell China, Autumn Moon*, and *Floating Life*

LIKE EVANS CHAN, Clara Law has fashioned a career in cinema that places her at the epicenter of patterns of migration within Greater China. In narratives that move among characters based in Europe, North America, Australia, and Asia, Law focuses on the relationship between gender and generational conflicts in her films. The depiction of what has come to be known as GenerAsian X in *Farewell, China* (1990), *Autumn Moon* (1992), and *Floating Life* (1996) reveals the way supposedly fixed identities become malleable within the diaspora and the particular way youth comes to bear on these fluctuations and personal transformations. All three films devote all or substantial portions of their plots to youth and young adults moving (or about to move) around the world. They journey from Japan to Hong Kong; from Hong Kong to Australia, Europe, and other destinations; from America to Hong Kong; from the People's Republic to America; and then often back again in the reverse direction. Law's films visualize these migrants in relation to ethnicity, class, and nationality so that issues of generation, age, sex, and gender become intertwined with shifting notions of the self as characters move around the globe.

GENERASIAN X AND THE GLOBAL CHINESE

The Euro-American notion of Generation X has become common within cultural discourse. It refers to the generation after the Baby Boomers, who, between 1989 and 1997, were in their late teens, twenties, or early thirties. Generation X is characterized as materialistic, jaded, worldly, cynical, uninterested in politics, casual about sex, and skeptical of personal commitment. Like many similar appellations, Generation X creates an image for consumption as it crafts a false sense of community among a group that can be targeted as consumers for specific products and services. Because of this, mention of this generation also implies a class position, that is, middle-class roots and decidedly bourgeois expectations. Generation X lives within a postmodern culture marked by a greater reliance on mobility, speed, and immediacy. Jet planes ferry bodies around the globe as satellite communications, computers, the Internet, and other new technologies fragment old alliances to create a bold new world for capitalists, consumers, and displaced workers.

Increasingly this generation has become a global entity for capitalist exploitation. MTV, Hollywood and Hong Kong action films, Japanese anime, computer games, Canto-pop and other world music, Benetton clothes and Nike shoes, the English-dominated but multiculturally inflected World Wide Web define the generation. Generation X exists within the contradictions of advanced capitalism, consuming global commodities while living within racially and ethnically isolated enclaves. Youth unites them as a market for transnational exploitation; new communication technologies help erode national barriers to further commercial penetration.

The addition of "Asian" into the mix to create GenerAsian X highlights many dramatic transformations involving young Asians around the world. Changes in immigration laws and patterns in the United States, Canada, Australia, and other parts of the world have made relocation for certain classes of people easier. An increased sense of regionalism in Europe, Latin America, Africa, and the Pacific Rim now competes with postcolonial feelings of identification with former colonizers and the neocolonial omnipresence of America. Transnational business links vie with decaying national interests. All these changes point to shifts in ethnic, racial, and other social alignments that are taken for granted by the generation that came of age in the latter part of the twentieth century.

Although American-based magazines such as *Yolk* and *A. Magazine* have helped to define GenerAsian X,[1] the concept has also garnered a certain global currency.[2] It has a common popular culture: a mixture of Hollywood, softened by multiculturalism, blended with an increasingly transnational Asian mass culture in which Jackie Chan can be lionized in Japan and anime can enthrall fans in the Philippines and Singapore. It shares a sense of separation from previous generations that battled against colonialism (including the internal colonialism of racism in America), wrestled with the impact of modernization (including immigration) on traditional ways of life, and fought against the ravages of American cultural imperialism.

GenerAsian X has a more fluid sense of identity. Postcolonial and postmodern, the combination of "Asian" with "Generation X" recognizes a separation based on racism and the legacy of colonialism while embracing the hybridity the condensation implies. On the move around the world, this is a polyglot generation in which English as a second language dominates much of the popular imagination. It is a generation marked by its class and class aspirations, defined by consumption and its ability to consume, forging an identity out of commodities. It dreams bourgeois dreams but finds itself young and in the streets, often marginalized and on the edge. Street gangs roam Hong Kong and Los Angeles; the supposedly overachieving model minority becomes the model majority in Taiwan, Korea, and Japan.

A significant part of GenerAsian X's cultural fabric comes from global Chinese culture. Hong Kong, as a major metropolis with a large culture industry, plays a major role. As a colonial, neocolonial, and postcolonial port with a mercurial identity, Hong Kong profits from its ability to blend British/British Commonwealth, European, American, Japanese, mainland Chinese, Taiwanese, Southeast Asian/Chinese diasporic elements into an Asian version of the melting pot for regional as well as international youth consumption. Though challenged by the PRC and the ROC, Hong Kong still sets a certain tone for global Chinese culture that has been difficult to displace. Even now, after 1997, Hong Kong still is associated with youth, modernity, a fast pace, and the *au currant*. Hence, Hong Kong and GenerAsian X have a peculiar affinity.

CLARA LAW'S GENERATION

Clara Law is not a member of GenerAsian X. However, she is a member of another generation with whom she shares certain affinities—the generation involved with Hong Kong cinema's New Wave. Although Stephen Teo rightly places her within what he calls the second wave of this movement,[3] Law shares many noteworthy aspects of her personal and professional career with others linked to both the first and second waves of Hong Kong's new cinema. Although Law is most often associated with her husband and collaborator, Eddie Fong (who wrote or co-wrote all three of the films under discussion here), it is also important to look at her oeuvre within the context of the work of two other acclaimed women directors associated with the Hong Kong New Wave, Ann Hui and Mabel Cheung. Although Cheung and Law are younger than Hui, they all share some striking similarities in their education, choice of genres, thematic preoccupations, and aesthetic interests. All three women have battled the odds to rise to prominence in a male-dominated industry. All have done advanced studies in the United Kingdom or the United states: Hui at the London Film School, Cheung at the University of Bristol and New York University, and Law at the National Film and Television School in England. They all worked in television, including stints at RTHK, before moving on to feature film production.[4] Cheung, like Law, normally works with a male collaborator; in Cheung's case, Alex Law. They are all comfortable with multilingual productions and subjects that cross national borders.

Over the years Hui, Cheung, and Law have tackled similar subject matter, often involving romance, melodrama, and female-centered narratives. More specifically, they have a preoccupation with themes of exile, nomadism, migration, split/ multiple/uncertain identities, and intergenerational conflicts.[5] Since the Joint Declaration, each has made at least one feature about life in the mainland. Hui's *Song of the Exile* (1990) and *My American Grandson* (1990) as well Cheung's *Eight Taels of Gold* (1990) deal with overseas Chinese going to the mainland. Law's *Farewell, China* and *Reincarnation of the Golden Lotus* (1989)[6] focus on mainland Chinese going abroad. Each has used her experiences living abroad as the basis for films on emigration from Hong Kong (e.g., Hui's *Song of the Exile*; Cheung's *Illegal Immigrant* [1985], *An Autumn's Tale* [1987]; and Law's *Floating Life*).[7] Hui and Law have also dealt with the historical and contemporary relationship between Hong Kong and Japan in *Song of the Exile* and *Autumn Moon*, respectively. Cheung has tackled the complex multinational history of modern China in her epic *The Soong Sisters* (1997), and the films of Hui and Law have been read, as much of the output of the Hong Kong film industry in recent years, as political allegory. (For more on all these films in relation to the broader treatment of the Chinese diaspora on screen and in relation to Chinese film and allegory, see Chapter 1.)

However, Hui, Cheung, and Law seem to be linked by more than their gender. They have a dedicated interest in exploring questions of identity within diaspora and a commitment to examining the meaning of Chineseness within the processes of globalization. To this end, personal relationships (between parents and children, among siblings, between husbands and wives as well as lovers) are used to look at global political, economic, social, and cultural dynamics. Hong Kong and its people provide the fulcrum for this investigation. The personal moves beyond the political to the global, and Hong Kong's 1997 fate becomes an emblem for more widespread changes. Law's summation of her life experience serves as an entry into her oeuvre:

> We Hongkong Chinese are more like an abandoned child, because we don't really have Hongkong. I mean, Hongkong will be taken back by the Chinese. I was born in Macao; I went to Hongkong when I was ten. Later, I went to England to study. Now I am trying to settle down here, in Australia with my family. The fact that we don't have a home weighs heavily on our minds.[8]

LAW'S MIGRATION TRILOGY AND THE POLITICS OF ALLEGORY

In "The New Hong Kong Cinema and the *Déjà Disparu*," Ackbar Abbas notes: "Almost every film made since the mid-eighties, regardless of quality or seriousness of intention, seems constrained to make some mandatory reference to 1997."[9] Clara Law, like Wong Kar-wai, Evans Chan, Peter Chan, and the other Hong Kong filmmakers examined in this book, offers no exception to this general rule. However, Abbas's assertion does not deny that these references are contradictory, politically ambivalent, and malleable. In the case of *Farewell, China*, *Autumn Moon*, and *Floating Life*, for example, it is difficult to tease out a singular narrative about the overseas Chinese, the fate of Hong Kong, or about the various national and political agendas of the parties involved. Instead, the films provide a postmodern acceptance of moral ambivalence, political vagary, nostalgia, fragmentation, and uncertainty of identity that is far removed from the national allegories and political optimism of an earlier generation.

The distinctive visual styles and narrative choices found in *Farewell, China*, *Autumn Moon*, and *Floating Life* help place these films within the category of postmodern allegory. They display a flatness and reliance on the surface of the image. Drawing on elements associated with modernism, the films create a pastiche of popular formulas (e.g., melodrama and romance) and high art flourishes. All three films vertiginously dissolve linear time and space in favor of the use of flashbacks, breaks in causality, shifts in perspective and narrative voice, and an episodic structure. A Brechtian alienation from the characters is achieved through the use of voiceover commentaries removed from on-screen events, the mediation of technology in interpersonal relationships (e.g., long-distance phone calls, video cameras, karaoke machines, etc.), and the multiple and contradictory roles played by several of the principal characters. Visually, the cinematography and mise-en-scène abstract the geographical locations through which the characters move. In

Farewell, China, the naturalistic presentation of rural China is contrasted with the monstrosity of New York, epitomized by a scene featuring a carnivalesque and decadent street theater performance. In *Autumn Moon*, repeated aerial shots of Hong Kong's high-rise housing complexes photographed at an extremely high angle from a gracefully moving plane coupled with the monochromatic color scheme help create a cityscape that provides a sense of abstraction, monotony, rigidity, and dehumanization. *Floating Life*'s use of title cards to announce changes in locations from various houses in Germany, Australia, and Hong Kong foregrounds place as an abstraction; that is, a concept illustrated by the images that follow of the intense sunlight engulfing the suburban house in Australia to the soft focus, muted colors, and moisture associated with the final abode pictured in Germany. Style dominates time, space, and character, and the image rules over narrative necessity.

Like many other allegories, *Farewell, China*, *Autumn Moon*, and *Floating Life* revolve around journeys. In *Farewell, China*, Zhao Nansheng (Tony Leung Ka-Fai) goes in search of his missing wife, Li Hong (Maggie Cheung), who has emigrated from mainland China to build a better life in New York City. Zhao meets up with Jane (Hayley Man Hei-Lin), an American-born Chinese street girl who has run away from home to search out an identity away from her Chinese American roots. In *Autumn Moon*, aptly named Tokio (Masatoshi Nagase) travels from Japan to Hong Kong in search of "authentic" Cantonese cuisine. He meets up with a teenage girl, Pui-Wai (Li Pui-Wai), who is on her own search for the meaning of love and commitment as she readies herself to leave Hong Kong, her self-absorbed boyfriend, and her self-sacrificing grandmother behind to join her parents who have already immigrated to Canada. In *Floating Life*, the Chan family leaves Hong Kong to seek out a better life in Germany and Australia. As in the other two films, a twenty-something man, in this case, Gar Ming (Anthony Wong), meets up with a younger woman, Apple (Nina Liu), who, like Jane in *Farewell, China*, has been raised in North America (Canada, in this case).

The journey in each film, however, seems to promote a different transnational allegory with Hong Kong both present and absent as a major player. *Farewell, China*, for example, ostensibly functions as a cautionary tale for those planning to emigrate from China to the West. Stephen Teo has compared it to Dante's *Inferno*,[10] and the film makes its descent into the underworld of New York City with the same sense of horror coupled with moral certitude as found in Dante's poem. A coproduction predicated on cooperation with the PRC, the ostensible allegory would appear to be clear: China represents home, hearth, and a certain Chinese identity free from racism (and colonialism); the West, in the form of New York, symbolizes the excesses of capitalism, the decadence of a rootless and materialistic lifestyle and, ultimately, death and madness. Characters from Hong Kong and Taiwan appear within the New York inferno to drive home the point that the West provides no safe haven for the Chinese emigrant. If Hong Kong as colony soon to become the Special Administrative Region is substituted for the wandering Chinese characters in the film, the allegory becomes even clearer—Hong Kong and its inhabitants are cautioned against wandering away from their Chinese roots.

The film's denouement pictures the dead body of Zhao stabbed to death by his insane wife, Li.[11] As the camera pulls away, the view of his body diminishes as a replica of the Goddess of Democracy looms over him in a square in New York's Chinatown. The image can be read as ironic, that is, in the seat of democratic freedom, the dispossessed are swallowed up by urban decadence. Tacitly, China is vindicated for its suppression of its own misguided youth in Tian'anmen. As the film closes with images of the Chinese countryside and Zhao and Li's child framed by the buildings of an alleyway in their small town, the future (with the hopes symbolized by the child) seems to reside in China.

However, this interpretation of *Farewell, China* misses several subtle and some not-so-subtle visual, dramatic, and narrative points in this film made during 1989 and screened just a few months after June 4. Although visually China is associated with domestic, rural images of family life, the place of China within the drama fulfills a different function. From the beginning of the film when Li asks for sympathy from a U.S. embassy bureaucrat because she is part of the lost generation victimized by the Cultural Revolution, the political excesses of Chinese government policies surface as explanations for the characters' apparently absurd actions throughout the film. Zhao and Li met during the Cultural Revolution. In the scene in which Zhao finally meets up with his wife in New York City, Li plays music from that era as she slips into a paranoid fantasy of eavesdropping officials and inconspicuous spies. They huddle together in the shadows on the floor of Li's apartment. Dramatically, it must be noted that the film's climax does not deal with the abuse Li suffered in the United States that had been graphically depicted throughout the film up to this point. Rather, Li's fevered imagination conjures up the excesses of the Cultural Revolution. The tragic fate of the doomed lovers, therefore, can be traced to China, rather than America.

In this case, what is not depicted and what could not be depicted due to censorship regulations impinging on the film as both a Chinese and a Hong Kong production are as important as what appears on screen. However, what is alluded to in the film conjures up Hong Kong's nightmares about China in the wake of the events of spring 1989 in Tian'anmen Square. The political excesses associated with an earlier generation stand in for the recent repression; the "victims" of the Cultural Revolution stand in for the students of Tian'anmen. Jane's ignorance of the Cultural Revolution masks her blindness to the 1989 student movement. The illegal and semi-legal students, artists, and intellectuals that people New York in the film remain mute on Tian'anmen; no one seeks political asylum. An entire generation is missing.

Hong Kong's explosion of public support for the student demonstrators is pushed aside. The sketchy inclusion of a poorly defined and arrogant English teacher from Hong Kong, who has settled in New York illegally, marks what is absent in the text. Hong Kong slips out of the picture as the anxiety surrounding the change in the colony's status increases.

This strategy of displacement, characteristic of political allegory, works to equate the Tian'anmen demonstrations with the Cultural Revolution; however, analogy does contain a certain degree of ambiguity. For example, the film seems to draw youth from the late 1960s to early 1970s and from the 1980s together in a scene in which Zhao explains his English name, Lincoln, to Jane. He says he chose the name because Lincoln was so honest to admit he chopped down the cherry tree; he states, "The Chinese of this generation don't dare face the truth." The statement is ambiguous, because Zhao could be talking about his own generation or the generation of students associated with the Tian'anmen demonstrations. His ignorance of American history and mythology (i.e., confusing George Washington and Abraham Lincoln), does not stop him from lionizing the American Dream of personal liberty, and this situates him as much in the latter as the former generation.

From this perspective, the film's denouement can be read differently. Faith in New York's Statue of Liberty and confidence in Beijing's Goddess of Democracy are equally misplaced. If New York is an inferno, the mainland is far from paradise. For Hong Kong, the prospect of being absorbed into a repressive and politically chaotic country brought up all the horror still associated with a Cold War fear of the "Red Chinese." The energy that went into depicting America as hell may be, then, the displaced emotion associated with what was a traumatic shock for many in Hong Kong. Although the film's Chinese title is innocuous and misleading, *The Season of Love in Another Land*, its English title, bids goodbye to China in no uncertain terms. However, *Farewell, China* must navigate murky waters. The film does display nostalgia for the authenticity of the mainland Chinese, for a sense of Chinese patriarchal tradition, and for the certainty of an enduring patrilineal descent; however, any faith in tradition is offset by fear of the repressive potential of the Chinese nation. Ultimately, the film remains politically ambivalent.

Autumn Moon at first glance also offers a neat, superficial allegory. Tokio leaves Japan to look for authentic Chineseness in Hong Kong. (The mainland and Taiwan are not on his itinerary.) He befriends the "spirit" of Hong Kong in the person of Pui-Wai, who acts as his guide. For her, McDonald's epitomizes "authentic" Hong Kong cuisine.[12] However, both eventually find Hong Kong and its authentic Chineseness in Pui-Wai's grandmother's kitchen. All manage to communicate through broken English, Chinese written characters (Han-zi) also found in written Japanese (kanji), and the links forged by the device of Tokio's camcorder. After parallel romantic and sexual disappointments and a shared concern for the ailing, hospitalized grandmother, Tokio and Pui-Wai solidify their fleeting, platonic relationship with a celebration of Mid-Autumn Festival, a Chinese holiday dedicated to the full autumn moon, the harvest, and family harmony.

Tokio notes a similarity to a dissimilar Japanese festival, O-Bon. This festival welcomes the spirits of the dead for a temporary visit to the land of the living and is more akin to the Chinese Pure Brightness Festival, also dedicated to the dead, than to the family- and moon-centered Mid-Autumn Festival. However, the point is made. The Japanese and the Chinese share a common Asian heritage and a common postmodern position of disaffection, fragmentation, and uncertain identity within advanced, global capitalism. Against the possibility of another "reunion" (i.e., Hong Kong with the PRC in 1997), Tokio and Pui-Wai find a sense of peace and harmony, as Hong Kong defines itself against a modern or premodern People's

Republic and as similar to a clearly postmodern Japan. Grandma has conveniently forgotten the Pacific war and the Japanese occupation,[13] and she gladly pours out her tale of self-sacrifice and authentic Chinese fortitude to be captured by Tokio's video camera, although the cameraman cannot understand her Cantonese monologue. Grandma embodies what must be left behind as Pui-Wai and her family move on with their lives away from a Hong Kong destined to revert to China. They escape, as well, from all China represents for the bourgeoisie of Hong Kong, that is, "authentic" Chinese poverty, outmoded customs, "backward," "primitive," rural sensibilities, and a collective past filled with real and imagined horrors. Grandma is loved as China may be loved as a homeland. However, both must be left behind as unsuitable for survival in the postmodern diaspora.

Given that the film is a coproduction, financed by Japanese money, and featuring Japanese acting talent,[14] it is not surprising that this film should pay homage to the relationship between Japan and Hong Kong. Stylistically, there are hints of Ozu, for example, in the use of cutaways to objects to halt the narrative and set a contemplative mood (e.g., the close-ups of the jars of preserved foods and traditional cooking implements in Grandma's kitchen and other similar set pieces within the mise-en-scène). A feeling for the bittersweet impermanence of love, beauty, and life itself, so fundamental to the Japanese aesthetic sensibility, permeates *Autumn Moon*. In addition, the poems Pui-Wai recites in her voiceover meditations throughout the film resemble Japanese haiku and point to a shared literary and cultural tradition. In her final voiceover, Pui-Wai recites the following poem she remembers from past Mid-Autumn celebrations with her deceased grandfather:

> When will the spring flower and the autumn moon fade?
> How much of the past do we know?
> At my home last night the east wind blew . . .
> I can't remember the rest.[15]

The east wind seems to blow from Japan in this case, and the past may need to be as faded and shadowy as the lines of the poem. However, this acceptance of a flawed memory has its function in the present moment captured by *Autumn Moon*. Memory must be selective[16] and home left as a collection of nostalgic feelings.

With the presentation of the cultural similarities between the hybridized, postmodern Japan and Hong Kong, there emerges a sense that Hong Kong really does not belong to China economically, historically, or culturally. The fantasy that Hong Kong is not Chinese and, therefore, can never be a part of China despite the fact of July 1, 1997, has its appeal. Chinese language, arts, food, and customs flow into a pan-Asian cultural melting pot and are fully appreciated by the Japanese tourist. However, this harmony is based on a double forgetfulness of both the Pacific war and the 1997 handover.

The monochromatic color scheme, repetitive camera movement, and abstract, dehumanizing patterns of the mise-en-scène also point to a less optimistic reading of the allegory. After all, Hong Kong is sick and dying like Pui-Wai's grandmother or destined to disappear into the Chinese diaspora like Pui-Wai and her boyfriend. While aestheticized through an association with changing seasons, falling leaves, growing up and growing old as part of the bittersweet cycle of human life, the connection to Hong Kong's political fate cannot be overlooked.

Floating Life presents an allegorical interpretation that seems, at first, to completely contradict the cautionary fable presented in *Farewell, China*. Like *Farewell, China*, *Floating Life* looks at ethnic Chinese emigrants trying to adjust to a new nation. In this case, the Chan family from Hong Kong finally acclimates to life in Germany and Australia. It can thus be read as the fruition of the situation described in *Autumn Moon*. Similar to Pui-Wai in *Autumn Moon*, Gar Ming, the Chans' eldest son, spends his final weeks in Hong Kong before emigrating.

In *Floating Life*, however, the overwhelming thrust of this Australian-produced film moves in the direction of embracing a new homeland.[17] The Chan family has successfully completed its journey, and all the family members establish roots in their new countries. At the conclusion of *Floating Life*, for example, the disturbed second sister, Bing (Annie Yip), has been recuperated through traditional Chinese means (i.e., familial affection and ancestor worship) and is pictured as pregnant and timidly walking in broad daylight at the side of her mother, Mrs. Chan (Cecilia Lee). The eldest daughter, Yen (Annette Shun Wah), and her family similarly find peace in a home with good feng shui in the German countryside. The plagues of Bing's career ambitions and the bad geographical orientation of the various abodes in Germany have been banished. Nostalgic moments for the remote homeland of China are curbed by comedy. When Mr. Chan (Edwin Pang) and an old friend meet briefly in Australia for ice cream, for example, their encounter has a tinge of comedy added by the voluptuous waitress dancing around the café. The parental generation, absent in *Autumn Moon*, becomes successfully resettled in *Floating Life*. The patriarchs huddle around a photograph of an ancestral home in China, but the photo represents a distant place, a possible burial place or retirement home, not the present moment of immigration. The men reminisce about their highly placed families that enjoyed a bountiful life before the 1949 revolution, but they are too young to be part of that past themselves, because their memories are of growing up in Hong Kong rather than of struggling in the mainland. Thus, the fate met by the characters in *Farewell, China* and the penetrating nostalgia evoked in *Autumn Moon* are both avoided in *Floating Life*.

In this film, a young child and a hopeful pregnancy symbolize life for the Chinese outside of China. Hong Kong, on the other hand, only promises death and decay. Gar Ming, for example, carries the burden of reburying his grandfather and burying the aborted fetus that he fathered with his Chinese American lover, Apple. Hong Kong becomes the land in which sex and death are inextricably linked, and it remains a mystery for the two younger Chan brothers, Yue and Chau (Toby Wong and Toby Chan), who prefer to speak English and have become accustomed to life in Australia.

However, the links between the throbbing fetus that lived, according to Gar Ming, for three seconds and the Crown Colony on the verge of reabsorption into the maternal body of China seem fairly obvious. In voiceovers, Gar Ming obsesses on the number and timing of his ejaculations and associates them with Hong Kong's imminent handover, "The pleasure still only lasts three seconds. Will it be the same in 1997? Where will I be in 1997?" Later, in another voiceover, as Gar Ming buries the fetus, it seems he could be talking about Hong Kong rather than his aborted flesh: "Three seconds of pleasure produces three inches of flesh. It throbs only once in its entire life. Its whole life is only one second. In one second, it experiences birth, aging, illness and death. . . . Too short . . . or too long? . . . It's not a piece of flesh. It's my child." Later, Gar Ming notes that he experiences the same pain looking at his parents that he feels when he thinks about the aborted fetus. Hong Kong is similarly associated with painful and ambivalent feelings. As Abbas has noted, after the Joint Declaration, Hong Kong's identity became transitional, neither British nor Chinese, but a place that could be construed as having its own autonomous identity briefly.[18] Hong Kong, however, has already disappeared (*déjà disparu*), because this autonomy was always a political impossibility.

The enduring visceral force of the throbbing fetus and its allegorical connections to Hong Kong grate against the ostensibly happy conclusion of this diasporic fantasy. Moreover, the emotive power of Mrs. Chan's final speech in the film also belies at least some of the optimism surrounding the film's dual happy endings. On her knees before the Chan family ancestor tablets, she begs forgiveness for neglecting her filial duties and for her daughter's neglect of her familial obligations in refusing to have children. She prays: "Why, after all these years of not having a homeland, we are used to hardship. Now, we have achieved our goal. The whole family is together in Australia—this paradise on earth. Why can't we have any joy? Why can't we put down our burden and plant our roots in this soil? Why?" Although, almost magically, Mrs. Chan's prayer is answered, the burning questions underlying it remain. The fact that the Chan family finds its true Chinese roots so far away from the new Special Administrative Region of Hong Kong, PRC, retains its bitter aspect. As the prayer and the earlier discussion of ancestral homes in the mainland point out, the Chan family is pictured here as Hong Kong immigrants as well as émigrés. Their right to a political voice or self-determination in Hong Kong is undercut by the comparative brevity of their sojourn there. Their children have inherited their rootlessness, and claims to a Hong Kong identity independent of China become difficult to substantiate.

Indeed, in all three films, Hong Kong slips gracefully out of the picture to resurface later as a "symptom"[19] of psychological imbalances associated with GenerAsian X. Taken together, the three films seem to be very confused politically. However, when this confusion is looked at as a symptom of what cannot be voiced in China, Hong Kong, Japan, or Australia, the relationship of these films to the ambivalence surrounding both Hong Kong as a geographical entity, GenerAsian X as a demographic entity, and the postmodern era comes to the surface.

GenerAsian X and the Politically Incorrect

In *Immigrant Acts*, Lisa Lowe posits a relationship between the process of decolonization postulated by Frantz Fanon in *The Wretched of the Earth* and the experience of immigration.[20] Fanon theorizes a dialectical relationship between assimilation and nationalism in the process of moving from colonial status to freedom in the third world. Lowe sees a similar dialectic operating within the Asian American community and, presumably, within other diasporic communities worldwide. She states:

> Although Fanon's treatise was cited in the 1960s as the manifesto for a nationalist politics of identity, rereading it in the 1990s, we ironically find his text to be the source of a serious critique of nationalism. Fanon argues that the challenge facing any movement that is dismantling colonialism (or a system in which one culture dominates another) is to provide for a new order that does not reproduce the social structure of the old system. This new order must avoid, he argues, the simple assimilation to the dominant culture's roles and positions by the emergent group, which would merely caricature the old colonialism, and it should be equally suspicious of an uncritical nativism or racialism that would appeal to essentialized notions of precolonial identity.[21]

Lowe goes on to point out Fanon's particular criticism of the national bourgeosie as a replacement for the European colonizer. She sees much of the same dynamic operating within the Asian American community in which cultural nationalism and assimilation ostensibly appear to be polar opposites when, in actuality, they work together to ensure the maintenance of hegemony. The bourgeois formation of this hegemony effectively excludes other classes and marginalizes women and other nondominant groups.

The bourgeois orientation of the films under discussion here seems clear. Virtually all of the principal characters fit squarely within the petit bourgeoisie or merchant classes as teachers, artists, and failed intellectuals in *Farewell, China*, as middle-class students and corporate businesspeople in *Autumn Moon*, and as retired merchants and corporate middle management employees in *Floating Life*. The films present the middle class as the norm, and the possibility of dropping from that class position is presented as horrific. This class nexus allows for the characters in all three films to travel, and thus the class dynamic of the global dispersal of people forms the backbone of all three films. As in many popular films, this class privilege does not go unchallenged, and the bourgeois world, both publicly and privately, is depicted as dehumanizing, senseless, inauthentic, and alienating. Thus the American Dream in *Farewell, China* is presented through the figure of Li Hong as the vacuous ravings of a madwoman who desperately hides her cons behind the mask of a successful businesswoman. In *Autumn Moon*, Tokio takes a holiday away from his Japanese corporation to look for something authentic and ends up at McDonald's and in bed with a woman whose corporate drudgery mirrors his own. His characteristic inventorying of all of his Hong Kong purchases via his video camera underscores his vapid obsession with commodities. *Floating Life* shows its characters consumed by their corporate jobs; for example, Gar Ming's insane hours speculating on the stock market and Bing's hysterical identification with her severe business suit as armor against the isolation and insecurity of being alone in a foreign country.

However, this critique does not belie these films' principal address to a middle-class audience within or necessarily affected by the Chinese diaspora. Because of this, it should come as no surprise that the films suffer from some of the ideological ills highlighted in Lowe's reading of Fanon. There is a tension between cultural nationalism and assimilation in all the films, between nostalgia for an authentic Chineseness and the self-deprecations associated with a denial of the self to assimilate into the cultural mainstream. Consequently, the films often appear to be politically incorrect in their depictions of sex, gender, race, ethnicity, age, and class.

Race and racism surface most disturbingly in *Farewell, China* and *Floating Life*. Although the Chinese migrants suffer from the racism of white society, they often display prejudice toward other people of color. Both films teeter-totter between presenting racial others as threats to the Chinese abroad and depicting internalized racism as the most debilitating consequence of leaving China/Hong Kong.

In *Farewell, China*, racism first surfaces in the institution of the United States government and its gate-keeping Immigration and Naturalization Service. After being repeatedly denied a student visa at the Guangzhou embassy near her southern Chinese home, Li Hong journeys to Shanghai with her husband and child to try again there. Her interview takes place in an impersonal office with the sole decoration of the U.S. flag. The male embassy worker is distant and condescending. Li Hong's request had been turned down earlier because she was considered "too pretty," and, presumably, a high risk for finding an American husband or drifting into prostitution. She vehemently states that she is now not pretty because she has had a baby in the intervening months since her last interview. Cynically, the official asks, "Did you have a baby in order to get a visa?" The film underscores the sexism and racism of U.S. immigration policy, but it also does nothing to negate the official's question, and, consequently, offers a complicit position with his moral judgment of Li Hong's character.

Moreover, the film depicts the internalized self-hatred stemming from Chinese exclusion from mainstream white middle-class society very directly. Zhao first encounters the toll American life has taken in terms of human dignity when his "friend" John, his first contact in New York whom he had known in the PRC, wakes him up in the middle of the night and throws him on the street out of fear of not being granted permanent residency if he is seen harboring an illegal alien. America, then, pits friend against friend ostensibly because of immigration status, but also because of the obviousness of Zhao's race.

Zhao, on the street in search of Li, meets up with Jane, who bears a striking resemblance to his wife. Detroit-born Jane speaks Toi San–inflected Cantonese mixed with English, which becomes her medium for communication with Zhao. To put it bluntly, she loathes being Chinese. She calls Zhao "E.T." to emphasize how alien he is in comparison to herself. When Li's wealthy sponsor in Long Island is less than helpful on their quest, she angrily calls him "a fucking Chink." Jane's internalized anti-Asian racism is linked to her background as a typically American child of separated parents and a weakened patriarchy. She associates her despised father with the smell of Chinese restaurants. Later in the film, she elaborates: "I hated having Chinese parents. I hated speaking Chinese. I even dyed my hair green and red and yellow, so I wouldn't look like a Chinese. Now, I'm happy. I'm free."

The chronicle of her life enfolds as a cliché of a dissolute youth. Jane went on the pill at ten, had an abortion at twelve, and had a baby girl given up for adoption at fourteen. Zhao asks, "Why have a child at all when you're so irresponsible?" Although Zhao may feel he is able to take the moral high ground with Jane, the film has already shown the viewer that he is cut from the same cloth, because he and his wife left their child behind in China. Indeed, the film draws a strong parallel between the morally bankrupt American-born Chinese and the equally morally bereft mainland Chinese. Throughout the film, Jane and Li Hong parallel one another in their internalized self-hatred, their ability to have a child and abandon it, their search for an ill-defined freedom, their dishonesty, their tendency to prostitute themselves, and their unselfconscious knack for leading men into their own self-destructive universe. Both characters are conflicted, caring, and brutally selfish. They hate themselves, hate being Chinese, and show the range of moral collapse suffered by the Chinese across continents. At the film's climax, Li Hong turns on her unsuspecting husband with whom she has just had a tearful reunion. When he wakes up in her bed, she shouts, "Shut up. We're not to speak Chinese here in my apartment. Is that clear? . . . Shut up, you fucking, stupid Chink. Speak English; this is the United States of America."

A similar ethnic self-deprecation marks Bing in *Floating Life*. Like Jane and Li Hong, Bing rails against Chinese culture because it prevents her from assimilating into mainstream Australian society. She refuses to speak Cantonese to her younger brothers, whom she browbeats with warnings that they will bring down all Asians in the eyes of Australians if they do not act in certain prescribed ways. She embodies the split of assimilation versus nationalism in her hysterical fear of Australian racism coupled with her equally intense fear that she is inadequate because of her race. Every action, then, becomes a contradiction. She and her brothers must prove the superiority of the Chinese immigrant by speaking impeccable English. She asks Yue and Chau, at one point, how many pages of the English dictionary they have memorized. For her, Australia is a land of poisonous snakes, ravenous pit bulls, skin cancer, clogged arteries, and endless hours of work that allow her to engage with her family only as a cultural policewoman, who denies them television, soft-core porn magazines, and fatty foods, the emblems of Western decadence. She yells at her younger brothers, "The house stinks. It's full of AIDS. You're here as immigrants, not to enjoy life!"

Internalizing this self-hatred, Yue and Chau consult a quack to enhance their height to be more attractive to the stately white Australian girls. By the time Gar Ming arrives in Australia, his youngest brother can barely understand and speak Cantonese. The youngest has stayed on with Bing and her husband out of fear, but Yue and their parents have abandoned the increasingly demanding Bing. Gar Ming refuses to let his youngest sibling escape and literally drags him kicking and screaming back to Mom and Dad.

Racism and the pains of immigration make this family dysfunctional. As Fanon's and Lowe's work shows, dealing with the effects of racism, colonialism, and immigration leads to pathology. Although less extreme, Yen's ways of dealing with life outside Hong Kong also show signs of being pathological. Apparently settled in Germany with a white husband, daughter, and supportive friends and in-laws, Yen suffers the same contradictory bind of assimilation and nationalism as her younger sister Bing. Like Bing, she is presented as a little crazy. Whereas Bing refuses to let her brothers speak Cantonese so that they can function as model Chinese in Australia, Yen is disappointed when her daughter, Mui Mui, complains about speaking Cantonese. Mui Mui notes that her father says that Cantonese is not "real" Chinese, because Mandarin is the official language of the People's Republic. Flustered, Yen replies that it is the only Chinese she knows. However, the relative inutility of speaking Cantonese in Germany, and by extension of being Chinese in Germany, surfaces.

Moreover, Chinese tradition becomes linked to psychological imbalance. Yen decides/realizes one day, for example, that her new apartment has bad feng shui and turns the household upside down rearranging furniture and seeking other remedies as dictated by this traditional Chinese environmental science. However, this feeling of malaise expands outside the home. Bing internalizes the threatening environment of Australia from radio reports, TV news, and the newspaper. When Yue and Chau introduce their life in Australia through a voiceover, they state that their first exposure to life there was "like a movie." "What movie?" the other inquires. "*Basic Instinct, Terminator, Jurassic Park*," comes the reply. *Floating Life* may be an immigration "comedy," but it has striking affinities with the science fiction, horror, and thriller genres. However, no actual racism or xenophobia in Australia is pictured in the film. Given that the film was funded by the federal government of Australia, the state government of Victoria, and the Special Broadcasting Service,[22] perhaps it should not come as a surprise that the vicious racism of Pauline Hansen does not figure in the script. Yen, in Germany, is the one who encounters racism directly, embodied by the figure of a skinhead with a swastika tattooed on his naked scalp. Although Yen has the courage to stand up to the skinhead's stares, she still develops a hysterical disease that makes her skin unbearably itchy. After the incident, she muses, "I live in Germany, but I'm not German. Where is my home?"

Pui-Wai in *Autumn Moon* seems to be in a similarly contradictory situation, since she is both at home and not at home in Hong Kong. She, too, is a divided figure—comfortable speaking English, more at home at McDonald's than at a Cantonese noodle shop, cosmopolitan and hybrid. Like all of the principal characters in these three films, she lives in an environment in which she must assimilate into a world dominated by British colonial vestiges, American transnational capitalism, and the myth of a Chinese cultural authenticity. Racism, then, operates in Hong Kong as well as abroad, because Pui-Wai must bow to certain assimilationist expectations on her way to Canada.

However, the depiction of racism in all three films is profoundly ambivalent. Although American, German, and Australian racism is clearly national, social, cultural, and institutional, the impact of that racism remains personal and pathological within the narrative. Political critique wanes. Also, as an extension of the nationalism Lowe's reading of Fanon warns against, an unselfconscious racism permeates representations of other minority groups. Perhaps the most striking case exists in *Farewell, China*. A dramatic turning point in the film occurs when Zhao tracks down Li's former employers in Harlem. To say the least, the African American community does not fare well in this sequence.

The carry-out in Harlem is hellish. A bullet-proof partition separates the Taiwanese couple who work frantically to fill the orders for the noisy African American clientele on the other side. The Taiwanese pop music in the kitchen vies with the customers' hip hop on the soundtrack. Zhao helps the couple lock up. A strong metal gate secures the business. They all rush to the car; the boss and his wife clutch that day's earnings and a handgun. The proprietor talks amiably with Zhao about working in Harlem. He prefers African Americans to whites, whom he classifies as snobs. "Actually, Harlem's quite peaceful," he says. However, the increasing panic in his wife's voice as the car refuses to start shows this to be false, and he finally admits to being afraid when "they're drunk."

When Zhao and his companions reach the safety of the couple's apartment, the proprietor's wife berates Zhao for allowing Li Hong to come to America alone: "Do you know what it's like not to have money for a tampon? To be raped?" At this point, the film takes on all the emotional energy of John Ford's *The Searchers* (1956).[23] The Chinese have settled on the frontier of Harlem to seek their fortune. Zhao has come in search of Li in a ghetto wilderness where she has been raped and brutalized by savages. Her purity has been compromised.

A flashback shows the Taiwanese proprietor and his wife in their carry-out. A woman's screams are heard outside; shadowy figures assault a woman. The proprietor takes out his gun to help the victim, but his wife stops him. Li Hong, beaten and hysterical, makes her way into the carry-out. She refuses to let her employers call the police because of her illegal immigration status, and she huddles under a table, sobbing, on the linoleum floor as the flashback ends. While the INS must take some of the blame for Li Hong's situation, the film, too, must take some blame for its own racist complicity. Like the natives in *The Searchers*, African Americans, purely by virtue of their race, act as signifiers of urban savagery and threats to Chinese purity. In condemning the racism of the U.S. government, the film legitimates the racist fears of a global Chinese audience that likely has learned the most about the American black community from Hollywood action films.

Race and racism are intimately connected with sex and gender in these films. If they can be read as cautionary tales for the Chinese abroad as well as celebrations of the enduring power of Chineseness, then they can also be read as cautionary tales for Chinese women and as celebrations of patriarchal tradition. The films have what can be called a postfeminist sensibility. Thus, a taken-for-granted equality for women in the business world, governmentally sanctioned reproductive freedom, and the availability of opportunities for higher education and travel roughly on a par with men are coupled with very conservative notions of sexual morality, femininity, domesticity, and the joy women find in their traditional gender roles. The postfeminist woman triumphs in the corporate, transnational workplace. However, she finds herself alienated, unfulfilled, and profoundly unhappy, longing nostalgically for an idealized patriarchy that never existed historically. When the postfeminist wins, in other words, she loses.

Generation X has been criticized often for benefiting from the fruits of the women's movement while cursing feminism. In *Farewell, China, Autumn Moon*, and *Floating Life*, this postfeminist sensibility casts its female characters in a suspect light. Women become the sites of moral laxity, potential cultural dissolution, and madness. Patriarchy is actively mourned, although the fact is accepted that it will not be resuscitated. In the case of these films, too, this postfeminism has a specifically transnational character. Bourgeois female labor finds favor in the transnational corporation blending the need for a polyglot education with cross-cultural savvy. Less committed to staying in place and garnering the rewards of a filial son, these Chinese women fit a niche in these transnational enterprises. Part model Asian worker and part exotic, eroticized ornament, Chinese women can be displayed as a denial of the exploitation of working-class Asian women in sweatshops around the globe. A scene in *Floating Life*, for example, shows Bing's warm acceptance into a transnational workplace when she is literally embraced by her white Australian colleagues. The female characters in these films travel in both a racialized and sexualized capitalist environment, and they sometimes benefit from the institutions that keep that world predominantly white, male, and middle class.

In *Farewell, China*, Li Hong takes on the persona of a successful transnational entrepreneur that masks her desperate life on the street. Her desire to separate herself from China and her Chinese husband and son marks a threat to the authenticity of Chinese identity as well as the prerogatives of the patriarchy. As a woman, she lives the dark side of American capitalism. She prostitutes herself to get ahead, for example, when she attempts to sell herself as a wife to an aging Chinatown laundry man. When the scheme goes awry because she cannot secure her divorce, she turns to running cons on the vulnerable, elderly Chinese of New York City.

Li Hong's alter ego Jane is literally a prostitute, and, through his association with her, Zhao becomes a pimp. Drunk and wearing the uniform of the street (i.e., jeans, leather jacket, and cigarette hanging from the lip), he hawks her on the streets, "Hey, fifteen-year-old Chinese girl, beautiful, clean, and sexy, $150." Here, *Farewell, China* meets another film indebted to *The Searchers*, *Taxi Driver* (1976), and as in that film, the flawed hero manages, really in spite of himself, to "rescue" the teenage prostitute. In this case, Jane comes to her senses after nearly having sex with Zhao, and she decides to return to her Detroit family and go "back to school." Just as Ethan (John Wayne) in *The Searchers* nearly kills Debbie (Natalie Wood), Zhao nearly penetrates Jane. However, both have a change of heart, and although Ethan and Zhao are both doomed in their respective films to wander away and die, they manage to allow for a glimmer of hope for the survival of patriarchal control of female sexuality. Li Hong has gone mad, but Jane has gone home.

In *Autumn Moon*, the situation is presented in more subtle ways. In this film, Pui-Wai and Miki (Maki Kiuchi) parallel one another as the two women in Tokio's life. Early in the film, Pui-Wai voices the idea that she represents a culture on the verge of dissolution, and as in *The Searchers*, that potential disappearance has sexual ramifications. She states in one of her numerous voice-overs: "In the past two years, most [of my Hong Kong friends] have emigrated. It will be my turn to go next year. By the time I'm twenty, we could all be married to foreigners." Threatened, Tokio represents an Asian masculinity in need of reform. In *Farewell, China*, Zhao starts out as a committed father and husband and becomes a bum. In *Autumn Moon*, Tokio starts out as a bum and becomes a devoted friend and reformed lover. At the beginning of the film, Tokio videotapes a woman he picks up for sex in the same way he obsessively tapes all the other possessions he acquires in Hong Kong. At first, Tokio treats Miki as one of his possessions. He remembers her as the sister of a former girlfriend but gets her confused with some other girl's sister, because women, equated with commodities, are inter-changeable for him. After having sex, they make a date for the next day; an empty table at the rendezvous point signals their lack of commitment to continuing their casual encounter. Divorced, Miki is committed to her corporate job, and she maintains a distance from men. After discussing young love with Pui-Wai and visiting her stoic grandmother in her hospital bed, Tokio pays a visit to Miki at her office. Now, with a softened Tokio, Miki becomes more than an interchangeable cipher after making love. In an intimate moment, Tokio talks about crying over *Bambi* (1942), and he reminisces about Miki's sister's breasts. Even this girl from his past takes on a new shape as Miki tells him of her sister's life with her husband and three children in Hawaii.

Pui-Wai's rendezvous with her boyfriend, however, is quite different. They fail to connect. Pui-Wai sits quietly by the hotel window as her boyfriend plays with his video game in bed. He only breaks the silence to talk about his plans in which both Pui-Wai and Hong Kong are noticeably absent. He will finish high school in the United States, double major in computer science and nuclear physics, and be sought after by American and Japanese transnationals. Ironically, Pui-Wai's boy-friend's self-absorption keeps her a virgin. The platonic connections the film favors over Tokio's womanizing ways win out as the film concludes with Tokio and Pui-Wai's chaste celebration of the Mid-Autumn family holiday.

At a time when families are scattering and filial connections to the elderly shattering, *Autumn Moon* hangs on to the memory of the Confucian, patriarchal order. Pui-Wai feeds her grandmother's cranky cat, even if she must leave her to live out her life alone and abandoned by her family, and she remembers her deceased grandfather during Mid-Autumn, even if she forgets his words. Similarly, Tokio's reminiscences with Miki and his celebration of Mid-Autumn as a sub-stitute for O-Ban reveal nostalgia for a traditional childhood as an analogue for a traditional cultural heritage. The postmodern moment may lay patriarchy to rest, but nostalgia for the patriarchy continues to be part of the cultural mix for GenerAsian X.

Floating Life pictures a similarly nostalgic view of Chinese patriarchal tradition. Female self-determination and sexual self-expression are depicted as threats that make racism and physical violence seem minor annoyances in comparison. Yen has difficulty continuing the Chinese language and traditions through her daughter in Germany. Bing hen-pecks her husband with the rest of the household in Australia, comes close to an adulterous affair when separated from him for business reasons, divides the family with her ultimatum to her two younger brothers, and generally disrespects her elder sister, mother, and father. Gar Ming is led astray by Apple, the free-spirited, Westernized temptress, who seduces him away from his obligation to marry and produce offspring.

Indeed, each member of the Chan family strays from his or her Confucian filial obligation. Even Mr. and Mrs. Chan neglect to pay their respects to their ancestors by not burning incense at the family shrine. The younger brothers split in their loyalties to the family. The narrative plays out the contradictions between Confucian order and assimilation into mainstream Australian society, between patriarchal prerogatives and feminist self-determination, between adhering to a traditional notion of Chineseness and accepting a cosmopolitan hybridity. As the narrative concludes, Tu Wei-Ming's vision of China on the periphery being free to be more Chinese than within the core of the People's Republic has triumphed. Bing has bowed down to her place within her husband's family by becoming pregnant. She and her mother can now control their threatening Australian environment (embodied by the neighbor's barking dog that they order to sit as they stroll past). Mr. Chan has settled into his own house with his wife and his three sons and designs a landscape and greenhouse reminiscent of his ancestral hall in the mainland. Even Mui Mui, in the last scene, finally gets her house and dreams of a time when her extended family in Australia will come and live there. "And maybe my baby, too" are her final words that clarify her own commitment to a sense of Chinese familial continuity.

Thus, *Farewell, China, Autumn Moon,* and *Floating Life* all recognize the political marks of postcolonialism, civil rights, feminism, the sexual revolution, the Cultural Revolution, the May–June 1989 demonstrations in Tian'anmen Square, and the Hong Kong 1997 change in sovereignty, consumerism, globalization, and the Chinese diaspora. However, while noting these momentous political, economic, social, and cultural changes, the films cling to conservative closures for their narrative conundrums. Women's sexuality, in particular, poses the most salient threat and is the element most harshly reined in as each film works through to its conclusion. Li Hong gives in to madness; Jane returns to her family; Pui-Wai retains her purity; her grandmother reconciles herself to her own expendability; Bing gets pregnant; Mrs. Chan enshrines the Chan ancestors properly; Yen finds her house and her daughter finds her dream of traditional family harmony. Miki finds a moment of solace with Tokio and a type of redemption. However, the insouciant Apple has her abortion and is discarded by the narrative as a dead-end. From this perspective, the films become morality tales for

GenerAsian X, warning of racism and cultural dissolution through the reconfigured presence of the liberated woman as the wanton vixen in need of a clear lesson. Narrative resolution rests on the elimination or recuperation of GenerAsian X's women for an uncertain patriarchal continuity of tradition within the Chinese diaspora.

8   Fighting Diaspora: The Legacy of Bruce and Brandon Lee in *Rapid Fire*

FROM ITS EARLIEST DAYS, American cinema has drawn on the presence of Chinese in the United States and Americans in China for its subject matter. Part of the wider depiction of Asia and Asians in American commercial film, the representation of China and the Chinese followed formulaic patterns characteristic of broader attitudes toward Asians within American society. As Eugene Franklin Wong has pointed out in his study *On Visual Media Racism: Asians in American Motion Pictures*,[1] Hollywood film has tended to lump Asian men into one of two categories, portraying them either as faithful eunuchs attending to the needs of their white masters or as barbaric heathens lusting after Anglo-American women. Although there have been exceptions to this general rule, Bruce Lee found the racism in Hollywood so deadening to his creative energies that he returned to Hong Kong to pursue his acting career and eventually become an internationally acclaimed star.[2] Following in his father's footsteps and trying to eke out a unique place for himself in the cinema, Brandon Lee created a star image that both adheres to and diverges significantly from the path taken by his father two decades before. While Bruce Lee stood as an emblem of justified revolt and vengeance for audiences of the dispossessed globally, Brandon Lee's image promised the possibility of assimilation as he began to make inroads into a racist film industry first in supporting and, shortly before his death in 1993 on the set of *The Crow* (1994), leading roles.

Rapid Fire (1992) is one of Brandon Lee's starring vehicles, and it can be used as a point of departure for understanding how Hollywood has rethought its depiction of Asian/Asian American identity as a consequence of changing patterns of immigration and in light of America's evolving relationship with the People's Republic of China. A pastiche of post-1989 Tian'anmen politics, oedipal ambivalence, ethnic gang wars, and urban paranoia, *Rapid Fire* self-consciously alludes to the connection between Brandon and his famous father within a drama that only thinly disguises its attempts to reconfigure Bruce Lee in his son's image. Rather than defying a racist society that attempts to destroy him, Brandon's character learns to accept his role as symbol of a new America, cleansed of its racism, by putting his martial arts talents and romantic energies in the service of the police. Throughout the course of its narrative, *Rapid Fire* voices concerns surrounding gender roles, ethnic identity, race, international politics, crime, and governmental corruption. The plot places these controversial issues on Brandon's shoulders in an attempt to reinvent an acceptable but nonthreatening multiethnic presence within Hollywood. Haunted by the ghost of Bruce Lee, this reconfigured masculinity, however, seems drained of affect, a postmodern simulation of an Asian American hero who has lost his original, justified anger.

By taking Brandon Lee in *Rapid Fire* as a case study in contemporary Hollywood attitudes toward Asia, the current commercial exploitation of China in the American cinema can be seen to closely parallel America's own inability to come to grips with rapidly changing attitudes toward race and gender domestically and globally. Lee's body functions as a spectacle that both acknowledges these social issues and drains them of significance within a postmodern reconfiguration of Lee (the son) replacing Lee (the father).

THE RELUCTANT HERO

Rapid Fire unfolds as a hybrid action-adventure/crime drama. It blazes no new narrative trails and stands as an example of contemporary postmodern Hollywood fiction. The plot involves battles between Chinese tongs and the Italian Mafia, criminals and the police, corrupt cops and honest civilians, and misunderstood rebels and figures of established authority. A reluctant hero,[3] a fairly standard (if interracial) love interest, and a crusty older policeman figure as protagonists and the usual, caricatured ethnics serve as the antagonists. Settings are both familiar and exotic, for example, the jungles of Southeast Asia, Tian'anmen, and the streets of Los Angeles and Chicago. Standard themes appear in the narrative—ethnicity and assimilation, justice and authority, capitalism and its excesses, familial obligation and political commitment, self-identity and the demands of the group or nation. Details directly recall other films—from Bruce Lee's trademark fighting gestures to snippets of music quoted from Sergio Leone's spaghetti Westerns. Nothing seems unfamiliar; like other postmodern films, *Rapid Fire* seeks to please through this all-encompassing familiarity of genre, narrative, gesture, dialogue, and star quality.

There is, however, something vaguely off. *Rapid Fire* copies classical Hollywood films but at a canted angle. In the opening credits, an ethereal Brandon Lee appears in a series of process shots that multiply his half-naked image, breaking down the integrity of his body. Within the diegesis, his character's centrality comes into question further through the device of a lengthy introductory sequence that delays the appearance of Jake Lo (Lee's character) as the film's principal protagonist. Although an episodic structure does tend to characterize the martial arts/action-adventure genre, this reluctance to produce a hero, even a reluctant hero like Jake Lo, seems out of keeping with the star-centered nature of the genre.

In fact, *Rapid Fire* appears at first to be a gangster film. The narrative opens in Asia with a meeting of two drug dealers. Tony Serrano (Nick Mancuso), a Chicago-based Mafioso, confronts Kinman "Tommy" Tau (Tzi Ma), a longtime associate, on his home turf, asking for a bigger percentage of their business. Although the sequence does allow for a display of Tau's staff fighting prowess as he takes out two of his underlings in a gambling competition for Serrano's enlightenment or entertainment, it does little to further the narrative. Moreover, elements of the mise-en-scène, for example, picturesque Buddha statues, Italian suits, lavish gestures (Tommy's invitation to fight by holding his staff out and Serrano spitting on the ground in refusal), make the villains appealing. Their glib remarks ("Fear the man, not the weapon," "Don't ask for what you can't take") gain weight through translation from Cantonese and Sicilian, adding an undeserved dramatic import by way of a certain exoticism. The delivery of the lines as well as the use of translation seem to allude again to a modernist alienation from the character, creating a postmodern distance from direct identification. This distance is reinforced by the fact that the scene ends with nothing having happened, with no real dramatic action having taken place. If anything, the sequence only serves to reduce the status of the hero, who seems to be overwhelmed by these spectacular adversaries.

In fact, Jake Lo is only introduced at the end of the following scene, as a spectator witnessing the enfolding spectacle of the events of June 1989 in Tian-'anmen. The scene dissolves to the famous photo of the Chinese demonstrator challenging an army tank by physically blocking its progress (see Chapter 1), which is being used as part of a campus demonstration in Los Angeles. Jake arrives on motorcycle in a plain white T-shirt and jeans. Like Marlon Brando or James Dean, he seems to strike a rebellious pose. A brief flashback, in black and white, sets up the connection. Images imitate familiar television news footage, for example, a row of bicycles collapse, demonstrators run in the streets from the army, and so on. In the middle of the chaos, Jake calls for his father. When he finally finds him, his father yells for Jake to go back, and Jake is pulled away as his father is crushed by a tank while trying to help a young woman trapped by fallen debris. In the present, when one of the young protesters tries to encourage Jake to join the demonstration, pointing to his father as a martyr, Jake replies in Cantonese that his father died for nothing and that politics is "bullshit."

Walking away from politics, the past, and the legacy of his father, Jake goes to art class. He is an art student, an observer. Although visually associated with other cinematic rebels (including, of course, Brandon's own father, Bruce), Jake's rebelliousness does not extend much beyond including a dragon in a drawing for a life study class. He shrugs off his teacher's admonition to draw what he sees and welcomes the opportunity to flirt with the young blonde model rather than concentrate on the class. Jake soon finds out, however, that the model's interest in him is only a ploy to lure him to attend a political fund-raiser, where he is the guest of honor as his father's son.

This scene also provides an important "structuring absence" within the film, that is, the absence of any reference to Jake's (Brandon's) mother. Although fans of Bruce and Brandon Lee know about the love affair between Linda and Bruce as well as the difficulties of their interracial marriage, the absence of any mention of Jake's mother leaves the character's identity less certain. Female characters hold out the unfulfilled promise of anchoring Jake's identity. However, the blonde appears, serves her mildly duplicitous plot function, and disappears. Even though another Caucasian love interest surfaces for Jake later, she functions more as one of the boys, her femininity minimized. This opens up the specular space for the contemplation of the male body without distraction. Here, as in the case of Bruce

Lee, the stigma of the Asian male body as feminine in comparison to white males is transformed into a positive attribute. Slender, lithe, sinewy, and smooth, Lee's body takes on attributes usually associated with females. While the other male characters are eager to act, Jake is an observer, stubbornly passive, stating his desire to stay out of any kind of involvement in anything throughout most of the film. As with most postmodern antiheroes, the protagonist's gender seems at first to be exaggerated. In this case, Jake Lo's fighting prowess and penchant for Hollywood rebel dress and pose seem to emphasize his masculinity. However, when the element of racial difference is added, Lo/Lee emerges as an icon that can subsume the feminine within itself. However, rather than calling for the reinvention of race, sex, and gender, postmodern androgyny banishes sexual politics. Gender is style rather than struggle—a fantasy of equality that may be utopian or simply a way of evacuating political anger from Hollywood films.

In addition to concretizing his ability to be assimilated into mainstream American culture, the fact that Jake is given a love interest also softens any threatening aspect to the gender blurring his physical presence may conjure up. Again, common in Hollywood actions films in which an emphasis on male physical prowess might threaten too great a homoerotic allure, the love interest keeps Jake within the realm of heterosexuality. Although Jake might be dull, passive, noncommittal, immature, and confused, he is coded as normal in opposition to the other characters that inhabit a world where women are at the periphery or banished completely.

The gangsters, the police, the Chinese protesters, and Jake's father occupy an environment that confuses and excludes Jake—and with reason. The blonde model leads Jake to the political fund-raiser, where she appears to be intimate with the other Chinese student who had admonished Jake earlier for not supporting his father's cause. However, this is not the last time Jake is duped. The party's host is Carl Chang (Michael Paul Chan), an associate of Tommy's, who has been targeted by Serrano in his bid to take over the drug market.

Although it makes narrative sense, because there needs to be some explanation for Jake's involvement with gangsters to get the plot moving, the ideology behind the narrative choice is startling. Chang explains his interest in the Chinese democracy movement: "Democracy, capitalism—it's all a good cause." Occurring in a media culture in which the interconnections between capitalism, Western democratic politics, and gangsters are taken for granted, the fact that the film seems to be saying that gangsters and prodemocracy Chinese protesters share a common set of values and interests slides by in the film without comment.

Given that capitalism is represented by drug traffickers and democracy by a corrupt federal government, Jake's inability to comprehend his father's involvement with all this seems more understandable than the narrative allows. The film simply takes for granted the U.S. government's right to send a Chinese American intelligence officer to Beijing to take an active role in promoting the overthrow of the Chinese government (or at least to advance a serious challenge to its policies) in the name of capitalism. No one broaches the potentially disturbing news that American and Chinese interests may not coincide and that Jake's father is a spy working for his adopted home, rather than exclusively in the interest of the Chinese demonstrators. No one in the film supports Jake's desire not to be involved with any of this.

Ideologically, the film takes for granted that democracy is positive, capitalism is good, drug trafficking is an unfortunate excess in an otherwise ideal system, and corruption can be held in check under the guidance and authority of a strong paternal presence. Chang's commitment to capitalism and democracy signals a postmodern politic within the film, where Jake's Vietnam-era suspicion of governmental intervention, capitalism, and American might exercised abroad is presented as retro and out of sync with a Reagan-Bush neoconservative ideology coded here as progressive.[4] Chang may be a gangster, but his political feelings are presented as appropriate in this post-Vietnam rewriting of history. A democratic, Americanized China must be good for business. Chang, like Jake's father, thoroughly identifies with the American cause.

Upstairs, another ideologically peculiar ethnic struggle takes place. Serrano sits behind Chang's desk, his face obscured by the shadows of the Venetian blinds—a classic gangster genre visual reference. Preparing to shoot Chang, Serrano claims his American heritage: "I'm an American and we know how to take things." Once again, the dark side of the American way surfaces; Serrano, coded already through gesture, dress, and language as alien, as Italian, sees himself as American when he is violently acquisitive. Chang attempts to use an antique Asian dagger to defend himself, misses, and is shot to death. Apparently, Asia loses its battle with America. However, the struggle really may not be between Asia and America. Chang has already demonstrated his commitment to democracy and capitalism, and so has Serrano. Jake is the "foreigner" who questions both. The plot swings into action when Jake, the observer, becomes the only eyewitness to Chang's murder. The rest of the film involves bringing Jake around so that he realizes his own personal commitment to this same path, to democracy, capitalism, and Americanism.

Oedipus in Diaspora

Although this path seems like the establishment of a more active identity for Jake, it actually involves the dissolving of his identity as the reluctant hero/young rebel into his father's role of crusader for the public good, champion of the American way. When the FBI agents introduce him to the boss Frank Stuart (Raymond J. Barry), for example, they discuss him only in relation to his father and his father's martial arts accomplishments, listing them as Wing Chun kung fu and Muay Thai. Paradoxically, the narrative road Jake travels as a character to become more closely identified with his father parallels the road Brandon follows as an actor inextricably connected to his father, Bruce.

However, whereas Bruce Lee was indeed a master of Wing Chun and had a familiarity with Muay Thai and other Asian fighting arts that he incorporated into his own system of Jeet Kune Do, he was anything but an American "career army" man. Instead, Bruce still serves as a symbol of rebellion against a racist America that failed to appreciate his talents. His starring vehicles, all made in Hong Kong,[5] present him as a model of justified anger against a political authority associated with a war in Asia that was labeled as racist, unjustified, immoral, and exploitative, serving the rich at the expense of the interests of the poor and working classes.

Jake's father represents an authority that Brandon's father spent his life struggling against. In using Brandon to fantastically reconstitute Bruce's marginalized Hollywood career, *Rapid Fire* rewrites history on yet another level. Hollywood allows Brandon to play a Bruce Lee substitute who refuses assimilation and who must be tricked, seduced, and beaten to accept a role that really was unavailable to his father, who became a rebel out of frustrated desire rather than choice. On this level, *Rapid Fire* operates as a fantasy of Bruce Lee in Hollywood, an image of Lee achieving what really eluded him throughout his life.

As in many postmodern Hollywood revisions of history, guilt becomes blame. Jake represents the unjustified, foolish, selfish rebel who fails to see the true value of the paternal authority he tries so desperately not to emulate. Brandon, on the other hand, seems to relish establishing his own career by physically quoting his father's style. When his leg is grabbed in a fight, he leaps up to kick with the other as Bruce did in *Enter the Dragon* (1973). Before a strike, Brandon, like Bruce, rolls his shoulder to distract an opponent. Also, as in Bruce's films, when he strikes a fatal blow, close-ups show a look of horror at his own ability to kill.

In one scene, Brandon breaks a stick in two to use like Filipino kali sticks, just like his father did in *Enter the Dragon*. Just as Bruce dressed up as a nerd with glasses to infiltrate the Japanese embassy in *Chinese Connection* (1972), Brandon dons similar attire and adjusts his glasses in exactly the same comical way as his father in a scene in the gangster's laundry in this film. Although Brandon does not adopt his father's characteristic vocalizations, the score fills this gap by imitating Bruce Lee's screeches instrumentally. At another point, Jake is asked to take his "fists of fury"—alluding to the title of a Bruce Lee film (1971)—outside after a fight.

However, the road the narrative takes in assigning blame to Jake (and through him ultimately to Bruce Lee and all the disenfranchised people he symbolizes globally) is a rocky one. This is a neoconservative text that recognizes the power of the social/political critique Lee embodies. Thus, though confused and misdirected, Jake's paranoia is not unfounded. When Jake is reluctant to go to Chicago to identify Serrano, one of the FBI agents threatens him with criminal prosecution on a trumped-up charge. Jake complains, "That's blackmail." The agent replies, "That's law enforcement." The film thus allows for a suspicion of authority to be voiced. It also allows this threat to be concretized as the corrupt Stuart tries unsuccessfully to have Jake assassinated. The corrupt agents even watch the 1960s TV version of *Batman* (1966–68) before their attack on Jake. Thus, the hero is presented as a camp figure. Style is drained of meaning, and the screen hero becomes a postmodern icon that the character Jake must either imitate or transcend.

Cynicism, paranoia, and ambivalence all figure prominently in postmodern Hollywood; however, the nostalgic desire for a time before the authority's feet of clay were discovered wins out over any criticism voiced. Jake may copy the past, but sincerity eventually overcomes the irony of the imitation. A conservative reading and a critical irony inhabit the same narrative. However, there is no dialectical tension between the two; both are drained of significance. The pleasures of the fantasy override any discursive struggle. The film makes it appear as if the battle has been waged and lost by both sides long ago.

Although the FBI may equate blackmail with law enforcement, the film provides an antidote to this poisonous portrayal of governmental authority in the next scene, which introduces Mace Ryan (Powers Boothe) and his local officers. Housed in an abandoned, dilapidated bowling alley, the righteous Chicago police stand in marked contrast to the corrupt federal agents. Karla Withers (Kate Hodge), who provides the love interest, is one of Ryan's staff members. Although in decay, the bowling alley provides the police unit with a warm atmosphere. The authority Ryan embodies is incorruptible and approachable, humanized by his constant frustration with the years spent pursuing Tommy Tau and his inability to hit a lone pin on one of the empty bowling alleys.

A similar atmosphere pervades Serrano's Italian restaurant. Although clean and elegant, there is an old-fashioned quality to the human organization of the space that parallels the feeling of loss and nostalgia conjured up by the older policeman at his bowling alley. In a second-storey loft area off of the main bar and restaurant, Serrano operates his business affairs while dining. Red wine and breadsticks mark his ethnicity. One of his minions relays phone messages from a pay phone nearby. The women sit away from the table, ornamental, without anything to add to the conversation or the plot. Serrano asks everyone to "think positive," providing the sudden death of Chicago's first African American mayor, Harold Washington, as an example of an unexpected, positive event. His vocal racism also helps place him in another era (although it is difficult to say whether Serrano complains about Washington because of his race or his honesty).

Still trusting Frank Stuart, Jake agrees to meet the agent in a secluded spot. Luckily, because of a phone tap, Ryan is there to rescue Jake from the set-up with Serrano's men. Driving uptown along Lake Shore Drive to confront Frank, Jake makes a parallel between Ryan and his father. "Christ, another hero," observes Jake as he guesses correctly that Ryan is divorced and totally consumed by his cause. The corrupt Stuart, on the other hand, still has his wife, who is there to witness the beating Jake gives him. Stuart is not "another hero" and quickly agrees to help Ryan use Serrano to get to Tommy Tau. Jake, of course, becomes the bait.

After getting off on the wrong foot with Karla (i.e., Jake had held her hostage at their first meeting, and Karla punched him to retaliate at their second meeting), Jake begins to bond with her while they plot Jake's role in the raid on Serrano's restaurant using a model of the location to help them. The control they have over the model is deceptive, of course, but it allows them to physically draw close and invites them to talk about their past. In fact, they seem like children playing with a doll's house. Jake complains bitterly about his father, "I never even knew why he was over there." Here, China and Vietnam have changed places historically. There was no American military presence in Beijing in 1989 (unless the film's director, Dwight H. Little, and the rest of *Rapid Fire*'s creative team know something no one else does). However, there are plenty of relatives of Vietnam veterans who still do not know "why he was over there." Historical boundaries dissolve so that emotional affect associated with one time and place can be transferred to another.

Actually, Jake never needs to understand his father's mission, because the narrative condenses the emotional affect associated with Jake's father with his feelings for Ryan as a father substitute. Karla observes, "Sounds like you hate him [Ryan] because he reminds you of your father." Because of this condensation of emotion and its displacement onto Ryan, the narrative need never explain why Jake's father "was over there." Instead, Ryan's far more understandable mission to bring the drug lords Serrano and Tau to justice simply needs to be accepted by the reluctant Jake.[6]

Just as he was seduced by the blonde model and taken in by the corrupt Frank Stuart, Jake allows himself to be seduced by Karla and taken in by Ryan. Even though Jake swears at Ryan in Cantonese in the next scene (translated indirectly as "he says he thinks he's in love with you" by one of Ryan's Chinese officers), the love element of the love-hate relationship has already been established and Jake is clearly, at this point, fighting with rather than against Ryan. His first order of business is to put corrupt authority behind him, which he does when he ridicules Frank as they walk to their rendezvous with Serrano. Frank states: "I take responsibility for my personal actions." Jake responds: "This isn't EST, Frank."

Next, Jake endures a beating from Serrano, who, in a kinky flourish, puts on a leather glove before striking, to help Ryan's plan. Unfortunately, even though Ryan manages to get the information he was looking for from the bug worn by Frank, the plan goes awry when the bug goes dead and his cue, "Nice doing business with you," does not ring true. Serrano is suspicious of Frank's lack of interest in money and notes, "The only time someone doesn't want money is when they want something else." Serrano takes out his pistol and shoots Frank. The sniper assigned to cover Serrano loses his shot, and chaos erupts when teargas is thrown in instead. Jake manages to vanquish all the mobsters that attack him and eventually brings Serrano to his knees, begging for mercy. Jake knocks him out and deposits him at Ryan's feet; he quips, "I hear they're looking for a police commissioner in Beirut."

The following sequence cross-cuts among three different locations, juxtaposing three quite different events: Jake and Karla in Karla's apartment looking at Jake's father's file and then making love; Serrano led to prison and then assassinated in his cell; and Ryan observing and failing to stop Tommy Tau's drug shipment. Following the violent spectacle of the showdown at Serrano's restaurant, the segment is anticlimactic. Each element of the sequence adds to a sense of repetition, rather than of release and exhilaration that might be expected to accompany a bedroom scene. Just as the guard says, "Welcome back, Mr. Serrano," as he escorts the prisoner into his cell, Jake, as expected, finds nothing new in the file Karla purloined. Karla repeats what everyone has been saying to Jake throughout the film: "Your father was doing what he thought was right. He died. It happens every day. Deal with it." Jake accepts this as foreplay. However, as their embraces are cross-cut with a montage of heroin transports and the stabbing of Serrano, the idea of sexual satisfaction seems remote. Although the focus is on the sensuality of Jake's body, for example, the musculature of his abdomen, the contours of his physique backlit in profile, the import of the scene seems to lie less in the display of sexuality then in the physical consummation of Jake's desire for acceptance within mainstream American society. When he critiques the government and rants against his father's politics, Jake really protests too much. His making love to Karla concretizes his full commitment to the government she works for and represents. America accepts him, and he finally gives himself body and soul to America through Karla.

By making love to Karla, Jake establishes his own stake in the American Dream. Instead of being the rebel looking for a new social order, he commits himself to the old order by following Ryan's lead, fulfilling the goals the older man cannot. Once dedicated to mainstream America, Jake cleans house, sweeping aside the excesses embodied by Serrano and Tau, as well as Frank Stuart, succeeding where both Ryan and his father failed. Although Jake does not bring democracy to China, he does rid American capitalism of the troublesome realities of corruption and drug trafficking, and he proves that racism is just a lingering irritation that can be eliminated as easily as the racist Serrano is erased from the plot. Ryan accepts Jake as a pseudo-son. "At least I didn't get that kid killed" is Ryan's way of expressing his supposedly deep feeling for Jake. Karla accepts Jake as a lover. Jake, then, moves into a newly constituted, enlightened American society. By the film's conclusion neither Jake nor the viewer should wonder about Jake's father. The reason for his death should be self-evident.

Finally, after all the efforts of the film have been spent tricking, trapping, coaxing, seducing, and generally brow-beating Jake into feeling guilty for distrusting the government that he blames for killing his father, Jake accepts America. However, despite all the plot time devoted to his forced welcome into the American mainstream, the fact of his racial/ethnic difference still disturbs the fantasy. He cannot be at peace in America until something Asian dies, so his final confrontation is with Tommy Tau. By killing Tau, Jake disposes of the alien presence within himself. Tau's Chinese ethnicity parallels Serrano's Italian exoticism. They both stand as excesses within a fiction that prizes homogeneity—for example, Jake's and Karla's androgyny, Jake's ordinary, "dull" dress and demeanor.

The final confrontation takes place in a Chinese laundry. In fact, it is the only direct contact Jake has with Tau at all. Ironically, the first step he takes to prove he is American and not Chinese is by impersonating a Chinese laundryman. Glasses held in place by a cord around his neck, a bandanna covering his head, clothing a size or two too small, and stooped posture create Jake's ethnic disguise. A guard confronts him. Jake responds in Cantonese, and the guard tells him to speak English. Jake collapses in front of the guard attempting to kowtow, thanking him vociferously and calling him "big brother." This display convinces the guard of Jake's authenticity, that he belongs.

However, this Chinese ethnic masquerade is simply a ruse. When Tau abducts both Ryan and Karla, Jake reveals his true identity by coming to the rescue. Ryan manages to help but gets shot in the process. Karla looks on helplessly. When Jake unbinds her, she is simply given the task of going for help. Jake transforms common objects (e.g., an aluminum clothes rack, scissors, and carts) found in the laundry into weapons to battle Tau's minions. Just as Bruce Lee often transformed the objects that marked his characters as underdogs into weapons to vanquish his enemies, Brandon takes up the clichéd icons associated with the Chinese laundryman to defeat his foes. However, in this case, Brandon's character is not really a worker; he is a privileged student, an artist, the son of a famous man. He does not use these objects to punish an exploitative boss, but rather takes them up as an homage, as part of his father's style, and rather than to further identify with the Chinese working man, to distance himself from that persona and show that that ethnic role is only a mask—to be discarded as quickly as possible.

Jake finally catches Tommy trying to escape on an El train platform. Since Jake's identity is always in question, Tommy, pulling out his knife, asks, "Who the fuck are you?" It is a good question. Jake's battles have been with men supposedly on his side, that is, with the young demonstrator, with Frank Stuart, with Ryan, and with the ghost of his father. Tommy has done nothing to Jake personally and really means nothing to him. Tommy is Ryan's adversary, not Jake's. Thus, the drama of the final confrontation is drained of affect. After a fight with long metal grappling rods, conjuring up both Tau's earlier fight with the staff and Bruce/Brandon's penchant for using workers' tools as weapons, Tommy is electrocuted while holding two of the weapons against the third rail. Although the death marks Jake's final act of commitment to Ryan's (and, by extension, his father's) cause, the spectacular death means little dramatically. Tommy never did find out who Jake was.

Although the death of Tommy may be somewhat anticlimactic, it does define Jake. His racial/ethnic difference has been used to further mainstream American interests. Tommy's laundry is in flames; the last vestiges of the disturbing aspects of ethnic exoticism destroyed with it. Jake rescues Ryan from the fire and assures Ryan that Tau is "one with his ancestors." When Jake remarks that he "had a good teacher" after Ryan compliments him, it remains unclear whether the teacher referred to is Ryan or Jake's father. It really makes little difference, however. The point has been made: Jake accepts paternal authority, recognizes himself as heir to his fathers' cause, and putting doubt and rebellion aside, accepts an American identity cleansed of the excesses of a capitalism gone criminal. Racial and gender differences remain marginal elements within the newly reconstituted American multicultural democracy.

Ryan and Karla joke that she was only using Jake to get to Ryan; as the disabled Ryan is hoisted into the ambulance, the oedipal fantasies played out with the passing of the father and the acquisition of the heroine as a prize simply parallel the acceptance of the ideology Ryan represents. A shot from the inside of the ambulance frames Jake on the outside. An off-screen voice asks, "Are you in or out?" Without hesitating, Jake replies, "We're in." He is "in." He gets the girl, gets the villain, gets the blessing of the older generation, and takes up the paternal authority promised by all.[7]

Star Power

However, even though Jake is clearly "in" in the fantasy world of *Rapid Fire*, is Brandon Lee "in" in Hollywood? Like Bruce, Brandon began his screen career in

American television (ironically in a spin-off from *Kung Fu*, the project his father coveted and was denied in favor of Euro-American actor David Carradine) and in Hong Kong features. In his final film, *The Crow*, he remains on the margins of the Hollywood feature. Shot in North Carolina, the film was so low budget that cost cuts and the lack of union rules may have contributed to the accident that led to Brandon's death on the set of gunshot wounds.

In *Rapid Fire*, Brandon stays squarely within his father's oeuvre, a self-conscious imitator, helped to achieve this duplication by some of his father's martial arts students. However, whereas Bruce's physical presence connoted resistance to racism, colonialism, and class exploitation, Brandon (half Asian and half white) is exploited here as an image of assimilation, acceptance, and reconciliation. The rebel's reluctance becomes the hero's acceptance of another's battle. In *Rapid Fire*, Brandon does not take up his father's causes, only his father's characteristic style. Narrative aside, perhaps it is this imitation of Bruce's physicality, of his definition of Asian masculinity as a rebellion against the American mainstream, that disturbs the film's neoconservative flirtations with justifying U.S. military/police intervention in Asia/Asian affairs—from Tian'anmen to the Golden Triangle heroin trade. Less a neoconservative icon of the new American hero, Brandon is a postmodern memento mori, a maudlin reminder of the struggles of the past and a fantasy that these battles have been concluded, a hope that the need for Bruce Lee no longer exists. Hollywood, through Brandon, reconstructs a Bruce Lee that never existed and allows Brandon to attempt to transcend him. However, as the body is drained of its anger, style becomes just a gesture drained of its significance, and it really does not matter whether Brandon is in or not.

9   In the Space of the Square:
The Gate of Heavenly Peace

Only when the square is awash with blood will the people of China open their eyes. Only then will they really be united. But how can I explain any of this to my fellow students?
　　—Chai Ling, student demonstrator

EVEN BEFORE THE FILM had its premiere at the New York Film Festival in 1995, Carma Hinton and Richard Gordon's *The Gate of Heavenly Peace* was embroiled in controversy. In *In the Red: On Contemporary Chinese Culture*, Geremie R. Barmé, one of the film's screenwriters, gives an account of the debate.[1] Carma Hinton provided Hsueh Hsiao-kuang, a Taiwanese journalist based in Hong Kong, with a rough cut of the film and supporting documents on the production. Clearly shocked by the May 28, 1989, interview that student demonstrator Chai Ling did with journalist Philip Cunningham, Hsueh wrote an article questioning the role extremist students played in provoking the violence that occurred on June 3–4. Chai, who had refused to be interviewed for *The Gate of Heavenly Peace*, responded to the article in the Taiwan-backed *World Journal* as well as in the dissident journals *Beijing Spring* and *Tiananmen*, questioning Hinton's motives and criticizing journalist Dai Qing, a prominently featured interviewee in the Hinton/Gordon film, who had also recently condemned Chai Ling's behavior. In fact, most of the inaugural issue of *Tiananmen* was devoted to a condemnation of the film.

Ironically, many of the barbs directed against Hinton involved her connection to the Chinese Communist Party. As the daughter of William Hinton, author of *Fanshen* and *Shenfan*,[2] massive, detailed studies in support of land reform in China after 1949, Carma Hinton was born in China and spent her youth and early adulthood there. Later, with her husband, Richard Gordon, Carma Hinton returned to China and produced several documentaries centered on life in Long Bow Village, where her father had conducted the preponderance of his research.[3] However, although Chai's dissident faction implied that Hinton was in league with the Communists, the People's Republic vociferously condemned the film as well. When Richard Pena, director of the New York Film Festival, refused to pull the film, Chinese authorities declined to allow Zhang Yimou to attend the festival to present his feature *Shanghai Triad*. The government also complained when the film was screened at Filmfest DC in Washington the following year.

As the voiceover narrator in *The Gate of Heavenly Peace* rightly points out: "Almost as soon as the struggle over Tian'anmen ended, the struggle over the story of what happened there began." The film itself is an important part of that struggle, and, as the invective flies at it from both the dissident camp and the official organs of the Chinese government, it provides a distinctive counterpoint to both positions. In fact, it argues for a redefinition of the contested space of the square and repositions the space in the global visual imagination. The "stars" of network television like Dan Rather as well as the "stars" of the demonstrations like Chai Ling, Wu'er Kaixi, and Wang Dan, and the government, such as Li Peng and Zhao Ziyang, drift to the edges of the struggle as the film places them in context as players in a larger drama that unfolds quite differently than it did in the Western press or through the official organs of the Chinese government.

When the Western media took up the demonstrations taking place in Beijing's Tian'anmen Square (Gate of Heavenly Peace Square) and created a global spectacle of youth, political struggle, and governmental repression, they created a specific vision of that place that erased its past history and current complexity. Clearly, the space defined by one of the largest public gathering spots in the world comprises more than the backdrop for the playing out of the drama of the decay of Communism, the emergence of the new world order, and the triumph of an American-flavored "democracy" against the forces of "totalitarianism." Tian'anmen Square represents centuries of Chinese imperial and republican history.[4] It serves as an emblem for the power of the Qing Dynasty and the shattering effects of the Boxer Rebellion, the struggles for national sovereignty and modernity represented by the May Fourth Movement of 1919, the establishment of the People's Republic in 1949, and the mass rallies of the Cultural Revolution (roughly 1966–76). This highly evocative national space has become a provocative transnational space in the wake of the events of May–June 1989. The events there had an impact far beyond the People's Republic, extending out to affect Hong Kong, Taiwan, Singapore, Chinese America, and the Chinese diaspora worldwide.

Despite the enormous amount of media material coming out of the square, few commentators have been able to sift through this information to come to an understanding of the spring events beyond a simple narrative of a justified demonstration against repression and unjustified oppression of peaceful protest. *The Gate of Heavenly Peace* comes as close as possible within the space of the cinema/TV screen to exploring the most salient and seminal aspects of this event. It deals with the incidents of spring 1989 within the local space of Beijing, the national space of the People's Republic, the international space of intergovernmental relations, the multinational spaces of corporate media, the transnational spaces of satellite communications, and the marginal, diasporic spaces of the Chinese exile community.

Unable to contain this continuing flood of information from the square, the filmmakers have gone beyond the space of film festival screens, NAATA video distribution, and PBS broadcast TV to cyberspace. With the establishment of *The Gate of Heavenly Peace* Web site (www.tsquare.tv), Tian'anmen has become a cyber entity and subject to a reconfiguration that perhaps more closely parallels the significance of this symbolic space that has already crossed so many borders within the public imagination. Struggles for control of the square and its political symbolic capital extend far beyond the physical parameters of Tian'anmen. *The*

Gate of Heavenly Peace project has become both part of this process of symbolically occupying the square and a site for a critical appraisal of the use of the
square as a place for the reconfiguration of relations of power among various
communities globally.

Thus, it comes as no surprise that Chai Ling, who had hung onto the occupation
of the square as tantamount to the student movement itself, and the government,
which had violently reoccupied the square, should square off against this film as
another attempt to occupy this space as a public platform for protest. Putting aside
the struggle to control the loudspeakers or the satellite news broadcasts from the
square, *The Gate of Heavenly Peace*'s Web site has transformed the unidirectional
nature of mass media into a less restrictive (though clearly limited) arena for the
dissemination of public political information. Although the film and the Web site
do not conceal the fact that they put forward a specific perspective on the 1989
events, the visual space the project occupies on film, video, and computer screens
opens up issues repressed by the Western media, the Chinese government, and
various factions within the dissident movement.

In "Tiananmen, Television and the Public Sphere: Internationalization of
Culture and the Beijing Spring of 1989," Craig Calhoun notes:

> The "Beijing Spring" of 1989 had both an intensive and an extensive relationship to
> space. It was intensively focused on Tiananmen Square. It seized that location, in-
> corporated its material symbols into a new drama, packed a million protesters into its
> confines. The movement lost coherence and intensity as a function of distance from
> the Square. At the same time, the movement existed in a "metatopical public space" of
> multinational media and indirect relationships to a world of diverse and far-flung
> actors. The movement's protagonists consciously addressed this world even though it
> had to seem distant, insubstantial and remote from their tangible experience.[5]

This chapter looks at the various ways in which the space of the square has been
reconfigured through this process and how *The Gate of Heavenly Peace* project
has intervened in the relations of power that have become inexorably linked to the
idea of Tian'anmen since 1989. Although a range of people protested in the square
in 1989, the focus of the media has been on the student demonstrators, and any
consideration of the events of that time must take into consideration the relationship between Chinese youth and the global politics of screen spectacles.

VISUALIZING THE SQUARE

The Gate of Heavenly Peace presents a picture of Tian'anmen Square as a space
intersected by local and global interests. In fact, a parallel exists between the way
the square functions as a space with very different and contradictory meanings at
the local, national, international, and transnational levels and the way the demonstrators conceive of their demands as both local and global, and thus spatial, in
nature. The film carefully points out that the movement included various strata of
Chinese society as well as supporters from outside of China and that all these
groups and individuals had different reasons for being in Tian'anmen Square that

spring. Factory workers attempting to create autonomous unions had very different motives than Dan Rather or Ted Koppel, for example, although support of democracy may have been a common rhetorical thread for all.

The Gate of Heavenly Peace opens with an implicit reminder that it operates in what Arjun Appadurai has called the mediascape, the transnational flow of images, by presenting a man with a camera around his neck prominent at the center of the composition, fleeing in a crowd from a fire in the background. The central position of the camera in the frame underscores the fact that another person, with a video camera in hand, photographs the scene as it unfolds. That image becomes part of the film. From the photograph not taken to the transnational screen that exhibits *The Gate of Heavenly Peace*, the June 1989 crackdown exists within the global flow of image culture, and, as such, may be linked more closely as a highly politicized image to what Appadurai calls the ideoscape: "Ideoscapes are also concatenations of images, but they are often directly political and frequently have to do with the ideologies of states and counterideologies of movements explicitly oriented to capturing state power or a piece of it."[6] For Appadurai, politics takes on a spatial dimension and ideology inevitably becomes part of transnational flows. Positioned with the demonstrators and against the violent power of the Chinese state, this footage allows the filmmakers to stand with the demonstrators and, with them, take possession of the square on screen for the world to see.

Over the image of the confrontation of the line of tanks in Beijing (discussed in Chapter 1), the female voice, who acts as the off-screen narrator for the film, comments: "Events do not deliver their meanings to us. They are always interpreted." The voice continues: "For millions who saw this scene all over the world, its meaning was clear. Here was human hope and courage challenging the remorseless machinery of state power. The Chinese government interpreted this scene just as simply, but differently." Almost imperceptibly, the film cuts to a Chinese documentary using the identical footage, but with a very different commentary. A male voice, also off-screen, states: "Anyone with common sense can see that if our tanks were determined to move on, this lone scoundrel could never have stopped them. This scene recorded on videotape flies in the face of Western propaganda. It proves that our soldiers exercised the highest degree of restraint."

Every image implies an interpretation, and *The Gate of Heavenly Peace* makes this explicit from the outset. The film has its own perspective that gradually emerges through the editing of the hours of footage that the filmmakers condensed into roughly three hours, the use of interviews, and the voiceover commentary that narrates the events. It sides with a certain constituency that supports the movement, favors moderates in the government like Zhao Ziyang, and criticizes extremists on both sides. The voiceover, for example, alludes to the film's suspicion of extreme positions: "When individuals stand up to power, they bring to the encounter the lessons that power has taught them and the harm it has done them. Merely to stand up does not free us from these things. Behind every gesture of hope and courage lies a life, a society, a history." As the film's argument unfolds, the point surfaces that the extremists in the dissident camp actually have a lot in common with the hardliners in the government. They try to stifle alternative positions, accuse their opponents of being traitors, and attempt to manipulate events to their advantage to maintain power. Perhaps even more than the old men in power, the demonstrators are "children of Mao," and they exhibit the legacy of Mao's romantic revolutionary idealism. Not surprisingly, the demonstrators grossly resent this comparison.

In fact, if one single incident inflamed the demonstrators more than anything else, it was an editorial that accused the movement of creating turmoil, a word that had been used to denounce the chaos associated with the Cultural Revolution. Because Deng Xiaoping was a victim of the Cultural Revolution, the word resonates with his deeply held fears of mass demonstrations of youth and turmoil in the streets as well. For the demonstrators, the word struck a nerve that went beyond its use to condemn the demonstrations as antigovernment, because it equated their group with the despised political movement orchestrated by Mao and the Gang of Four.[7] Ironically, this was also the word used to condemn Deng Xiaoping when, mourning Zhou Enlai's death in 1976, the people of Beijing went to Tian'anmen to advocate for reform. Because Deng was considered Zhou's protégé, he was blamed for the demonstrations and again ousted from power. The 1989 demonstrators were outraged that Deng would dare condemn them with the same rhetoric that had been used to denounce him in 1976 and, with the editorial, symbolically turn his back on many who had previously supported him. This, along with a general opposition to corruption and excess, solidified various factions into a movement. However, the film does seem to acknowledge as true what the demonstrators vociferously protested against; specifically, the protesters did share a political history with those whom they opposed and were marked by that association. As a result of this lesson in power politics, many voices became lost in the struggle to dominate the square.

In an attempt to counter this silencing of different perspectives, the film brings to the fore many voices marginalized within the movement as well as within the international press, including the perspectives of workers attempting to form independent unions and relatives of the victims of government violence.[8] Many political analysts have noted the destructive aspect of Deng's policies, including Richard Levy, who states:

> I think there's a real analogy between Deng and Reagan. Both encouraged the most short term, individualistic, material motives with no analysis or concern for either the long-term or the collective interests of those same people. Both Deng's and Reagan's policies could, in fact, produce short term payoffs for certain strata, in material ways, at the expense of very long term, negative consequences for a larger number of people.[9]

While demonstrators were outraged by government corruption and backdoor manipulation of the system, some groups wanted wider and accelerated reforms that would include elections and an independent press. Others wanted a bigger slice of the booming economy and a relaxation of government interference in business. Peasants, largely out of the square and out of the picture, make a few cameo appearances to petition for the redress of local grievances or bring food in support of the demonstrators; however, they say little.

The vast majority of China's industrial workers, unlike the peasants who have unevenly lost or gained from Deng's reforms, have suffered the most from reform and China's entry into the global economy, but they appear in the film primarily as supporters of the student leaders. However, the workers and students do not share the same basic goals. Although this is mentioned in *The Gate of Heavenly Peace*, the implications of this fact remain largely unexplored as the students' demands for greater freedom of expression, more campus self-governance, and implicitly a bigger slice of the economic pie for the college-educated after graduation take center stage. In *Virtual Geography: Living with Global Media Events*, McKenzie Wark observes:

> The students are largely indifferent or hostile to the nascent workers' movement, despite the many acts of solidarity performed by the workers' groups over the course of the event. Many of the students risk nothing more than bad job assignments for participation in the movement. Rebel workers may more likely be executed.[10]

The film emphasizes the tensions among the students and intellectuals over tactics within the square, rather than looking closely at the ideological splits within the movement based on class. Later, the largest schism to emerge involves those students, like Chai Ling and Li Lu,[11] who advocate the overthrow of the government and those who wish to return to their campuses, like Wang Dan, to continue to agitate for gradual reform. Occupying the square meant different things for different people, just as the square itself signified very different things as it appeared on screens around the world.

The square, although a single location, functions in many different ways as a space. For the locals, it serves as a large park to fly kites or go out for a stroll. Local merchants work the square selling snacks and souvenirs. Police patrol it, and cleaning crews maintain it. Nationally, it serves as the seat of government power. Although the actual offices of the upper cadres do not rest on the square, the Great Hall of the People serves as the official site of government functions. Considered sacred ground, it celebrates the Communist Party with Mao's tomb and the Monument to the Martyrs of the Revolution. Beyond this, the square embodies the Chinese nation-state with the Gate of Heavenly Peace that dates back to imperial dynastic rule. As a site of mass rallies and pilgrimages of peasants from the provinces, the square unifies the nation and also links that identity to the extra-national existence of the Communist movement. Portraits of Marx, Engels, Lenin, and Stalin, as well as Mao, grace the square and link the national interests of the state with the goals of the Communist Party. In spite of, but also in a sense as a result of, the Sino-Soviet split in the 1950s, the square occupies a prominent place as an international symbol of Communism—with or without the addition of Deng's Chinese characteristics.

Within the Chinese diaspora, the square, like the Great Wall, serves as a symbol of Chineseness, a transnational space related to an ethnic identity that transcends both the People's Republic as a nation and the Chinese Communist Party as the governing entity of a sovereign state. The square represents a common history, culture, and tradition that go beyond the nation to include Chinese around the globe. However, the square is also transnational in another respect. With the opening of China to global trade, Tian'anmen Square signifies a new travel destination, the center of a new market for world goods, and the doorway for the exploitation of Chinese labor, natural resources, and consumer spending. When Bob Hope (shown in *The Gate of Heavenly Peace*) visits Tian'anmen Square, he opens the space up to transnational flows of people, capital, and images. The square represents the global investment in China, and any demonstrations in the square take on a significance that goes far beyond the Chinese nation-state.

The Gate of Heavenly Peace strips away these layers of meaning to uncover the significance of the square as a historical place as well as a present location with local, national, transnational, and global dimensions. Two interviewees, journalist Dai Qing and former party official Ge Yang, talk about the significance of the square in modern Chinese history, and they mention the symbolic gesture of Mao moving the seat of power from behind the closed Gate of Heavenly Peace out into the square, marking a dramatic shift from the occult power of the old regime to the open exercise of the will of the people assembled in the public square. In a massive building campaign, Mao expanded the square to its present gigantic dimensions and symbolically enlarged the masses of people who could be rallied in his support publicly in the square.

The film emphasizes the political dimensions of the square's history in relation to the legacy of the various student movements that held demonstrations in Tian'anmen. Given the 1989 demonstrations took place during the same year as the seventieth anniversary of the May Fourth movement and the fortieth anniversary of the founding of the People's Republic of China, the importance of the square to both of those events figures prominently in the documentary. It was also the tenth anniversary of the 1978–79 "democracy wall" movement, which in many ways helped solidify Deng's power when dissident Wei Jingsheng was sentenced to a long prison term for asking for more freedom of speech.

As the voiceover points out that the students were "consciously" associating themselves with the history of student protests in the square, the film cuts from the stone plaque that commemorates the May Fourth demonstrations on the Monument to the Martyrs of the Revolution to a shot of a 1989 demonstrator with a megaphone standing at the base of the monument. In fact, ceremonies held to celebrate the anniversary of the May Fourth movement, which also demanded democratic reform and an opening to Western ideas, fueled the 1989 protests. The film points out that the students involved with the May 4, 1919, demonstrations protested against the signing of the Treaty of Versailles at the end of World War I that gave concessions to Japan at the expense of Chinese interests. With students wearing Marlboro caps and Wu'er Kaixi asking for the ability to buy a pair of Nike shoes as one of his demands, the call for national interests plays less of a role in the 1989 movement than in 1919. Although the students in both eras share a common desire for change, democratic process, and the opening of China to positive Western influences, the critique of Deng's policies as exposing China to global capitalist exploitation does not seem to be a pillar of the 1989 movement as national political interests had been in 1919.

In fact, although *The Gate of Heavenly Peace* acerbically comments on Deng Xiaoping's visit to the United States, picturing him in a cowboy hat and showing him saluted by Bob Denver who wishes him luck with his "new long march to modernization," the film pulls away from noting any critique the 1989 demonstrators may have of the processes of Americanization and the negative impact of China's entry into the global economy. Rather, the voiceover simply ironically remarks that the Americans seemed relieved after Deng's historic visit that "the Chinese are just like us; they want what we want. And, maybe we can sell it to them." Certainly, for many in the United States, the agitation against Deng's government came as a surprise, because unlike the movements in Eastern Europe, Chinese dissent had not been on the American media radar screen. However, Western media quickly coopted the demonstrators' call for greater freedom as more American popular culture, consumer goods, fewer controls on the press and the market, and a more open playing field for U.S. political and economic interests.

The film presents three possible views of Deng's policies in relation to Americanization and transnational capitalism. The first sees his policies as being superficial and not allowing democracy (on the Euro-American model) to follow on the heels of capitalism. The second sees no hope for freedom under the current system and agitates for its overthrow. The third places the onus on Deng's program of modernization itself for the current ills of China by allowing the dismantling of socialist guarantees involving work and social welfare. Although the third position receives some attention in the first part of the film, particularly through the presentation of Deng's visit to America and the commentary of some of the interviewees involved with the autonomous workers' union, the preponderance of the film presents the battle between the first two positions and the struggle for possession of the square, physically and symbolically.

Like the demonstrations in 1976 that began with memorials in Tian'anmen on the occasion of Zhou Enlai's death, the 1989 demonstrations began with the public mourning of the passing of reform advocate Hu Yaobang. Ousted from the leadership supposedly because of his advocacy of bourgeois liberalism, Hu became a symbol of the need for greater reform, the end of corruption, and a more open approach to the exercise of political power. As such, for workers, students, and intellectuals, he served as a rallying point. As one of the interviewees in the film points out, mourning for Hu allowed for a public gathering of people to discuss their own lives and concerns.

Although many of these concerns were local in nature (e.g., demands for reform of aspects of campus life at Beijing's institutions of higher education, the formation of local unions, etc.), bringing these issues to the square immediately put them on the national agenda. One interviewee, Wu Guogang, identified as a former government official, succinctly articulates the disjuncture between the local and the national when he remarks that many reformers, inspired by Zhao Ziyang, were agitating for local elections. However, the students and intellectuals were more interested in the bigger picture of "saving China," and local cadres were very reluctant to give up the power they enjoyed. For Wu, the catapulting of the local to the national level did little to help the cause of reform.

When the students presented their petition on their knees to the government, no official came out to acknowledge the demonstrators, and many in Beijing were outraged when they saw images of the kneeling students. Although the violent scuffles that ensued were not televised, the demonstrations could not be ignored during the official memorial for Hu Yaobang, and global TV reported the protests. In an interview in the film, Wu'er Kaixi states: "We petitioned them like loyal subjects—kneeling down like subjects petitioning the emperor—but it's fair to say the government virtually crumbled under the weight of our knees."

With this image of kneeling students, the movement went from the local and national to international media event. Educator and critic Liu Xiaobo explains that when he saw the news reportage of this event, he purchased a plane ticket to return to Beijing, and the transnational circulation of images as well as people began to fuel the movement. BBC and VOA radio broadcasts helped spur similar demonstrations in other urban centers. As Wark notes:

> Beijing student demonstrations sometimes take on the appearance of a global positive feedback loop: a few thousand students demonstrate at Tiananmen; foreign journalists report it; Voice of America radio relays that report and amplifies it, saying that hundreds of thousands of students demonstrated; students pick up the broadcast, and while many of them are suspicious of the American versions of the event, it rings truer than the Chinese press reports, so it becomes a self-fulfilling prophecy.[12]

The April 26 *People's Daily* editorial accusing the demonstrators of creating "turmoil" also brought the protests to a new level, stimulating broader national and international interest in the movement. The level of spectacle intensified, and educator Liang Xiaoyan says that the atmosphere resembled a carnival as people came out in droves to see the students' "big show."

With the anniversary of the May Fourth Movement and Soviet leader Mikhail Gorbachev's visit on May 15, the international visibility of the demonstrations intensified. Posters appeared in English and Russian in the square. Equivocation within the government led to a loosening of restrictions on the press, and some journalists joined the demonstrations with posters warning the public "not to believe everything you read." Although Zhao Ziyang had mollified some of the demonstrators, others decided to go on a hunger strike to keep the momentum going. The ceremony to mark the first visit by a Soviet head of state to China since 1959 was moved from Tian'anmen to the airport, and the demonstrators remained in the square, in the international spotlight of the world media, "upstaging" Gorbachev.

As shots of ambulances taking away dehydrated hunger strikers filled the screens, people from all over China began to flood the square to show support. Although, locally, they did not represent either the "officially" elected representatives of the state supported student organizations or the "unofficial" members of the association of independent student unions, the hunger strikers held center stage for the nation and began to act as a beacon for transnational support of the protests.

The film's voiceover notes: "The spectacle was overwhelming and highly photogenic. . . . The foreign press in Beijing to cover the Sino-Soviet summit walked into the biggest international media story ever reported out of China."

The Gate of Heavenly Peace offers the images that began to create a transnational spectacle that transcended any specific local or even national demands of the demonstrators. A sweatshirt emblazoned with "We shall overcome" refers to a very different call for civil rights in the United States but links Tian'anmen with America. The V-sign moves between 1940s-era victory to the 1960s and a call for peace. In Tian'anmen, it may signify victory for some, peace for others, or simply act as a transcultural bond with the ubiquitous TV cameras from around the world. Marlboro and McDonald's logos dot the televisual compositions, and again their significance seems to float as emblems of China's call for increased international contact, for greater openness to the global market, or as a sign of the students' superficial lust for consumer goods. For Wu'er Kaixi, the seemingly contradictory demands seamlessly blend together: "So what do we want? Nike shoes, lots of free time to take our girlfriends to a bar, the freedom to discuss an issue with someone and get a little respect from society."

When Li Peng finally met with the hunger strikers, several wearing their hospital gowns, on television, the movement had already broken away from any putative leadership. Speaking directly to Li Peng, Wu'er Kaixi, pale and clearly dehydrated, warned that no one could guarantee that the square could be cleared if a single hunger striker objected. Li Peng squirmed in his chair on national and international TV screens, and Zhao Ziyang, defeated, made his last public appearance in the square that evening to apologize for the failure of his political reforms. Martial law in force, the lines of communication again shifted to the local level as brigades of motorcyclists went back and forth between the troops and the square to report on any military movements. Portions of the square open to the loudspeakers began to broadcast letters from disgruntled workers, and the students enjoyed the growing support of peasants and smaller merchants as well.

As the leadership of the movement split over tactics, the rank-and-file pulled together. The voiceover states: "In the vast square, in this space designed to make the many feel as one, a space dedicated to the manufacturing of public life. The personal gesture now became significant. Each small act of generosity seeming to prophesize a new way of living together, a new civility. It was a feeling as intense as it was transitory." However, moments that indicated the disintegration of the movement began to appear on screen as well, for example, images of the bloodied bodies resulting from factional violence. Demoralized by dwindling resources, poor sanitation, and increased infighting, Wang Dan organized a meeting and negotiated an end to the occupation of the square effective May 30. Chai Ling agreed to leave the square, but she changed her mind soon afterward. The student leaders, as the film points out, found it difficult to gauge their constituency. New demonstrators began to pour in from all over China, eager to stay in the square, and the students who had had enough simply left quietly.

Another factor also had a dramatic impact on the movement. Popular entertainers in Hong Kong held a benefit concert to support the Tian'anmen demonstrators. If Liu Xiaobo's journey from the United States to Beijing represented a trickle of support for the movement by Chinese living abroad, the Hong Kong Songs for Democracy concert opened a floodgate. In addition, the nature of the support changed. Ethnic Chinese from Hong Kong, Taiwan, and other places within the diaspora showed their encouragement by trekking to the square or sending money and supplies. Chai Ling rightly predicted: "We will mobilize Chinese people around the world to protest martial law."

As the local conditions worsened, the transnational power of the demonstrations strengthened. The Central Art Academy put up its statue of the Goddess of Democracy in the square, facing the portrait of Mao over the Gate of Heavenly Peace. Although the significance of the statue seemed transparent to world news reporters who saw a rekindling of the Statue of Liberty's flame in support of democracy for China, the actual interpretations of the figure varied dramatically. Some of the artists claimed influence from Soviet realism in their depiction of the model worker citizen as the standard-bearer of the nation.[13] Rey Chow saw another image that played into Western notions of a feminized China, and she compared the depiction of the statue in Tian'anmen by the media to *King Kong*'s (1933) depiction of the white damsel under siege by a big hairy ape. In her scenario, the "white" Western soul of China in the form of the white female statue, supported by the "good natives," comes under threat from the primitive, dark heart of the despotic "Orient" in the form of the ape-like Communist Party leadership. She calls it the *King Kong* syndrome: "This is the cross-cultural syndrome in which the 'Third World,' as the site of the 'raw' material that is 'monstrosity,' is produced for the surplus value of spectacle, entertainment, and spiritual enrichment for the 'First World.'"[14]

The Gate of Heavenly Peace poses these questions as it presents the Goddess on screen: "What does democracy mean? What was it coming to mean in China? What could it be made to mean? If democracy came to China, what would she look like? Whose features would she wear?" Pointing out that Mao also called for mass democracy with the camera closing in on the eyes of the Mao portrait in Tian'anmen, the film comments on the fundamentally Maoist aspect of much of the movement's rhetoric, pulling the statue away from international associations with either Russia or the United States and equating the statue instead, mirror-like, with Mao.

Adding to the spectacle, Taiwanese pop singer Hou Dejian decided, along with Liu Xiaobo, to wage another hunger strike. Staking a claim to a prime location at the base of the Monument to the Martyrs of the Revolution, Liu and Hou were joined by a handful of other nonstudent demonstrators. In a peculiar twist of logic, they went on a hunger strike to try to convince the students to leave the square. Of course, these luminaries, particularly Hou, who was famous not only for his music but also for his controversial decision to leave Taiwan and take up residence in the PRC, only served to draw more media and more students into the square at the same moment that Deng planned to unleash the military. However, these hunger strikers were also instrumental in negotiating a retreat from the square for many of the students, which may have averted further bloodshed. On June 4, the Goddess of Democracy fell, the troops came into the square, and Hinton and Gordon had to dig deep for the footage they uncovered on events of the night of June 3–4. The home video footage and the European TV footage they unearthed confirm the troops firing on civilians and the tanks rolling into Tian'anmen. However, controversy continues among eyewitnesses as to the actual number of dead in the square.

Because no figure of the casualties has been agreed on, *The Gate of Heavenly Peace* focuses on the loss of Professor Ding Zilin's son. The sad loss of this teenage boy and his mother's search for some sort of justice or explanation for his death stand in for the tragedy of many others. Many featured in the documentary were arrested and spent time in prison, including Wang Dan, Liu Xiaobo, and Dai Qing. Also, in the aftermath, global media continued to play a contradictory role. Although some reporters took precautions to conceal the identity of their sources, others were not as careful, and several people were arrested after appearing on the news outside of China. Surveillance cameras, which had been set up to control traffic before the demonstrations, now provided another source for the identification of participants in the demonstrations. Many, like Chai Ling and Wu'er Kaixi, managed to leave the country. Others, like Hou Dejian, were deported. After passing through Taiwan, Hou, in fact, ended up in Australia.

The Gate of Heavenly Peace concludes on a photo of Ding's son and the mother's thoughts about a suitable final resting place for his ashes. Thus, the film ends with a memorial to the loss of young life and the tragic consequences of June 4. However, *The Gate of Heavenly Peace* does not rest but expands out of the confines of the film/video screen to cyberspace. Embedded in the Web site, a drawn map of the square links the various parts of the space to the different meanings the square holds for *tai ji quan* practitioners and Young Pioneers, for tourists (including cybertourists, presumably) and for government officials.

The site complements the film in many important ways. It enables the cyber-visitor to get a sense of the space of the square physically with a literal overview and a feeling for the place of the square historically with a detailed chronology and links to articles on the history of Tian'anmen. Also, the site includes extensive commentary on the role of global media in the square, providing insights into aspects of the protests that the documentary, which focuses primarily on the perspective of the demonstrators, does not address in depth. Although the site does not provide a discussion board or other type of public forum for discussion, e-mail access to many involved in the production of the film and the Web site can be found.

However, the promise of the cybersquare, the cinematic square, the video square, and the physical square never fully materializes as a public forum for continuing dissent. Just as most in China find it difficult to journey to Beijing to make their voices heard, access to the Internet requires a certain degree of education, proximity to a town or city with Internet availability, and the leisure time necessary to pursue a life online. Even for those comfortable with the digital realm and living outside the firewalls set up to block politically sensitive sites in the People's Republic, the cyberspace occupied by *The Gate of Heavenly Peace* and

FIGURE 41. Screen grab of the cybersquare from *The Gate of Heavenly Peace* Web site. The Tian'anmen Square cybertour. (Courtesy of Carma Hinton. © Long Bow Group, Inc. All rights reserved.)

related sites on human rights, political dissidents, and politics in China diminish in comparison with sites devoted to tourism, business opportunities, and other commercial Chinese ventures. As Ralph A. Litzinger points out in "Screening the Political: Pedagogy and Dissent in *The Gate of Heavenly Peace*," even if access to dissident sites were not blocked by government firewalls, many who frequent China's cybercafés would still not hit on these sites:

> These cyber cafes do not seem to be providing spaces for subversion or radicalism, and most users do not look for sites such as Amnesty International or HumanRights.com ... Internet cafes are arguably providing spaces for the construction and pursuit of new desires, and these desires seem to be closely linked to China's burgeoning consumer economy and to the fascination with certain kinds of commodities.[15]

The global marketplace has transformed the cybersquare and the actual square in China into a site of capitalist consumption, a place for tourism, and the transformation of "China" itself into a commodity. As Dai Jinhua astutely points out, there is nothing innocent about the appropriation of the word "square," *guang chang*, as a synonym for "shopping plaza" in the wake of the spring 1989 events:

> The particular guangchang where the student demonstration was crushed in 1989 has become a deeply complex taboo: it symbolizes the socialist system but also the toppling of that system. So to name a commercial plaza a guangchang, to change the political meaning of guangchang, or at the very least to mask the significance of

FIGURE 42. *The Gate of Heavenly Peace* Web site provides the following caption: "There are a number of kiosks set up around the Square for tourists to grab a photo opportunity and commemorate their visit by having themselves snapped with Tiananmen Gate in the background. For many tourists—here as at famous sites throughout the world—it is a case of not *cogito* but rather *KODAK ergo sum.*" (Courtesy of Carma Hinton. © Long Bow Group, Inc. All rights reserved.)

political mass movements with a happy shoppers' heaven, is a transformation that is by no means innocent.[16]

However, it must be kept in mind that there never existed a clear dichotomy between, as Wu'er Kaixi put it, a desire for "Nike shoes" and "the freedom to discuss an issue with someone and get a little respect from society." The bourgeois public sphere has always contained both, and the freedom to choose among an array of commodities has often been on a par with the ability to speak out against oppression. However, within the "marketplace of ideas," political hegemony remains operative, and, as most states with capitalist economies know all too well, the marketplace can all too easily overshadow any ideas competing for political, economic, social, or cultural power. Chinese cyberspace and physical space have been opened to the transnational flow of the global economy, and the meaning of any square in China has been transformed as a result. However, other public spaces, outside of Beijing, have also been transformed by the legacy of June 4, 1989, and Hong Kong's Victoria Park, in the heart of the supposedly apolitical port marked by British colonialism, has hosted a number of incarnations of the Goddess of Democracy and other memorials to the Tian'anmen demonstrators.[17]

YOUTH CULTURE, SPECTACLE, AND THE SQUARE

The types of cultural capital that circulate in the square vary, and not all of them can be too quickly dismissed as lacking in any glimmer of dissent or opposition.

Although commodified in a particular way to appeal to viewers outside of China, the spectacle that emerged from the 1989 demonstrations contains enormous contradictions. The songs that the demonstrators sang during the occupation of the square, for example, point to a wide range of competing interpretations—many of them running counter to the Western scenario of advocacy for a 1776-style bourgeois American Revolution in China. Although rock signers Cui Jian and Hou Dejian each turned up in the square to contribute an "anthem" to the movement, the one song that appeared to galvanize the preponderance of the protesters was the "Internationale."[18]

Though the song would seem to mean more to those in the transnational corporate sweatshops making the Nike shoes than to many of the students who could only envision wearing them, the fact that the crowd should hit on this song seems to point to something that goes beyond a simple explanation of childhood Communist indoctrination. In the musical call for the workers of the world to rise up against oppression, the "Internationale" provides not only a song that the demonstrators were all certain to know but also a reminder of the importance of the support of the workers to the protests as well as highlighting the reform element of the movement's agenda by situating itself within international socialist culture rather than outside it. However, in virtually all accounts of the demonstrations, May 1, May Day, International Labor Day, remains invisible—overshadowed by May 4.

In fact, if the "Internationale" links the movement to the international Left, other songs favored by the demonstrators emphasized connections to Chinese history and, specifically, national interests. For example, harkening back to the May Fourth Movement and demonstrations against Japanese incursions into Chinese territory, some of the students sang, "Fellow students, be strong, shoulder the weight of our nation." Going back to the demonstrators' youth, "I Love Beijing, Tian'anmen," a Young Pioneers' favorite, emphasized the local dimension of the protests as well as highlighting the importance of youth and the place of Tian'anmen within the popular Chinese national imagination.

However, music also highlighted key differences among the demonstrators. In *The Gate of Heavenly Peace*, the generation gap, for example, is palpable. While teacher Liang Xiaoyan complained about the rowdy rock music in Tian'anmen, Wu'er Kaixi criticized the older intellectuals who had come to the square and condescendingly addressed the students as children. Clearly, the appearance of Cui Jian in the square spoke to the students and younger workers in a way it did not to the older supporters of the movement. Although Cui's "Nothing to My Name" has nothing to do with political protest directly, it resonates deeply with the students' feelings about their situation in China:

> I want to give you my hope
> I want to help make you free
> But you always laugh at me
> For I have nothing to my name.[19]

Although the vagabond lover tries to get his girlfriend to elope with him, she laughs because he has nothing. The promise of Deng's modernization of China has left many, like the song's protagonist, behind. However, youth culture also opens up the possibility of freedom from the push toward consumerism—a vague, but definite call for liberation.[20]

In the film, Hou Dejian links the demonstrations to international youth culture and rock's call for personal liberation:

> Popular music, of course, came from the West. When young people try to express themselves, to sing about their own concerns, it is really a form of liberalization. That's why this music played a very important role during the movement. When someone takes part in a rock concert, that kind of crazy feeling is all about self-liberation and about self-expression.

Hou's analysis of the centrality of rock music to the demonstrations differs greatly from the associations conjured up by the "Internationale" or "I Love Beijing, Tian'anmen." Linking the students to, in Hou's view, "Western" notions of individual freedom and self- (rather than collective) expression, the movement takes on a dimension that articulates a connection to transnational youth culture and becomes a generational protest against the old guard broadly defined to go beyond Li Peng and outside the circles of government.

However, Hou's contribution to the music in the square speaks more to transnational, ethnic solidarity, to the importance of the global Chinese to the local events in Tian'anmen and the national events within the People's Republic, than to the demonstrators as part of a global youth culture that goes beyond Greater China. His top-selling song, "Children of the Dragon," for example, refers directly to the plight of the Chinese throughout history. Ironically, when the tanks were on their way to the square, Hou sang "The Beautiful Chinese" to honor the presentation of "a beautiful image of the Chinese to the rest of the world," self-consciously addressing the image of China broadcast by satellite worldwide.

Accompanied by an acoustic guitar, the song takes on the quality of an American protest song from the 1960s. Again, the transcultural presentation of an American-style folk song by a Taiwanese singer to support a movement for national reform by a local Beijing group of students resonates temporally and spatially for those tracking the event around the world.

The Gate of Heavenly Peace refers to one last song, He Yong's "Garbage Dump," a raw punk piece, as it accounts for the malaise that hit China's youth particularly hard after June 1989:

> People are like insects,
> All fighting one another.
> We eat our conscience,
> And we shit ideology.[21]

Although many students went back to school hoping to be able to buy a pair of Nike shoes after graduation, others tuned society out and dropped out into the underground. The raw anger and flirtation with nihilism of punk rock spoke to the post-1989 generation in profound ways. While drug addiction and other maladies increased, the avant garde also surged with creative energies that fueled the work of Sixth Generation filmmakers, visual artists, and creative writers.[22] Protest took on new forms.

AFTER JUNE 4

Youth formed the heart of the 1989 protests, and youth culture continues to serve as a barometer of the nature of dissent in China. As the self-appointed leader of the students, Chai Ling represents her generation for the world media. However, the question remains as to whether or not Chai Ling hijacked the movement. Perhaps Chai Ling receives too prominent a place in *The Gate of Heavenly Peace*, out of proportion to the actual power she had to keep the students in the square or move them out.[23] In some respects, she overshadows the other demonstrators and continues to exert inordinate influence on the dissidents in exile.

However, in her interview with Philip Cunningham presented in the film, she appears neither as a goddess of democracy nor as the bloodthirsty coward who plans to leave the square before it is awash in the demonstrators' blood. Rather, she seems to be young, afraid, and naive. In the photograph taken of her dressed to leave Beijing and go into hiding next to the TV playing an image of her crying during the interview, she looks like any other hopeful student, wearing her backpack, ready to go overseas. In fact, she changed her mind and stayed in the square, just as earlier she had changed her mind about calling for a halt to the demonstrations.

Caught up in the momentum of the moment, she saw the interest of the global media and the influx of money, supplies, and support from Hong Kong, Taiwan, and the overseas Chinese. She also saw the supporters from abroad and the students from the countryside come into the square as the more seasoned veterans had had enough and were returning to their campuses. Although the older hunger strikers like Liu Xiaobo and Hou Dejian may have done much more harm than good by staying close to the Monument of the Martyrs of the Revolution to agitate for the students to leave the square as the tanks rolled, they present themselves as the voice of reason, after the fact, in the film. However, if twenty-three-year-old Chai Ling understood that staying in the square in defiance of martial law would inevitably lead to bloodshed, it seems likely that the more mature Liu and Hou would understand this point just as well.

In fact, the controversy surrounding when to stay and when to go does not lead very far in an understanding of the movement and its importance. Calling for the overthrow of the government after the declaration of martial law and as soldiers began to mobilize on the outskirts of Beijing may have seemed reasonable at the moment and may even continue to be a reasonable response for some to the violent occupation of the square on June 4. However, after the event, the government successfully shifted public attention from the political to the economic dimension of Deng's reforms. As Ding Zilin's futile efforts to get some recognition of her son's death indicate, Deng had closed the book on the aspect of reform that included the redress of wrongs done by the government during the Cultural Revolution and earlier political campaigns like the Anti-Rightist Movement, and he would not reopen it to consider the innocent victims of the June military action. However, Deng, reinvigorating reform economics in 1992, continued to expand his economic policies, foreign investment poured in, and collective control of the economy continued to erode.

In fact, the workers took the brunt of the crackdown. The "hooligans" tried and executed for setting fire to the troop buses and throwing rocks came inordinately from their ranks. During the June action, they also had the highest incidence of casualties as they attempted to stop the troops before they overran the square. Whereas censorship regulations, restrictions on travel, and other constraints on intellectual freedom have their ups and downs, workers suffer constantly and inescapably from the erosion of social services, unemployment, and exploitation by transnational firms. The urban workers, the displaced peasants, and the newly impoverished from all classes bear the weight of reform on their backs, and they had the most to lose with the failure of the 1989 demonstrations. Whether Chai Ling or Li Peng go down in history as villains or not does not belie the important point that economic reform had its big losers who were not helped by the 1989 protests.

The shift of significance of the square as a public political forum to the square as a transnational marketplace encapsulates the struggle for the public sphere that occurs globally between the voices for democracy and the forces of capitalist expansion. As Tian'anmen exists on the Internet as a place for political discourse, it exists in Beijing as a site for international tourism and the display of China's entry into the global marketplace. Ironically, within Beijing and within China's national imaginary, Tian'anmen looms large, but within cyberspace, it occupies only a tiny corner of virtual geography overwhelmed by commercial interests. In an interview with Ian Buruma in Boston, Chai Ling, attending Harvard Business School, spoke of wanting to liberate China via the Internet and of hoping to get rich to "fix" China.[24] In the cyberagora, politics takes a back seat to consumerism, and the political sphere continues to shrivel.

FROM TIAN'ANMEN TO TIMES SQUARE AND BACK AGAIN

Using two widely publicized political events to frame a period of dramatic change within the Chinese world, this book has looked at how global screen culture has shaped various conceptions of China from Beijing in spring 1989 to Hong Kong on July 1, 1997, from the Tian'anmen demonstrations to the change of sovereignty of Britain's last major colony. In 1993, the Times Square shopping mall opened in the Causeway Bay area of central Hong Kong. As annual demonstrations continued to mark the anniversary of June 4 in Hong Kong's Victoria Square, Times Square appeared as an emblem of the marketplace. Like Times Square, New York City, this multistory shopping mall provides a visual marker of the edges of the Chinese world—far from Beijing, removed from the power of the Chinese state, within the ephemeral world of commercial advertising, brand names, and mammoth images of consumer products.

However, it is too easy to structure global China around these two spatial nodes. Within Tian'anmen at the height of the demonstrations, student leaders like Wu'er Kaixi peppered their rhetoric with references to Nike shoes, and Marlboro and McDonald logos found their way into newscasts broadcast via commercial satellites to the world. Also, in Times Square, in the heart of Manhattan's entertainment district, refugee art students from Beijing began to eke out a living painting caricatures of tourists and selling trinkets on the street. Tian'anmen serves as a marketplace, and Times Square hosts political exiles. The easy spatial, temporal, and political distinctions dissolve as China moves from a cultural and political center in Tian'anmen to the edges, and those edges turn out to be the center of the Western imagination—the Marlboro cowboy riding over the heads of shoppers, Calvin Klein briefs massive above the neon lights, electronic bulletins flashing the news framed by American-based conglomerates in Times Square. However, within that Times Square core, other images circulate of Jackie Chan as the kung fu comic, Michelle Yeoh as the Bond girl, and John Woo and Ang Lee as the new masters of action cinema. The screens remain reassuringly Orientalist while promising multiculturalism and fulfilling the potential of the American Dream for all men and women of the world.

However, other Chinese figures appear in Times Square as well. In Peter Chan's *Comrades: Almost a Love Story*,[25] the "illegal alien" Li Qiao (Maggie Cheung) escapes from the INS, inspired by spotting the quintessentially Chinese Xiao-Jun (Leon Lai), the mainland bumpkin, on a bicycle weaving through New York traffic in Times Square. In the heart of capitalist Times Square, dwarfed by commercial billboards and skyscrapers, Li Qiao finds her inspiration to resist in a vision of her comrade from the PRC. In *Crossings* (see Chapter 6), filmmaker Evans Chan brings his "barbarians," marginalized within the Chinese world by the vicissitudes of politics (e.g., the Cultural Revolution and the 1997 change in sovereignty of Hong Kong), their gender (e.g., as women victimized by "wrong loves"), their family histories (e.g., as mixed-race and non-Han Chinese), and their class (e.g., as educated professionals who can move, but at a price and with limitations, within the transnational economy), to a meeting close to the signature neon billboards of New York's Times Square. As "barbarians" leaving China behind to "invade" New York, they move into a different Chinese world. They become part of a diaspora in which anti-Asian violence becomes a question of American racism and sexism and the legacy of Tian'anmen turns into a question of U.S. foreign policy. If Tian'anmen can become a tourist destination, then Times Square can contain the seeds of an evolving political identity within transnational China.

Interview with Carma Hinton

What prompted you to begin The Gate of Heavenly Peace *project?*

I think I was motivated to do this project because of the way the U.S. press portrayed the entire incident. At that point in my life, I was very reluctant to take on a project of that scope and complexity. I had a new baby, I was finishing my dissertation, looking for a job, and I did not want to take any big risks.

Some of the reasons why I finally pushed myself to do the film involved the fact that I was in the United States watching television in 1989. What bothered me was that as the event became bigger, a lot of the Western reporters who had been in China for a long time and who knew Chinese were brushed aside. Big television personalities took over as the anchors. They did not know Chinese, they did not know China, but they knew how to package, they knew how to draw viewers, and they knew how to do the perfect sound bite. Because of the competition in the news industry, the networks were compelled to one-up one another in order to get the new tidbit in the next morning's few minutes allotted to China. The adventures of the American news personalities became the story, and it became ever more simplistic. The slogans, which were most meaningful to the U.S. audience, became the focus, and little effort was made to explore what democracy and freedom might have meant to the Chinese. The true heroes became the American anchorpeople who discovered the great story. I thought that something was not right here.

Also, presenting images of the students as these innocent, totally pure little angels and the government as this monolithic block of bad people does not illuminate what was really going on. In both camps, there were intense struggles. I knew this because I spoke to people on the phone at the time. If there was a nice-looking student who could speak good English, he or she would become a much more important subject than a worker who shied away from the camera. The worker may have been more afraid of retaliation than the student, or the worker did not know any English, or whatever. The media selected their own heroes and leaders of the Chinese movement. I was quite bothered by all of that.

Another thing that really bothered me had to do with how the U.S. media dealt with the interviews. Before the interviewee even finished an idea, much less than a sentence, sometimes midsentence, midsyllable—cut! Since I know Chinese, it was very grating to have somebody cut off in midsyllable. I felt that these voices should have been heard. The images that became iconic—the man in front of the tank, the Goddess of Democracy, Tian'anmen Square—meant something to the participants. The images meant different things to different people. The networks were much better when they reported U.S. stories. They could tolerate more gray areas. Whereas, when it came to China, it had to be black and white. We decided in the film, right off the bat, not to talk to any Western commentators of the event.

Once we decided to do a film and we studied the news footage closely, it all looked alike. Because the news reporters had the same approach in getting certain angles and certain people, there was a certain formula. For example, when the twelve intellectuals went to Tian'anmen Square to express support for the students' intentions and celebrate their courage, they also wanted to warn the students that if they took the protest to extremes, they might make it more difficult for the forces inside the Party sympathetic to their cause to help them. The intellectuals were worried. The cameramen, who didn't know Chinese, simply did close-up shots on each new person who took the mike and then turned the camera toward the audience. Since each of the intellectuals began each speech with high praise for the students, only those portions of their speeches were captured in close-up shots, with good sound. There were no shots with good picture or sound of their warnings and advice.

Fortunately, we were able to find a lot of home video footage. These amateur camera people filmed with a very different purpose. The camera followed specific people for a much longer time, so an entire process unfolded. The technical quality was much worse, but the content was infinitely richer. However, it was difficult to find this footage, since we were still trying to interview people in China, so we had to keep a low profile, and only make quiet inquiries.

We had to make many difficult choices during the editing process. I'll use the April 20 incident to illustrate this. Three days earlier, on April 17, the students had submitted a seven-point petition to the government. On the nights of the 18th and the 19th, the students staged a sit-in at Xinhuamen Gate, the entrance to the government compound, to demand a reply. A clash between the police and the students was reported to have occurred around dawn on the 20th, following the second night of the sit-in. The government claimed that the crowd had tried to push their way into Xinhuamen, and that some policemen had had their faces bloodied in the resulting confrontation. The independent student union issued statements denying that the students had ever tried to force their way into Xinhuamen Gate, and saying that the police had beat up the students.

We found home video footage shot on the afternoon of April 20, showing students gathering in Tian'anmen Square, where they told crowds of people what had happened earlier that morning. The first speaker was Wu'er Kaixi, who was very flamboyant and gave many colorful descriptions of how the police brutally broke into the students' ranks and beat them up. He implied that the students had simply been sitting there when the police charged in.

Around 4:45 in the morning a thousand or so police and soldiers brutally broke into our ranks. There were about four or five hundred of us, students as well as other citizens. The police savagely beat us up. They also beat up other citizens. They injured countless people! And they had their hands all over our female classmates! For example, if a boy and a girl were together, they would gang up on the girl and beat her up. That's what these police did! Two or three of them beat up one of us. I even saw five or six of them beat up one person. A Hong Kong reporter was beat up. One woman reporter, also from Hong Kong, had her camera grabbed by police. They pulled out the film and exposed it! This is what they mean by democracy!

The next speaker, Zhou Yongjun, gave a much longer, more detailed account of events. He said that the students were orderly at first, but then some latecomers got too excited and tried to push their way into Xinhuamen Gate. He said that he persuaded them to stop. Then the police gave the students an ultimatum to leave before 4:45 AM of the morning of the 20th. When the students stayed past 4:45 AM, the police came to remove them and put them on buses. Some angry students broke the windows on the bus with their fists. Broken glass flew on the heads and faces of the police. Zhou stated that the police kicked open the bus door and tried to arrest those students, but he said to their commanding officer, "You'd better not arrest them because arresting students would make the police look very bad." So the police let all of the students go. Zhou said that at that point a crowd of onlookers that was still gathered further down the street was shouting slogans. So after leaving the students, the police, on their way back to Xinhuamen Gate, attacked and beat up people in that crowd.

So this long stretch of home video contained two different accounts of what had happened. Zhou Yongjun spoke slowly, in great detail. He denounced the police, but he did not leave out facts that made the students look less than perfect. Wu'er Kaixi, on the other hand, was an emotional speaker who knew how to push all the right buttons to get the crowd stirred up. Unlike Zhou, he did not mention any actions by the students that might have contributed to the conflict.

The way two people from the same side of a conflict could give such different accounts about an incident only hours after it had occurred was very interesting. We wanted to include both accounts in our film, not only to tell the story of the April 20 incident, but also to raise the issue of how history is constructed. But Zhou Yongjun's account was too long to show in its entirety, and without any footage of the actual incident that he was describing, there was no way to edit down his talk. Wu'er Kaixi's account, in contrast, was electrifying; he takes over the screen, and he is exciting to watch. To follow Wu'er Kaixi's energetic scene with Zhou Yongjun's plodding account would have caused the energy of our film to sag. We thought about switching the order of the speakers in order to preserve both accounts. But the fast-fading daylight on that rainy afternoon made the switch look artificial, raising problems about authenticity. Furthermore, April 20 was only a short moment in a long story about the 1989 protest movement, and we couldn't afford to spend too much time on it. After trying long and hard to make the scene work, we finally decided that we had to cut out Zhou Yongjun. To let Wu'er Kaixi's story stand alone as our film's coverage of the April 20 incident, however, would have been obviously one-sided.

Thus, in order to address what Zhou Yongjun had described, i.e., how some students had provoked the police, we came up with an alternative. While we didn't have any footage of the second night of the sit-in, leading up to the morning of the 20th, we did have footage from the first night of the sit-in, which showed students trying to push their way into Xinhuamen Gate. We had also interviewed a worker, Han Dongfang, who had been there that night and described what he saw: "The students surged towards the gate a number of times, so I went over to the big red columns." We were able to vividly illustrate Han Dongfang's story with footage of the exact scenes that he was describing. He spoke to the students:

I called out to them, "I'm a worker. I've been a soldier myself, and I think what you're doing is very risky. This is the seat of the highest power in the nation. If you storm in, the government will have every reason to mow you down." I said, "To sacrifice yourselves like this is completely meaningless. We should use other methods to achieve our goals." I told people to stop pushing, to sit down and wait. Eventually the crowd settled down. There were no clashes that night. I didn't go there the following night, but I heard that there had been a clash.

In this way we were able to keep the April 20 story within a reasonable length, while retaining some of its complexity. It was not a perfect solution, but we felt that this was the best we could do with the materials we had in order to accommodate both the pacing of the film and the multiple perspectives we were trying to show.

Could you talk about how you present Tian'anmen Square as a visual element within the film?

In the film, Tian'anmen Square functions as a multifaceted structural device. Tian'anmen Square is both a physical space and a symbolic space. Space involves *nei* and *wai*, the inside and the outside. The square becomes the inside, and everything else becomes the outside. The movement becomes the inside, and everything else becomes the outside. Even the symbolic meaning of that square has a certain outside-inside dynamic. For the Communist Party, the square is the nei, and the wai wants to get a hold of it. The concepts of inside and outside appeal to the Party. Throughout the film, for example, we contrasted the emperor, who was hidden inside the Forbidden City, with the Communist Party, who claimed to represent the people and open the square up for the masses. Yet the leader is always up on the podium, and the masses are all looking up to him. There are all these complex spatial arrangements of symbolism of power, of control, and of countercontrol. Even in the protest movement, there was an inside and an outside. For example, the students took the center of the square, while the workers had their headquarters on the periphery, near the public bathroom.

With extension into cyberspace, we hope to accommodate what the film cannot include in two or three hours' time. The Web is nonlinear. We can do a better job of not privileging the single narrative, but presenting a multilevel narrative. Very early on in the project, we had that idea. Even as we began to gather and log our footage, we thought about the right organization so that we could eventually put more material up on the Web. Our Web site is still very small scale compared to what we envision the Web site could do. We are still designing new templates for plugging in other material. We are experimenting with new forms of presentation. Beyond *The Gate of Heavenly Peace*, we hope to create a digital encyclopedia of twentieth-century China. Of course, we wouldn't be able to cover everything, but we have some strong material covering many important periods and topics.

April 14, 2002

Notes

NOTES TO CHAPTER 1

1. It is useful to note that Murdoch really has had his sights set on China for some time. See "Murdoch, the Middle Kingdom, and the Media," *Peekabooty*, March 11, 2003; available online at www.peek-a-booty.org/pbhtml/article.php?sid=15.

2. See Mike Chinoy, *China Live: Two Decades in the Heart of the Dragon* (Atlanta: Turner Publishing, 1997).

3. Jenny Kwok Wah Lau, "*Ju Dou:* A Hermeneutical Reading of Cross-Cultural Cinema," *Film Quarterly* 45:2 (Winter 1991–92), p. 3. Also quoted in Rey Chow, *Primitive Passions: Visuality, Sexuality, Ethnography, and Contemporary Chinese Cinema* (New York: Columbia University Press, 1995), p. 166. Jenny Lau also looks at the same scene in "*Ju Dou:* An Experiment in Color and Portraiture in Chinese Cinema," in Linda C. Erhlich and David Desser, eds., *Cinematic Landscapes: Observations on the Visual Arts and Cinema of China and Japan* (Austin: University of Texas Press, 1994), p. 137. This particular moment has been analyzed in a number of different contexts; see Shuqin Cui, "Gendered Perspective: The Construction and Representation of Subjectivity and Sexuality in *Ju Dou,*" in Sheldon Hsiao-peng Lu, ed., *Transnational Chinese Cinemas: Identity, Nationhood, Gender* (Honolulu: University of Hawaii Press, 1997), pp. 303–30; Jerome Silbergeld, *China into Film: Frames of Reference in Contemporary Chinese Cinema* (London: Reaktion Books, 1999), chap. 6; Sheila Cornelius (with Ian Haydn Smith), *New Chinese Cinema: Challenging Representations* (London: Wallflower Press, 2002), chap. 4; Claire Huot, *China's New Cultural Scene: A Handbook of Changes* (Durham, NC: Duke University Press, 2000), chap. 4; and Yingjin Zhang, *Screening China: Critical Interventions, Cinematic Reconfigurations, and the Transnational Imaginary in Contemporary Chinese Cinema* (Ann Arbor: Center for Chinese Studies, University of Michigan, 2002), chap. 6. Zhang Yimou discusses *Ju Dou* in several of the interviews collected in Frances Gateward, ed., *Zhang Yimou Interviews* (Jackson: University Press of Mississippi, 2001).

4. Dai Jinhua, *Cinema and Desire: Feminist Marxism and Cultural Politics in the Work of Dai Jinhua*, eds. Jing Wang and Tani E. Barlow (London: Verso, 2002), p. 56.

5. Looking at *Ju Dou* as an allegory of June 4 is critiqued by W. A. Callahan, "Gender, Ideology, Nation: *Ju Dou* in the Cultural Politics of China," *East-West Film Journal* 7:1 (January 1993), pp. 52–80.

6. For more on this point, see Sheldon Hsiao-peng Lu, "National Cinema, Cultural Critique, Transnational Capital: The Films of Zhang Yimou," in *Transnational Chinese Cinemas*, pp. 105–36. See also Chen Xiaoming, "The Mysterious Other: Postpolitics in Chinese Film," trans. Liu Kang and Anbin Shi, *boundary 2* 24:3 (Fall 1997), pp. 123–41.

7. Chow, *Primitive Passions*, p. 149. For more on the "Zhang Yimou model," see Tonglin Lu, *Confronting Modernity in the Cinemas of Taiwan and Mainland China* (New York: Cambridge University Press, 2002), chap. 5.

8. David Morley and Kevin Robins, *Spaces of Identity: Global Media, Electronic Landscapes and Cultural Boundaries* (London: Routledge, 1995), p. 141.

9. Ibid, p. 144.

10. Jean Baudrillard, "The Ecstasy of Communication," trans. John Johnston, in Hal Foster, ed., *The Anti-Aesthetic: Essays on Postmodern Culture* (Post Townsend, WA: Bay Press, 1983), p. 133.

11. John Berger, *Ways of Seeing* (London: BBC and Penguin Books, 1972).

12. Xudong Zhang, *Chinese Modernism in the Era of Reforms: Cultural Fever, Avant-Garde Fiction, and the New Chinese Cinema* (Durham, NC: Duke University Press, 1997), p. 386.

13. Chris Berry, "A Nation T(w/o)o: Chinese Cinema(s) and Nationhood(s)," *East-West Film Journal* 7:1 (January 1993), p. 25.

14. For a discussion of the importance of this series to an understanding of Tian'anmen in 1989, see Bérénice Reynaud, "New Visions, New Chinas: Video-Art, Documentation, and the Chinese Modernity in Question," in Michael Renov and Erika Suderburg, eds., *Resolutions: Contemporary Video Practices* (Minneapolis: University of Minnesota, 1996), pp. 229–57. This essay also includes detailed discussion of video works from around the world that comment on the spring 1989 events. For more on *River Elegy*, see Jing Wang, *High Culture Fever: Politics, Aesthetics, and Ideology in Deng's China* (Berkeley: University of California Press, 1996), chap. 3; Xiaomei Chen, "Occidentalism as Counter-discourse: *He Shang* in Post-Mao China," *Critical Inquiry* 18 (1992), pp. 686–712.

15. For more on American political rhetoric surrounding Chinese politics and its implications, see Richard Madsen, "China in the American Imagination," *Dissent* (Winter 1998), pp. 54–59.

16. For a study of the critical reception of this film, see Faye Zhengxing, "Has the Movie *Red Corner* Driven China into Its Corner?" *Asian Cinema* 12:1 (Spring–Summer 2001), pp. 117–28.

17. For a detailed discussion of Xie's *Opium War*'s production history and analysis of the film in relation to contemporary Chinese politics, see Zhiwei Xiao, "The Opium War in the Movies: History, Politics and Propaganda," *Asian Cinema* 11:1 (Spring/Summer 2000), pp. 68–83; Rebecca E. Karl, "The Burdens of History: *Lin Zexu* (1959) and *The Opium War* (1997)," in Xudong Zhang, ed. *Whither China?: Intellectual Politics in Contemporary China* (Durham, NC: Duke University Press, 2001), pp. 229–62.

18. Esther C. M. Yau, "Introduction: Hong Kong Cinema in a Borderless World," in Esther C. M. Yau, ed. *At Full Speed: Hong Kong Cinema in a Borderless World* (Minneapolis: University of Minnesota Press, 2001), pp. 16–17.

19. Stephen Teo, *Hong Kong Cinema: The Extra Dimensions* (London: BFI, 1997), p. 207.

20. Esther Yau, "Border Crossing: Mainland China's Presence in Hong Kong Cinema," in Nick Browne, Paul G. Pickowicz, Vivian Sobchack, and Esther Yau, eds., *New Chinese Cinemas: Forms, Identities, Politics* (New York: Cambridge University Press, 1994), p. 181.

21. John Lent, *The Asian Film Industry* (Austin: University of Texas Press, 1990), p. 118. For more on film censorship in the PRC and Hong Kong, see Tony Rayns, "The Well Dries Up," *Index on Censorship: Hong Kong Goes Back* 26:1 (January–February 1997), pp. 89–94.

22. Law Kar, ed., *Hong Kong New Wave: Twenty Years After*, 23rd Hong Kong International Film Festival (Hong Kong: Provisional Urban Council, 1999).

23. Sam Ho, ed., *The Swordsman and His Jiang Hu: Tsui Hark and Hong Kong Film* (Hong Kong: Hong Kong Film Archive, 2002).

24. Lisa Odham Stokes and Michael Hoover, *City on Fire: Hong Kong Cinema* (New York: Verso, 1999), p. 261.

25. See Law Kar, ed., *Transcending the Times: King Hu and Eileen Chang, 22nd Hong Kong Film Festival* (Hong Kong: Provisional Urban Council, 1998).

26. For an overview of Hong Kong films on Vietnam, see Tony Williams, "Hong Kong Cinema, the Boat People, and *To Liv(e)*," *Asian Cinema* 11:1 (Spring/Summer 2000), pp. 131–42.

27. For a discussion of the latter two films, see Julian Stringer, "Cultural Identity and Diaspora in Contemporary Hong Kong Cinema," in Darrell Y. Hamamoto and Sandra Liu, eds., *Countervisions: Asian American Film Criticism* (Philadelphia: Temple University Press, 2000), pp. 298–312.

28. Paul Virilio, *The Aesthetics of Disappearance*, trans. Philip Beitchman (New York: Semiotext[e], 1991).

29. Ackbar Abbas, *Hong Kong: Culture and Politics of Disappearance* (Minneapolis: University of Minnesota Press, 1997). For more on Hong Kong's nostalgia cinema, see Natalia Chan Sui Hung, "Rewriting History: Hong Kong Nostalgia Cinema and Its Social Practice," in Poshek Fu and David Desser, eds., *The Cinema of Hong Kong: History, Arts, Identity* (New York: Cambridge University Press, 2000), pp. 253–272; Linda Chiu-han Lai, "Film and Enigmatization: Nostalgia, Nonsense, and Remembering," in Esther C. M. Yau, ed., *At Full Speed: Hong Kong Cinema in a Borderless World* (Minneapolis: University of Minnesota Press, 2001), pp. 231–50.

30. For another perspective on Hong Kong film in relation to 1997, see Sheldon H. Lu, "Filming Diaspora and Identity: Hong Kong and 1997," in Fu and Desser, eds., *The Cinema of Hong Kong*, pp. 273–88.

31. Woo quoted in Christopher Heard, *Ten Thousand Bullets: The Cinematic Journey of John Woo* (Los Angeles: Lone Eagle, 2000), pp. 88–89. For a discussion of the impact of June 1989 on Woo's oeuvre as well as other Hong Kong action films, see Julian Stringer, " 'Your Tender Smiles Give Me Strength': Paradigms of Masculinity in John Woo's *A Better Tomorrow* and *The Killer*," *Screen* 38:1 (Spring 1997), pp. 25–41. Also mentioned in Robert Hauke, "John Woo's Cinema of Hyperkinetic Violence: From *A Better Tomorrow* to *Face/Off*," *Film Criticism* 24:1 (Fall 1999), pp. 39–59.

32. Paula Kalina interview with Trinh T. Minh-ha, "Flowers Repression," in Trinh T. Minh-ha, *Cinema Interval* (New York: Routledge, 1999), p. 206.

33. For an overview of the political ties of specific Hong Kong film companies, see Hector Rodriguez, "Organizational Hegemony in the Hong Kong Cinema," *Post Script* 19:1 (Fall 1999), pp. 107–19. For more on the transnational character of Hong Kong film, see Kwai-Cheung Lo, "Transnationalization of the Local in Hong Kong Cinema of the 1990s," in Yau, ed., *At Full Speed*, pp. 261–76. On the "Taiwan factor," see Liang Hai-chiang, "Hong Kong Cinema's 'Taiwan Factor,' " in Law Kar, ed., *Fifty Years of Electric Shadows, 21st Hong Kong International Film Festival*, trans. Yatsen Chan (Hong Kong: Urban Council, 1997), pp. 158–63. For Hong Kong's influence on PRC film, see Hu Ke, "The Influence of Hong Kong Cinema on Mainland China," trans. Grace Ng and Stephen Teo, in Kar, ed., *Fifty Years of Electric Shadows*, pp. 171–78.

34. For more on this point, see Bérénice Reynaud, *A City of Sadness* (London: BFI, 2002).

35. For the definitive study of *A City of Sadness*, see Abé Mark Nornes and Yeh Yueh-yu, *Narrating National Sadness: Cinematic Mapping and Hypertextual Dispersion*, available online at http://cinemaspace.berkeley.edu/papers/cityofsadness/index.html. For a discussion of *A City of Sadness* within the context of developments in contemporary Taiwanese cinema, see Douglas Kellner, "New Taiwan Cinema in the 80s," *Jump Cut* 42

(December 1998), pp. 101–15; and June Yip, "Constructing a Nation: Taiwanese History and the Films of Hou Hsiao-hsien," in Lu, ed., *Transnational Chinese Cinemas*, pp. 139–68.

36. Gilles Deleuze, *Cinema 2: The Time-Image*, trans. Hugh Tomlinson and Robert Galeta (Minneapolis: University of Minnesota Press, 1989), p. xi.

37. See Ien Ang, "Can One Say No to Chineseness? Pushing the Limits of the Diasporic Paradigm," *boundary 2* 25:3 (Fall 1998), pp. 223–42; and Allen Chun, "Fuck Chineseness: On the Ambiguities of Ethnicity as Culture as Identity," *boundary 2* 23:2 (Summer 1996), pp. 111–38.

38. For a detailed discussion of issues surrounding Chinese transnationalism and diaspora, see Donald M. Nonini and Aihwa Ong, "Introduction: Chinese Transnationalism as an Alternative Modernity," in Aihwa Ong and Donald Nonini, eds., *Ungrounded Empires: The Cultural Politics of Modern Chinese Transnationalism* (New York: Routledge, 1997), pp. 3–33. For a specific discussion of the issue of the "nation" as it relates to Chinese cinema, see Chris Berry, "If China Can Say No, Can China Make Movies? Or, Do Movies Make China? Rethinking National Cinema and National Agency," *boundary 2* 25:3 (Fall 1998), pp. 129–50.

39. For a review of these and other documentaries on Tian'anmen, see Pauline Chen, "Screening History: New Documentaries on the Tiananmen Events in China," *Cineaste* 22:1 (Winter 1996), p. 18ff. Available online at www.lib.berkeley.edu/mrc/tianamen.html.

40. For a detailed examination of this scene from *Beijing Bastards* in the context of the relationship between Chinese film and the creation of the public sphere, see Stephanie Hemelryk Donald, *Public Secrets, Public Spaces: Cinema and Civility in China* (Lanham, MD: Rowman and Littlefield, 2000). For more on the notion of a public sphere after 1989, see Xudong Zhang, "Nationalism, Mass Culture, and Intellectual Strategies in Post-Tiananmen China," in Zhang, ed. *Whither China?*, pp. 315–48.

41. For an insightful critique of *Hibiscus Town* in relation to Deng's economic policies, see Andrew Kipnis, "Anti-Maoist Gender: *Hibiscus Town*'s Naturalization of a Dengist Sex/Gender/Kinship System," *Asian Cinema* 8:2 (Winter 1996/1997), pp. 66–75.

42. See Suzie Sau Fong Young, "Encountering (China, My) Sorrow," *Asian Cinema* 10:1 (Fall 1998), pp. 107–11. More recently, Dai has made *Balzac and the Little Chinese Seamstress* (2002) also about the Cultural Revolution. Both films were made possible by European financing.

43. For a detailed analysis of the series' reception in post-1989 China, see Jianying Zha, *China Pop: How Soap Operas, Tabloids, and Bestsellers Are Transforming a Culture* (New York: New Press, 1995).

44. Although much of this film is set in the 1950s, it deals with the same issues that characterized the 1960s as well, see Darrell William Davis, "Borrowing Postcolonial: Wu Nien-Chen's *Dou-san* and the Memory Mine," *Post Script* 20:2-3 (Winter/Spring and Summer 2001), pp. 94–114. Chaoyang Liao, "Borrowed Modernity: History and the Subject in *A Borrowed Life*," *boundary 2* 24:3 (Fall 1997), pp. 225–45.

45. For a detailed discussion of this film, see Tonglin Lu, *Confronting Modernity in the Cinemas of Taiwan and Mainland China* (New York: Cambridge University Press, 2002), chap. 7.

46. For more on *Song of the Exile*, see Patricia Brett Erens, "Crossing Borders: Time, Memory, and the Construction of Identity in *Song of the Exile*," *Cinema Journal* 39:4 (Summer 2000), pp. 43–59. See also Chua Siew-Keng, "The Politics of 'Home': *Song of the Exile*," *Jump Cut* 42 (December 1998), pp. 90–93; Tony Williams, "Border-Crossing

Melodrama: *Song of the Exile*," *Jump Cut* 42 (December 1998), pp. 94–100; and Freda Freidberg, "Border Crossings: Ann Hui's Cinema," *Senses of Cinema*, September 2002, available online at www.sensesofcinema.com/contents/02/22/hui.html. For a discussion of the film in relation to Ann Hui's oeuvre, see Elaine Yee Lim Ho, "Women on the Edges of Hong Kong Modernity: The Films of Ann Hui," in Mayfair Mei-Hui Yang, ed., *Spaces of Their Own: Women's Public Sphere in Transnational China* (Minneapolis: University of Minnesota Press, 1999), pp. 162–87; and Patricia Brett Erens, "The Film Work of Ann Hui," in Fu and Desser, eds., *The Cinema of Hong Kong*, pp. 176–95.

47. Sek Kei, "Hong Kong Cinema from June 4 to 1997," trans. Stephen Teo, in Law, ed., *Fifty Years of Electric Shadows*, p. 120.

48. Shanghai, too, has the longest continuous history of film production in the Chinese-speaking world. For an overview of Shanghai's continuing importance as a media center, see Mayfair Mei-hui Yang, "Mass Media and Transnational Subjectivity in Shanghai: Notes on (Re)Cosmopolitanism in a Chinese Metropolis," in Ong and Nonini, eds., *Ungrounded Empires* pp. 287–319.

49. For an analysis of *Peach Blossom Land*, see Jon Kowallis, "The Diaspora in Postmodern Taiwan and Hong Kong Film: Framing Stan Lai's *Peach Blossom Land* with Allen Fong's *Ah Ying*," in Lu, ed., *Transnational Chinese Cinemas*, pp. 169–86.

50. Lisa Odham Stokes and Michael Hoover, "Resisting the Stage: Imaging/Imagining Ruan Lingyu in Stanley Kwan's *Actress*," *Asian Cinema* 11:2 (Fall/Winter 2000), p. 93. See also Julian Stringer, "*Centre Stage*: Reconstructing the Bio-Pic," *CineAction* 42, (1997), pp. 28–39; Shuqin Cui, "Stanley Kwan's *Centre Stage*: The (Im)possible Engagement between Feminism and Postmodernism," *Cinema Journal* 34:4 (Summer 2000), pp. 60–80. For more on the historical relationship between Hong Kong and Shanghai film see Law Kar, ed., *Cinema of Two Cities: Hong Kong-Shanghai, 18th Hong Kong International Film Festival* (Hong Kong: Urban Council, 1994).

51. Needless to say, the movie does not follow the infamous biography of the sisters too closely: Sterling Seagrave, *The Soong Dynasty* (New York: Harper and Row, 1985). The film also suffered from the heavy hand of the censors; see Stokes and Hoover, *City on Fire*, p. 267; Bérénice Reynaud, *Nouvelles Chines/Nouveaux cinémas* (Paris: Cahiers du cinéma, 1999), p. 136.

52. See Peter X Feng, "Decentering the Middle Kingdom: *China—Land of my Father, The Way to my Father's Village, Made in China*," *Jump Cut* 42 (December 1998), pp. 122–34.

53. Shu-Mei Shih, "Gender and a Geopolitics of Desire: The Seduction of Mainland Women in Taiwan and Hong Kong Media," in Yang, ed., *Spaces of Their Own*, pp. 278–307. Also, see Li-Mei Chang, "Whose Fatal Ways: Mapping the Boundary and Consuming the Other in Border Crossing Films," *Asian Journal of Communication* 11:2 (2001), pp. 39–57.

54. See Sheldon H. Lu, "Soap Opera in China: The Transnational Politics of Visuality, Sexuality, and Masculinity," *Cinema Journal* 40:1 (Fall 2000), pp. 25–47. Dai Jinhua, *Cinema and Desire: Feminist Marxism and Cultural Politics in the Work of Dai Jinhua*, eds. Jing Wang and Tani E. Barlow (London: Verso, 2002), chap. 7. Lydia H. Liu, "*Beijing Sojourners in New York*: Postsocialism and the Question of Ideology in Global Media Culture," *positions: east asian cultures critique* 7:3 (Winter 1999), pp. 764–97. For more on the changing role of television in China, see James Lull, *China Turned On: Television, Reform and Resistance* (New York: Routledge, 1991); Junhao Hong, "Reconciliation between Openness and Resistance: Media Globalization and New Policies of China's Television in the 1990s," in Georgette Wang, Jan Servaes, and Anura Goonasekera, eds., *The*

New Communications Landscape: Demystifying Media Globalization (New York: Routledge, 2000), pp. 288–306; and Michael Curtin, "Hong Kong Meets Hollywood in the Extranational Arena of the Culture Industries," in Kwok-Kan Tam, Wimal Dissanayake, and Terry Siu-han Yip, eds., *Sights of Contestation: Localism, Globalism and Cultural Production in Asia and the Pacific* (Hong Kong: Chinese University Press, 2002), pp. 79–109.

55. For example, Wong Kar-Wai/Shanghai–Hong Kong; Peter Chan/Thailand–United States–Hong Kong; Edward Yang/Shanghai–Taiwan–United States–Taiwan; Wayne Wang/Hong Kong–United States; Chen Kaige/PRC–USA; Richard Fung/Trinidad–Ireland–Canada; John Woo/Guangzhou–Hong Kong–California, and so on.

56. Aihwa Ong, *Flexible Citizenship: The Cultural Logics of Transnationality* (Durham, NC: Duke University Press, 1999).

57. See Tony Williams, "Under 'Western Eyes': The Personal Odyssey of Huang Fei-Hong in *Once upon a Time in China*," *Cinema Journal* 40:1 (Fall 2000), pp. 3–24. For more on the series, see Yang Ming-Yu, *China: Once upon a Time/Hong Kong 1997—A Critical Study of Contemporary Hong Kong Martial Arts Film*, Ph.D. dissertation, University of Maryland, College Park, 1995. Hector Rodriguez, "Hong Kong Popular Culture as an Interpretive Arena: The Huang Feihong Film Series," *Screen* 38:1 (Spring 1997), pp. 1–24.

58. For more on global flow, see Arjun Appadurai, *Modernity at Large: Cultural Dimensions of Globalization* (Minneapolis: University of Minnesota Press, 1996).

59. Jerry White, "The Films of Ning Ying: China Unfolding in Miniature," *CineAction* 42 (February 1997), pp. 2–9.

60. For a discussion of this film in relation to Deng's policies, see Monica Hulsbus, "On the Oppositional Politics of Chinese Every Day Practices," *CineAction* 42 (February 1997), pp. 10–14.

61. For more on *The Troubleshooters* and some of these other films, see Esther C. M. Yau, "International Fantasy and the 'New Chinese Cinema,'" *Quarterly Review of Film and Video* 14:3 (April 1993), pp. 95–107; Wang, *High Culture Fever*, chap. 7; Claire Huot, *China's New Cultural Scene: A Handbook of Changes* (Durham, NC: Duke University Press, 2000), chap. 2; and Reynaud, *Nouvelles Chines*, chap. 4.

62. On the depiction of the overseas Chinese on global screens, see Law Kar, ed., *Overseas Chinese Figures in Cinema, 16th Hong Kong International Film Festival* (Hong Kong: Urban Council, 1992).

63. See Silbergeld, *China into Film*, chapter 3. See also Ann S. Anagnost, *National Past-Times: Narrative, Representation, and Power in Modern China* (Durham, NC: Duke University Press, 1997), chap. 6.

64. For an analysis of guan xi in relation to Xie Fei's *Black Snow* (1989), see Stephanie Hemelryk Donald, *Public Secrets, Public Spaces: Cinema and Civility in China* (Lanham, MD: Rowman and Littlefield, 2000), pp. 125–28.

65. Tu Wei-ming, "Cultural China: The Periphery as Center," in Tu Wei-Ming, ed., *The Living Tree: The Changing Meaning of Being Chinese Today* (Stanford, CA: Stanford University Press, 1994), pp. 1–34.

66. For a detailed critique, see Arif Dirlik, "Confucius in the Borderlands: Global Capitalism and the Reinvention of Confucianism," *boundary 2* 22:3 (Autumn 1995), pp. 229–73.

67. Sheldon Lu, "Historical Introduction: Chinese Cinemas (1896–1996) and Transnational Film Studies," in Lu, ed., *Transnational Chinese Cinemas*, pp. 18–19. For a discussion of the dialectical pulls of nationalism and capitalism in contemporary Chinese

societies, see Aihwa Ong, "Chinese Modernities: Narratives of Nation and of Capitalism," in Ong and Nonini, eds., *Ungrounded Empires*, pp. 171–202. For an overview of the use of the concept of "Greater China," see Harry Harding, "The Concept of Greater China: Themes, Variations, and Reservations," in David Shambaugh, ed., *Greater China: The Next Superpower?* (New York: Oxford University Press, 1995), pp. 8–34.

68. Peter Hitchcock, "Mao to the Market," in Zhang, ed., *Whither China?*, p. 273. See also Arif Dirlik, "Critical Reflections on 'Chinese Capitalism' as Paradigm," *Identities* 3 (January 1997), pp. 303–30.

69. See Christina Klein, *Cold War Orientalism: Asia in the Middlebrow Imagination, 1945–1961* (Berkeley: University of California Press, 2003). For more on the transnational dimension of Woo's action films, see Anne Ciecko, "Transnational Action: John Woo, Hong Kong, Hollywood," in Lu, ed., *Transnational Chinese Cinemas*, pp. 221–38.

70. See Stringer, "Your Tender Smile Gives Me Strength"; Jillian Sandell, "Reinventing Masculinity: The Spectacle of Male Intimacy in the Films of John Woo," *Film Quarterly* 49:4 (Summer 1996), pp. 23–34; Tony Williams, "Space, Place, and Spectacle: The Crisis Cinema of John Woo," *Cinema Journal* 36:2 (Winter 1997), pp. 67–84; and Anthony Enns, "The Spectacle of Disabled Masculinity in John Woo's 'Heroic Bloodshed' Films," *Quarterly Review of Film and Video* 17:2 (June 2000), pp. 137–45.

71. Wena Poon, "*Chinese Box*," *Film Quarterly* 52:1 (Fall 1998), pp. 31–34.

72. For more on Ang Lee's vision of the Chinese patriarchy, see Wei Ming Dariotis and Eileen Fung, "Breaking the Soy Sauce Jar: Diaspora and Displacement in the Films of Ang Lee," in Lu, ed., *Transnational Chinese Cinemas*, pp. 187–220; Shu-Mei Shih, "Globalisation and Minoritisation: Ang Lee and the Poltics of Flexibility," *New Formations* 40 (2000), pp. 86–101; and Cynthia Liu, "'To Love, Honor, and Dismay': Subverting the Feminine in Ang Lee's Trilogy of Resuscitated Patriarchs," *Hitting Critical Mass: A Journal of Asian American Cultural Criticism* 3:1 (Winter 1995), pp. 1–60.

73. Lu, "Historical Introduction," p. 23. This trope has been explored by many scholars working on the depiction of women in Chinese cinema; see Rey Chow, *Woman and Chinese Modernity: The Politics of Reading between West and East* (Minneapolis: University of Minnesota Press, 1991); and Shuqin Cui, *Women through the Lens: Gender and Nation in a Century of Chinese Cinema* (Honolulu: University of Hawaii Press, 2003). For more on the category of "woman" in relation to the Chinese state, see Tani Barlow, "Theorizing Woman: Funü, Guojia, Jiating (Chinese Women, Chinese State, Chinese Family)," in Inderpal Grewal and Caren Kaplan, eds., *Scattered Hegemonies: Postmodernity and Transnational Feminist Practices* (Minneapolis: University of Minnesota Press, 1994), pp. 173–96.

74. Inderpal Grewal and Caren Kaplan, "Introduction: Transnational Feminist Practices and Questions of Postmodernity," in Grewal and Kaplan, eds., *Scattered Hegemonies*, p. 7. For an overview of current theorizations of nationalism, globalization, Marxism, and feminism, see Lisa Lowe and David Lloyd, "Introduction," in Lisa Lowe and David Lloyd, eds., *The Politics of Culture in the Shadow of Capital* (Durham, NC: Duke University Press, 1997), pp. 1–32.

75. For an overview, see Wendy Arons, "'If Her Stunning Beauty Doesn't Bring You to Your Knees, Her Deadly Drop Kick Will': Violent Women in the Hong Kong Kung Fu Film," in Martha McCaughey and Neal King, eds., *Reel Knockouts: Violent Women in the Movies* (Austin: University of Texas Press, 2001), pp. 27–51. See also Bey Logan, *Hong Kong Action Cinema* (Woodstock, NY: Overlook Press, 1995), chap. 9.

76. Sometimes billed as Michelle Khan, Michelle Yeoh, originally from Malaysia, has established herself as one of Hong Kong's foremost martial arts heroines. See Tony

Williams, "Michelle Yeoh, 'Under Eastern Eyes,'" *Asian Cinema* 12:2 (Fall/Winter 2001), pp. 119–31; Anne T. Ciecko and Sheldon H. Lu, "The Heroic Trio: Anita Mui, Maggie Cheung, Michelle Yeoh—Self-Reflexivity and the Globalization of the Hong Kong Action Heroine," *Post Script* 19:1 (Fall 1999), pp. 70–86.

77. As do the martial heroines in Disney's *Mulan* (1998) and Ang Lee's *Crouching Tiger, Hidden Dragon* (2000), both outside the scope of this study because of its timeframe.

78. For a discussion of Communist Puritanism and its impact on Chinese screen culture, see Cui, *Women through the Lens*. See also Mayfair Mei-hui Yang, "From Gender Erasure to Gender Difference: State Feminism, Consumer Sexuality, and Women's Public Sphere in China," in Yang, ed., *Spaces of Their Own*, pp. 35–67. Yang also looks at contemporary Chinese women's search to get in touch with their repressed feminine sexuality in her documentary, *Through Chinese Women's Eyes* (1997).

79. See Renee Tajima, "Asian Women's Images in Film: The Past Sixty Years," in Pearl Bowser, ed., *In Color: Sixty Years of Images of Minority Women in the Media, 1921–1981* (New York: Third World Newsreel, 1983), pp. 26–29.

80. See Eugene Franklin Wong, *On Visual Media Racism: Asians in the American Motion Pictures* (New York: Arno Press, 1978).

81. See Judith Butler, *Gender Trouble: Feminism and the Subversion of Identity* (New York: Routledge, 1990).

82. For a discussion of the importance of costume in this film, see Amelie Hastie, "Fashion, Femininity, and Historical Design: The Visual Texture of Three Hong Kong Films," *Post Script* 19:1 (Fall 1999), pp. 52–69.

83. Bhaskar Sarkar, "Hong Kong Hysteria: Martial Arts Tales from a Mutating World," in Yau, ed., *At Full Speed*, p. 170. Also, see Lenuta Giukin, "Boy-Girls: Gender, Body, and Popular Culture in Hong Kong Action Movies," in Murray Pomerance, ed., *Ladies and Gentlemen, Boys and Girls: Gender in Film at the End of the Twentieth Century* (Albany: SUNY Press, 2001), pp. 54–69.

84. Esther C. M. Yau, "Introduction: Hong Kong Cinema in a Borderless World," in Yau, ed., *At Full Speed*, p. 7.

85. For a detailed discussion of these three films, see Andrew Grossman, "Better Beauty through Technology: Chinese Transnational Feminism and the Cinema of Suffering," *Bright Lights Film Journal* 35 (January 2002), available online at www.brightlightsfilm.com/35/chinesefeminism1.html. For more on *Intimates*, see Helen Hok-sze Leung, "Queerscapes in Contemporary Hong Kong Cinema," *positions: east asia cultures critique* 9:2 (Fall 2001), pp. 423–48. More recently, *Fish and Elephant* (2001) has been hailed as the first lesbian feature made in the People's Republic. There has been an explosion of recent scholarship on Chinese queer studies, queer youth, Asian American queer studies, and queer media studies; for example, see Robin Bernstien and Seth Silberman, eds. *Generation Q: Gays, Lesbians, and Bisexuals Born Around 1969's Stonewall Riots Tell Their Stories of Growing Up in the Age of Information* (LA: Alyson, 2000); Chris Berry, "Sexual DisOrientations: Homosexual Rights, East Asian Films, and Postmodern Postnationalism" in Xiaoping Tang and Stephen Snyder, eds. *Pursuit of Contemporary East Asian Culture* (Boulder: Westview, 1996), pp. 157–82; David L. Eng and Alice Y. Hom, eds. *Q & A: Queer in Asian America* (Philadelphia: Temple U. Press, 1998); Andrew Grossman, ed. *Queer Asian Cinema: Shadows in the Shade* (NY: Haworth Press, 2000); Gordon Brent Ingram, "Marginality and the Landscape of Erotic Alien(nations)," in Gordon Brent Ingram, Anne Marie Bouthillette, and Tolanda Retter, eds., *Queers in Space: Communities, Public Places, Sites of Resistance* (Seattle: Bay Press, 1997), pp. 27–52;

Lancaster, Roger N. and Michaela di Leonardo, eds. *The Gender Sexuality Reader: Culture, History, Political Economy* (NY: Routledge, 1997); Fran Martin and Chris Berry, "Queer'N'Asian on the Net: Syncretic Sexualities in Taiwan and Korean Cyberspaces," *Critical InQueeries* 2:1 (June 1998), pp. 67–93; Fran Martin, *Situating Sexualities: Queer Representation in Taiwanese Fiction, Film and Public Culture* (Hong Kong: Hong Kong University Press, 2003); Nitaya Masavisut, George Simson, and Larry E. Smith, eds. *Gender and Culture in Literature and Film East and West: Issues of Perception and Interpretation*, (Honolulu: University of Hawaii Press, 1994); Eve Oishi, "Bad Asians: New Film and Video by Queer Asian American Artists," in Darrell Y. Hamamoto and Sandra Liu, eds. *CounterVisions: Asian American Film Criticism* (Philadelphia: Temple U. Press, 2000), pp. 221–244; Gerard Sullivan and Peter A. Jackson, eds. *Gay and Lesbian Asia: Culture, Identity, Community* (Hayworth Press, 2001).

86. For a detailed analysis of the film, see Chris Berry, "Staging Gay Life in China: *East Palace, West Palace*," *Jump Cut* 42 (December 1998), pp. 84–89.

87. For more on films from China's Sixth Generation, see Shuqin Cui, "Working from the Margins: Urban Cinema and Independent Directors in Contemporary China," *Post Script* 20:2–3 (Winter/Spring and Summer 2001), pp. 77–93; Jenny Kwok Wah Lau, "Globalization and Youthful Subculture: The Chinese Sixth-Generation Films at the Dawn of the New Century," in Jenny Kwok Wah Lau, ed., *Multiple Modernities: Cinemas and Popular Media in Transcultural East Asia* (Philadelphia: Temple University Press, 2003), pp. 13–27; and Reynaud, *Nouvelles Chines*, chap. 5.

88. For a critique of gender in this film and *Beijing Bastards*, see Stephanie Donald, "Symptoms of Alienation," *Continuum: Journal of Media and Cultural Studies* 12:1 (1998), pp. 91–103.

89. For a discussion of this film and the rest of Fruit Chan's 1997 trilogy as exemplars of Deleuze's notion of minor cinema, see Ka-Fai Yau, "Cinema 3: Towards a 'Minor Hong Kong Cinema,'" *Cultural Studies* 15:3–4 (2001), pp. 543–63.

90. Hamid Naficy, *An Accented Cinema: Exilic and Diasporic Filmmaking* (Princeton, NJ: Princeton University Press, 2001); and Hamid Naficy, "Phobic Spaces and Liminal Panics: Independent Transnational Film Genre," in Rob Wilson and Wimal Dissanayake, eds., *Global/Local: Cultural Production and the Transnational Imaginary* (Durhan, NC: Duke University Press, 1996), pp. 119–44.

91. For more on the various ways in which films in Taiwan have been funded, see *20th Anniversary of Taiwanese New Cinema* (Taipei: Taipei Golden Horse Festival Executive Committee, 2002).

92. For a discussion of the relation between state financing, foreign investment, and contemporary Chinese film, see Paul G. Pickowicz, "Velvet Prisons and the Political Economy of Chinese Filmmaking," in Deborah S. Davis, Richard Kraus, Barry Naughton, Elizabeth J. Perry, eds., *Urban Spaces in Contemporary China: The Potential for Autonomy and Community in Post-Mao China* (New York: Woodrow Wilson Center Press and Cambridge University Press, 1995), pp. 193–220.

93. See Yingjin Zhang, *Screening China: Critical Interventions, Cinematic Reconfigurations, and the Transnational Imaginary in Contemporary Chinese Cinema* (Ann Arbor: Center for Chinese Studies, University of Michigan, 2002).

94. Patricia R. Zimmermann, *States of Emergency: Documentaries, Wars, Democracies* (Minneapolis: University of Minnesota Press, 2000).

95. John Hess and Patricia Zimmermann, "Transnational Documentaries: A Manifesto," *Afterimage* (January/February 1997), p. 11.

96. See Gina Marchetti, "Cinema Frames, Videoscapes, and Cyberspace: Exploring Shu Lea Cheang's *Fresh Kill*," *positions: east asia cultures critique*, 9:2 (Fall 2001), pp. 401–22.

97. Laura U. Marks, *The Skin of the Film: Intercultural Cinema, Embodiment, and the Senses* (Durham, NC: Duke University Press, 2000), pp. 6–7.

98. Ella Shohat and Robert Stam, *Unthinking Eurocentrism: Multiculturalism and the Media* (New York: Routledge, 1994), p. 48.

99. For a discussion of Hong Kong film fans and Internet use, see David Bordwell, *Planet Hong Kong: Popular Cinema and the Art of Entertainment* (Cambridge, MA: Harvard University Press, 2000). For an overview of the transnational market for Hong Kong cinema, see Cindy Hing-Yuk Wong, "Cities, Cultures and Cassettes: Hong Kong Cinema and Transnational Audiences," *Post Script* 19:1 (Fall 1999), pp. 87–106.

100. Ian Buruma, *Bad Elements: Chinese Rebels from Los Angeles to Beijing* (New York: Random House, Vintage, 2001), p. 112.

101. Zillah Eisenstein, *Global Obscenities: Patriarchy, Capitalism, and the Lure of Cyberfantasy* (New York: New York University Press, 1998), p. 69. Chapter 5 of this book includes a discussion of the UN Beijing Conference on Women held in 1995. Although not as widely covered as June 30–July 1, 1997, in Hong Kong, global media channels were on hand to witness women calling for international rights—many advocating political positions antithetical to the national interests of the PRC.

NOTES TO CHAPTER 2

1. Born in Taiwan, the popular Lin has starred in a number of films in Hong Kong as well.

2. For a discussion of the relationship between romanticism and postmodernism in Hong Kong cinema, see Chuck Kleinhans, "Terms of Transition: The Action Film, Postmodernism, and Issues of an East-West Perspective," in Jenny Kwok Wah Lau, ed., *Multiple Modernities: Cinemas and Popular Media in Transcultural East Asia* (Philadelphia: Temple University Press, 2003), pp. 167–78.

3. See Ackbar Abbas, "The Erotics of Disappointment," in Jean-Marc Lalanne, David Martinez, Ackbar Abbas, and Jimmy Ngai, eds., *Wong Kar-Wai* (Paris: Dis Voir, 1997), pp. 39–81; Curtis K. Tsui, "Subjective Culture and History: The Ethnographic Cinema of Wong Kar-Wai." *Asian Cinema* 7:2 (Winter 1995), pp. 93–124; Lisa Odham Stokes and Michael Hoover, *City on Fire: Hong Kong Cinema* (New York: Verso, 1999). Although he favors other lines of inquiry, David Bordwell does acknowledge the prevalence of this interpretation in *Planet Hong Kong: Popular Cinema and the Art of Entertainment* (Cambridge, MA: Harvard University Press, 2000).

4. In addition to the above, see Tsung-Yi Huang, "*Chungking Express*: Walking with a Map of Desire in the Mirage of the Global City," *Quarterly Review of Film and Video* 18:2 (April 2001), pp. 129–42.

5. Gregory L. Ullmer, "The Object of Post-Criticism," in Hal Foster, ed., *The Anti-Aesthetic: Essays on Postmodern Culture* (Port Townsend, WA: Bay Press, 1993), pp. 83–110.

6. Craig Owens, "The Allegorical Impulse: Toward a Theory of Postmodernism," *October* 12 (Spring 1980), pp. 66–86, and part II, *October* 13 (Summer 1980), pp. 59–80.

7. Fredric Jameson, *Postmodernism, or, The Cultural Logic of Late Capitalism* (Durham, NC: Duke University Press, 1991).

8. See Jerome Silbergeld, *China into Film: Frames of Reference in Contemporary Chinese Cinema* (London: Reaktion Books, 1999), p. 111.

9. For more on Hong Kong censorship, see chapter 1 in this book as well as John A. Lent, *The Asian Film Industry* (Austin: University of Texas Press, 1990). See also Tan See Kam, "Ban(g)! Ban(g)! Dangerous Encounter—1st Kind: Writing with Censorship," *Asian Cinema* 8:1 (Spring 1996), pp. 83–108.

10. Jameson, *Postmodernism*, p. 168. Jameson has been embroiled in controversy because of his notion that all third world texts are necessarily national allegories; see Fredric Jameson, "Third World Literature in the Era of Multinational Capitalism," *Social Text* 15 (Fall 1986), pp. 65–68. His use of the term to discuss the shifting and contingent nature of postmodern texts differs somewhat from his insistence on looking at all texts from the third world as national allegories, and *Chungking Express* vacillates between the two senses of the term because it seems to allegorize Hong Kong as a place contested by various national interests as well as allegorize the postmodern condition of late capitalism in Hong Kong.

11. Ewa Mazierska and Laura Rascaroli, "Trapped in the Present: Time in the Films of Wong Kar-Wai," *Film Criticism* 25:2 (Winter 2000–2001), p. 8.

12. Jeremy Hansen, "Creative Chaos: The Disorganized World of Wong Kar-wai," in Stefan Hammond, ed., *Hollywood East: Hong Kong Movies and the People Who Make Them* (Lincolnwood, IL: Contemporary Books, 2000), p. 49.

13. For a discussion of the career of Faye Wong, see Anthony Fung and Michael Curtin, "The Anomalies of Being Faye (Wong): Gender Politics in Chinese Popular Music," *International Journal of Cultural Studies* 5:3 (September 2002), pp. 263–90.

14. Actually, Takeshi Kaneshiro has a Japanese father and a Chinese mother; he was raised in Taipei and educated in an American school there.

15. See Ackbar Abbas, *Hong Kong: Culture and the Politics of Disappearance* (Minneapolis: University of Minnesota Press, 1997). The film's director, Wong Kar-wai, is himself a "mainlander" born in Shanghai who moved to Hong Kong as a child and has older siblings who had stayed behind, unable to leave during the Cultural Revolution.

16. Actually Lau Wai-Keung started as director of photography for *Chungking Express* before Doyle came on board.

17. Robert M. Payne, "Ways of Seeing Wild: The Cinema of Wong Kar-Wai," *Jump Cut* 44 (Fall 2001); available online at www.ejumpcut.org/archive/jc44.2001/payne%20for%site/wongkarwai1.html.

18. See Huang, "*Chungking Express*: Walking with a Map of Desire."

19. Hamid Naficy, *An Accented Cinema: Exilic and Diasporic Filmmaking* (Princeton, NJ: Princeton University Press, 2001), p. 32.

20. See William H. Overholt, *The Rise of China: How Economic Reform Is Creating a New Superpower* (New York: Norton, 1993), p. 215.

21. Karl Marx, *Capital: A Critique of Political Economy, Vol. I : The Process of Capitalist Production*, trans. Samuel Moore and Edward Aveling, ed. Frederick Engels (New York: International, 1967), p. 72. For more on the nature of the commodity, see Arjun Appadurai, "Introduction: Commodities and the Politics of Value," in Arjun Appadurai, ed., *The Social Life of Things* (Cambridge: Cambridge University Press, 1986), pp. 3–63; and John Frow, *Time and Commodity Culture: Essays in Cultural Theory and Postmodernity* (New York: Oxford University Press, 1997), chap. 3. For a discussion of the representation of the commodity in intercultural cinema, see Laura U. Marks, *The Skin of the Film: Intercultural Cinema, Embodiment, and the Senses* (Durham, NC: Duke University Press, 2000), chap. 2.

22. Fredric Jameson, "Postmodernism and Consumer Society," in Hal Foster, ed. *The Anti-Aesthetic: Essays on Postmodern Culture* (Port Townsend, WA: Bay Press, 1983). pp. 111–25.

23. In *Once upon a Time in China and America* (1997), this saying cropped up in a speech given by Wong Fei-hung that put a gathering of Chinatown gamblers fast to sleep.

24. Richard J. Barnet and John Cavanagh, *Global Dreams: Imperial Corporations and the New World Order* (New York: Touchstone, Simon and Shuster, 1994).

25. Chuck Stephens, "Time Pieces: Wong Kar-Wai and the Persistence of Memory," *Film Comment* 32:1 (January–February 1996), p. 12ff.

26. Patrick E.Tyler, "In China, Letting a Hundred Films Wither," *New York Times*, December 1, 1996.

27. Although the Opium War is taught to all receiving a Chinese education, I am often struck by the ignorance of those outside of China as to the roots of the international drug trade and its relationship to imperialism. I still encounter the odd individual who admits that he or she thought the British fought the Opium War to keep opium from coming into Britain from China, rather than the other way around. At least since the fall of the Qing Dynasty, Lin Zexu has been used as a model hero, fighting imperialism as well as official corruption in China. Numerous films have been made about his career; most praise his efforts to fight against the corruption and stupidity of the Qing court. As in Xie Jin's account, most of these historical depictions favor Qing villains over foreign devils as the true culprits in China's humiliation during the nineteenth century. For an account of Xie's film in relation to earlier renderings of the war, see Li Cheuk-To, "*Yapian Zhanzheng* (The *Opium War*)," *Cinemaya* 38 (Autumn 1997), pp. 30–31; Zhiwei Xiao, "The Opium War in the Movies: History, Politics and Propaganda," *Asian Cinema* 11:1 (Spring/Summer 2000), pp. 68–83; and Rebecca E. Karl, "The Burdens of History: Lin Zexu (1959) and The *Opium War* (1997)," in Xudong Zhang, ed., *Whither China? Intellectual Politics in Contemporary China* (Durham, NC: Duke University Press, 2001), pp. 229–62. For more specific information on the version made during the Japanese occupation of China, see David Desser, "From the Opium War to the Pacific War: Japanese Propaganda Films of World War II," *Film History* 7:1 (Spring 1995), pp. 32–48; and Poshek Fu, "The Ambiguity of Entertainment: Chinese Cinema in Japanese-Occupied Shanghai, 1941 to 1945," *Cinema Journal* 37:1 (Fall 1997), pp. 66–84.

28. I have pointed out elsewhere that one of the few avenues available to those outside the bourgeoisie to enjoy the vilification and destruction of capitalists and their goods is in fantasies about drugs and the drug trade. See Gina Marchetti, "Action-Adventure as Ideology," in Ian Angus and Sut Jhally, eds., *Cultural Politics in Contemporary America* (New York: Routledge, Chapman and Hall, 1989), pp. 182–97.

29. More than one version of *Chungking Express* is in distribution. This particular scene differs in other versions of the film.

30. Hong Kong cinema has a certain fascination with Taiwanese triads, see Chapter 4 for more on the history of Taiwanese gangsters' notoriety.

31. Fredric Jameson, *The Geopolitical Aesthetic: Cinema and Space in the World System* (Bloomington: Indiana University Press, 1995), p. 154.

32. Curtis K. Tsui, "Subjective Culture and History: The Ethnographic Cinema of Wong Kar-Wai," *Asian Cinema* 7:2 (Winter 1995), p. 115.

33. For more on different aspects of space in the city of Hong Kong, see Abbas, *Hong Kong*, chap. 4.

34. It has been noted that the British colonial administration encouraged all kinds of migrations of labor, from its own administrators coming from the United Kingdom to

boatloads of Indian convicts and Chinese coolies (*ku-li*—literally "bitter labor"). Governing the motley, polyglot assortment in the colonies helped solidify British power by keeping races, religions, and ethnic groups at odds, meeting only on the common ground established under British authority, law, and the English language.

35. This fact is mentioned in an interview with Tony Rayns, "Poet of Time," *Sight and Sound* 5:9 (September 1995), pp. 12–16. Supposedly, the image of the toy plane taking off and landing on skin comes from an old Pan Am commercial.

36. Cheese is a running joke in the film *The Soong Sisters* (1997).

37. For more on the depiction of commodities in *Chungking Express*, see Stokes and Hoover, *City on Fire*, pp. 195–200.

38. Rey Chow, *Woman and Chinese Modernity: The Politics of Reading between West and East* (Minneapolis: University of Minnesota Press, 1991), p. 27.

39. Rayns, "Poet of Time," p. 13.

40. Ibid., pp. 13–14.

41. For a detailed discussion of the use of music in Wong's films, see Yeh Yueh-Yu, "A Life of Its Own: Musical Discourse in Wong Kar-Wai's Films," *Post Script* 19:1 (Fall 1999), pp. 120–36, and Yeh Yueh-yu, "Cause without a Rebel: Musical Discourse in the Films of Wong Kar Wai," in *1996 Taipei Golden Horse Film Festival Catalogue/Anthology* (Taipei: Golden Horse Film Festival, 1996), pp. 150–55.

42. Abbas, *Hong Kong*, p 57.

43. Sigmund Freud, "Fetishism" (1927), in Philip Rieff, ed., *Sexuality and the Psychology of Love* (New York: Collier Books, Macmillan, 1978), pp. 214–19.

44. Gayle Rubin, "The Traffic in Women: Notes on the 'Political Economy' of Sex," in Rayna R. Reiter, ed., *Toward an Anthropology of Women* (New York: Monthly Review Press, 1975), pp. 157–210.

45. Chow, *Woman and Chinese Modernity*, p. 11.

46. Ella Shohat and Robert Stam, *Unthinking Eurocentrism: Multiculturalism and the Media* (New York: Routledge, 1994).

47. Sumiko Higashi, *Cecil B. DeMille and American Culture: The Silent Era* (Berkeley: University of California Press, 1994).

48. Larry May, *Screening out the Past: The Birth of Mass Culture and the Motion Picture Industry* (Chicago: University of Chicago Press, 1983).

49. Gina Marchetti, *Romance and the "Yellow Peril": Race, Sex, and Discursive Strategies in Hollywood Fiction* (Berkeley: University of California Press, 1993), chap. 6.

50. For more on *Double Happiness*, see Edward O'Neill, "Asian American Filmmakers: The Next Generation? Identity, Mimicry and Transtextuality in Mina Shum's *Double Happiness* and Quentin Lee and Justin Lin's *Shopping for Fangs*," *Cineaction* 42 (February 1997), pp. 50–62.

51. Other films have looked at Chinatown sweatshops in the garment industry, including Marva Nabili's *Nightsongs* (1984) and Sylvia Chang's *Siao Yu* (1995).

52. Pam Tom takes up similar themes in her film *Two Lies* (1989), in which a mother and daughter find themselves in conflict over the mother's eye-widening operation.

53. A point made by Bordwell, *Planet Hong Kong*, p. 284.

54. For a discussion of the reception of the film in Hong Kong, see Gary W. McDonogh and Cindy Hing-Yuk Wong, "Orientalism Abroad: Hong Kong Readings of *The World of Suzie Wong*," in Daniel Bernardi, ed., *Classic Hollywood, Classic Whiteness* (Minneapolis: University of Minnesota Press, 2001), pp. 210–42.

55. For more on the appropriation of commodities as subcultural resistance, see Dick Hebdige, *Subculture: The Meaning of Style* (London: Methuen, 1979).

56. The extraordinarily successful pop diva is sometimes referred to as Teresa Tang. In point of fact, she shares the same surname, Deng, with Deng Xiaoping, and her name in *pin yin* is Deng Lijun.

57. Kwai-Cheung Lo, "Transnationalization of the Local in Hong Kong Cinema of the 1990s," in Esther C. M. Yau, ed., *At Full Speed: Hong Kong Cinema in a Borderless World* (Minneapolis: University of Minnesota Press, 2001), p. 270 and 272. For more on the centrality of Teresa Teng to *Comrades'* narrative, see Linda Chiu-han Lai, "Film and Enigmatization: Nostalgia, Nonsense, and Remembering," in Yau, ed. *At Full Speed*, pp. 231–50; and Sheldon H. Lu, "Filming Diaspora and Identity: Hong Kong and 1997," in Poshek Fu and David Desser, eds., *The Cinema of Hong Kong: History, Arts, Identity* (New York: Cambridge University Press, 2000), pp. 273–88. For more on the popularity of Hong Kong and Taiwanese popular culture among people from the PRC, see Thomas B. Gold, "Go with Your Feelings: Hong Kong and Taiwan Popular Culture in Greater China," in David Shambaugh, ed., *Greater China: The Next Superpower?* (New York: Oxford University Press, 1995), pp. 255–73.

58. Fung and Curtin, "The Anomalies of Being Faye (Wong)," also make some interesting comparisons between Teresa Teng and Faye Wong.

NOTES TO CHAPTER 3

1. Anne T. Ciecko and Sheldon H. Lu, "*Ermo*: Televisuality, Capital and the Global Village," *Jump Cut* 42 (December 1998), p. 77.

2. Ibid, p. 81.

3. Beth Notar, "Blood Money: Woman's Desire and Consumption in *Ermo*," *Asian Cinema* 12:2 (Fall/Winter 2001), p. 143.

4. See also Sun Wanning, "Women in the City: Mobility, Television and the Choices of Being Modern," *Asian Journal of Communication* 11:2 (2001), pp. 18–38.

5. For a detailed look at the political and economic repercussions of 1989, see Joseph Fewsmith, *China since Tiananmen: The Politics of Transition* (New York: Cambridge University Press, 2001).

6. For an overview of many of the video works associated with this documentary movement, see Bérénice Reynaud, "New Visions/New Chinas: Video-Art, Documentation, and the Chinese Modernity in Question," in Michael Renov and Erika Suderberg, eds., *Resolutions: Contemporary Video Practices* (Minneapolis: University of Minnesota Press, 1996), pp. 229–57; and Bérénice Reynaud, *Nouvelles Chines/ Nouveaux cinémas* (Paris: Cahiers du cinéma, 1999), chap. 6, which includes a brief discussion of *Out of Phoenix Bridge*. See also Dai Jinhua, "A Scene in the Fog: Reading the Sixth Generation Films," trans. Yiman Wang, in Dai Jinhua, *Cinema and Desire: Feminist Marxism and Cultural Politics in the Work of Dai Jinhua*, eds. Jing Wang and Tani E. Barlow (London: Verso, 2002), pp. 71–98. For more on feminist documentary practices in general, see: Diane Carson, Linda Dittmar, and Janice R. Welsch, eds., *Multiple Voices in Feminist Film Criticism* (Minneapolis: University of Minnesota Press, 1994); Alexandra Juhasz, ed., *Women of Vision: Histories in Feminist Film and Video* (Minneapolis: University of Minnesota Press, 2001); Julia Lesage, "The Political Aesthetics of the Feminist Documentary Film," *Quarterly Review of Film Studies*, No 3 (Fall 1978), pp. 507–23; Diane Waldman and Janet Walker, eds., *Feminism and Documentary* (Minneapolis; University of Minnesota Press, 1999).

7. Many of these films are based on books by novelist Wang Shuo, including *The Troubleshooters* (1988). See Jing Wang, *High Culture Fever: Politics, Aesthetics, and Ideology in Deng's China* (Berkeley: University of California Press, 1996).

8. For more information on the film, see the director's note, *"A Little Life Opera,"* *International Forum of New Cinema*, February 1997, available online at www.fdk-berlin.de/forum97/f088e.html.

9. For more on the history of filmmaking in China before and after 1949, see Jay Leyda, *Dianying—Electric Shadows: An Account of Film and the Film Audience in China* (Cambridge, MA: MIT Press, 1972); and Paul Clark, *Chinese Cinema: Culture and Politics since 1949* (Cambridge: Cambridge University Press, 1987).

10. For a discussion of the relationship between gender and class in Chinese films of the 1950s, see Esther C. M. Yau, "Compromised Liberation: The Politics of Class in Chinese Cinema of the Early 1950s," in David E. James and Rick Berg, eds., *The Hidden Foundation: Cinema and the Question of Class* (Minneapolis: University of Minnesota Press, 1996), pp. 138–71.

11. A film like *Third Sister Liu* (1961) fits somewhere between the two genres.

12. For an account of migrant labor in China, see Dorothy J. Solinger, "The Floating Population in the Cities: Markets, Migration, and the Prospects for Citizenship," in Susan D. Blum and Lionel M. Jensen, eds., *China off Center: Mapping the Margins of the Middle Kingdom* (Honolulu: University of Hawaii Press, 2002), pp. 273–88; and Huang Ping, "Recent Trends in Peasant Out-Migrations in Contemporary China," trans. Erica Brindley and Joshua Goldstein, in Meaghan Morris and Brett de Bary, eds., *"Race" Panic and the Memory of Migration* (Hong Kong: Hong Kong University Press, 2001), pp. 131–70.

13. Siqin Gaowa is one of the PRC's most respected actresses, and she has starred in a number of award-winning dramas, including Xie Jin's *Garlands at the Foot of the Mountain* (1985) and films by Hong Kong directors Stanley Kwan (*Full Moon in New York*, 1989) and Yim Ho (*Homecoming*, 1984; *The Day the Sun Turned Cold*, 1994).

14. In Chinese-language cinema, the mentally retarded often stand as allegorical symbols of the backwardness of the Chinese nation. Thus, Dunzi functions less as a character and more as a sign of a dysfunctional nation as does the young retarded boy who literally bites the hand that feeds him in Hong Kong director Ann Hui's *Song of the Exile* (1990). Zhang Yuan's *Mama* (1992), however, provides a marked contrast to this depiction of the mentally handicapped in Chinese-language cinema.

15. Jerome Silbergeld, *China into Film: Frames of Reference in Contemporary Chinese Cinema* (London: Reaktion Books, 1999), p. 183. Emphasis in original.

16. Xiaobing Tang, "Configuring the Modern Space: Cinematic Representations of Beijing and Its Politics," *East-West Film Journal* 8:2 (July 1994), pp. 47–69.

17. See Darrell Davis and Yeh Yueh-yu, "Warning! Category III: The Other Hong Kong Cinema," *Film Quarterly* 54.4 (Summer 2001), pp. 12–26.

18. Ning Ying's *For Fun* (1992) deals with a group of retirees who adore Chinese opera.

19. The cell phone, or *da ge da* (literally "big brother big"), has been a marker of success in the Chinese world since it first appeared. Replacing the beeper as a sign of being so connected and in demand that the owner must be able to be reached at any time of day and under any circumstances, the cell phone also has particular importance in the People's Republic as a status symbol because private phone lines are still at a premium. The cell phone is also a sign of China's entry into postmodernity, because it can operate without the modern infrastructure of telephone wires and government-controlled telephone exchanges.

Bouncing off satellites, cell phone communication leap frogs beyond China's lagging infrastructure to enable global business connections to flourish.

20. For some, the opera sisterhood also means freedom from men, and some contemporary films have dealt with lesbian relationships within the opera world, including *The Silent Thrush* (Cheng Sheng-fu, Taiwan, 1992), *Song of the Goddess* (Ellen Pau, Hong Kong, 1993) and the experimental short *Suet-Sin's Sisters* (Yau Ching, 1999).

21. Rey Chow, *Primitive Passions: Visuality, Sexuality, Ethnography, and Contemporary Chinese Cinema* (New York: Columbia University Press, 1995).

22. Laura Marks, *The Skin of the Film: Intercultural Cinema, Embodiment, and the Senses* (Durham, NC: Duke University Press, 2000), p. 105.

23. Chow, *Primitive Passions*, p. 19.

24. Ibid., p. 38.

NOTES TO CHAPTER 4

1. Robert Warshow, *The Immediate Experience* (Cambridge, MA: Harvard University Press, 2001), p. 101.

2. Aihwa Ong, *Flexible Citizenship: The Cultural Logics of Transnationality* (Durham: Duke University Press, 1999), p. 162.

3. Warshow, *The Immediate Experience*.

4. Ibid., p. 102.

5. See Andrew Bergman for more on the parallel between the gangster and "legitimate" businessmen. Andrew Bergman, *We're in the Money: Depression America and Its Films* (New York: New York University Press, 1971).

6. Sterling Seagrave, *Lords of the Rim* (London: Corgi, Bantam, 1995), p. 143–44.

7. See Sterling Seagrave, *The Soong Dynasty* (New York: Harper and Row, 1985).

8. See Abé Mark Nornes and Yeh Yueh-yu, *City of Sadness*, online publication available at http://cinemaspace.berkeley.edu/papers/cityofsadness/table.html, as well as Bérénice Reynaud, *City of Sadness* (London: BFI, 2003). For more on Hou's films, see Tonglin Lu, *Confronting Modernity in the Cinemas of Taiwan and Mainland China* (New York: Cambridge University Press, 2002); Hector Rodriquez, *The Cinema in Taiwan: Identity and Political Legitimacy*, Ph. D. dissertation, New York University, 1995; Shiao-Ying Shen, *Permutations of the Foreigner: A Study of the Works of Edward Yang, Stan Lai, Chang Yi, and Hou Hsiao-hsien*, Ph.D. dissertation, Cornell University, Ithaca, NY, 1995; Kwok-kan Tam and Wimal Disssanayake, *New Chinese Cinema* (Oxford: Oxford University Press, 1998); William Tay, "The Ideology of Initiation: The Films of Hou Hsiao-hsien," in Nick Browne, Paul G. Pickowicz, Vivian Sobchack, and Esther Yau, eds., *New Chinese Cinemas: Forms, Identities, Politics* (New York: Cambridge University Press, 1994); Yeh Yueh-Yu, "Politics and Poetics of Hou Hsiao-hsien's Films," *Postscript* 20:2 and 3 (Winter/ Spring and Summer 2001), pp. 61–76; and June Yip, "Constructing a Nation: Taiwanese History and the Films of Hou Hsiao-hsien," in Sheldon Hsiao-peng Lu, ed., *Transnational Chinese Cinemas: Identity, Nationhood, Gender* (Honolulu: University of Hawaii Press, 1997), pp. 169–86. Lu, Rodriquez, Shen, Tay, Tam, and Dissanayake also discuss Edward Yang's oeuvre.

9. For an overview of this year in relation to the political economy of contemporary Taiwan, see Willem Van Kemenade, *China, Hong Kong, Taiwan, Inc.*, trans. Dianne Webb (New York: Vintage, 1997).

10. For more on *hei jin*/black gold, see Allen T. Cheng, "The Curse of 'Black Gold,'" *Asia Week*, March 17, 2000, vol. 26 no. 10. Available online at www.asiaweek.com/asiaweek/ magazine/2000/03317/nat.4taiwan.kmt.html. *Black Gold* (a.k.a. *Island of Greed*, Michael and Johnny Mak, 1997) shows Hong Kong film's interest in the specifically Taiwanese circulation of black gold on the island. Several other Hong Kong films depict Taiwan's infamous gangster subculture; see, Liang Hai-chiang, "Hong Kong Cinema's 'Taiwan Factor,'" in Law Kar, ed., *Fifty Years of Electric Shadows, 21st Hong Kong Internatinal Film Festival*, trans. Yatsen Chan (Hong Kong: Urban Council, 1997), pp. 158–63.

11. "Taiwan's Dirty Business," *Asia, Inc.*, April 1997, available online at http:// members.tripod.com/~orgcrime/taiwantsdirtybusiness.htm.

12. See Pierre Bourdieu, *Distinction: A Social Critique of the Judgment of Taste*, trans. Richard Nice (Cambridge, MA: Harvard University Press, 1984).

13. See Sarah Thornton, *Club Cultures: Music, Media and Subcultural Capital* (Hanover: Wesleyan University Press, 1996).

14. See Mike Featherstone, *Undoing Culture: Globalization, Postmodernism and Identity* (London: Sage, 1995); and Jan Nederveen Pieterse, "Globalization as Hybridization," in Mike Featherstone, Scott Lash, and Roland Robertson, eds., *Global Modernities*. (London: Sage, 1995), pp. 45–68.

15. Edward Yang has stated that the character of Winston Chen, although fictionalized, is based on a childhood acquaintance of his; see "Director's Note," online at www.usc.edu/ isd/archives/asianfilm/taiwan/mahjong/synopsis.html.

16. Taiwan Democratic Progressive Party, "A Look Back at the DPP's Decade in the Street," *Taiwan International Review* 2: 5 (September–October 1996); available online at www.taiwandc.org/dpp/099604.htm.

17. Lu, *Confronting Modernity*, p. 119.

18. The Japanese-style tattoos also pay tribute to the film's Japanese backers as does the appearance of actress/pop singer Annie Shizuka Inoh, born in Taiwan but educated in Japan. Yang's *Mahjong* also enjoyed Japanese financial backing. For more on the transnational business relations that shape contemporary Chinese-language film, see Lu, *Transnational Chinese Cinemas*. For an insightful account of Hou's relationship to his Japanese backers, critics, and audience, see Yeh, "Politics and Poetics of Hou Hsiao-hsien's Films."

19. For a more detailed discussion of this image, see Yeh's contribution to Yeh Yueh-Yu, Shen Shiao-Ying, Li Zhen-Ya, and Lin Wen-Chi, "Symposium on *Goodbye South Goodbye*," *Chinese/Foreign Literature* 26:10 (March 1998), pp. 65–73. Unpublished translation by Qu Jiao-Jie.

20. For a study of cross-straits guan xi in action, see Hsing You-Tien, "Building Guanxi across the Straits: Taiwanese Capital and Local Chinese Bureaucrats," in Aihwa Ong and Donald Nonini, eds., *Ungrounded Empires: The Cultural Politics of Modern Chinese Transnationalism* (New York: Routledge, 1997), pp. 143–64.

21. Ong, *Flexible Citizenship*, p. 117.

22. Stephanie Hemelryk Donald, *Public Secrets, Public Spaces: Cinema and Civility in China* (Lanham, MD: Rowman and Littlefield, 2000), pp. 127–28.

23. Mayfair Yang, *Gifts, Favors, and Banquets: The Art of Social Relationships in China* (Ithaca, NY: Cornell University Press, 1994), p. 111.

24. Shelley Kraicer and Lisa Roosen-Runge, "Edward Yang: A Taiwanese Independent Filmmaker in Conversation," *CineAction* 47 (September 1998), p. 53.

25. Yang, *Gifts, Favors, and Banquets*, p. 115.

26. Although the Japanese workplace forms the basis for her study, many of Kondo's observations about role-playing in daily life in *Crafting Selves* resonate with the discussion of guan xi here. See Dorinne K. Kondo, *Crafting Selves: Power, Gender, and Discourses of Identity in a Japanese Workplace* (Chicago: University of Chicago Press, 1990).

27. This is also similar to the ways in which people perform gender and sexuality as discussed in Judith Butler, *Gender Trouble: Feminism and the Subversion of Identity* (New York: Routledge, 1990); Judith Butler, *Bodies That Matter: On the Discursive Limits of "Sex"* (New York: Routledge, 1993).

28. Quoted in Chiao Hsiung-Ping (Peggy), "Edward Yang, *Mahjong*: Urban Trials," *Cinemaya* 33 (Summer, 1996), pp. 24–27.

29. For an insightful discussion of rock and roll, Taiwan, and other films by Edward Yang, see Yeh Yueh-Yu, "A National Score: Popular Music and Taiwanese Cinema," Ph.D. dissertation, University of Southern California, 1995.

30. Fredric Jameson, "Postmodernism and Consumer Society," in Hal Foster, ed., *The Anti-Aesthetic: Essays on Postmodern Culture* (Seattle: Bay Press, 1983), pp. 111–25.

31. For a detailed discussion of the centrality of the karaoke club within the Chinese diasporan business circles, see Hsing, "Building Guanxi across the Straits."

32. See Tay, "The Ideology of Initiation." for a discussion of youth in Hou's oeuvre.

33. For more on the use of music in this film see Yeh, *A National Score*.

34. A point made by Jameson in his discussion of *The Terrorizer* (see *The Geopolitical Aesthetic: Cinema and Space in the World System* [Bloomington: Indiana University Press, 1995]) and reiterated by Zhang in his discussion of Taipei as a cine-city. For more on Yang's depiction of Taipei, see Lu, *Confronting Modernity*.

35. Chia Yi City Government Web site, www.chiayi.gov/tw/english.htm.

36. Yingjin Zhang, *Screening China: Critical Interventions, Cinematic Reconfigurations, and the Transnational Imaginary in Contemporary Chinese Cinema* (Ann Arbor: Center for Chinese Studies, University of Michigan, 2002), p. 309.

37. Jameson, *The Geopolitical Aesthetic*.

NOTES TO CHAPTER 5

1. Chua Beng-Huat, "Culture, Multiracialism, and National Identity in Singapore," in Chen Kuan-Hsing, ed., *Trajectories: Inter-Asia Cultural Studies* (London: Routledge, 1998), p. 186. Although the author does not include a discussion of the formation of modern Singapore as a nation-state, it is useful to look at Benedict Anderson, *Imagined Communities* (New York: Verso, 1991) for a discussion of the relationship between colonialism and modernity in the formation of nations in Southeast Asia, including the colonial history of Singapore.

2. For an incisive commentary on Asian values in the Singaporean context, see Chua Beng-Huat, "'Asian Values' Discourse and the Resurrection of the Social," *positions* 7:2 (1999), pp. 573–92.

3. It must be remembered that the Cathay Organization and the Shaw Brothers have strong roots in Singapore that date back to the British colonial era as film exhibitors, regional distributors, and producers. For more on the history of film in Singapore, see Jan Uhde and Yvonne Ng Uhde, *Latent Images: Film in Singapore* (New York: Oxford University Press, 2000).

4. For more on Chinese transnational cinema, see Sheldon Hsiao-peng Lu, ed., *Transnational Chinese Cinemas: Identity, Nationhood, Gender* (Honolulu: University of

Hawaii Press, 1997). For a detailed discussion of Singapore's role in current formations of transnational Chinese cinema, see Tan See Kam, Michael Lee, and Annette Aw, "Contemporary Singapore Filmmaking: History, Policies, and Eric Khoo," *Jump Cut* 46 (Summer 2003), available online at www.ejumpcut.org/currentissue/12storeys/index.html.

5. For more information on *Mee Pok Man* and *Twelve Storeys* as well as Khoo's complete oeuvre, visit the Zhao Wei Company Web site at www.zhaowei.com. See also Uhde and Uhde, *Latent Images*; Tan, Lee, and Aw, "Contemporary Singapore Filmmaking," and Audrey Wong, "Considering the 'Singapore Film,'" *Arts Issue* 7, National University of Singapore's Centre for the Arts, available online at www.nus.edu.sg/nusinfo/cfa/artsmag/arts7-4sfilm1.html. For more information on film in relationship to other mass media in Singapore (including information on censorship), see David Birch, *Singapore Media: Communication Strategies and Practices* (Melbourne, Australia: Longman Cheshire, 1993) and Tan Yew Soon and Soh Yew Peng, *The Development of Singapore's Modern Media Industry* (Singapore: Times Academic Press, 1994). For information on Singapore's film industry in relation to other Asian cinema industries, see John Lent, *The Asian Film Industry* (Austin: University of Texas Press, 1990). For information on the short film culture that Khoo helped shape, see Philip Cheah, "Singapore Shorts," *Cinemaya* 28–29 (1995), pp. 30–31.

6. Scholars working in a range of disciplines have taken up the subject of postmodernism and Greater China. For example, see Arif Dirlik and Zhang Xudong, eds., "Postmodernism and China: A Special Issue," *boundary 2* 24:3 (Fall 1997).

7. In fact, it is difficult not to see Meng as an imitation Lee Kuan Yew, with his combination of British colonial roots, evidenced by his command of English, and "Asian values," as he mouths neo-Confucianist government propaganda. It must be kept in mind that Lee was British educated and came from an ethnic Chinese family that favored English. Lee learned Mandarin as an adult to break from his own as well as Singapore's colonial status. For more on Lee Kuan Yew and his successor, Goh Chok Tong, see Greg Sheridan, *Tigers: Leaders of the New Asia-Pacific* (St. Leonards, Australia: Allen and Unwin, 1997).

8. Singlish is English laced with Malay and Chinese words from various dialects, strongly accented, with grammatical formations frequently closer to Chinese than English.

9. The fingernail may also point to cocaine use or the affectation of "cool" based on the assumption that he snorts cocaine from the nail.

10. Given the taboos surrounding homosexuality in Singapore and the increasingly frank treatment of this issue in Chinese-language cinema transnationally, it is not unreasonable to conjecture that this unnamed suicide may be gay and thus as distressed by the heterosexist patriarchy as the other characters. San San's sexual orientation could also be an unstated factor. For more on sexuality and secret lives in *Twelve Storeys*, see Michael Lee, "Dead Man Gazing: Posthumous Voyeurism in *12 Storeys*, or 'Splacing' Singapore's Official and Unofficial Discourses," *Asian Cinema* (Fall/Winter 2000), pp. 99–131.

11. For more on the crisis in the sex-gender system in Singapore, see Geraldine Heng and Janadas Devan, "State Fatherhood: The Politics of Nationalism, Sexuality, and Race in Singapore," in Roger N. Lancaster and Michaela di Leonardo, eds., *The Gender Sexuality Reader: Culture, History, Political Economy* (New York: Routledge, 1997), pp. 107–21.

12. David Harvey, *The Condition of Postmodernity* (Oxford: Basil Blackwell Press, 1989), p. 66.

13. Wong, "Considering the 'Singapore Film.'" The importance of the HDB flat in *Twelve Storeys* is also discussed in Nazir Keshvani's review of the film, in *Cinemaya* 35 (1997), pp. 26–28.

14. Michel Foucault, *Discipline and Punish: The Birth of the Prison*, trans. Alan Sheridan (New York: Vintage, 1979). For a somewhat different reading of Foucault in relation to Khoo, see Lee, "Dead Man Gazing."

15. Stan Sesser, *The Lands of Charm and Cruelty: Travels in Southeast Asia* (New York: Vintage, 1994). The riots between the Chinese and Malays in July 1964 in particular had lasting ramifications not only internally but with Singapore's relationship to Malaysia.

16. The seedy hotel in *Mee Pok Man* is called the 7th Storey, again missing the elevator cutoff by a single floor.

17. Khoo's films not only feature punk music, they take on a punk sensibility inflected by a contradictory mix of youthful exuberance, anger, rebelliousness, and nihilism. Joe Ng, who plays the mee pok man, is a member of a band, The Padres, for example, and his stage persona carries over into his performance. See Philip Cheah's review of *Mee Pok Man*, in *Cinemaya* 30 (1995), p. 25. For the definitive study of music in Chinese-language films, see Yeh Yueh-Yu, *Phantom of the Music: Song Narration and Chinese-Language Cinema* (in Chinese) (Taipei: Yuan Liu, 2000).

18. Chinese American architect I. M. Pei has been responsible for some of the architectural similarities between Western cities like New York and Asian cities like Hong Kong. A point brought out by C. J. W-L. Wee, "Contending with Primordialism: The 'Modern' Construction of Postcolonial Singapore," *positions* 1: 3 (1993), p. 715–43.

19. Mike Featherstone, *Undoing Culture: Globalization, Postmodernism and Identity* (London: Sage, 1995), p. 96.

20. Wee, "Contending with Primordialism," p. 717.

21. Recently, there has been some relaxation of this rule. In 1998, for example, *Mad Phoenix* was allowed to be exhibited in Cantonese, because it dealt with Cantonese opera and would be very difficult to dub. A further historical note needs to be added as well. The Mandarin campaign as an antidote for Westernization displaces an earlier distrust of Mandarin as the language of Communism.

22. See John Thornton Caldwell, *Televisuality: Style, Crisis, and Authority in American Television* (New Brunswick, NJ: Rutgers University Press, 1995).

23. Top-rated situation comedy produced by the Television Corporation of Singapore (TCS) in the mid-1990s.

24. Although the taxi driver is a marginal figure in *Mee Pok Man* and *Twelve Storeys*, Khoo did go on to produce a TV series called *Drive* that more prominently featured taxis.

25. Fredric Jameson, "Postmodernism and Consumer Society," in Hal Foster, ed., *The Anti-Aesthetic: Essays on Postmodern Culture* (Port Townsend, WA: Bay Press, 1993), pp. 111–25.

26. See the Internet Movie Database, online at http://us.imdb.com/title?0120116.

27. Singapore Airlines is probably Singapore's most globally visible government-run enterprise. The stewardess, like the presence of Shell Oil, in Khoo's films tacitly signals the importance of Singapore's geographic location to its success as a transportation center.

28. There are many excellent studies of the sex trade/sex tourism in Southeast Asia, including Thanh-Dam Truong, *Sex, Money, and Morality: Prostitution and Tourism in Southeast Asia* (London: Zed Books, 1990); Eliza Noh, "'Amazing Grace, Come Sit on My Face,' or Christian Ecumenical Representations of the Asian Sex Tour Industry," *positions* 5:2 (1997), pp. 439–65; among others. For more on the Asian sex industry in a global perspective, see Cynthia Enloe, *Bananas, Beaches and Bases: Making Feminist Sense of International Politics* (Berkeley: University of California Press, 1990).

29. Although Bogdanovich was welcome to film in Singapore, the finished film offended the censors and was banned from exhibition for almost two decades. The film was eventually shown at the Singapore International Film Festival in 1997.

30. See Gina Marchetti, *Romance and the "Yellow Peril": Race, Sex, and Discursive Strategies in Hollywood Fiction* (Berkeley: University of California Press, 1993).

31. For a broader perspective, see Roland B. Tolentino, "Bodies, Letters, Catalogs: Filipinas in Transnational Space," *Social Text* 14:3 (Fall 1996), pp. 49–76.

32. For a discussion of Filipino cinematic representation of overseas women workers, including Contemplacion, see Bliss Lim, "True Fictions: Women's Narratives and Historical Trauma," *Velvet Light Trap* 45 (Spring 2000), pp. 62–75.

33. The presence of Chinese merchants in the area goes back centuries; however, it was Sir Stamford Raffles's settlement of Singapore in 1819 that brought it into the larger economy of imperial England. With that came laborers from China and India. The influx of the Chinese during the colonial period was particularly dramatic and created complex social stratification. Perhaps the most striking division involved the Peranakans, established descendents of Chinese and Malay marriages who kept certain Chinese customs, did not convert to Islam, and spoke Malay. They saw themselves as distinct from the overseas Chinese born in China and were often vastly better off in terms of both cultural and actual capital. For example, the traditionally patrilocal Chinese adopted the matrilocal Malay custom of the newlyweds living with the wife's family to solidify their roots in the local community to considerable economic advantage. For the definitive account of the relationship of the British Empire to the Chinese diaspora, as well as Chinese emigration in other parts of the world, see Lynn Pan, *Sons of the Yellow Emperor: A History of the Chinese Diaspora* (New York: Kodansha International, 1990).

34. L. H. M. Ling, "Sex Machine: Global Hypermasculinity and Images of the Asian Woman in Modernity," *positions* 7:2 (1999), p. 296.

35. Shih Shu-mei, "Gender and a Geopolitics of Desire: The Seduction of Mainland Women in Taiwan and Hong Kong Media," in Mayfair Mei-Hui Yang, ed., *Spaces of Their Own: Women's Public Sphere in Transnational China* (Minneapolis: University of Minnesota Press, 1999), pp. 278–307.

36. Around the time of *Twelve Storeys'* release, there was a minor controversy surrounding the screening of Carma Hinton's *Gate of Heavenly Peace* at the Singapore International Film Festival. Even in 1997, the events of 1989 in Tian'anmen remained a touchy subject for the censors.

37. Sesser, *The Lands of Charm and Cruelty*, p. 5.

38. The PAP has been in power in Singapore since 1959, before it became a sovereign entity after its split from Malaysia in 1965.

39. See Tania Modleski, *Feminism without Women: Culture and Criticism in a "Postfeminist" Age* (New York: Routledge, 1991).

40. See the distinction drawn between *gui* and *shen* in the entry on ghosts in Wolfram Eberhard, *A Dictionary of Chinese Symbols: Hidden Symbols in Chinese Life and Thought*, trans. G. L. Campbell (London: Routledge, 1986), pp. 128–29.

NOTES TO CHAPTER 6

1. Chan strikes a delicate balance between Asian and Asian American cinema culture as well. For a discussion of the differences between the two, see Luis Francia, "Asian

Cinema and Asian American Cinema: Separated by a Common Language," *Cinemaya* 9 (Autumn 1990), pp. 36–39.

2. For more on the film and its depiction of the controversy surrounding the Vietnamese refugees in Hong Kong, see Tony Williams, "Hong Kong Cinema, the Boat People, and *To Liv(e)*," *Asian Cinema* 11: 1 (Spring/Summer 2000), pp. 131–42.

3. For an insightful reading of *Crossings*, see Tony Williams, "*Crossings*: A Transnational Cinematic Text," *Asian Cinema* 11:2 (Fall/Winter 2000), pp. 67–75.

4. Marina Heung, "Small Triumphs: The New Asian Woman in American Cinema," *Cinemaya* 35 (1997), p. 33.

5. The transnational dimension of Chinese film has been noted by a number of film scholars, including Sheldon Lu, ed., *Transnational Chinese Cinemas: Identity, Nationhood, Gender* (Honolulu: University of Hawaii Press, 1997); and Steve Fore, "Golden Harvest Films and the Hong Kong Movie Industry in the Realm of Globalization." *Velvet Light Trap* 34 (Fall 1994), pp. 40–58.

6. Fredric Jameson, *The Geopolitical Aesthetic: Cinema and Space in the World System* (Bloomington: Indiana University Press, 1995), p. 151.

7. Evans Chan, "Forward to *To Liv(e)*," in Tak-wai Wong, ed., *Evans Chan's To Liv*(e): *Screenplay and Essays* (Hong Kong: University of Hong Kong, Department of Comparative Literature, 1996), p. 6. For more on the international new wave, see Robert Kolker, *The Altering Eye: Contemporary International Cinema* (New York: Oxford University Press, 1983).

8. Patricia Brett Erens, "The Aesthetics of Protest: Evans Chan's *To Liv(e)*, in Wong, *Evans Chan's To Liv*(e), pp. 109–16.

9. Peter Wollen, "Godard and Counter Cinema: *Vent d'est*," in his *Readings and Writings: Semiotic Counter-Strategies* (London: Verso, 1982), pp. 79–91.

10. The idea of location has been hotly debated in critical theory and cultural studies circles. See Caren Kaplan, "The Politics of Location in Transnational Feminist Practice," in Inderpal Grewal and Caren Kaplan, eds., *Scattered Hegemonies: Postmodernity and Transnational Feminist Practices* (Minneapolis: University of Minnesota Press, 1994).

11. Rey Chow, *Writing Diaspora: Tactics of Intervention in Contemporary Cultural Studies* (Bloomington, Indiana University Press, 1993).

12. Quote taken from the published screenplay, in Wong, *Evans Chan's To Liv*(e), p. 35.

13. Ibid., p. 49.

14. See Antonio Gramsci, *Selections from the Prison Notebooks* (New York: International Publishers, 1971).

15. Edward Said, *Culture and Imperialism* (New York: Random House, 1994).

16. Gayatri Chakravorty Spivak, *The Post-Colonial Critic: Interviews, Strategies, Dialogues* (New York: Routledge, 1990).

17. Homi Bhabha, *The Location of Culture* (London: Routledge, 1994).

18. See Kuan-hsing Chen, "The Formation of a Diasporic Intellectual: An Interview with Stuart Hall," in David Morley and Kuan-Hsing Chen, eds., *Stuart Hall: Critical Dialogues in Cultural Studies* (New York: Routledge, 1996). See also Stuart Hall, "New Ethnicities," in David Morley and Kuan-Hsing Chen, eds., *Stuart Hall: Critical Dialogues in Cultural Studies* (New York: Routledge, 1996).

19. Evans Chan, "Forward to *To Liv(e)*," in Wong, *Evans Chan's To Liv*(e), p. 5.

20. Quote taken from the published screenplay, Chan in Wong, *Evans Chan's To Liv*(e), p. 61.

21. For a more extensive discussion of Chan's films in the context of Hong Kong's alternative arts, see Hector Rodriguez, "The Fragmented Commonplace: Alternative Arts and Cosmopolitanism in Hong Kong," in Jenny Kwok Wah Lau, ed., *Multiple Modernities: Cinemas and Popular Media in Transcultural East Asia* (Philadelphia: Temple University Press, 2003), pp. 128–48.

22. For more on the depiction of overseas Chinese in the cinema globally, see Law Kar, ed., *Overseas Chinese Figures in Cinema*. Hong Kong: 16th Hong Kong International Film Festival, 1992.

23. Bhabha, *The Location of Culture*, p. 170.

NOTES TO CHAPTER 7

1. Both magazines are American-based publications designed for the Asian American community. However, given the Web presence of these publications and similar ones directed to English-speaking people of Asian descent, it is not far-fetched to see their appeal to Asians elsewhere who share a common global culture dominated by American media. See GenerAsian Life Web site, http://home.inreach.com/asunaro.

2. The 1998 Singapore International Film Festival, for example, featured a sidebar on GenerAsian X films.

3. Stephen Teo, *Hong Kong Cinema: The Extra Dimensions* (London: BFI, 1997).

4. Stephen Teo, ed., *Hong Kong Cinema in the Eighties: A Comparative Study with Western Cinema*. The 15th Hong Kong International Film Festival, Hong Kong Urban Council, 1991.

5. For an excellent discussion of these border crossings between the PRC and Hong Kong on film, see Esther Yau, "Border Crossing: Mainland China's Presence in Hong Kong Cinema," in Nick Browne, Paul Pickowicz, Vivian Sobchack, and Esther Yau, eds., *New Chinese Cinemas: Forms, Identities, Politics* (New York: Cambridge University Press, 1994).

6. For a detailed examination of this film, see Steve Fore, "Tales of Recombinant Femininity: *Reincarnation of the Golden Lotus*, the *Chin P'ing Mei*, and the Politics of Melodrama in Hong Kong," *Journal of Film and Video* 45:4 (Winter 1993), pp. 57–70.

7. Law's *The Other Half and the Other Half* (1988), set in Hong Kong, deals with similar issues. Law and Fong as a team have also made a short contribution to the omnibus film *Erotique* (1994), on the topic of waiting to emigrate, called "Wonton Soup." See Tan See Kam, Justin Clemens, and Eleanor Hogan, "Clara Law: Seeking an Audience outside Hong Kong," *Cinemaya* 25/26 (Autumn–Winter 1994–95), pp. 50–54. See also the interview with Clara Law in Miles Wood, *Cine East: Hong Kong Cinema through the Looking Glass* (Surrey, U.K.: FAB Press,1998).

8. Kam, Clemens, and Hogan, "Clara Law," p. 51.

9. Ackbar Abbas, *Hong Kong: Culture and the Politics of Disappearance* (Minneapolis: University of Minnesota Press, 1997), p. 24.

10. Teo, *Hong Kong Cinema: The Extra Dimensions*, p. 186.

11. For more on Maggie Cheung's portrayal of Li, see Augusta Lee Palmer and Jenny Kwok Wah Lau, "Of Executioners and Courtesans: The Performance of Gender in Hong Kong Cinema of the 1990s," in Jenny Kwok Wah Lau, ed., *Multiple Modernities: Cinemas and Popular Media in Transcultural East Asia* (Philadelphia: Temple University Press, 2003), pp. 203–21.

12. For a detailed analysis of this scene and a thorough reading of the film, see Steve Fore, "Time-Traveling under an *Autumn Moon*," *Post Script* 17:3 (Summer

1998), pp. 34–46. For another detailed analysis of the film, see Audrey Yue, "Migration-as-Transition: Pre-Post-1997 Hong Kong Culture in Clara Law's *Autumn Moon*," *Intersections: Gender, History, and Culture in the Asian Context* 4 (September 2000), available online at www.she.murdoch.edu.au/intersections/issue4/yue.html. For more on *Autumn Moon* in relation to its depiction of the city of Hong Kong, see Stephen Rowley, "*Autumn Moon* and Urban Bewilderment," *Cinephobia* (1998), online at http://home.mira.net/~satadaca.postmod1.htm.

13. A point made by critic Evans Chan in a private e-mail correspondence with me in spring 1998.

14. As Steve Fore points out in his article, it was produced as part of a series financed by Japan called Asian Beat. See Fore, "Time-Traveling under an *Autumn Moon*."

15. Fore translates the poem somewhat differently in his article. I am relying on the subtitles provided by the edition of the film produced for video release in the United States.

16. As in Ann Hui's *Summer Snow*, in which Alzheimer's disease provides a convenient way for memory to be erased.

17. See Chris Berry, "*Floating Life*," *Cinemaya* 33 (Summer 1996), pp. 35–36; Stephen Teo, "*Floating Life*: The Heaviness of Moving," *Senses of Cinema* 12 (February–March 2001), available online at www.sensesofcinema.com/contents/01/12/floating.html.; and David L. Eng, "Melancholia/Postcoloniality: Loss in *The Floating Life*," *Qui Parle* 11:2 (Fall/Winter 1999), pp. 137–150.

18. Abbas, *Hong Kong*.

19. In Zizek's sense of the term; see Slavoj Zizek, *Enjoy Your Symptom!: Jacques Lacan in Hollywood and Out* (New York: Routledge, 2001), or in Jameson's sense of a "political unconscious" in Fredric Jameson, *The Political Unconscious* (Ithaca, NY: Cornell University Press, 1982).

20. Lisa Lowe, *Immigrant Acts: On Asian American Cultural Politics* (Durham, NC: Duke University Press, 1996); Frantz Fanon, *The Wretched of the Earth*, trans. Constance Farrington (New York: Grove Press, 1986).

21. Lowe, *Immigrant Acts*, p. 73.

22. Presentation by Clara Law reported in Law Kar, ed., *Fifty Years of Electric Shadows: Report of Conference on Hong Kong Cinema*. Hong Kong: 21st Hong Kong International Film Festival, Urban Council of Hong Kong, 1997, p. 39.

23. For more on the connection between *Farewell, China* and *The Searchers*, see Tony Williams, "Transnational Stardom: The Case of Maggie Cheung Man-yuk," *Asian Cinema* 14:2 (Fall/Winter 2003), pp. 180–96.

NOTES TO CHAPTER 8

1. Eugene Franklin Wong, *On Visual Media Racism: Asians in American Motion Pictures* (New York: Arno, 1978). For more on the depiction of Asian males in American culture, see Jachinson Chen, *Chinese American Masculinities: From Fu Manchu to Bruce Lee* (New York: Routledge, 2001).

2. There are many published biographies of Bruce Lee, including John Little, ed., *Bruce Lee: The Celebrated Life of the Golden Dragon* (Boston: Charles E. Tuttle, 2000), which features Lee's life using extensive quotations from the star, and Michael Jahn, *Dragon: The Bruce Lee Story* (New York: Jove, 1993), which was made into a feature film.

3. See Robert B. Ray, *A Certain Tendency of the Hollywood Cinema, 1930–1980* (Princeton, NJ: Princeton University Press, 1985).

4. For more on the links between masculinity and politics in neoconservative ideology, see Susan Jeffords, *The Remasculinization of America: Gender and the Vietnam War* (Bloomington: Indiana University Press, 1989); Susan Jeffords, *Hard Bodies: Hollywood Masculinity in the Reagan Era* (New Brunswick, NJ: Rutgers University Press, 1994); and Yvonne Tasker, *Spectacular Bodies: Gender, Genre and the Action Cinema* (New York: Routledge, 1993). For more on race, ethnicity, and the body in film, see Chris Holmlund, *Impossible Bodies: Femininity and Masculinity at the Movies* (New York: Routledge, 2002). For more on action cinema and Chinese/Chinese American masculinity, see: Amy Kashiwabara, "Vanishing Son: The Appearance, Disappearance, and Assimilation of the Asian-American Man in American Mainstream Media" (Berkeley: University of California, 1996) http://www.lib.berkeley.edu/MRC/Amydoc.html; Verina Glaessner, *Kung Fu: Cinema of Vengeance* London: Lorrimer, 1974; Chuck Kleinhans, "Terms of Transition: The Action Film, Postmodernism, and Issues of an East-West Perspective," in Jenny Kwok Wah Lau, ed., *Multiple Modernities: Cinemas and Popular Media in Transcultural East Asia* (Philadelphia: Temple University Press, 2003), pp. 167–178; Kwai-Cheung Lo, "Muscles and Subjectivity: A Short History of the Masculine Body in Hong Kong Popular Culture," *Camera Obscura* 39 (September 1996), pp. 104–125; Gina Marchetti, "Du péril jaune à la menace rouge" and "Les acteurs asiatiques, du déni au défi," trans. Stéphane Roques, *L'Asie à Hollywood*, ed. Charles Tesson, Claudine Paquot, and Roger Garcia (Paris: Cahiers du Cinéma, in conjunction with the 54th Locarno International Film Festival, 2001), pp. 12–33, 34–47; Gina Marchetti, "Ethnicity, the Cinema, and Cultural Studies," in *Unspeakable Images: Ethnicity and the American Cinema*, ed. Lester Friedman (Urbana: U. of Illinois Press, 1991), pp. 277–307; Gina Marchetti, "America's Asia: Hollywood's Construction, Deconstruction, and Reconstruction of the 'Orient'," *Out of the Shadows: Asians in American Cinema*, ed. Roger Garcia (Milan, Italy: Edizioni Olivares, produced in conjunction with the 54th Locarno International Film Festival, 2001), pp. 37–57; Meaghan Morris, "Learning from Bruce Lee: Pedagogy and Political Correctness in Martial Arts Cinema," Matthew Tinkcom and Amy Villarejo, eds. *Keyframes: Popular Cinema and Cultural Studies* (London: Routledge, 2001), pp. 171–186; Gary Okihiro, *Margins and Mainstreams: Asians in American History and Culture* (Seattle: University of Washington Press, 1994); Vijay Prashad, "Bruce Lee and the Anti-Imperialism of Kung Fu: A Polycultural Adventure," *positions: east asia cultures critique* 11:1 (Spring 2003), pp. 51–90; Vijay Prashad, *Everybody Was Kung Fu Fighting: Afro-Asian Connections and the Myth of Cultural Purity* (Boston: Beacon, 2001); Yvonne Tasker, "Fists of Fury: Discourses of Race and Masculinity in the Martial Arts Cinema," in Harry Stecopoulos and Michael Uebel, eds. *Race and the Subject of Masculinities* (Durham, NC: Duke, 1997), pp. 315–336; Jeff Yang, Dina Gan, Terry Hong, *Eastern Standard Time : A Guide to Asian Influence on American Culture from Astro Boy to Zen Buddhism* (Mariner Books, 1997).

5. *Enter the Dragon* (1973) is a Hong Kong–U.S. coproduction between Golden Harvest and Warner Bros., which is the closest Bruce Lee came to a completed Hollywood film.

6. Using drug trafficking as a metaphor for capitalist corruption and switching from political struggles to wars on crime are established tropes within the action-adventure genre. See Gina Marchetti, "Action-Adventure as Ideology," in Ian Angus and Sut Jhally, eds., *Cultural Politics in Contemporary America* (New York: Routledge, Chapman and Hall, 1989), pp. 182–97.

7. It is striking how similar this post-1989 fantasy is to pre–Vietnam War era cold war fantasies of American might abroad coupled with promises of domestic racial harmony. See

Christina Klein, *Cold War Orientalism: Asia in the Middlebrow Imagination, 1945–1961* (Berkeley: University of California Press, 2003).

NOTES TO CHAPTER 9

1. Geremie R. Barmé, *In the Red: On Contemporary Chinese Culture* (New York: Columbia University Press, 1999).

2. William Hinton, *Fanshen: A Documentary of Revolution in a Chinese Village* (New York: Vintage Books, Random House, 1966) and William Hinton, *Shenfan: The Continuing Revolution in a Chinese Village* (New York: Vintage Books, Random House, 1983).

3. See Hong Jing-Yi, *A Study of Cross-Cultural Factors in Selected Documentaries about China*, Ph.D. dissertation, University of Maryland, College Park, 1991.

4. For the definitive history of protests in the square, see Jonathan D. Spence, *The Gate of Heavenly Peace: The Chinese and Their Revolution, 1895–1980* (New York: Penguin, 1981).

5. Craig Calhoun, "Tiananmen, Television and the Public Sphere: Internationalization of Culture and the Beijing Spring of 1989," *Public Culture* 2:1 (Fall 1989), p. 55. Several excellent analyses have been conducted on the impact of global media on the 1989 Tian'anmen protests, see *Turmoil at Tiananmen: A Study of U.S. Press Coverage of the Beijing Spring of 1989*, Joan Shorenstein Barone Center on the Press, Politics and Public Policy, John F. Kennedy School of Government, Harvard University, June 1992, included on *The Gate of Heavenly Peace* Web site.

6. Arjun Appadurai, *Modernity at Large: Cultural Dimensions of Globalization* (Minneapolis: University of Minnesota Press, 1996), p. 36.

7. In fact, this editorial led to the publication of literature on why the demonstrators had nothing in common with the Cultural Revolution. See "China's Patriotic Democracy Movement and the Cultural Revolution," Beijing University, Department of Theory and Information Dissemination Committee, May 3, 1989, translated and reprinted in *Radical America* 22:4 (July–August 1988, published September 1, 1989), pp. 16–18. Barmé analyzes the Mao-inspired rhetoric of Chai Ling and some of the other dissidents in *In the Red*.

8. There are several excellent accounts of the involvement of workers in the spring 1989 demonstrations, including Wang Shaoguang, "Deng Xiaoping's Reform and the Chinese Workers' Participation in the Protest Movement of 1989," *Research in Political Economy* 13 (1992), pp. 163–97, available online at www.cuhk.edu.hk/gpa/wang_files/worker.pdf; Andrew G. Walder and Gong Xiaoxia, "Workers in the Tiananmen Protests: The Politics of the Beijing Workers' Autonomous Federation," *Australian Journal of Chinese Affairs* 29 (January 1993), available on *The Gate of Heavenly Peace* Web site.

9. Ann Withorn, "Democracy, Lies and Videotape: Reflections on China—An Interview with Richard Levy," *Radical America* 23:2–3 (April–September 1989/published October 1990), p. 70.

10. McKenzie Wark, *Virtual Geography: Living with Global Media Events* (Bloomington: Indiana University Press, 1994), p. 114.

11. Both have varied their positions over time; see Li Lu, *Moving the Mountain: My Life in China—From the Cultural Revolution to Tiananmen Square* (London: Macmillan, 1990). This book formed the basis for Michael Apted's 1994 documentary with the same title.

12. Wark, *Virtual Geography*, p. 147.

13. For information on the inspiration for the statue, see Wark, *Virtual Geography*, p. 118.

14. Rey Chow, "Violence in the Other Country: Preliminary Remarks on the 'China Crisis,' June 1989," *Radical America* 22:4 (July–August 1988, published September 1, 1989), p. 25. Chow reprises her use of the King Kong syndrome to analyze media depictions of July 1, 1997, Hong Kong change in sovereignty as well; Rey Chow, "King Kong in Hong Kong: Watching the 'Handover' from the U.S.A.," *Social Text* 55, 16:2 (Summer 1998), pp. 93–108.

15. Ralph A. Litzinger, "Screening the Political: Pedagogy and Dissent in *The Gate of Heavenly Peace*," *positions: east asia cultures critique* 7:3 (Winter 1999), p. 833.

16. Dai Jinhua, *Cinema and Desire: Feminist Marxism and Cultural Politics in the Work of Dai Jinhua*, eds. Jing Wang and Tani E. Barlow (London: Verso, 2002), p. 220.

17. David Clarke, *Hong Kong Art: Culture and Decolonization* (London: Reaktion Books, 2001).

18. Peter Miller's documentary, *The Internationale* (2001), looks briefly at the singing of the song by the 1989 demonstrators in Tian'anmen. For a discussion of the "Internationale" as part of a broader critique of international revolt against globalization, including a brief discussion of Tian'anmen, see Michael Hardt and Antonio Negri, *Empire* (Cambridge, MA: Harvard University Press, 2000).

19. Andrew F. Jones has made an interesting observation about some similarities between the lyrics for "Internationale" and "Nothing to My Name." See Andrew F. Jones, "The Politics of Popular Music in Post-Tiananmen China," in Susan D. Blum and Lionel M. Jensen, eds., *China Off Center: Mapping the Margins of the Middle Kingdom* (Honolulu: University of Hawaii Press, 2002), p. 301.

20. For detailed examinations of rock and popular music in post-1989 China, see Claire Huot, *China's New Cultural Scene: A Handbook of Changes* (Durham, NC: Duke University Press, 2000); Gregory B. Lee, *Troubadours, Trumpeters, Troubled Makers: Lyricism, Nationalism, and Hybridity in China and Its Others* (Durham, NC: Duke University Press, 1996); and Jeroen de Kloet, "Marx or Market: Chinese Rock and the Sound of Fury," in Jenny Kwok Wah Lau, ed., *Multiple Modernities: Cinemas and Popular Media in Transcultural East Asia* (Philadelphia: Temple University Press, 2003), pp. 28–52.

21. The lyrics are translated a bit differently in de Kloet, "Marx or Market," p. 28.

22. See Harry H. Kuoshu, "*Beijing Bastards*, the Sixth Generation Directors, and 'Generation-X' in China," *Asian Cinema* 10:2 (Spring–Summer 1999), pp. 18–28. For a discussion of the avant garde in China after 1989, see Sheldon Hsiao-peng Lu, "Art, Culture, and Cultural Criticism in Post-New China," *New Literary History* 28:1 (1997), pp. 111–33.

23. A similar point is made by Edward Friedman, "*The Gate of Heavenly Peace*," *Journal of Asian Studies* 56:2 (May 1997), pp. 582–84.

24. Ian Buruma, *Bad Elements: Chinese Rebels from Los Angeles to Beijing* (New York: Random House, Vintage, 2001), p. 10.

25. See Chapter 2. For more on New York in Hong Kong cinema, see Staci Ford, "Hong Kong Film Goes to America," paper presented at *Hong Kong/Hollywood at the Borders: Alternative Perspectives, Alternative Cinemas*, University of Hong Kong, April 2, 2004.

Bibliography

Abbas, Ackbar. "The Erotics of Disappointment," in Jean-Marc Lalanne, David Martinez, Ackbar Abbas, and Jimmy Ngai, eds., *Wong Kar-Wai* (Paris: Dis Voir, 1997), pp. 39–81.

Abbas, Ackbar. *Hong Kong: Culture and Politics of Disappearance* (Minneapolis: University of Minnesota Press, 1997).

Anagnost, Ann S. *National Past-Times: Narrative, Representation, and Power in Modern China* (Durham, NC: Duke University Press, 1997).

Anderson, Benedict. *Imagined Communities* (New York: Verso, 1991).

Ang, Ien. "Can One Say No to Chineseness? Pushing the Limits of the Diasporic Paradigm," *boundary 2* 25:3 (Fall 1998), pp. 223–42.

Angus, Ian and Sut Jhally, eds. *Cultural Politics in Contemporary America* (NY: Routledge, Chapman and Hall, Inc., 1989).

Anonymous. "China's Patriotic Democracy Movement and the Cultural Revolution," Beijing University, Department of Theory and Information Dissemination Committee, May 3, 1989, translated and reprinted in *Radical America* 22:4 (July–August 1988, published September 1, 1989), pp. 16–18.

Anonymous. "Taiwan's Dirty Business," *Asia, Inc.*, April 1997; available online at http://members.tripod.com/~orgcrime/taiwansdirtybusiness.htm.

Anonymous. "Murdoch, the Middle Kingdom, and the Media," *Peekabooty*, March 11, 2003, available online at www.peek-a-booty.org/pbhtml/article.php?sid=15.

Appadurai, Arjun. *The Social Life of Things* (Cambridge: Cambridge University Press, 1986).

Appadurai, Arjun. "Introduction: Commodities and the Politics of Value," in Arjun Appadurai, ed., *The Social Life of Things* (Cambridge: Cambridge University Press, 1986), pp. 3–63.

Appadurai, Arjun. *Modernity at Large: Cultural Dimensions of Globalization* (Minneapolis: University of Minnesota Press, 1996).

Arons, Wendy. "'If Her Stunning Beauty Doesn't Bring You to Your Knees, Her Deadly Drop Kick Will': Violent Women in the Hong Kong Kung Fu Film," in Martha McCaughey and Neal King, eds., *Reel Knockouts: Violent Women in the Movies* (Austin: University of Texas Press, 2001), pp. 27–51.

Atkins, Thomas R., ed. *Graphic Violence on the Screen* (New York: Simon and Shuster, 1976).

Barlow, Tani. "Theorizing Woman: Funü, Guojia, Jiating (Chinese Women, Chinese State, Chinese Family)," in Inderpal Grewal and Caren Kaplan, eds., *Scattered Hegemonies: Postmodernity and Transnational Feminist Practices* (Minneapolis: University of Minnesota Press, 1994), pp. 173–96.

Barmé, Geremie R. *In the Red: On Contemporary Chinese Culture* (New York: Columbia University Press, 1999).

Barnet, Richard J., and John Cavanagh. *Global Dreams: Imperial Corporations and the New World Order* (New York: Touchstone, Simon and Shuster, 1994).

Baudrillard, Jean. "The Ecstasy of Communication," trans. John Johnston, in Hal Foster, ed., *The Anti-Aesthetic: Essays on Postmodern Culture* (Post Townsend, WA: Bay Press, 1983), pp. 126–34.

Berger, John. *Ways of Seeing.* (London: BBC and Penguin, 1972).

Bergman, Andrew. *We're in the Money: Depression America and Its Films* (New York: New York University Press, 1971).

Bernardi, Daniel, ed. *The Birth of Whiteness: Race and the Emergence of United States Cinema,* (New Brunswick, NJ: Rutgers University Press, 1996).

Bernardi, Daniel, ed., *Classic Hollywood, Classic Whiteness* (Minneapolis: University of Minnesota Press, 2001).

Bernstein, Matthew, and Gaylyn Studlar, eds. *Visions of the East: Orientalism in Film* (New Brunswick, NJ: Rutgers University Press, 1997).

Bernstien, Robin, and Seth Silberman, eds. *Generation Q: Gays, Lesbians, and Bisexuals Born around 1969's Stonewall Riots Tell Their Stories of Growing Up in the Age of Information* (Los Angeles: Alyson, 2000).

Berry, Chris. "A Nation T(w/o)o: Chinese Cinema(s) and Nationhood(s)," *East-West Film Journal* 7:1 (January 1993), pp. 24–51.

Berry, Chris. "Taiwanese Melodrama Returns with a Twist in *The Wedding Banquet,*" *Cinemaya* 21 (Autumn 1993), pp. 52–54.

Berry, Chris. "*Floating Life,*" *Cinemaya* 33 (Summer 1996), pp. 35–36.

Berry, Chris. "Sexual DisOrientations: Homosexual Rights, East Asian Films, and Postmodern Postnationalism," in Xiaoping Tang and Stephen Snyder, eds., *Pursuit of Contemporary East Asian Culture* (Boulder: Westview, 1996), pp. 157–82.

Berry, Chris. "If China Can Say No, Can China Make Movies? Or, Do Movies Make China? Rethinking National Cinema and National Agency," *boundary 2* 25:3 (Fall 1998), pp. 129–50.

Berry, Chris. "Staging Gay Life in China: *East Palace, West Palace,*" *Jump Cut* 42 (December 1998), pp. 84–89.

Berry, Chris. "Asian Values, Family Values: Film, Video, and Lesbian and Gay Identities," in Gerard Sullivan and Peter A. Jackson, eds., *Gay and Lesbian Asia: Culture, Identity, Community* (New York: Hayworth Press, 2001), pp. 211–231.

Bhabha, Homi. *The Location of Culture* (London: Routledge, 1994).

Birch, David. *Singapore Media: Communication Strategies and Practices* (Melbourne, Australia: Longman Cheshire, 1993).

Blum, Susan D., and Lionel M. Jensen, eds. *China off Center: Mapping the Margins of the Middle Kingdom* (Honolulu: University of Hawaii Press, 2002).

Bordwell, David. *Planet Hong Kong: Popular Cinema and the Art of Entertainment* (Cambridge, MA: Harvard University Press, 2000).

Bourdieu, Pierre. *Distinction: A Social Critique of the Judgment of Taste,* trans. Richard Nice (Cambridge, MA: Harvard University Press, 1984).

Browne, Nick, Paul G. Pickowicz, Vivian Sobchack, and Esther Yau, eds. *New Chinese Cinemas: Forms, Identities, Politics* (New York: Cambridge University Press, 1994).

Buruma, Ian. *Bad Elements: Chinese Rebels from Los Angeles to Beijing* (New York: Random House, Vintage, 2001).

Butler, Judith. *Gender Trouble: Feminism and the Subversion of Identity* (New York: Routledge, 1990).

Butler, Judith. *Bodies That Matter: On the Discursive Limits of "Sex"* (New York: Routledge, 1993).

Calhoun, Craig. "Tiananmen, Television and the Public Sphere: Internationalization of Culture and the Beijing Spring of 1989," *Public Culture* 2:1 (Fall 1989), pp. 54–71.

Callahan, W. A. "Gender, Ideology, Nation: *Ju Dou* in the Cultural Politics of China," *East-West Film Journal* 7:1 (January 1993), pp. 52–80.

Carson, Diane, Linda Dittmar, and Janice R. Welsch, eds. *Multiple Voices in Feminist Film Criticism* (Minneapolis: University of Minnesota Press, 1994).

Chan, Evans. "Forward to *To Liv(e)*," in Tak-wai Wong, ed., *Evans Chan's To Liv(e): Screenplay and Essays* (Hong Kong: University of Hong Kong, Department of Comparative Literature, 1996).

Chan Sui Hung, Natalia. "Rewriting History: Hong Kong Nostalgia Cinema and Its Social Practice," in Poshek Fu and David Desser, eds., *The Cinema of Hong Kong: History, Arts, Identity* (New York: Cambridge University Press, 2000), pp. 253–72.

Chang, Li-Mei. "Whose Fatal Ways: Mapping the Boundary and Consuming the Other in Border Crossing Films," *Asian Journal of Communication* 11:2 (2001), pp. 39–57.

Cheah, Philip. "Singapore Shorts," *Cinemaya* 28–29 (1995), pp. 30–31.

Cheah, Philip. "Review of *Mee Pok Man*," *Cinemaya* 30 (1995), p. 25.

Chen Kuan-Hsing. "The Formation of a Diasporic Intellectual: An Interview with Stuart Hall," in David Morley and Kuan-Hsing Chen, eds., *Stuart Hall: Critical Dialogues in Cultural Studies* (New York: Routledge, 1996), pp. 484–503.

Chen Kuan-Hsing, ed. *Trajectories: Inter-Asia Cultural Studies* (London: Routledge, 1998).

Chen, Jachinson. *Chinese American Masculinities: From Fu Manchu to Bruce Lee* (New York: Routledge, 2001).

Chen, Pauline. "Screening History: New Documentaries on the Tiananmen Events in China," *Cineaste* 22:1 (Winter 1996), p. 18ff. Available online at www.lib.berkeley.edu/mrc/tianamen.html.

Chen Xiaomei. "Occidentalism as Counterdiscourse: *He Shang* in Post-Mao China," *Critical Inquiry* 18 (1992), pp. 686–712.

Chen Xiaoming. "The Mysterious Other: Postpolitics in Chinese Film," trans. Liu Kang and Anbin Shi, *boundary 2* 24:3 (Fall 1997), pp. 123–41.

Cheng, Allen T. "The Curse of 'Black Gold,'" *Asia Week* 26:10 (March 17, 2000), available online at www.asiaweek.com/asiaweek/magazine/2000/0317/nat.4taiwan.kmt.html.

Chiang, Mark. "Coming Out into the Global System: Postmodern Patriarchies and Transnational Sexualities in *The Wedding Banquet*," in David L. Eng and Alice Y. Hom, eds., *Q & A: Queer in Asian America* (Philadelphia: Temple University Press, 1998), pp. 374–95.

Chiao Hsiung-Ping. "Bruce Lee: His Influence on the Evolution of the Kung Fu Genre," *Journal of Popular Film and Television* 9:1 (1981), pp. 30–42.

Chiao Hsiung-Ping (Peggy). "Edward Yang, *Mahjong*: Urban Trials," *Cinemaya* 33 (Summer 1996), pp. 24–27.

Chiao, Peggy. "White Terror and the Formosa Incident: Introspections on Recent Political Film from Taiwan," *Cinemaya* 32 (Spring 1996), pp. 22–24.

Chinoy, Mike. *China Live: Two Decades in the Heart of the Dragon* (Atlanta: Turner, 1997).

Chou Wah-Shan, "Homosexuality and the Cultural Politics of *Tongzhi* in Chinese Societies," in Gerard Sullivan and Peter A. Jackson, eds., *Gay and Lesbian Asia: Culture, Identity, Community* (New York: Hayworth Press, 2001), pp. 27–64.

Chow, Rey. "Violence in the Other Country: Preliminary Remarks on the 'China Crisis,' June 1989," *Radical America* 22:4 (July–August 1988, published September 1, 1989), pp. 23–32.

Chow, Rey. *Woman and Chinese Modernity: The Politics of Reading Between West and East* (Minneapolis: University of Minnesota Press, 1991).

Chow, Rey. *Writing Diaspora: Tactics of Intervention in Contemporary Cultural Studies* (Bloomington, Indiana University Press, 1993).

Chow, Rey. *Primitive Passions: Visuality, Sexuality, Ethnography, and Contemporary Chinese Cinema* (New York: Columbia University Press, 1995).

Chow, Rey. "King Kong in Hong Kong: Watching the 'Handover' from the U.S.A.," *Social Text* 55, 16:2 (Summer 1998), pp. 93–108.

Chow, Rey. *Ethics after Idealism: Theory-Culture-Ethnicity-Reading* (Bloomington: Indiana University Press, 1998).

Chua, Beng-Huat. "Culture, Multiracialism, and National Identity in Singapore," in Chen Kuan-Hsing, ed. *Trajectories: Inter-Asia Cultural Studies* (London: Routledge, 1998), pp. 186–205.

Chua Beng-Huat. "'Asian Values' Discourse and the Resurrection of the Social," *positions: east asia cultures critique* 7:2 (1999), pp. 573–92.

Chua Ling-Yen. "The Cinematic Representation of Asian Homosexuality in *The Wedding Banquet*," *Journal of Homosexuality* 36:3–4 (1999), pp. 99–112.

Chua Siew-Keng. "The Politics of 'Home': *Song of the Exile*," *Jump Cut* 42 (December 1998), pp. 90–93.

Chun, Allen. "Fuck Chineseness: On the Ambiguities of Ethnicity as Culture as Identity," *boundary 2* 23:2 (Summer 1996), pp. 111–38.

Ciecko, Anne. "Transnational Action: John Woo, Hong Kong, Hollywood," in Sheldon Hsiao-peng Lu, ed., *Transnational Chinese Cinemas: Identity, Nationhood, Gender* (Honolulu: University of Hawaii Press, 1997), pp. 221–38.

Ciecko, Anne T., and Sheldon H. Lu. "*Ermo*: Televisuality, Capital and the Global Village," *Jump Cut* 42 (December 1998), pp. 77–83.

Ciecko, Anne T., and Sheldon H. Lu. "*The Heroic Trio*: Anita Mui, Maggie Cheung, Michelle Yeoh—Self-Reflexivity and the Globalization of the Hong Kong Action Heroine," *Postscript* 19:1 (Fall 1999), pp. 70–86.

Clark, Paul. *Chinese Cinema: Culture and Politics since 1949* (Cambridge: Cambridge University Press, 1987).

Clarke, David. *Hong Kong Art: Culture and Decolonization* (London: Reaktion Books, 2001).

Clifford, James. "Traveling Cultures," in Lawrence Grossberg, Cary Nelson, and Paula Treichler, eds., *Cultural Studies* (New York: Routledge, 1992), pp. 96–116.

Clouse, Robert. *The Making of Enter the Dragon* (Burbank: Unique, 1987).

Cornelius, Sheila (with Ian Haydn Smith). *New Chinese Cinema: Challenging Representations* (London: Wallflower Press, 2002).

Cui, Shuqin. "Gendered Perspective: The Construction and Representation of Subjectivity and Sexuality in *Ju Dou*," in Sheldon Hsiao-peng Lu, ed. *Transnational Chinese Cinemas: Identity, Nationhood, Gender* (Honolulu: University of Hawaii Press, 1997), pp. 303–30.

Cui, Shuqin. "Stanley Kwan's *Centre Stage*: The (Im)possible Engagement between Feminism and Postmodernism," *Cinema Journal* 34:4 (Summer 2000), pp. 60–80.

Cui, Shuqin. "Working from the Margins: Urban Cinema and Independent Directors in Contemporary China," *Post Script* 20:2–3 (Winter/Spring and Summer 2001), pp. 77–93.

Cui, Shuqin. *Women through the Lens: Gender and Nation in a Century of Chinese Cinema* (Honolulu: University of Hawaii Press, 2003).

Curtin, Michael. "Hong Kong Meets Hollywood in the Extranational Arena of the Culture Industries," in Kwok-Kan Tam, Wimal Dissanayake, and Terry Siu-han Yip, eds., *Sights of Contestation: Localism, Globalism and Cultural Production in Asia and the Pacific* (Hong Kong: Chinese University Press, 2002), pp. 79–109.

Dai Jinhua. "Rewriting Chinese Women: Gender Production and Cultural Space in the Eighties and Nineties," in Mayfair Mei-Hui Yang, ed., *Spaces of Their Own: Women's Public Sphere in Transnational China* (Minneapolis: University of Minnesota Press, 1999), pp. 191–206.

Dai Jinhua. "A Scene in the Fog: Reading the Sixth Generation Films," trans. Yiman Wang, in Dai Jinhua, *Cinema and Desire: Feminist Marxism and Cultural Politics in the Work of Dai Jinhua*, eds. Jing Wang and Tani E. Barlow (London: Verso, 2002), pp. 71–98.

Dai Jinhua. *Cinema and Desire: Feminist Marxism and Cultural Politics in the Work of Dai Jinhua*, eds. Jing Wang and Tani E. Barlow (London: Verso, 2002).

Dariotis, Wei Ming, and Eileen Fung. "Breaking the Soy Sauce Jar: Diaspora and Displacement in the Films of Ang Lee," in Sheldon Hsiao-peng Lu, ed., *Transnational Chinese Cinemas: Identity, Nationhood, Gender* (Honolulu: University of Hawaii Press, 1997), pp. 187–220.

Davis, Darrell William. "Borrowing Postcolonial: Wu Nien-Chen's *Dou-san* and the Memory Mine," *Post Script* 20:2–3 (Winter/Spring and Summer 2001), pp. 94–114.

Davis, Darrell, and Yeh Yueh-yu. "Warning! Category III: The Other Hong Kong Cinema," *Film Quarterly* 54.4 (Summer 2001), pp. 12–26.

Davis, Deborah S., Richard Kraus, Barry Naughton, Elizabeth J. Perry, eds. *Urban Spaces in Contemporary China: The Potential for Autonomy and Community in Post-Mao China* (New York: Woodrow Wilson Center Press and Cambridge University Press, 1995).

Deleuze, Gilles. *Cinema 2: The Time-Image*, trans. Hugh Tomlinson and Robert Galeta (Minneapolis: University of Minnesota Press, 1989).

Desser, David. "From the Opium War to the Pacific War: Japanese Propaganda Films of World War II," *Film History* 7:1 (Spring 1995), pp. 32–48.

Desser, David. "The Kung Fu Craze: Hong Kong Cinema's First American Reception," in Poshek Fu and David Desser, eds., *The Cinema of Hong Kong: History, Arts, Identity* (New York: Cambridge University Press, 2000), pp. 19–43.

Dirlik, Arif. "Confucius in the Borderlands: Global Capitalism and the Reinvention of Confucianism," *boundary 2* 22:3 (Autumn 1995), pp. 229–73.

Dirlik, Arif. "Critical Reflections on 'Chinese Capitalism' as Paradigm," *Identities* 3 (January 1997), pp. 303–30.

Dirlik, Arif, and Zhang Xudong, eds. "Postmodernism and China: A Special Issue," *boundary 2* 24:3 (Fall 1997).

Donald, Stephanie. "Symptoms of Alienation," *Continuum: Journal of Media and Cultural Studies* 12:1 (1998), pp. 91–103.

Donald, Stephanie Hemelryk. *Public Secrets, Public Spaces: Cinema and Civility in China* (Lanham, MD: Rowman and Littlefield, 2000).

Dorfman, Ariel. *The Empire's Old Clothes: What the Lone Ranger, Babar, and Other Innocent Heroes Do to Our Minds* (New York: Pantheon Books, 1983).

Du Bois, W.E.B. *The Souls of Black Folk*, ed. Henry Louis Gates Jr. and Terri Hume Oliver (New York: Norton, 1999).

Eberhard, Wolfram. *A Dictionary of Chinese Symbols: Hidden Symbols in Chinese Life and Thought*, trans. G. L. Campbell (London: Routledge, 1986).

Eisenstein, Zillah. *Global Obscenities: Patriarchy, Capitalism, and the Lure of Cyber-fantasy* (New York: New York University Press, 1998).

Eng, David L. "Melancholia/Postcoloniality: Loss in *The Floating Life*," *Qui Parle* 11:2 (Fall/Winter 1999), pp. 137–50.

Eng, David L., and Alice Y. Hom, eds. *Q & A: Queer in Asian America* (Philadelphia: Temple University Press, 1998).

Enloe, Cynthia. *Bananas, Beaches and Bases: Making Feminist Sense of International Politics* (Berkeley: University of California Press, 1990).

Enns, Anthony. "The Spectacle of Disabled Masculinity in John Woo's 'Heroic Blood-shed' Films," *Quarterly Review of Film and Video* 17:2 (June 2000), pp. 137–45.

Erens, Patricia Brett. "The Aesthetics of Protest: Evans Chan's *To Liv(e)*," in Tak-wai Wong, ed., *Evans Chan's To Liv(e): Screenplay and Essays* (Hong Kong: University of Hong Kong, Department of Comparative Literature, 1996), pp. 109–16.

Erens, Patricia Brett. "Crossing Borders: Time, Memory, and the Construction of Identity in *Song of the Exile*," *Cinema Journal* 39:4 (Summer 2000), pp. 43–59.

Erens, Patricia Brett. "The Film Work of Ann Hui," in Poshek Fu and David Desser, eds., *The Cinema of Hong Kong: History, Arts, Identity* (New York: Cambridge University Press, 2000), pp. 176–95.

Fanon, Frantz. *Black Skin, White Masks*, trans. Charles Lam Markmann (New York: Grove Press, 1967).

Fanon, Frantz. *The Wretched of the Earth*, trans. Constance Farrington (New York: Grove Press, 1986).

Featherstone, Mike. *Undoing Culture: Globalization, Postmodernism and Identity* (London: Sage, 1995).

Featherstone, Mike Scott Lash, and Roland Robertson, eds. *Global Modernities* (London: Sage, 1995).

Feng, Peter X "In Search of Asian American Cinema," *Cineaste* 21:1–2 (Winter–Spring 1995), p. 32 ff., available online at www.lib.berkeley.edu/mrc/insearchofasian.html.

Feng, Peter X "Being Chinese American, Becoming Asian American: *Chan Is Missing*," *Cinema Journal* 35:4 (1996), pp. 88–118.

Feng, Peter X "Decentering the Middle Kingdon: *China—Land of My Father* (Felicia Lowe, 1979), *The Way to My Father's Village* (Richard Fung, 1988), *Made in China* (Lisa Hsia, 1986)," *Jump Cut* 42 (December 1998), pp. 122–34.

Feng, Peter X *Identities in Motion: Asian American Film and Video* (Durham, NC: Duke University Press, 2002).

Feng, Peter X, ed. *Screening Asian Americans* (New Brunswick, NJ: Rutgers University Press, 2002).

Fewsmith, Joseph. *China since Tiananmen: The Politics of Transition* (New York: Cambridge University Press, 2001).

Fong, Allen, "*A Little Life Opera*," *International Forum of New Cinema*, February 1997; available online at www.fdk-berlin.de/forum97/f088e.html.

Fong-Torres, Ben. *The Rice Room: Growing up Chinese-American: From Number Two Son to Rock 'N' Roll* (New York: Penguin, Plume, 1995).

Ford, Staci. "Hong Kong Film Goes to America," paper presented at *Hong Kong/Hollywood at the Borders: Alternative Perspectives, Alternative Cinemas*, University of Hong Kong, April 2, 2004.

Fore, Steve. "Tales of Recombinant Femininity: *Reincarnation of the Golden Lotus*, the *Chin P'ing Mei*, and the Politics of Melodrama in Hong Kong," *Journal of Film and Video* 45:4 (Winter 1993), pp. 57–70.

Fore, Steve. "Golden Harvest Films and the Hong Kong Movie Industry in the Realm of Globalization," *Velvet Light Trap* 34 (Fall 1994), pp. 40–58.

Fore, Steve. "Time-Traveling under an *Autumn Moon*," *Post Script* 17:3 (Summer 1998), pp. 34–46.

Foster, Gwendolyn Audrey. *Women Filmmakers of the African and Asian Diaspora* (Carbondale: Southern Illinois University Press, 1997).

Foster, Hal, ed. *The Anti-Aesthetic: Essays on Postmodern Culture* (Post Townsend, WA: Bay Press, 1983).

Foucault, Michel. *Discipline and Punish: The Birth of the Prison,* trans. Alan Sheridan (New York: Vintage, 1979).

Francia, Luis. "Asian Cinema and Asian American Cinema: Separated by a Common Language," *Cinemaya* 9 (Autumn 1990), pp. 36–39.

Freidberg, Freda. "Border Crossings: Ann Hui's Cinema," *Senses of Cinema* (September 2002); available online at www.sensesofcinema.com/contents/02/22/hui.html.

Freud, Sigmund. "Fetishism" (1927), in Philip Rieff, ed., *Sexuality and the Psychology of Love* (New York: Collier, Macmillan, 1978), pp. 214–19.

Friedman, Edward. "*The Gate of Heavenly Peace,*" *Journal of Asian Studies* 56:2 (May 1997), pp. 582–84.

Frow, John. *Time and Commodity Culture: Essays in Cultural Theory and Postmodernity* (New York: Oxford University Press, 1997).

Fu, Poshek. "The Ambiguity of Entertainment: Chinese Cinema in Japanese-Occupied Shanghai, 1941 to 1945," *Cinema Journal* 37:1 (Fall 1997), pp. 66–84.

Fu, Poshek, and David Desser, eds. *The Cinema of Hong Kong: History, Arts, Identity* (New York: Cambridge University Press, 2000).

Fung, Anthony, and Michael Curtin. "The Anomalies of Being Faye (Wong): Gender Politics in Chinese Popular Music," *International Journal of Cultural Studies* 5:3 (September 2002), pp. 263–90.

Garcia, Roger, ed. *Out of the Shadows: Asians in American Cinema* (Milan, Italy: Edizioni Olivares, produced in conjunction with the 54th Locarno International Film Festival, 2001).

Gateward, Frances, ed. *Zhang Yimou Interviews* (Jackson: University Press of Mississippi, 2001).

Giukin, Lenuta. "Boy-Girls: Gender, Body, and Popular Culture in Hong Kong Action Movies," in Murray Pomerance, ed., *Ladies and Gentlemen, Boys and Girls: Gender in Film at the End of the Twentieth Century* (Albany: SUNY, 2001), pp. 54–69.

Glaessner, Verina. *Kung Fu: Cinema of Vengeance*. London: Lorrimer, 1974.

Gold, Thomas B. "Go with Your Feelings: Hong Kong and Taiwan Popular Culture in Greater China," in David Shambaugh, ed., *Greater China: The Next Superpower?* (New York: Oxford University Press, 1995), pp. 255–73.

Gramsci, Antonio. *Selections from the Prison Notebooks* (New York: International, 1971).

Grewal, Inderpal, and Caren Kaplan. "Introduction: Transnational Feminist Practices and Questions of Postmodernity," in Inderpal Grewal and Caren Kaplan, eds., *Scattered Hegemonies: Postmodernity and Transnational Feminist Practices* (Minneapolis: University of Minnesota Press, 1994), pp. 1–33.

Grewal, Inderpal, and Caren Kaplan, eds. *Scattered Hegemonies: Postmodernity and Transnational Feminist Practices* (Minneapolis: University of Minnesota Press, 1994).

Grossberg, Lawrence, Cary Nelson, and Paula Treichler, eds. *Cultural Studies* (New York: Routledge, 1992).

Grossman, Andrew. "Better Beauty through Technology: Chinese Transnational Feminism and the Cinema of Suffering," *Bright Lights Film Journal* 35 (January 2002); available online www.brightlights.com/35/chinesefeminism1.html.

Grossman, Andrew. "'Beautiful Publicity': An Introduction to Queer Asian Film," Andrew Grossman, ed., *Queer Asian Cinema: Shadows in the Shade* (New York: Haworth Press, 2000), pp. 1–29.

Grossman, Andrew, ed. *Queer Asian Cinema: Shadows in the Shade* (New York: Haworth Press, 2000).

Hagedorn, Jessica. "Asian Women in Film: No Joy, No Luck," *Ms.* (January/February 1994), pp. 74–79.

Hall, Stuart. "New Ethnicities," in David Morley and Kuan-Hsing Chen, eds., *Stuart Hall: Critical Dialogues in Cultural Studies* (New York: Routledge, 1996), pp. 441–49.

Hamamoto, Darrell Y. *Monitored Peril: Asian Americans and the Politics of TV Representation* (Minneapolis: University of Minnesota Press, 1994).

Hamamoto, Darrell Y., and Sandra Liu, eds. *Coutervisions: Asian American Film Criticism* (Philadelphia: Temple University Press, 2000).

Hammond, Stefan, ed. *Hollywood East: Hong Kong Movies and the People Who Make Them* (Lincolnwood, IL: Contemporary Books, 2000).

Hansen, Jeremy. "Creative Chaos: The Disorganized World of Wong Kar-wai," in Stefan Hammond, ed., *Hollywood East: Hong Kong Movies and the People Who Make Them* (Lincolnwood, IL: Contemporary Books, 2000), pp. 37–55.

Harding, Harry. "The Concept of Greater China: Themes, Variations, and Reservations," in David Shambaugh, ed., *Greater China: The Next Superpower?* (New York: Oxford University Press, 1995), pp. 8–34.

Hardt, Michael, and Antonio Negri. *Empire* (Cambridge, MA: Harvard University Press, 2000).

Harvey, David. *The Condition of Postmodernity* (Oxford: Basil Blackwell Press, 1989).

Hastie, Amelie. "Fashion, Femininity, and Historical Design: The Visual Texture of Three Hong Kong Films," *Post Script* 19:1 (Fall 1999), pp. 52–69.

Hauke, Robert. "John Woo's Cinema of Hyperkinetic Violence: From *A Better Tomorrow* to *Face/Off*," *Film Criticism* 24:1 (Fall 1999), pp. 39–59.

Heard, Christopher. *Ten Thousand Bullets: The Cinematic Journey of John Woo* (Los Angeles: Lone Eagle, 2000).

Hebdige, Dick. *Subculture: The Meaning of Style* (London: Methuen, 1979).

Heng, Geraldine, and Janadas Devan. "State Fatherhood: The Politics of Nationalism, Sexuality, and Race in Singapore," in Roger N. Lancaster and Michaela di Leonardo, eds., *The Gender Sexuality Reader: Culture, History, Political Economy* (New York: Routledge, 1997), pp. 107–21.

Hess, John, and Patricia Zimmermann. "Transnational Documentaries: A Manifesto," *Afterimage* (January/February 1997), pp. 10–14.

Heung, Marina. "Small Triumphs: The New Asian Woman in American Cinema," *Cinemaya* 35 (1997), pp. 29–33.

Higashi, Sumiko. *Cecil B. DeMille and American Culture: The Silent Era* (Berkeley: University of California Press, 1994).

Hinton, William. *Fanshen: A Documentary of Revolution in a Chinese Village* (New York: Vintage Books, Random House, 1966).

Hinton, William. *Shenfan: The Continuing Revolution in a Chinese Village* (New York: Vintage Books, Random House,1983).

Hitchcock, Peter. "Mao to the Market," in Xudong Zhang, ed., *Whither China?: Intellectual Politics in Contemporary China* (Durham, NC: Duke University Press, 2001), pp. 263–284.

Ho, Elaine Yee Lim. "Women on the Edges of Hong Kong Modernity: The Films of Ann Hui," in Mayfair Mei-Hui Yang, ed. *Spaces of Their Own: Women's Public Sphere in Transnational China* (Minneapolis: University of Minnesota Press, 1999), pp. 162–87.

Ho, Sam, ed. *The Swordsman and His Jiang Hu: Tsui Hark and Hong Kong Film* (Hong Kong: Hong Kong Film Archive, 2002).

Holmlund, Chris. *Impossible Bodies: Femininity and Masculinity at the Movies* (New York: Routledge, 2002).

Hong Jing-Yi. *A Study of Cross-Cultural Factors in Selected Documentaries about China.* Ph.D dissertation, University of Maryland, College Park, 1991.

Hong, Junhao. "Reconciliation between Openness and Resistance: Media Globalization and New Policies of China's Television in the 1990s," in Georgette Wang, Jan Servaes, and Anura Goonasekera, eds., *The New Communications Landscape: Demystifying Media Globalization* (NY: Routledge, 2000), pp. 288–306.

Hong, Peter Y. "New Voices Emerge to Tell the Story of Ordinary Americans," *Los Angeles Times*, May 23, 1998 p. 2; www.sound2cb.com/education/teaching/ucla/voices. html.

Hsing You-Tien. "Building Guanxi across the Straits: Taiwanese Capital and Local Chinese Bureaucrats," in Aihwa Ong and Donald Nonini, eds., *Ungrounded Empires: The Cultural Politics of Modern Chinese Transnationalism* (New York: Routledge, 1997), pp. 143–64.

Hu Ke. "The Influence of Hong Kong Cinema on Mainland China," trans. Grace Ng and Stephen Teo, in Law Kar, ed., *Fifty Years of Electric Shadows*, *21st Hong Kong International Film Festival*, trans. Yatsen Chan (Hong Kong: Urban Council, 1997), pp. 171–78.

Huang Ping. "Recent Trends in Peasant Out-Migrations in Contemporary China," trans. Erica Brindley and Joshua Goldstein, in Meaghan Morris and Brett de Bary, eds., *"Race" Panic and the Memory of Migration* (Hong Kong: Hong Kong University Press, 2001), pp. 131–70.

Huang, Tsung-Yi. "*Chungking Express*: Walking with a Map of Desire in the Mirage of the Global City," *Quarterly Review of Film and Video* 18:2 (April 2001), pp. 129–42.

Hulsbus, Monica. "On the Oppositional Politics of Chinese Every Day Practices," *CineAction* 42 (February 19917), pp. 10–14.

Huot, Claire. *China's New Cultural Scene: A Handbook of Changes* (Durham, NC: Duke University Press, 2000).

Ingram, Gordon Brent, Anne Marie Bouthillette, and Tolanda Retter, eds., *Queers in Space: Communities, Public Places, Sites of Resistance* (Seattle: Bay Press, 1997).

Ingram, Gordon Brent. "Marginality and the Landscape of Erotic Alien(nations)," in Gordon Brent Ingram, Anne Marie Bouthillette, and Tolanda Retter, eds., *Queers in Space: Communities, Public Places, Sites of Resistance* (Seattle: Bay Press, 1997), pp. 27–52.

Jahn, Michael. *Dragon: The Bruce Lee Story* (New York: Jove, 1993).

James, David E., and Rick Berg, eds. *The Hidden Foundation: Cinema and the Question of Class* (Minneapolis: University of Minnesota Press, 1996).

Jameson, Fredric. *The Political Unconscious* (Ithaca, NY: Cornell University Press, 1982).

Jameson, Fredric. "Postmodernism and Consumer Society," in Hal Foster, ed., *The Anti-Aesthetic: Essays on Postmodern Culture* (Port Townsend, WA: Bay Press, 1983), pp. 111–25.

Jameson, Fredric. "Third World Literature in the Era of Multinational Capitalism," *Social Text* 15 (Fall 1986), pp. 65–68.

Jameson, Fredric. *Postmodernism, or, The Cultural Logic of Late Capitalism* (Durham, NC: Duke University Press, 1991).

Jameson, Fredric. *The Geopolitical Aesthetic: Cinema and Space in the World System* (Bloomington: Indiana University Press, 1995).

Jeffords, Susan. *The Remasculinization of America: Gender and the Vietnam War* (Bloomington: Indiana University Press, 1989).

Jeffords, Susan. *Hard Bodies: Hollywood Masculinity in the Reagan Era* (New Brunswick, NJ: Rutgers University Press, 1994).

Jones, Andrew F. "The Politics of Popular Music in Post-Tiananmen China," in Susan D. Blum and Lionel M. Jensen, eds., *China Off Center: Mapping the Margins of the Middle Kingdom* (Honolulu: University of Hawaii Press, 2002), pp. 291–307.

Juhasz, Alexandra, ed. *Women of Vision: Histories in Feminist Film and Video* (Minneapolis: University of Minnesota Press, 2001).

Kaplan, Caren. "The Politics of Location in Transnational Feminist Practice," in Inderpal Grewal and Caren Kaplan, eds., *Scattered Hegemonies: Postmodernity and Transnational Feminist Practices* (Minneapolis: University of Minnesota Press, 1994), pp. 137–52.

Kaplan, Caren. *Questions of Travel: Postmodern Discourses of Displacement* (Durham, NC: Duke University Press, 1996).

Karl, Rebecca E. "The Burdens of History: *Lin Zexu* (1959) and *The Opium War* (1997)," in Xudong Zhang, ed., *Whither China?: Intellectual Politics in Contemporary China* (Durham, NC: Duke University Press, 2001), pp. 229–62.

Kashiwabara, Amy. "Vanishing Son: The Appearance, Disappearance, and Assimilation of the Asian-American Man in American Mainstream Media," Berkeley: University of California, 1996; available online at www.lib.berkeley.edu/mrc/amydoc.html.

Kellner, Douglas. "New Taiwan Cinema in the 80s," *Jump Cut* 42 (December 1998), pp. 101–15.

Keshvani, Nazir. Review of *Twelve Storeys*, *Cinemaya* 35 (1997), pp. 26–28.

Kim, Elaine H. *Asian American Literature: An Introduction to the Writings and Their Social Context* (Philadelphia: Temple University Press, 1982).

Kinder, Marsha, ed. *Kids' Media Culture* (Durham: Duke University Press, 1999).

Kingston, Maxine Hong. *The Woman Warrior: Memoirs of a Girlhood Among Ghosts* (New York: Vintage, 1975).

Kipnis, Andrew. "Anti-Maoist Gender: *Hibiscus Town*'s Naturalization of a Dengist Sex/Gender/Kinship System," *Asian Cinema* 8:2 (Winter 1996/1997), pp. 66–75.

Klein, Christina. *Cold War Orientalism: Asia in the Middlebrow Imagination, 1945–1961* (Berkeley: University of California Press, 2003).

Kleinhans, Chuck. "Class in Action," in David E. James and Rick Berg, eds., *The Hidden Foundation: Cinema and the Question of Class* (Minneapolis: University of Minnesota Press, 1996), pp. 240–63.

Kleinhans, Chuck. "Terms of Transition: The Action Film, Postmodernism, and Issues of an East-West Perspective," in Jenny Kwok Wah Lau, ed., *Multiple Modernities: Cinemas and Popular Media in Transcultural East Asia* (Philadelphia: Temple University Press, 2003), pp. 167–78.

Kloet, Jeroen de. "Marx or Market: Chinese Rock and the Sound of Fury," in Jenny Kwok Wah Lau, ed., *Multiple Modernities: Cinemas and Popular Media in Transcultural East Asia* (Philadelphia: Temple University Press, 2003), pp. 28–52.

Kolker, Robert. *The Altering Eye: Contemporary International Cinema* (New York: Oxford University Press, 1983).

Kondo, Dorinne K. *Crafting Selves: Power, Gender, and Discourses of Identity in a Japanese Workplace* (Chicago: University of Chicago Press, 1990).

Kowallis, Jon. "The Diaspora in Postmodern Taiwan and Hong Kong Film: Framing Stan Lai's *Peach Blossom Land* with Allen Fong's *Ah Ying*," in Sheldon Hsiao-peng Lu, ed. *Transnational Chinese Cinemas: Identity, Nationhood, Gender* (Honolulu: University of Hawaii Press, 1997), pp. 169–86.

Kraicer, Shelley, and Lisa Roosen-Runge. "Edward Yang: A Taiwanese Independent Filmmaker in Conversation," *CineAction* 47 (September 1998), pp. 48–55.

Kuoshu, Harry H. "*Beijing Bastards*, the Sixth Generation Directors, and 'Generation-X' in China," *Asian Cinema* 10:2 (Spring–Summer 1999), pp. 18–28.

Lai, Linda Chiu-han. "Film and Enigmatization: Nostalgia, Nonsense, and Remembering," in Esther C. M. Yau, ed., *At Full Speed: Hong Kong Cinema in a Borderless World* (Minneapolis: University of Minnesota Press, 2001), pp. 231–50.

Lalanne, Jean-Marc, David Martinez, Ackbar Abbas, and Jimmy Ngai. *Wong Kar-Wai* (Paris: Dis Voir, 1997).

Lancaster, Roger N., and Michaela di Leonardo, eds. *The Gender Sexuality Reader: Culture, History, Political Economy* (New York: Routledge, 1997).

Lau, Jenny Kwok Wah. "*Ju Dou*: A Hermeneutical Reading of Cross-Cultural Cinema," *Film Quarterly* 45:2 (Winter 1991–92), pp. 2–10.

Lau, Jenny Kwok Wah. "*Ju Dou*: An Experiment in Color and Portraiture in Chinese Cinema," Linda C. Erhlich and David Desser, eds., *Cinematic Landscapes: Observations on the Visual Arts and Cinema of China and Japan* (Austin: University of Texas Press, 1994), pp. 127–48.

Lau, Jenny Kwok Wah. "Globalization and Youthful Subculture: The Chinese Sixth-Generation Films at the Dawn of the New Century," in Jenny Kwok Wah Lau, ed., *Multiple Modernities: Cinemas and Popular Media in Transcultural East Asia* (Philadelphia: Temple University Press, 2003), pp. 13–27.

Lau, Jenny Kwok Wah, ed., *Multiple Modernities: Cinemas and Popular Media in Transcultural East Asia* (Philadelphia: Temple University Press, 2003).

Law Kar, ed. *Overseas Chinese Figures in Cinema*, 16th Hong Kong International Film Festival (Hong Kong: Urban Council, 1992).

Law Kar, ed. *Cinema of Two Cities: Hong Kong-Shanghai*, 18th Hong Kong International Film Festival (Hong Kong: Urban Council, 1994).

Law Kar, ed. *Fifty Years of Electric Shadows: Report of Conference on Hong Kong Cinema*, 21st Hong Kong International Film Festival (Hong Kong: Urban Council of Hong Kong, 1997).

Law Kar, ed. *Transcending the Times: King Hu and Eileen Chang*, 22nd Hong Kong Film Festival (Hong Kong: Provisional Urban Council, 1998).

Law Kar, ed. *Hong Kong New Wave: Twenty Years After*, 23rd Hong Kong International Film Festival (Hong Kong: Provisional Urban Council, 1999).

Lee, Gregory B. *Troubadours, Trumpeters, Troubled Makers: Lyricism, Nationalism, and Hybridity in China and Its Others* (Durham, NC: Duke University Press, 1996).

Lee, Michael. "Dead Man Gazing: Posthumous Voyeurism in *12 Storeys*, or 'Splacing' Singapore's Official and Unofficial Discourses?," *Asian Cinema* (Fall/Winter 2000), pp. 99–131.

Lent, John A. *The Asian Film Industry* (Austin: University of Texas Press, 1990).

Leong, Russell, ed. *Moving the Image: Independent Asian Pacific American Media Arts* (Los Angeles: UCLA Asian American Studies Center and Visual Communications, 1991).

Lesage, Julia. "The Political Aesthetics of the Feminist Documentary Film," *Quarterly Review of Film Studies*, No 3 (Fall 1978), pp. 507–23.

Leung, Helen Hok-sze. "Queerscapes in Contemporary Hong Kong Cinema," *positions: east asia cultures critique* 9:2 (Fall 2001), pp. 423–48.

Lewis, Jon, ed. *The End of Cinema as We Know It: American Film in the Nineties* (NY: New York University Press, 2001).

Leyda, Jay. *Dianying—Electric Shadows: An Account of Film and the Film Audience in China* (Cambridge, MA: MIT Press, 1972).

Li Cheuk-To. "*Yapian Zhanzheng* (*The Opium War*)," *Cinemaya* 38 (Autumn 1997), pp. 30–31.

Li Lu. *Moving the Mountain: My Life in China—From the Cultural Revolution to Tiananmen Square* (London: Macmillan, 1990).

Li, Siu Leung. "Kung Fu: Negotiating Nationalism and Modernity," *Cultural Studies* 15:3/4 (2001), pp. 515–42.

Liang Hai-chiang. "Hong Kong Cinema's 'Taiwan Factor,'" in Law Kar, ed., *Fifty Years of Electric Shadows*, *21st Hong Kong International Film Festival*, trans. Yatsen Chan (Hong Kong: Urban Council, 1997), pp. 158–63.

Liao, Chaoyang. "Borrowed Modernity: History and the Subject in *A Borrowed Life*," *boundary 2* 24:3 (Fall 1997), pp. 225–45.

Lii, Ding-Tzann. "A Colonized Empire: Reflections on the Expansion of Hong Kong Films in Asian Countries," in Kuan-Hsing Chen, ed., *Trajectories: Inter-Asia Cultural Studies* (London: Routledge, 1998), pp. 122–41.

Lim, Bliss Cua. "Spectral Times: The Ghost Film as Historical Allegory," *positions: east asian cultures critique* 9:2 (Fall 2001), pp. 287–329.

Lim, Bliss. "True Fictions: Women's Narratives and Historical Trauma," *Velvet Light Trap* 45 (Spring 2000), pp. 62–75.

Ling, L.H.M. "Sex Machine: Global Hypermasculinity and Images of the Asian Woman in Modernity," *positions: east asian cultures critique* 7:2 (1999), pp. 1–30.

Little, John, ed. *Bruce Lee: The Celebrated Life of the Golden Dragon* (Boston: Charles E. Tuttle, 2000).

Litzinger, Ralph A. "Screening the Political: Pedagogy and Dissent in *The Gate of Heavenly Peace*," *positions: east asia cultures critique* 7:3 (Winter 1999), pp. 827–50.

Liu, Cynthia. "'To Love, Honor, and Dismay': Subverting the Feminine in Ang Lee's Trilogy of Resuscitated Patriarchs," *Hitting Critical Mass: A Journal of Asian American Cultural Criticism* 3:1 (Winter 1995), pp. 1–60.

Liu, Lydia H. "*Beijing Sojourners in New York*: Postsocialism and the Question of Ideology in Global Media Culture," *positions: east asian cultures critique* 7:3 (Winter 1999), pp. 764–97.

Liu, Timothy. "*The Outcasts*: A Family Romance," in Andrew Grossman, ed., *Queer Asian Cinema: Shadows in the Shade* (New York: Haworth Press, 2000), pp. 233–36.

Lo, Kwai-Cheung. "Double Negations: Hong Kong Cultural Identity in Hollywood's Transnational Representations," *Cultural Studies* 15: 3/4 (2001), pp. 464–85.

Lo, Kwai-Cheung. "Muscles and Subjectivity: A Short History of the Masculine Body in Hong Kong Popular Culture," *Camera Obscura* 39 (September 1996), pp. 104–25.

Lo, Kwai-Cheung. "Transnationalization of the Local in Hong Kong Cinema of the 1990s," in Esther C. M. Yau, ed., *At Full Speed: Hong Kong Cinema in a Borderless World* (Minneapolis: University of Minnesota Press, 2001), pp. 261–76.

Logan, Bey. *Hong Kong Action Cinema* (Woodstock, NY: Overlook Press, 1995).

Lowe, Lisa. *Immigrant Acts: On Asian American Cultural Politics* (Durham, NC: Duke University Press, 1996).

Lowe, Lisa and David Lloyd, "Introduction," in Lisa Lowe and David Lloyd, eds., *The Politics of Culture in the Shadow of Capital* (Durham, NC: Duke University Press, 1997), pp. 1–32.

Lowe, Lisa, and David Lloyd, eds. *The Politics of Culture in the Shadow of Capital* (Durham, NC: Duke University Press, 1997).

Lu, Sheldon. "Historical Introduction: Chinese Cinemas (1896–1996) and Transnational Film Studies," in Sheldon Hsiao-peng Lu, ed. *Transnational Chinese Cinemas: Identity, Nationhood, Gender* (Honolulu: University of Hawaii Press, 1997), pp. 1–31.

Lu, Sheldon H. "Filming Diaspora and Identity: Hong Kong and 1997," in Poshek Fu and David Desser, eds., *The Cinema of Hong Kong: History, Arts, Identity* (New York: Cambridge University Press, 2000), pp. 273–88.

Lu, Sheldon H. "Soap Opera in China: The Transnational Politics of Visuality, Sexuality, and Masculinity," *Cinema Journal* 40:1 (Fall 2000), pp. 25–47.

Lu, Sheldon. "Hong Kong Diaspora Film: From Exile to Wrong Love to Flexible Citizenship and Transnationalism," paper presented at *Year 2000 and Beyond: History, Technology and Future of Transnational Chinese Film and TV—The Second International Conference on Chinese Cinema*, Hong Kong Baptist University, April 19, 2000.

Lu, Sheldon H. "Hong Kong Diaspora Film and Transnational TV Drama: From Homecoming to Exile to Flexible Citizenship," *Postscript* 20:2 and 3 (Winter/Spring and Summer 2001), pp. 137–46.

Lu, Sheldon Hsiao-peng. "Art, Culture, and Cultural Criticism in Post-New China," *New Literary History* 28:1 (1997), pp. 111–33.

Lu, Sheldon Hsiao-peng. "National Cinema, Cultural Critique, Transnational Capital: The Films of Zhang Yimou," in Sheldon Hsiao-peng Lu, ed. *Transnational Chinese Cinemas: Identity, Nationhood, Gender* (Honolulu: University of Hawaii Press, 1997), pp. 105–36.

Lu, Sheldon Hsiao-peng, ed. *Transnational Chinese Cinemas: Identity, Nationhood, Gender* (Honolulu: University of Hawaii Press, 1997).

Lu, Tonglin. *Confronting Modernity in the Cinemas of Taiwan and Mainland China* (New York: Cambridge University Press, 2002).

Lull, James. *China Turned On: Television, Reform and Resistance* (New York: Routledge, 1991).

Ma, Eric K. W. "Television and Orientalism," in Toby Miller, ed., *Television Studies* (London: British Film Institute, 2002), pp. 123–27.

Ma, Sheng-Mei. *The Deathly Embrace: Orientalism and Asian American Identity* (Minneapolis: University of Minnesota Press, 2000).

Madsen, Richard. "China in the American Imagination," *Dissent* (Winter 1998), pp. 54–59.

Magnan-Park, Aaron Han Joon. "Imagining Communities of the 'Yet-to-be-Fully-National': Hong Kong Action Cinema's Engagement with a Globalized Transnational Imaginary," in Michael Strysick, ed., *The Politics of Community* (Aurora, CO: Davies Group, 2002), pp. 151–79.

Marchetti, Gina. "Class, Ideology and Commercial Television: An Analysis of *The A-Team*," *Journal of Film and Video* 39:2 (Spring 1987), pp. 19–28.

Marchetti, Gina. "Action-Adventure as Ideology," in Ian Angus and Sut Jhally, eds., *Cultural Politics in Contemporary America* (New York: Routledge, Chapman and Hall, 1989), pp. 182–97.

Marchetti, Gina. "The Blossoming of a Revolutionary Aesthetic: Xie Jin's *Two Stage Sisters*," *Jump Cut* 34 (March 1989), pp. 95–106.

Marchetti, Gina. "Ethnicity, the Cinema, and Cultural Studies," in Lester Friedman, ed., *Unspeakable Images: Ethnicity and the American Cinema* (Urbana: University of Illinois Press, 1991), pp. 277–307.

Marchetti, Gina. *Romance and the "Yellow Peril": Race, Sex, and Discursive Strategies in Hollywood Fiction* (Berkeley: University of California Press, 1993).

Marchetti, Gina. "Cinema Frames, Videoscapes, and Cyberspace: Exploring Shu Lea Cheang's *Fresh Kill*," *positions: east asia cultures critique* 9:2 (Fall 2001), pp. 401–22.

Marchetti, Gina. "Du péril jaune à la menace rouge" and "Les acteurs asiatiques, du déni au défi," trans. Stéphane Roques, in Charles Tesson, Claudine Paquot, and Roger Garcia, eds., *L'Asie à Hollywood*, (Paris: Cahiers du Cinéma, in conjunction with the 54th Locarno International Film Festival, 2001), pp. 12–33, 34–47.

Marchetti, Gina. "America's Asia: Hollywood's Construction, Deconstruction, and Reconstruction of the 'Orient,'" in Roger Garcia, ed., *Out of the Shadows: Asians in American Cinema* (Milan, Italy: Edizioni Olivares, produced in conjunction with the 54th Locarno International Film Festival, 2001), pp. 37–57.

Marcuse, Herbert. *Eros and Civilization: A Philosophical Inquiry into Freud* (New York: Beacon Press, 1974).

Marks, Laura U. *The Skin of the Film: Intercultural Cinema, Embodiment, and the Senses* (Durham, NC: Duke University Press, 2000).

Martin, Fran. *Situating Sexualities: Queer Representation in Taiwanese Fiction, Film and Public Culture* (Hong Kong: Hong Kong University Press, 2003).

Martin, Fran, and Chris Berry. "Queer'N'Asian on the Net: Syncretic Sexualities in Taiwan and Korean Cyberspaces," *Critical InQueeries* 2:1 (June 1998), pp. 67–93.

Marx, Karl. *Capital: A Critique of Political Economy, Vol.I : The Process of Capitalist Production*, trans. Samuel Moore and Edward Aveling, ed. Frederick Engels (New York: International, 1967).

Masavisut, Nitaya, George Simson, and Larry E. Smith, eds. *Gender and Culture in Literature and Film East and West: Issues of Perception and Interpretation* (Honolulu: University of Hawaii Press, 1994).

May, Lary. *Screening Out the Past: The Birth of Mass Culture and the Motion Picture Industry* (Chicago: University of Chicago Press, 1983).

Mazierska, Ewa, and Laura Rascaroli. "Trapped in the Present: Time in the Films of Wong Kar-Wai," *Film Criticism* 25:2 (Winter 2000–2001), pp. 2–20.

McCaughey, Martha, and Neal King, eds. *Reel Knockouts: Violent Women in the Movies* (Austin: University of Texas Press, 2001).

McDonogh, Gary W., and Cindy Hing-Yuk Wong. "Orientalism Abroad: Hong Kong Readings of *The World of Suzie Wong*," in Daniel Bernardi, ed., *Classic Hollywood, Classic Whiteness* (Minneapolis: University of Minnesota Press, 2001), pp. 210–42.

Miller, Toby, ed. *Television Studies* (London: British Film Institute, 2002).

Mitchell, Katharyne. "In Whose Interest? Transnational Capital and the Production of Multiculturalism in Canada," in Rob Wilson and Wimal Dissanayake, eds., *Global/ Local: Cultural Production and the Transnational Imaginary* (Durham, NC: Duke University Press, 1996), pp. 219–52.

Mitchell, Katharyne. "Transnational Subjects: Constituting the Cultural Citizen in the Era of Pacific Rim Capital," in Aihwa Ong and Donald Nonini, eds., *Ungrounded Empires: The Cultural Politics of Modern Chinese Transnationalism* (New York: Routledge, 1997), pp. 228–56.

Modleski, Tania. *Feminism without Women: Culture and Criticism in a "Postfeminist" Age* (New York: Routledge, 1991).

Morley, David, and Kevin Robins. *Spaces of Identity: Global Media, Electronic Landscapes and Cultural Boundaries* (London: Routledge, 1995).

Morley, David, and Kuan-Hsing Chen, eds. *Stuart Hall: Critical Dialogues in Cultural Studies*. (New York: Routledge, 1996).

Morris, Meaghan. "Learning from Bruce Lee: Pedagogy and Political Correctness in Martial Arts Cinema," in Matthew Tinkcom and Amy Villarejo, eds., *Keyframes: Popular Cinema and Cultural Studies* (London: Routledge, 2001), pp. 171–86.

Morris, Meaghan and Brett de Bary, eds. *"Race" Panic and the Memory of Migration* (Hong Kong: Hong Kong University Press, 2001).

Moy, James S. *Marginal Sights: Staging the Chinese in America* (Iowa City: University of Iowa Press, 1993).

Mulvey, Laura. "Visual Pleasure and Narrative Cinema," *Screen* 16:3 (Autumn 1975), pp. 6–18.

Naficy, Hamid. "Phobic Spaces and Liminal Panics: Independent Transnational Film Genre," in Rob Wilson and Wimal Dissanayake, eds., *Global/Local: Cultural Production and the Transnational Imaginary* (Durham, NC: Duke University Press, 1996), pp. 119–44.

Naficy, Hamid. *An Accented Cinema: Exilic and Diasporic Filmmaking* (Princeton, NJ: Princeton University Press, 2001).

Noh, Eliza. "'Amazing Grace, Come Sit on My Face,' or Christian Ecumenical Representations of the Asian Sex Tour Industry," *positions: east asia cultures critique* 5:2 (1997), pp. 439–65.

Nonini, Donald M., and Aihwa Ong. "Introduction: Chinese Transnationalism as an Alternative Modernity," in Aihwa Ong and Donald Nonini, eds., *Ungrounded Empires: The Cultural Politics of Modern Chinese Transnationalism* (New York: Routledge, 1997), pp. 3–33.

Nornes, Abé Mark, and Yeh Yueh-yu. *Narrating National Sadness: Cinematic Mapping and Hypertextual Dispersion*, online document available at http://cinemaspace .berkeley.edu/papers/cityofsadness/index.html.

Notar, Beth. "Blood Money: Woman's Desire and Consumption in *Ermo*," *Asian Cinema* 12:2 (Fall/Winter 2001), pp. 132–53.

Oishi, Eve. "Bad Asians: New Film and Video by Queer Asian American Artists," in Darrell Y. Hamamoto and Sandra Liu, eds., *CounterVisions: Asian American Film Criticism* (Philadelphia: Temple University Press, 2000), pp. 221–44.

Okihiro, Gary. *Margins and Mainstreams: Asians in American History and Culture* (Seattle: University of Washington Press, 1994).

O'Neill, Edward. "Asian American Filmmakers: The Next Generation? Identity, Mimicry and Transtextuality in Mina Shum's *Double Happiness* and Quentin Lee and Justin Lin's *Shopping for Fangs*," *CineAction* 42 (February 1997), pp. 50–62.

Ong, Aihwa. "Chinese Modernities: Narratives of Nation and of Capitalism," in Aihwa Ong and Donald Nonini, eds., *Ungrounded Empires: The Cultural Politics of Modern Chinese Transnationalism* (New York: Routledge, 1997), pp. 171–202.

Ong, Aihwa, and Donald M.Nonini, eds. *Ungrounded Empires: The Cultural Politics of Modern Chinese Transnationalism* (New York: Routledge, 1997).

Ong, Aihwa. *Flexible Citizenship: The Cultural Logics of Transnationality* (Durham, NC: Duke University Press, 1999).

Overholt, William H. *The Rise of China: How Economic Reform Is Creating a New Superpower* (New York: Norton, 1993).

Owens, Craig. "The Allegorical Impulse: Toward a Theory of Postmodernism," *October* 12 (Spring 1980), pp. 66–86, and Part II, *October* 13 (Summer 1980), pp. 59–80.

Palmer, Augusta Lee, and Jenny Kwok Wah Lau. "Of Executioners and Courtesans: The Performance of Gender in Hong Kong Cinema of the 1990s," in Jenny Kwok Wah Lau, ed., *Multiple Modernities: Cinemas and Popular Media in Transcultural East Asia* (Philadelphia: Temple University Press, 2003), pp. 203–21.

Palumbo-Liu, David, ed. *The Ethnic Canon: Histories, Institutions, and Interventions*, (Minneapolis: University of Minnesota Press, 1995).

Pan, Lynn. *Sons of the Yellow Emperor: A History of the Chinese Diaspora* (New York: Kodansha International, 1990).

Parker, Andrew, Mary Russo, Doris Sommer, and Patricia Yaeger, eds. *Nationalisms and Sexualities* (New York: Routledge, 1992).

Payne, Robert M. "Ways of Seeing Wild: The Cinema of Wong Kar-Wai," *Jump Cut* 44 (Fall 2001); available online at www.ejumpcut.org/archive/jc44.2001/payne%20for%20site .wongkarwai1.html.

Pickowicz, Paul G. "Velvet Prisons and the Political Economy of Chinese Filmmaking," in Deborah S. Davis, Richard Kraus, Barry Naughton, Elizabeth J. Perry, eds., *Urban Spaces in Contemporary China: The Potential for Autonomy and Community in Post-Mao China* (New York: Woodrow Wilson Center Press and Cambridge University Press, 1995), pp. 193–220.

Pieterse, Jan Nederveen. "Globalization as Hybridization," in Mike Featherstone, Scott Lash, and Roland Robertson, eds., *Global Modernities* (London: Sage, 1995), pp. 45–68.

Pomerance, Murray, ed. *Ladies and Gentlemen, Boys and Girls: Gender in Film at the End of the Twentieth Century* (Albany: SUNY, 2001).

Poon, Wena. "*Chinese Box*," *Film Quarterly* 52:1 (Fall 1998), pp. 31–34.

Prashad, Vijay. *Everybody Was Kung Fu Fighting: Afro-Asian Connections and the Myth of Cultural Purity* (Boston: Beacon, 2001).

Prashad, Vijay. "Bruce Lee and the Anti-Imperialism of Kung Fu: A Polycultural Adventure," *positions: east asia cultures critique* 11:1 (Spring 2003), pp. 51–90.

Ray, Robert B. *A Certain Tendency of the Hollywood Cinema, 1930–1980* (Princeton, NJ: Princeton University Press, 1985).

Rayns, Tony. "*The Wedding Banquet,*" *Sight and Sound* 3:10 (October 1993), p. 56.

Rayns, Tony. "Poet of Time," *Sight and Sound* 5:9 (September 1995), pp. 12–16.

Rayns, Tony. "Confrontations," *Sight and Sound* 7:3 (1997), pp. 14–18.

Rayns, Tony. "The Well Dries Up," *Index on Censorship: Hong Kong Goes Back* 26:1 (January–February 1997), pp. 89–94.

Reiter, Rayna R., ed. *Toward an Anthropology of Women* (New York: Monthly Review Press, 1975).

Renov, Michael, and Erika Suderburg, eds. *Resolutions: Contemporary Video Practices* (Minneapolis: University of Minnesota Press, 1996).

Reynaud, Bérénice "New Visions, New Chinas: Video-Art, Documentation, and the Chinese Modernity in Question," in Michael Renov and Erika Suderburg, eds., *Resolutions: Contemporary Video Practices* (Minneapolis: University of Minnesota Press, 1996), pp. 229–57.

Reynaud, Bérénice. *Nouvelles Chines/Nouveaux cinémas* (Paris: Cahiers du cinéma, 1999).

Reynaud, Bérénice. *A City of Sadness* (London: BFI, 2002).

Rieff, Philip, ed., *Sexuality and the Psychology of Love* (New York: Collier Books, Macmillan, 1978).

Rodriguez, Hector. *The Cinema in Taiwan: Identity and Political Legitimacy.* Ph.D. dissertation. New York University, 1995.

Rodriguez, Hector. "Hong Kong Popular Culture as an Interpretive Arena: The Huang Feihong Film Series," *Screen* 38:1 (Spring 1997), pp. 1–24.

Rodriguez, Hector. "Organizational Hegemony in the Hong Kong Cinema," *Post Script* 19:1 (Fall 1999), pp. 107–19.

Rodriguez, Hector. "The Fragmented Commonplace: Alternative Arts and Cosmopolitanism in Hong Kong," in Jenny Kwok Wah Lau, ed., *Multiple Modernities: Cinemas and Popular Media in Transcultural East Asia* (Philadelphia: Temple University Press, 2003), pp. 128–48.

Rojas, Carlos. "Specular Failure and Spectral Returns in Two Films with Maggie Cheung (and One Without)," *Senses of Cinema* 12 (February–March 2001); available online at www.sensesofcinema.com/contents/01/12/cheung.html.

Rowley, Stephen. "*Autumn Moon* and Urban Bewilderment," *Cinephobia* (1998); online document available at http://home.mira.net/~satadaca/postmod1.htm.

Rubin, Gayle. "The Traffic in Women: Notes on the 'Political Economy' of Sex," in Rayna R. Reiter, ed., *Toward an Anthropology of Women* (New York: Monthly Review Press, 1975), pp. 157–210.

Russell, Catherine. *Experimental Ethnography: The Work of Film in the Age of Video* (Durham, NC: Duke University Press, 1999).

Said, Edward W. *Orientalism* (New York: Random House, 1979).

Said, Edward W. *Culture and Imperialism* (New York: Vintage, 1993).

Sandell, Jillian. "Reinventing Masculinity: The Spectacle of Male Intimacy in the Films of John Woo," *Film Quarterly* 49:4 (Summer 1996), pp. 23–34.

Sang, Tze-Lan Deborah. "Feminism's Double: Lesbian Activism in the Mediated Public Sphere of Taiwan," in Mayfair Mei-Hui Yang, ed., *Spaces of Their Own: Women's Public Sphere in Transnational China* (Minneapolis: University of Minnesota Press, 1999), pp. 132–61.

Sarkar, Bhaskar. "Hong Kong Hysteria: Martial Arts Tales from a Mutating World," in Esther C. M. Yau, ed., *At Full Speed: Hong Kong Cinema in a Borderless World* (Minneapolis: University of Minnesota Press, 2001), pp. 159–76.

Seagrave, Sterling. *The Soong Dynasty* (New York: Harper and Row, 1985).

Seagrave, Sterling. *Lords of the Rim* (London: Corgi, Bantam, 1995).

Sedgwick, Eve K. *Epistemology of the Closet* (Berkeley: University of California Press, 1990).

Sek Kei. "Hong Kong Cinema from June 4 to 1997," trans. Stephen Teo, in Law Kar, ed., *Fifty Years of Electric Shadows, 21st Hong Kong International Film Festival* (Hong Kong: Urban Council, 1997), pp. 120–25.

Sesser, Stan. *The Lands of Charm and Cruelty: Travels in Southeast Asia* (New York: Vintage, 1994).

Shambaugh, David, ed., *Greater China: The Next Superpower?* (New York: Oxford University Press, 1995).

Shen, Shiao-Ying. *Permutations of the Foreign/er: A Study of the Works of Edward Yang, Stan Lai, Chang Yi, and Hou Hsiao-hsien.* Ph.D. dissertation. Cornell University, Ithaca, NY, 1995.

Sheridan, Greg. *Tigers: Leaders of the New Asia-Pacific* (St. Leonards, Australia: Allen and Unwin, 1997).

Shih, Shu-Mei. "Gender and a Geopolitics of Desire: The Seduction of Mainland Women in Taiwan and Hong Kong Media," in Mayfair Mei-Hui Yang, ed., *Spaces of Their Own: Women's Public Sphere in Transnational China* (Minneapolis: University of Minnesota Press, 1999), pp. 278–307.

Shih, Shu-Mei. "Globalisation and Minoritisation: Ang Lee and the Politics of Flexibility," *New Formations* 40 (2000), pp. 86–101.

Shohat, Ella, and Robert Stam. *Unthinking Eurocentrism: Multiculturalism and the Media* (New York: Routledge, 1994).

Siegel, Marc. "The Intimate Spaces of Wong Kar-wai," in Esther C. M. Yau, ed., *At Full Speed: Hong Kong Cinema in a Borderless World* (Minneapolis: University of Minnesota Press, 2001), pp. 277–94.

Silbergeld, Jerome. *China into Film: Frames of Reference in Contemporary Chinese Cinema* (London: Reaktion Books, 1999).

Soe, Valerie. "Fighting Fire with Fire: *Detournement*, Activism, and Video Art," in Darrell Y. Hamamoto and Sandra Liu, eds., *Countervisions: Asian American Film Criticism* (Philadelphia: Temple University Press, 2000), pp. 177–85.

Solinger, Dorothy J. "The Floating Population in the Cities: Markets, Migration, and the Prospects for Citizenship," in Susan D. Blum and Lionel M. Jensen, eds., *China off Center: Mapping the Margins of the Middle Kingdom* (Honolulu: University of Hawaii Press, 2002), pp. 273–88.

Spence, Jonathan D. *The Gate of Heavenly Peace: The Chinese and Their Revolution, 1895–1980* (New York: Penguin, 1981).

Spivak, Gayatri Chakravorty. *The Post-Colonial Critic: Interviews, Strategies, Dialogues* (New York: Routledge, 1990).

Stecopoulos, Harry, and Michael Uebel, eds. *Race and the Subject of Masculinities* (Durham, NC: Duke University Press, 1997).

Stephens, Chuck. "Time Pieces: Wong Kar-Wai and the Persistence of Memory," *Film Comment* 32:1 (January–February 1996), pp. 12ff.

Stokes, Lisa Odham, and Michael Hoover. *City on Fire: Hong Kong Cinema* (New York: Verso, 1999).

Stokes, Lisa Odham, and Michael Hoover, "Resisting the Stage: Imaging/Imagining Ruan Lingyu in Stanley Kwan's *Actress*," *Asian Cinema* 11:2 (Fall/Winter 2000), pp. 92–98.

Stringer, Julian. "'Your Tender Smiles Give Me Strength': Paradigms of Masculinity in John Woo's *A Better Tomorrow* and *The Killer*," *Screen* 38:1 (Spring 1997), pp. 25–41.

Stringer, Julian. "Cultural Identity and Diaspora in Contemporary Hong Kong Cinema," in Darrell Y. Hamamoto and Sandra Liu, eds., *Coutervisions: Asian American Film Criticism* (Philadelphia: Temple University Press, 2000), pp. 298–312.

Stringer, Julian. "*Centre Stage*: Reconstructing the Bio-Pic," *CineAction* 42 (1997), pp. 29–39.

Strysick, Michael, ed. *The Politics of Community* (Aurora, CO: Davies Group, 2002).

Sullivan, Gerard, and Peter A. Jackson, eds. *Gay and Lesbian Asia: Culture, Identity, Community* (New York: Hayworth Press, 2001).

Sun Wanning. "Women in the City: Mobility, Television and the Choices of Being Modern," *Asian Journal of Communication* 11:2 (2001), pp. 18–38.

Taiwan Democratic Progressive Party. "A Look Back at the DPP's Decade in the Street," *Taiwan International Review* 2:5 (September–October 1996); available online at www.taiwandc.org/dpp/099604.htm.

Tajima, Renee. "Asian Women's Images in Film: The Past Sixty Years," in Pearl Bowser, ed., *In Color: Sixty Years of Images of Minority Women in the Media, 1921–1981* (New York: Third World Newsreel, 1983), pp. 26–29.

Tam, Kwok-kan, and Wimal Dissanayake. *New Chinese Cinema* (Oxford: Oxford University Press, 1998).

Tam, Kwok-Kan, Wimal Dissanayake, and Terry Siu-han Yip, eds. *Sights of Contestation: Localism, Globalism and Cultural Production in Asia and the Pacific* (Hong Kong: Chinese University Press, 2002).

Tambling, Jeremy. *Wong Kar-Wai's* Happy Together (Hong Kong: University of Hong Kong Press, 2003).

Tan See Kam. "Ban(g)! Ban(g)! Dangerous Encounter—1st Kind: Writing with Censorship," *Asian Cinema* 8:1 (Spring 1996), pp. 83–108.

Tan See Kam, Justin Clemens, and Eleanor Hogan. "Clara Law: Seeking an Audience Outside Hong Kong," *Cinemaya* 25/26 (Autumn–Winter 1994–95), pp. 50–54.

Tan See Kam, Michael Lee, and Annette Aw. "Contemporary Singapore Filmmaking: History, Policies, and Eric Khoo," *Jump Cut* 46 (Summer 2003); available online at www.ejumpcut.org/currentissue/12storeys/index.html.

Tan Yew Soon, and Soh Yew Peng. *The Development of Singapore's Modern Media Industry* (Singapore: Times Academic Press, 1994).

Tang, Xiaobing. "Configuring the Modern Space: Cinematic Representations of Beijing and Its Politics," *East-West Film Journal* 8:2 (July 1994), pp. 47–69.

Tang, Xiaoping, and Stephen Snyder, eds. *Pursuit of Contemporary East Asian Culture* (Boulder: Westview Press, 1996).

Tasker, Yvonne. *Spectacular Bodies: Gender, Genre and the Action Cinema* (New York: Routledge, 1993).

Tasker, Yvonne. "Fists of Fury: Discourses of Race and Masculinity in the Martial Arts Cinema," in Harry Stecopoulos and Michael Uebel, eds., *Race and the Subject of Masculinities* (Durham, NC: Duke University press, 1997), pp. 315–36.

Tay, William. "The Ideology of Initiation: The Films of Hou Hsiao-hsien," in Nick Browne, Paul G. Pickowicz, Vivian Sobchack, and Esther Yau, eds., *New Chinese Cinemas: Forms, Identities, Politics* (New York: Cambridge University Press, 1994), pp. 151–59.

Teo, Stephen. *Hong Kong Cinema: The Extra Dimensions* (London: BFI, 1997).

Teo, Stephen. "*Floating Life*: The Heaviness of Moving," *Senses of Cinema* 12 (February–March 2001); available online at www.sensesofcinema.com/contents/01/12/floating.html.

Teo, Stephen, ed., *Hong Kong Cinema in the Eighties: A Comparative Study with Western Cinema, 15th Hong Kong International Film Festival* (Hong Kong Urban Council, 1991).

Tesson, Charles, Claudine Paquot, and Roger Garcia, eds. *L'Asie à Hollywood* (Paris: Cahiers du Cinéma, in conjunction with the 54th Locarno International Film Festival, 2001).

Thornton, Sarah. *Club Cultures: Music, Media and Subcultural Capital* (Hanover: Wesleyan University Press, 1996).

Tinkcom, Matthew, and Amy Villarejo, eds. *Keyframes: Popular Cinema and Cultural Studies* (London: Routledge, 2001).

Tolentino, Roland B. "Bodies, Letters, Catalogs: Filipinas in Transnational Space," *Social Text* 14:3 (Fall 1996), pp. 49–76.

Trinh T. Minh-ha, *Cinema Interval* (New York: Routledge, 1999).

Truong, Thanh-Dam. *Sex, Money, and Morality: Prostitution and Tourism in Southeast Asia* (London: Zed Books, 1990).

Tsang, Daniel C. "Notes on Queer 'N Asian Virtual Sex," *Amerasia Journal* 20:1 (1994), pp. 117–28.

Tsui, Curtis K. "Subjective Culture and History: The Ethnographic Cinema of Wong Kar-Wai," *Asian Cinema* 7:2 (Winter 1995), pp. 93–124.

Tu Wei-Ming. "Cultural China: The Periphery as Center," in Tu Wei-Ming, ed., *The Living Tree: The Changing Meaning of Being Chinese Today* (Stanford, CA: Stanford University Press, 1994), pp. 1–34.

Tu Wei-Ming, ed. *The Living Tree: The Changing Meaning of Being Chinese Today* (Stanford, CA: Stanford University Press, 1994).

Tuan, Mia. *Forever Foreigners or Honorary Whites? The Asian Ethnic Experience Today* (New Brunswick, NJ: Rutgers University Press, 1998).

Turmoil At Tiananmen: A Study of U.S. Press Coverage of the Beijing Spring of 1989 (Joan Shorenstein Barone Center on the Press, Politics and Public Policy, John F. Kennedy School of Government, Harvard University, June 1992), included on *The Gate of Heavenly Peace* Web site (www.tsquare.tv).

20th Anniversary of Taiwanese New Cinema (Taipei: Taipei Golden Horse Festival Executive Committee, 2002).

Tyler, Patrick E. "In China, Letting a Hundred Films Wither," *New York Times* (December 1, 1996), pp. 1, 26–30.

Uhde, Jan, and Yvonne Ng Uhde. *Latent Images: Film in Singapore* (New York: Oxford, 2000).

Ullmer, Gregory L.,"The Object of Post-Criticism," in Hal Foster, ed., *The Anti-Aesthetic: Essays on Postmodern Culture* (Port Townsend, WA: Bay Press, 1993), pp. 83–110.

Van Kemenade, Willem. *China, Hong Kong, Taiwan, Inc.*, trans. Dianne Webb (New York: Vintage, 1997).

Virilio, Paul. *The Aesthetics of Disappearance*, trans. Philip Beitchman (New York: Semiotext[e], 1991).

Walder, Andrew G., and Gong Xiaoxia. "Workers in the Tiananmen Protests: The Politics of the Beijing Workers' Autonomous Federation," *The Australian Journal of Chinese Affairs*, No. 29 (January 1993), is available on *The Gate of Heavenly Peace* Web site, http:/www.tsquare.tv/links/Walder.html.

Waldman, Diane and Janet Walker, eds., *Feminism and Documentary* (Minneapolis; University of Minnesota Press, 1999).

Wang, Georgette, Jan Servaes, and Anura Goonasekera, eds. *The New Communications Landscape: Demystifying Media Globalization* (New York: Routledge, 2000).

Wang, Jing. *High Culture Fever: Politics, Aesthetics, and Ideology in Deng's China* (Berkeley: University of California Press, 1996).

Wang Shaoguang. "Deng Xiaoping's Reform and the Chinese Workers' Participation in the Protest Movement of 1989," *Research in Political Economy* 13 (1992), pp. 163–97; available online at www.cuhk.edu.hk/gpa/wang_files/worker.pdf.

Wark, McKenzie. *Virtual Geography: Living with Global Media Events* (Bloomington: Indiana University Press, 1994).

Warshow, Robert. *The Immediate Experience* (Cambridge, MA: Harvard University Press, 2001).

Wee, C.J.W-L. "Contending with Primordialism: The 'Modern' Construction of Postcolonial Singapore," *positions: east asia cultures critique* 1:3 (1993), pp. 715–43.

White, Jerry. "The Films of Ning Ying: China Unfolding in Miniature," *CineAction* 42 (February 19917), pp. 2–9.

Williams, Tony. "Space, Place, and Spectacle: The Crisis Cinema of John Woo," *Cinema Journal* 36:2 (Winter 1997), pp. 67–84.

Williams, Tony. "Border-Crossing Melodrama: *Song of the Exile*," *Jump Cut* 42 (December 1998), pp. 94–100.

Williams, Tony. "*Crossings*: A Transnational Cinematic Text," *Asian Cinema* 11:2 (Fall/Winter 2000), pp. 67–75.

Williams, Tony. "Under 'Western Eyes': The Personal Odyssey of Huang Fei-Hong in *Once Upon a Time in China*," *Cinema Journal* 40:1 (Fall 2000), pp. 3–24.

Williams, Tony. "Hong Kong Cinema, the Boat People, and *To Liv(e)*," *Asian Cinema* 11:1 (Spring/Summer 2000), pp. 131–42.

Williams, Tony. "Michelle Yeoh, 'Under Eastern Eyes,'" *Asian Cinema* 12:2 (Fall/Winter 2001), pp. 119–31.

Williams, Tony. "Transnational Stardom: The Case of Maggie Cheung Man-yuk," *Asian Cinema* 14:2 (Fall/Winter 2003), pp. 180–96.

Wilson, Rob, and Wimal Dissanayake, eds. *Global/Local: Cultural Production and the Transnational Imaginary* (Durham, NC: Duke University Press, 1996).

Withorn, Ann. "Democracy, Lies and Videotape: Reflections on China—An Interview with Richard Levy," *Radical America* 23:2–3 (April–September 1989/published October 1990), pp. 61–75.

Wollen, Peter. "Godard and Counter Cinema: *Vent d'est*," in *Readings and Writings: Semiotic Counter-Strategies* (London: Verso, 1982), pp. 79–91.

Wong, Audrey. "Considering the 'Singapore Film,'" *Arts Issue* 7, National University of Singapore's Centre for the Arts; online document available at www.nus.edu.sg/nusinfo/cfa/artsmag/arts7-4sfilm1.htm.

Wong, Cindy Hing-Yuk. "Cities, Cultures and Cassettes: Hong Kong Cinema and Transnational Audiences," *Post Script* 19:1 (Fall 1999), pp. 87–106.

Wong, Eugene Franklin. *On Visual Media Racism: Asians in the American Motion Pictures* (New York: Arno Press, 1978).

Wong, Tak-wai, ed. *Evans Chan's* To Liv(e): *Screenplay and Essays* (Hong Kong: University of Hong Kong, Department of Comparative Literature, 1996).

Wood, Miles. *Cine East: Hong Kong Cinema through the Looking Glass* (Surrey, U.K.: FAB Press, 1998).

Wu, Frank H. *Yellow: Race in America beyond Black and White* (New York: Basic Books, 2002).

Wu, William F. *The Yellow Peril: Chinese Americans in American B Fiction, 1850–1940* (Hamden, CT: Archon, 1982).

Wyatt, Justin. "Marketing Marginalized Cultures: *The Wedding Banquet*, Cultural Identities, and Independent Cinema of the 1990s," *The End of Cinema as We Know It: American Film in the Nineties*, ed. Jon Lewis (NY: New York University Press, 2001), pp. 61–71.

Xiao, Zhiwei. "The Opium War in the Movies: History, Politics and Propaganda," *Asian Cinema* 11:1 (Spring/Summer 2000), pp. 68–83.

Yang, Edward. "Director's Note," online document available at www.usc.edu/isd/archives/asianfilm/taiwan/mahjong/synopsis.html.

Yang, Jeff, Dina Gan, Terry Hong, *Eastern Standard Time: A Guide to Asian Influence on American Culture from Astro Boy to Zen Buddhism* (Boston, MA: Mariner Books, 1997).

Yang, Mayfair. *Gifts, Favors, and Banquets: The Art of Social Relationships in China* (Ithaca, NY: Cornell University Press, 1994).

Yang, Mayfair Mei-hui. "Mass Media and Transnational Subjectivity in Shanghai: Notes on (Re)Cosmopolitanism in a Chinese Metropolis," in Aihwa Ong and Donald Nonini, eds., *Ungrounded Empires: The Cultural Politics of Modern Chinese Transnationalism* (New York: Routledge, 1997), pp. 287–319.

Yang, Mayfair Mei-hui. "From Gender Erasure to Gender Difference: State Feminism, Consumer Sexuality, and Women's Public Sphere in China," in Mayfair Mei-Hui Yang, ed., *Spaces of Their Own: Women's Public Sphere in Transnational China* (Minneapolis: University of Minnesota Press, 1999), pp. 35–67.

Yang, Mayfair Mei-Hui, ed. *Spaces of Their Own: Women's Public Sphere in Transnational China* (Minneapolis: University of Minnesota Press, 1999).

Yang Ming-Yu. *China: Once Upon a Time/Hong Kong 1997—A Critical Study of Contemporary Hong Kong Martial Arts Film*, Ph.D. dissertation, University of Maryland, College Park, 1995.

Yau, Esther. "Border Crossing: Mainland China's Presence in Hong Kong Cinema," in Nick Browne, Paul G. Pickowicz, Vivian Sobchack, and Esther Yau, eds., *New Chinese Cinemas: Forms, Identities, Politics* (New York: Cambridge University Press, 1994), pp. 180–201.

Yau, Esther C. M. "International Fantasy and the 'New Chinese Cinema,'" *Quarterly Review of Film and Video* 14:3 (April 1993), pp. 95–107.

Yau, Esther C. M. "Compromised Liberation: The Politics of Class in Chinese Cinema of the Early 1950s," in David E. James and Rick Berg, eds., *The Hidden Foundation: Cinema and the Question of Class* (Minneapolis: University of Minnesota Press, 1996), pp. 138–71.

Yau, Esther C. M. "Introduction: Hong Kong Cinema in a Borderless World," in Esther C. M. Yau, ed., *At Full Speed: Hong Kong Cinema in a Borderless World* (Minneapolis: University of Minnesota Press, 2001), pp. 1–28.

Yau, Esther C. M., ed. *At Full Speed: Hong Kong Cinema in a Borderless World* (Minneapolis: University of Minnesota Press, 2001).

Yau, Ka-Fai. "Cinema 3: Towards a 'Minor Hong Kong Cinema,'" *Cultural Studies* 15:3–4 (2001), pp. 543–63.

Yeh Yueh-Yu. *A National Score: Popular Music and Taiwanese Cinema*, Ph.D. dissertation, University of Southern California, 1995.

Yeh Yueh-Yu. "Cause Without a Rebel: Musical Discourse in the Films of Wong Kar Wai," in *1996 Taipei Golden Horse Film Festival Catalogue/Anthology* (Taipei: Golden Horse Film Festival, 1996), pp. 150–55.

Yeh Yueh-Yu. "A Life of Its Own: Musical Discourse in Wong Kar-Wai's Films," *Post Script* 19:1 (Fall 1999), pp. 120–36.

Yeh Yueh-Yu. *Phantom of the Music: Song Narration and Chinese-language Cinema* (in Chinese) (Taipei: Yuan Liu, 2000).

Yeh Yueh-Yu. "Politics and Poetics of Hou Hsiao-hsien's Films," *Post Script* 20:2 and 3 (Winter/Spring and Summer 2001), pp. 61–76.

Yeh Yueh-Yu, Shen Shiao-Ying, Li Zhen-Ya, and Lin Wen-Chi. "Symposium on *Goodbye South Goodbye*," *Chinese/Foreign Literature* 26:10 (March 1998), pp. 65–73. Unpublished translation by Qu Jiao-Jie.

Yip, June. "Constructing a Nation: Taiwanese History and the films of Hou Hsiao-hsien," in Sheldon Hsiao-peng Lu, ed., *Transnational Chinese Cinemas: Identity, Nationhood, Gender* (Honolulu: University of Hawaii Press, 1997), pp. 139–68.

Young, Suzie Sau Fong. "Encountering (China, My) Sorrow," *Asian Cinema* 10:1 (Fall 1998), pp. 107–11.

Yue, Audrey. "Migration-as-Transition: Pre-Post-1997 Hong Kong Culture in Clara Law's *Autumn Moon*," *Intersections: Gender, History, and Culture in the Asian Context* 4 (September 2000); available online at www.she.murdoch.edu.au/intersections/issue4/yue.html.

Zha, Jianying. *China Pop: How Soap Operas, Tabloids, and Bestsellers Are Transforming a Culture* (New York: New Press, 1995).

Zhang, Xudong. *Chinese Modernism in the Era of Reforms: Cultural Fever, Avant-Garde Fiction, and the New Chinese Cinema* (Durham, NC: Duke University Press, 1997).

Zhang, Xudong. "Nationalism, Mass Culture, and Intellectual Strategies in Post-Tiananmen China," in Xudong Zhang, ed., *Whither China? Intellectual Politics in Contemporary China* (Durham, NC: Duke University Press, 2001), pp. 315–48.

Zhang, Xudong, ed. *Whither China?: Intellectual Politics in Contemporary China* (Durham, NC: Duke University Press, 2001).

Zhang, Yingjin. *Screening China: Critical Interventions, Cinematic Reconfigurations, and the Transnational Imaginary in Contemporary Chinese Cinema* (Ann Arbor: Center for Chinese Studies, University of Michigan, 2002).

Zhengxing, Faye. "Has the Movie *Red Corner* Driven China into Its Corner?" *Asian Cinema* 12:1 (Spring–Summer 2001), pp. 117–28.

Zimmermann, Patricia. *Reel Families: A Social History of Amateur Film* (Bloomington: Indiana University Press, 1995).

Zimmermann, Patricia R. *States of Emergency: Documentaries, Wars, Democracies* (Minneapolis: University of Minnesota Press, 2000).

Zizek, Slavoj. *Enjoy Your Symptom!: Jacques Lacan in Hollywood and Out* (New York: Routledge, 2001).

Index